Sociology of Higher Education

Sociology of Higher Education

Contributions and Their Contexts

Edited by
Patricia J. Gumport

The Johns Hopkins University Press
Baltimore

All rights reserved. Published 2007
Printed in the United States of America on acid-free paper
9 8 7 6 5 4 3 2 1

Chapter 1 © 1973 American Sociological Association

The Johns Hopkins University Press
2715 North Charles Street
Baltimore, Maryland 21218-4363
www.press.jhu.edu

Library of Congress Cataloging-in-Publication Data

Sociology of higher education : contributions and their contexts / Patricia J. Gumport, Editor.
  p. cm.
Includes bibliographical references and index.
ISBN-13: 978-0-8018-8614-0 (hardcover : alk. paper)
ISBN-13: 978-0-8018-8615-7 (pbk. : alk. paper)
ISBN-10: 0-8018-8614-7 (hardcover : alk. paper)
ISBN-10: 0-8018-8615-5 (pbk. : alk. paper)
1. Education, Higher—Social aspects. 2. Educational sociology. I. Gumport, Patricia J.
LC191.9.S63 2007
306.43'2—dc22

                              2006039544

A catalog record for this book is available from the British Library.

Contents

Preface

It has been more than thirty years since Burton Clark's (1973) comprehensive assessment of sociology of higher education, a field then young but gaining in momentum. In his essay, published in *Sociology of Education*, Clark takes on the role of cartographer, locating major domains of inquiry and their borders. He characterizes the sociology of higher education as having emerged in the years following World War II with two major foci, educational inequality and the effects of college on students, and two literatures that were smaller at the time, on the academic profession and on governance and organization. Looking to the field's prospective developments, he foresees great possibilities for probing more deeply along these lines of inquiry and extending them. It is a generative nexus: the convergence of a sociological concern and a practical problem in higher education. Even so, he cautions researchers against what he characterizes as several possible wrong turns. He pointedly warns researchers not to focus so much on the needs of practitioners that the field becomes "a managerial sociology," not to be preoccupied with quantitative measurement of determinants, "tunnel vision riveted on the trivial," or lapse into qualitative vignettes that would reduce "scholarly discipline to journalistic play" (Clark 1973, pp. 10–12 in this volume).

This book begins where Clark left off. What happened over the next three decades? Research in each of the initial four domains advanced, the organizing categories themselves were reshaped, and several new lines of inquiry emerged in the context of dramatic societal, institutional, and organizational changes during the last quarter of the twentieth century. Surprisingly, in spite of this impressive expansion of what we have come to consider "the sociology of higher education," there has been no comprehensive effort to assess the field since Clark's 1973 article. The time is ripe for doing so; indeed, such an effort is long overdue.

This volume has three major objectives: (1) to characterize the evolution of sociology of higher education as a field of study over those thirty years; (2) to examine the societal, organizational, and professional contexts that have played a role in shaping distinct areas of specialization within the field; and (3) to consider prospects for the future, including factors shaping the legitimacy, vitality, and institutionalization of specific lines of inquiry, as pursued by faculty located in education and sociology departments.

Research in the sociology of higher education straddles these two organizational and intellectual locations. One aim of this book is to strengthen the bridge between them, and the chapter authors were selected with this in mind. Several authors have taught in both education and sociology departments (often with a courtesy appointment in one or the other) and have published in journals targeted for each audience. Their chapters reflect scholarly sensibilities informed by this mix. Yet the authors' career histories and intellectual biographies also reveal their primary immersion in one or the other—that is, in literatures and discourses that lean more heavily toward sociology or higher education, respectively. Nonetheless these scholars share a common ground, having witnessed key changes in the institutional realities of higher education worldwide: demographic, economic, ideological, organizational, political, and professional—to name a few dimensions of evolution and conflict affecting the phenomena that are the foci of inquiry in these chapters.

The book is organized into three major parts. Part I consists of points of departure: The first chapter reprints Clark's (1973) article from *Sociology of Education* as a springboard for reflecting upon the development of major intellectual currents within the sociology of higher education. The second—editorial—chapter revisits Clark's initial assessment of the field and discusses the societal and organizational forces that shaped the field's evolution over the next thirty years. The rest of the book is divided into two major parts, with chapters that include references to conceptual and empirical work considered foundational to each line of inquiry.

Part II has four chapters that address each of the four major domains Clark originally identified as core areas of inquiry within sociology of higher education, as cited above: the study of educational inequality, college effects, the academic profession, and colleges and universities as organizations. Each chapter traces developments since 1970 and reflects upon the range of social and intellectual forces that account for developments in that area. The authors show how these lines of inquiry have been inspired by changes in higher education itself and also by a rich reservoir of conceptual, empirical, and methodological resources from within sociology's specializations. In Chapters Three and Four—on inequality and college impact, respectively—the authors weave together literature that illuminates higher education's role in stratification and socialization, while Chapter Five examines research on faculty and the academic workplace that draws heavily on the sociology of professions and the sociology of work. To characterize the massive literatures addressing higher education's organizational dynamics, the author of Chapter Six both narrows and broadens the literature review, by confining the discussion to colleges and universities as organizations and by including foundational concepts that span social science disciplines beyond sociology (political science, anthropology, social psychology, and management). Although Clark's initial mapping conjoined the study of academic organization with that of governance, in this volume governance is treated in Chapter Five's discussion of the academic workplace and in Chapter Ten's review of sociological frameworks for policymaking.

Part III examines the field's broader landscape, where scholars have pursued new directions for inquiry. Chapters delve into four specializations: the analysis of higher education as an institution, the study of academic and departmental practices, the study of diversity, and research on higher education policy. (Some other lines of inquiry that are not treated in these chapters are discussed in Chapters 2 and 12, the editorial chapters.) The above four specializations were selected for in-depth review because they are among the most recognizable and institutionalized lines of inquiry within contemporary course offerings and publications and at professional associations where researchers present papers on topics within the purview of the sociology of higher education. Each chapter's author discusses the prominent lines of scholarly development, the influence of broader contexts on the research itself, and the prospects for future work in the field.

The study of higher education as an institution (Chapter 7) has occupied scholars' attention for several decades. The developments within institutional theory of greatest interest to higher education drew questions and concepts from major social theorists like Émile Durkheim and Max Weber, and these lines of inquiry gained momentum during the 1970s. Since then this work has been very generative, shedding light on local organizational and broader institutional dynamics relevant to each of the substantive domains in this volume, especially inquiry into the social construction of the rational myths that support higher education's taken-for-granted structures and practices. Enthusiasm for this area's tremendous conceptual versatility and its power to explain institutional processes has led to its advancement by faculty with a range of objectives: by scholars whose principal aim is to advance theoretical and empirical literature in the study of institutions and by researchers and teachers who seek to apply its concepts to illuminate powerful legitimation and change dynamics at one or more levels of higher education—whether global, transnational, national, or state, organizational, interor intraorganizational, interpersonal or cognitive levels. One line of inquiry, neoinstitutional theory, explores the potential for strategic organizational behavior likely to garner legitimacy. This has been of particular interest to higher education researchers who seek to identify courses of action for practitioners coping with environmental change.

The literature on academic departments (reviewed in Chapter 8) has emerged from the study of academic organizations and governance, as well as from the study of the academic profession—research that has intensified with changes in the nature of academic work and higher education's organizational forms. Work on diversity (discussed in Chapter 9) initially took shape from concepts and tools developed in the study of educational inequality and the study of college impact. Still in its infancy, the study of diversity and diverse learning environments has been galvanized by major demographic, political, and legal changes, with ensuing widespread recognition of this agenda's significance. Higher education policy research (characterized in Chapter 10) has recently come into focus as an arena for sociological analysis by researchers interested in politics and as a deeper inquiry into governance dynamics, especially policymaking within public higher education. As in the chapter on the study of organizations, the literature review extends beyond sociology, citing policy process theories in political science, where scholars have found approaches useful for examining who controls the higher education enterprise and how policy and agenda setting occurs in different contexts.

Part IV concludes the volume with two chapters. Burton Clark's brief essay, written in 2006, more than thirty years after his initial article, offers some pointed advice for future directions in the sociology of higher education. Rather than emphasizing the potential for convergence, Clark diagnoses an "acute" disconnect between research and practice. Although he initially cautioned against focusing too much on the immediate needs of practitioners, in this piece he decidedly favors the practical side, even irreverently chiding those who "aim to generate 'theory,' ensuring turgid prose" that is ignored by practitioners. Here he pushes researchers to be problem driven, not only in their selection of topics worthy of study but also in formulating their findings and conclusions. While he has long argued the merits of case study approaches, at this point he advocates a particular form of sociological inquiry: he urges researchers to learn from those in the field, listen to higher education practitioners who have valuable firsthand knowledge, and develop research that will help them surmount their challenges by identifying what works in practice. Some readers may find this ironic, given that Clark earlier advocated otherwise and located many of his own conceptual and empirical contributions within theoretically informed sociological traditions, as citations in the chapters to come will reveal. Be that as it may, we believe the balance among our chapters not only does justice to the field's foundational roots and the mix of concerns informed by sociological theories and practical realities but also suggests where and how Clark's practical orientation may find traction in future developments.

In the concluding editorial chapter, I weave together some themes from the prior chapters and further examine prospects for the future. What factors constrain or facilitate the sociology of higher education's further development in the early decades of the twenty-first century? How do the pressures add up for faculty in education and sociology, respectively? Is there support for a range of research objectives, from original contributions to sociology to the application of sociological theory and methods to questions of practice and policy? My discussion of the contextual factors shaping developments in the sociology of higher education is informed by premises in the sociology of knowledge: it treats the advancement of knowledge in this field as effected not only by the ideas themselves but also by the academic settings in which researchers work. These settings include the academic reward system for tenure and promotion, as well as the defining characteristics of professional associations and academic departments where faculty reside. In looking ahead, I argue that the sociology of higher education faces major constraints that work against its institutionalization as a field of study. However, the advancement of knowledge within distinct lines of inquiry is by no means dependent upon the recognition that they constitute a field per se. Researchers demonstrate much interest in and support for several particular lines of inquiry, as the book makes clear. Furthermore, promising new and timely avenues of pursuit beckon, as Chapter Twelve will elucidate.

We hope that the book becomes a valuable resource for researchers dedicated to the advancement of the sociology of higher education as well as for students in both education and sociology. Faculty, department chairs, and deans should also find this book helpful in their quest to learn more about the contours of the field, as they assess the research contributions of faculty colleagues and graduate students. We hope that the range of insight these contributions offer will significantly enhance the knowledge and understanding available for all the above participants in our enterprise.

I close with a public acknowledgment to those who made major contributors to this volume. To the chapter authors, I appreciate your role in this team and your patience through the editing process. I sincerely hope that you are satisfied with our collective effort. Together we want to convey warmest thanks to Jacqueline Wehmueller at the Johns Hopkins University Press for supporting our work and giving us the opportunity to publish it here. To Mary Kay Martin, we offer much appreciation for your careful editing and good cheer.

Finally, we dedicate this volume to Burton R. Clark, not only for providing a map of the field but also for his own scholarly contributions over subsequent decades. His work has been valuable for each of us, albeit in different ways, and we hope it will be inspirational for generations to come. I personally first encountered Clark's work in 1983, as a doctoral student, finding his book on higher education systems tucked at the back of a library bookshelf. That book, along with his other work and the opportunity to work directly with him for two years at UCLA, fundamentally changed my thinking about higher education—its structures, processes, traditions, values, identities, discourses, and unique contributions to society. We have all seen through his eyes the unlimited potential in studying this complex enterprise as sociologists of higher education. For his steady stream of insights, his support in launching my career, and his ongoing collegiality, I am most grateful. My life and work have been deeply enriched, as have ours all.

I POINTS OF DEPARTURE

1 Development of the Sociology of Higher Education

BURTON R. CLARK

A sociology of higher education has emerged in the quarter-century since World War II. It is now a field with several important streams of interest: the two major foci of educational inequality beyond the secondary level and the social-psychological effects of college on students, and smaller literatures on the academic profession and governance and organization. In the 1970s, some parts of the field face the danger of expensive trivialization, others of substituting playful journalism for scholarly discipline. Encouraging prospects for the near future include more extensive development of comparative studies and analyses with historical depth. A useful additional step would be to counter the dominant instrumental definitions of education with approaches that center on the values, traditions, and identities—the expressive components—of educational social systems.

My purposes here are to review the development to date of the sociological study of higher education and, upon that base, to assess the strengths and weaknesses of current research and to point the prospects for the future. The review is selective and the assesesment biased by personal perception and preference. I would like to err in being open and catholic, since there are so many ways that sociological study of colleges and universities can render us more sensitive in coping with immediate problems as well as contribute to theory and method in sociology. But, in a limited essay, it is necessary to categorize roughly the work of the past and to highlight the more salient work. It is also realistic to face the fact of limited talent and resources as we turn to the

This article was first published in *Sociology of Education* 1973, vol. 46 (winter): 2–14. It is reprinted here by permission of the American Sociological Association.

future and to emphasize one or two perspectives that might best correct the defects of our current efforts.

The Past and the Present

The emergence and substantial growth of a sociology of higher education have followed from the extensive educational expansion of the period since the end of World War II, especially that of the last decade, in semideveloped and developed nations around the world. The higher learning became problematic to social analysts as it became more important to the general population as well as to economic and governmental elites. The move toward mass participation in higher education has strained the traditional internal ordering of educational affairs. New demands have caused great problems of adapting externally to fast-changing sectors of society. The various demands, new and old, often pull in opposite directions: a dynamic, advanced economy, fueled by governmental concern about national strength, presses for a rationalization of training while a highly volatile culture of youth, fueled by the needs of the mass media and a youth industry, argues against such technical rationality, preferring a logic of sentiment and identity. Such strains, seemingly basic and reflected in various conflicts and disturbances, have led scholars to turn with wonderment, and often with some anguish, to the serious study of their own world. The 1960s saw a revitalization of the study of education in economics, political science, history, organizational analysis—and sociology.

We need only to look back a few years to see how recent is our concern. In the United States, we have had colleges since colonial days and universities since the last quarter of the nineteenth century. General sociology developed about the turn of the century and was a viable enterprise with a number of subfields by the 1920s. But among the subfields the sociology of education was a fragile enterprise until at least the 1950s; and within it, thought and analysis centered on the elementary and secondary levels. In its early state, the field was called "educational sociology," and its main journal was the *Journal of Educational Sociology*. It was based in teachers colleges and the social foundations divisions of schools of education at the universities, where its task was to aid in the preparation of teachers and administrators for the public schools. One historical review of sociological inquiry in education in the period 1917 to 1940 speaks of three subgroups: a general sociology group, concerned with the development of sociology; a policy group, interested in setting educational values and effecting social reform through the training of teachers and administrators; and a social technology group, seeking to develop a practitioner role around technical prescription on educational methods (Richards 1969). Not one of these groups was successful in developing a prominent position either within education or sociology; and, of note for our purposes, none paid serious attention to higher education. The proper subject matter was the school, not the college and university.

We may connect two types of pre–World War II literature to the modern sociology of higher education. For one, broad statements in sociology and anthropology offered an undifferentiated view of education of all levels and types as a means of cultural transmission, socialization, social control, or social progesss (Durkheim 1922; Cooley 1956; Ross 1928; Ward 1906). Of the broad approaches, Durkheim's seemingly conservative view of education as a dependent element in a slowly evolving web of institutions has been the most noted: education is "a collection of practices and institutions that have been organized slowly in the course of time, which are comparable with all the other social institutions and which express them, and which, therefore, can no more be changed at will than the structure of the society itself" (Durkheim 1922, p. 65). Such statements, elaborating the basic sociological truth of the interdependence of social institutions, now seem both more appropriate, in the round, for 1900 than 1970 and for the elementary school than the university. Their import lay in establishing the terms of discussion for a long period, and even today they remain useful in recalling the specialist to the broadest conceptions of the social functions of education. Secondly, certain specific statements about higher education became established as classics but stood for decades in lonely isolation. The foremost instance in the basic theoretical literature is composed of Max Weber's statements on "Science as a Vocation" and "The 'Rationalization' of Education and Training," in which, following from his general insight on the rise of bureaucracy and specialization, he portrayed the tension between the generalist and the specialist—"the struggle of the 'specialist type of man' against the older type of 'cultivated man' "—as basic to many modern educational problems (Weber 1946, p. 243). In retrospect, a highly useful line of inquiry could have developed three or four decades ago from the Weberian perspective on education, bureaucracy, and culture; but instead we have a notable instance of discontinuity in social research. The second instance of the striking specific classical statement was Thorstein Veblen's angry blast at the influence of businessmen and their mentality in the control and administration of colleges and universities, in his *The Higher Learning in America,* originally published in 1918 (Veblen 1954). Veblen apparently was not followed for thirty years, until Hubert P. Beck's work *Men Who Control Our Universities* appeared in 1947 (Beck 1947). Noting this discontinuity, we can well wish that Veblen had taken apprentices or had attracted followers whose work in turn would have established momentum in the analysis of power and control in higher education. A third instance of work that stood by itself for a long time was Logan Wilson's dissertation on university professors, published in 1942 as *The Academic Man: A Study in the Sociology of a Profession* (Wilson 1942). There was no follow-up on this promising topic for a decade and a half, until Caplow and McGee's *The Academic Marketplace,* 1958, and still today we do not have a book-length treatment of the university professor that is as serious and systematic as Wilson's effort of almost thirty years ago.

It is not until the 1960s that we discern a serious sociology of higher education in the sense of a subfield with a steady flow of writing and a specialty in which students take training, pursue it for a number of years, and accept a professional label. Two main directions of effort have become firmly institutionalized in these few short years, each representing a convergence of a sociological concern and a practical problem. The first stream is the study of inequality in education beyond the high school, particularly the search for the sources of inequality in social class, race, ethnicity, and sex. Inequality remains the root concern in the sociology of education around the world.

In American sociology, the basic field of stratification, concerned with class and race, was the base from which there developed a disciplined, empirically minded thrust into the study of education. In the 1930s and 1940s, a series of now-classic community studies (Lynd 1929, 1937; Warner 1941; Hollingshead 1949) dramatized the impact of social class on the mobility of the young in the elementary and secondary school, including who finished high school and thus qualified for college. This sociological concern developed in the 1950s and 1960s into a serious tradition of statistical analysis (for example, see the work of William Sewell and his students—Sewell 1966, 1967), and this concern followed mass education up into the college level. We now have an extensive journal literature of the social determinants of aspiration and achievement that includes the collegiate as well as the secondary and elementary levels of education, with increasing refinement around the issues germane to open admission and differentiation of institutions and tracks within a mass system, for example, who goes to what kind of college and who completes the various degree levels. Here ideas on various overt and covert forms of channeling students and hence affecting seriously their social mobility have enlivened the literature and anticipated some current criticisms of schooling, for example, the cooling-out function of certain practices in colleges (Clark 1960), the difference between sponsored and contest forms of formal selection in educational systems (Turner 1968), and the effects of counselors' categories of thought as labels placed on the young (Cicourel and Kitsuse 1963).

The second stream is the study of the effects of the college years on the character, belief, and thought of students. An early study here was T. M. Newcomb's analysis of the effect of Bennington College on its girls (Newcomb 1943), a classic work in social psychology. The topic was picked up again in the 1950s when Nevitt Sanford and his associates attempted a longitudinal examination of personality development in Vassar girls, a study that was only weakly sociological (Sanford 1962); and a group of Cornell sociologists compared the attitudes and values of students at eleven colleges and universities, noting some differences between public and private institutions in inputs and apparent effects (Goldsen et al. 1960). Since 1960, there has been a rapidly growing body of sociological writing, beginning with the study of Howard Becker and colleagues on the subculture of medical students (Becker et al. 1961) and the essay by Clark and Trow on types of undergraduate subcultures (see Newcomb and Wilson 1966). Among the best studies reported later in the decade were the analysis of Becker, Geer, and Hughes of students' orientations to making the academic grade (1968) and the remarkable reanalysis of Bennington College by Newcomb a quarter-century after his first study (1967). The study of life inside the campus and of its effects on the values, attitudes, and achievements of the student has become established rapidly, fueled by practical concerns of professors and administrators as well as the professional influence of senior investigators on colleagues and students. Research in this area also converges with that of psychologists who have been developing an even more extensive and intensive literature of the effect—or noneffect—of college on students (see Feldman and Newcomb 1970).

Bordering on, and often converging with, this interest in student life is the late great concern with the causes of student disturbances. Stemming from the growing sense of academic crisis in the years since 1964, the writings on student unrest have come in waves from successively embattled campuses as all factions leaped to their pens and have been therefore long on ideology and short on research. This interest may yet find steady and creative academic bases in political sociology, for example, in the comparative study of student movements (Lipset 1966; Martinelli and Cavalli 1970), and in the study of student life as related to the organization and governance of the college and univeristy (Yamamoto 1968; Kruytbosch and Messinger 1970). But militant student action is a highly volatile phenomenon—witness the relative quiet of 1970–71—and its academic pursuit remains unsteady. A concern that escalated rapidly with the front-page headlines also may subside rapidly if student news becomes relegated again to the page behind the want ads or is assigned low priority as a campus problem when such matters as finance and faculty rights come to the fore.

Beyond these two main lines of inquiry, each of which centers on students, we may note two additional efforts that are otherwise focused. One is the study of "academic man," or higher education as a profession. Here we have the early study of Logan Wilson, noted above; some thoughts by Riesman on academic disciplines as power groups (1956); the efforts of Lazarsfeld and Thielens in *The Academic Mind* to study social scientists in a time of crisis (1958); the reflections of Caplow and McGee on the vagaries of the academic marketplace (1958); the delineation by John D. Donovan of *The Academic Man in the Catholic College* (1964); and the current, largely unpublished work of Talcott Parsons and Gerald M. Platt on "The American Academic Profession." Work is going forward in this line in other countries; for example, the extensive investigation undertaken in the mid-1950s in West Germany, reported in Plessner (1956) and the study by Halsey and Trow of the academic man in Britain. Most past work in this line has been conceptually ad hoc; but since there is now a thriving sociology of occupations and professions, the study of academic man can play effectively against this literature, for example, on the strain between professional and bureaucratic orientations and the tensions common to the roles of professional men in complex organizations (cf. Clark 1966).

The second subsidiary path takes the organizations of higher education as the units for study. Here conceptual leads have come from the literature on organization theory to which all the social sciences have contributed and the sociological field of complex organizations. The work includes the study of the dilemmas of the open door college (Clark 1960); the analysis of university goals (Gross and Grambsch 1968); the creation of new perspectives on academic authority and power, including that of a subculture of administrators (Lunsford 1970; Baldridge 1971); the tensions of public experimental colleges (Riesman, Gusfield, and Gamson 1970); and developmental analysis of organizational character and institutional self-belief (Clark 1970). The organizational studies commonly are case studies oriented to exploration and discovery rather than to validation. Varying in rigidity, they shade off into journalistic vignettes and the writings of administrators and students of higher education that are not particularly sociological in intent or style.

This line of inquiry also extends at a more macrocosmic level into the organizations of sets of colleges and universities, including national systems of higher education. Here our appetites were whetted early by the skillful and provocative essays of Joseph Ben David, the Israeli sociologist, on the effects of major structural differences among the systems of the most advanced industrial societies on flexibility, innovation, and change (Ben David 1962). Riesman has portrayed the rank-ordering and imitating propensities of the American system as a snakelike procession (Riesman 1956); and Jencks and Riesman, within a wide-ranging description of the variety of colleges and universities in the American system, have interpreted the rise to power of professional scholars and scientists as the fundamental academic revolution of recent times (Jencks and Riesman 1968). We have had an occasional illuminating country case study of a country outside of the advanced nations, as in Philip Foster's analysis of education and social status in Ghana (Foster 1965). An educational literature on national systems has grown rapidly in the 1960s, but much of it remains in the general terms of manpower need, quantitative educational expansion, and national planning. The surveys of national systems have at least provided basic descriptive information comparatively assembled, on an ever larger number of systems of higher education (e.g., OECD 1970), providing a base for more conceptually focused comparative inquiry.

The Future

Relatively young and unformed fields of study often are torn between intensive effort in one or two main lines of research and a desire to wander around testing the ground to find new and more sensitive approaches. The intensive effort allows us to refine empirically a few concepts and improve a few methods, with the possibility that we may finally pin something down. The wandering effort allows us to leapfrog from one idea to another, accelerating the conceptual game, with the possibility that we will come up with an exciting idea. These contradictory approaches are evident in the sociology of higher education, and each, with its evident virtues, carries its own dangers for the decade or two ahead.

The first approach has the danger of an inbred tradition of work, with increasing tunnel vision riveted on the trivial. The two most established lines of research mentioned earlier, those of educational inequality and college impact, will face this danger in the 1970s. The study of educational inequality is fast becoming a detailed and technical business in which only a few analysts, equipped with the latest statistical techniques, are competent. A tricky and complex problem does indeed call for the greatest possible methodological sophistication. But down that road also comes the career devoted to improving the reliability and validity of instruments of highly specific application. Our colleagues in educational psychology can attest to the stultifying and dead-end pitfalls of that particular academic procession.

In the study of college impact, we already have a relatively massive but trivial literature (cf. Feldman and Newcomb's review of 1,500 studies). If at last we have stopped attempting to measure the effects of specific courses on students, we seemingly still are stuck with a commitment to measure ever more carefully the year by year effect of one college after another—or perhaps several hundred of them simultaneously—on a host of specific attitudes. But the effort to sort out the determinants and the outcomes, particularly to comprehend the interactions between student inputs and campus structures, is increasingly costly in time and money. Is it worth it? Is it worth it for social science? It is helpful to stand back and recall that a fundamental if not the basic effect of college is to make college graduates out of high school graduates. Here the change is one hundred percent in the surviving cohort: none of those entering college but all those receiving the degree are socially defined as college graduates. As John Meyer has put it, this is what colleges socially are chartered to do, to alter social statuses with this particular self- and public definition (Meyer 1972). The consequences of the definition are enormous. In Meyer's terms: "Whether or not the student has learned anything—[and, we might add, become a little less religious or a little more liberal]—his job prospects, income potential, access to political and civil service positions, marital prospects, and other opportunities, are greatly altered" (Meyer 1972, p. 110). Here the fundamental sociological thesis is that college effects occur primarily not at the level of attitudes and values but in the allocation of statuses and roles. This plausible argument should give some pause to those who would spend research fortunes on highly sophisticated, five-year, input-throughput-output analyses of small changes in specific values. In any event, the more sustained lines of work in the sociology of higher education already need this kind of direct challenging of their relative importance and possible contribution.

The second approach, that of the wandering analytical gypsy, will carry in the 1970s the danger of a game of vignettes. For many of us, it is more fun to go find another interesting case about which to write an interpretive story than to plug along in one vein seeking replication or the hard data of comparison. The result of drifting too far in this direction is a maximum of zig and zag, a minimum of accumulation, and even a reduction of scholarly discipline to journalistic play. The temptation is to be clever, even sardonic: the provocative phrase, rather than the truth, will set us free. Thus we are right on one page and wrong on the next, and only a few informed people are able to distinguish the one from the other. We shall see much of this form of quasi-sociological writing in the 1970s, and what at one time is a fresh and useful ethnography can become a tiresome description of an endless number of tribes and a tangle of uncorrected interpretations. The ethnography will need conceptual focus and the hard criticism of those who insist on some systematic data.

The research of the 1970s clearly will include much comparative analysis, in line with the general drift of sociology toward comparative study, a development that should help correct the myopia that comes from too many days spent on scale reliability or on vignettes of the American college. The comparative work will entail a variety of analytical interests, for example, inequalities in access, student life, institutional resilience and change, and governance and management of national systems. We also will gain from more historical investigation. The written history of higher education has been improving rapidly (cf. Hofstadter and Metzger 1955; Rudolph 1962; Veysey 1965); there are young scholars who seem equally at home in sociology and history; and general sociology is clearly no longer uncomfortable with historical perspectives and materials. Historical studies instruct us about educational systems of the past, connections between educational trends and change in other sectors of society, and, most important for sociologists, the past-to-present development of existing systems. Developmental analysis carried out over decades of time can highlight fundamental institutional trajectories and hence suggest the potentialities and limitations of current institutional forms as they face new demands.

As one attempts to estimate the future for the lines of inquiry identified above, a latent common problem in approach and perspective becomes more manifest: how can the sociology of higher education take cues from, and make returns to, the concerns of educational practitioners without becoming a managerial sociology? It is not that we are so easily bought but that we are so much involved. Since education prepares the young for later life and professor-researchers are part of the training corps, we tend to perceive and define education in instrumental terms. Like administrators and reformers, we want to know who gets in and who gets out, what the students have learned and whether their personal character has been affected. Educational questions not only too easily set the sociological questions, but they also become voiced around immediate needs of administration and public policy, for example, what specific issues are disturbing the students and hence what manipulations of structure and procedure will be advantageous? Even when our attitude is critical of present practice, we are still in the stance of defining the ends of educational work and arranging practices to be effective means to those ends.

One way to contain this tendency in part is to see higher education through the definitions presented by students and other subordinate actors, an approach practiced by Howard Becker and others in the symbolic interaction school of thought. A second way is to play against instrumental terms by seeking the expressive aspects of the system. Though colleges and universities begin as purposive formal organizations, they become, in varying degree, social institutions heavy with affect and nonrational involvement. For faculty and administrators, there are loyalties and lifestyles of the employing institution and the national discipline. For students, there are the feelings of group attachment or detachment that are constructed in the meeting of personal and institutional character. Research on attitudes and values of students and professors catches some of the personal side of expressive phenomena.

What lags is research on institutional and system capacities to embody certain values in the thought and lifestyles of an evolving group. Macro-system analysis need not be limited to inputs and outputs and managerial manipulation of administrative structure. Compared to most other classes of complex organizations, colleges and universities apparently have a high propensity to order themselves through normative bonds and emotional commitment. We move toward a fuller understanding of their nature as we bring into view their variations as systems that at a given time are ends in themselves. We seek then for the evolution of value systems that give meaning to the lives of participants. We seek how the organized social system unconsciously absorbs the individual into a collectivity, promoting personal satisfaction in return. We seek group and institutional identities.

In historical connection, the present natural interest in effective delivery of educational services links well with the Weberian interest in bureaucratic rationality and the role of education in the certification of training. The corrective perspective emphasized here, in contrast, is rooted more in the Durkheimian concern with the role of morality and sentiment in social order. Durkheim saw schools as miniature societies that have their own particular moralities, ones developed over time as institutional character emerges as a reaction to institutional function. If colleges and universities as well as schools are places where society recreates (and develops) itself in the young, then their values, traditions, and collective identities appropriately can be placed at the center of sociological attention.

References

Astin, A. 1970. "The Methodology of Research on College Impact," pts. 1–2. *Sociology of Education* 43 (3–4): 223–54, 437–48.

Baldridge, J. V. 1971. *Power and Conflict in the University.* New York: John Wiley.

Beck, H. P. 1947. *Men Who Control Our Universities.* New York: King's Crown Press.

Becker, H. S., B. Geer, and E. C. Hughes. 1968. *Making the Grade: The Academic Side of College Life.* New York: Wiley.

Becker, H. S., B. Geer, E. C. Hughes, and A. L. Strauss. 1961. *Boys in White: Student Culture in Medical School.* Chicago: University of Chicago Press.

Ben David, J., and A. Sloczower. 1962. "Universities and Academic Systems in Modern Societies." *European Journal of Sociology* 3:45–84.

Caplow, T., and R. J. McGee. 1958. *The Academic Marketplace*. New York: Basic Books.

Cicourel, A. V., and J. I. Kitsuse. 1963. *The Educational Decision-Makers*. Indianapolis: Bobbs-Merrill.

Clark, B. R. 1960. *The Open Door College*. New York: McGraw-Hill.

——. 1966. "Organizational Adaptation to Professionals." In *Professionalization*, ed. H. M. Vollmer and D. L. Mills, 282–91. Englewood Cliffs, NJ: Prentice-Hall.

——. 1970. *The Distinctive College: Antioch, Reed, and Swarthmore*. Chicago: Aldine.

Cooley, C. H. 1956. *Two Major Works: Social Organization* and *Human Nature and the Social Order*. Glencoe, IL: Free Press (originally published in 1909 and 1902).

Donovan, J. D. 1964. *The Academic Man in the Catholic College*. New York: Sheed and Ward.

Durkheim, E. 1922. *Education and Society*. Translated by Sherwood D. Fox. Glencoe, IL: Free Press (1956).

Feldman, K. A., and T. M. Newcomb. 1970. *The Impact of College on Students*. 2 vols. San Francisco: Jossey-Bass.

Foster, P. 1965. *Education and Social Change in Ghana*. Chicago: University of Chicago Press.

Goldsen, K., M. Rosenberg, R. M. Williams, and E. A. Suchman. 1960. *What College Students Think*. New York: D. Van Nostrand.

Gross, E. G., and P. V. Grambsch. 1968. *University Goals and Academic Power*. Washington, DC: American Council on Education.

Halsey, A. H., and M. Trow. 1971. *The British Academics*. Cambridge, MA: Harvard University Press.

Hofstadter, R., and W. P. Metzger. 1955. *The Development of Academic Freedom in the United States*. New York: Columbia University Press.

Hollingshead, A. B. 1959. *Elmtown's Youth*. New York: John Wiley.

Jencks, C., and D. Riesman. 1968. *The Academic Revolution*. Garden City, NY: Doubleday.

Kruytbosch, C. E., and S. L. Messinger, eds. 1970. *The State of the University: Authority and Change*. Beverly Hills, CA: Sage.

Lazarsfeld, P. F., and W. Thielens Jr. 1958. *The Academic Mind*. New York: Free Press of Glencoe.

Lipset, S. M., ed. 1966. *Student Politics*. Special issue of *Comparative Education Review* 10 (June).

Lunsford, F. 1970. "Authority and Ideology in the Administered University." In *The State of the University: Authority and Change*, ed. C. E. Kruytbosch and S. L. Messinger. Beverly Hills, CA: Sage.

Lynd, S., and H. M. Lynd. 1929. *Middletown*. New York: Harcourt, Brace.

———. 1937. *Midletown in Transition*. New York: Harcourt, Brace.

Martinelli, A., and A. Cavalli. 1970. "Toward a Conceptual Framework for the Comparative Analysis of Student Movements." Paper presented at seventh World Congress of Sociology, Varna, Bulgaria.

Meyer, J. W. 1972. "The Effects of the Institutionalization of Colleges in Society." In *College and Student: Selected Readings in the Social Psychology of Higher Education*, edited by K. A. Feldman, 109–26. New York: Pergamon.

Newcomb, T. M. 1943. *Personality and Social Change*. New York: Dryden.

Newcomb, T. M., K. E. Koenig, R. Flacks, and D. P. Warwick. 1967. *Persistence and Change: Bennington College and Its Students after Twenty-five Years*. New York: Wiley.

Newcomb, T. M., and E. K. Wilson, eds. 1966. *College Peer Groups*. Chicago: Aldine.

OECD (Organisation for Economic Co-operation and Development). 1970. *Development of Higher Education, 1950–1967: Statistical Survey*. Paris: OECD.

Parsons, T., and G. M. Platt. 1969. "The American Academic Profession: A Pilot Study." Typescript.

Plessner, H., ed. *Untersuchungen zur Lage der Deutschen Hochschullehrer*. Gottingen: Vandenhoeck und Ruprescht.

Richards, R. R. 1969. "Perspectives on Sociological Inquiry in Education, 1917–1940." Ph.D. dissertation. University of Wisconsin.

Riesman, D. 1956. *Constraint and Variety in American Education*. Lincoln: University of Nebraska Press.

Riesman, D., J. Gusfield, and Z. Gamson. 1970. *Academic Values and Mass Education: The Early Years of Oakland and Monteith*. Garden City, NY: Doubleday.

Ross, E. 1901. *Social Control*. New York: Macmillan (1928).

Rudolph, F. 1962. *The American College and University*. New York: Alfred A. Knopf.

Sanford, N., ed. 1962. *The American College*. New York: John Wiley.

Sewell, W. H., and J. M. Armer. 1966. "Neighborhood Context and College Plans." *American Sociological Review* 31:159–68.

Sewell, W. H., and V. P. Shah. 1967. "Socioeconomic Status, Intelligence, and the Attainment of Higher Education." *Sociology of Education* 40:1–23.

Turner, Ralph H. 1960. "Sponsored and Contest Mobility and the School System." *American Sociological Review* 25:855–67.

Veblen, T. 1918. *The Higher Learning in America*. Stanford, CA: Academic Reprints (1954).

Veysey, L. R. 1965. *The Emergence of the American University*. Chicago: University of Chicago Press.

Ward, L. F. 1906. *Applied Sociology*. Boston: Ginn.

Warner, W. L., and P. S. Lunt. 1941. *The Social Life of a Modern Community.* New Haven, CT: Yale University Press.

Weber, M. 1946. *From Max Weber: Essays in Sociology.* Translated and edited by H. H. Gerth and C. Wright Mills. New York: Oxford University Press.

Wilson, L. 1942. *The Academic Man: A Study in the Sociology of a Profession.* New York: Oxford University Press.

Yamamoto, K., ed. 1968. *The College Student and His Culture: An Analysis.* Boston: Houghton Mifflin.

2 Sociology of Higher Education
An Evolving Field

PATRICIA J. GUMPORT

This chapter sets the stage for the book chapters. I begin with a discussion of Clark's characterization of the sociology of higher education circa 1970. Then I review the societal and organizational contexts that have played a role in shaping the major areas of specialization within the field.

A cartographer's representation should be read as an approximation of prevailing ideas. Charting the contours of a field at any given point is a tall order, in part because categories of inquiry are inherently dynamic. That is, the categories themselves are in flux, and particular labels affixed to them have an inescapable historical specificity. There is also the earlier question of how much research on a topic warrants its recognition as constituting a category in its own right. Perceptions of major categories of ideas—and their relative positions in the field—are filtered through subjective appraisals of what is deemed most worthy of study. Making such determinations presents challenges to researchers reviewing literatures, instructors constructing syllabi, and students exploring the conceptual and empirical foundations of a field. Such challenges have been foremost in the minds of this book's chapter authors and the editor, and one can surmise this was also the case for Clark himself.

Clark's Early Perspective

In his 1973 article, Clark characterizes the field in terms in use at the time. He identifies two major areas of inquiry, "the study of educational inequality beyond the secondary level" and "the social-psychological effects of college on students," as well as two "smaller literatures" (p. 3 in this volume) focused on "the study of 'academic man,' or higher education as a profession," and "the organizations of higher education as the units of study" (p. 8). The latter, he notes, extends earlier work to "a more macrocosmic level," including national systems of higher education (p. 9). A closer look at his observations is instructive. I quote from the original to convey his meaning and to familiarize the reader with the terminology of that era.

According to Clark, societal conditions spurred interest in the sociology of higher education. After World War II, higher education in the United States became more important to the general public as well as to "economic and government elites" (p. 4). Not only were enrollments increasing dramatically but new and at times competing demands on colleges and universities challenged them to adapt their organizational structures and functions. At the time, faculty in the social sciences showed considerable interest in studying education, but their focus was primarily on schools, not on colleges or universities. The exceptions to this Clark calls classics that "stood for decades in lonely isolation" (1973, p. 5 in this volume)—such as Weber's (1918) lecture "Science as a Vocation," Veblen's (1918) *The Higher Learning in America,* and later Wilson's (1942) *The Academic Man.*

Clark points to literature foundational to American sociology that offered unlimited conceptual possibilities to anchor the study of higher education: for example, Weber on bureaucracy and rationalization; Durkheim on collective identities, social control, and the evolution of societal structure; and the Lynds' and Hollingshead's studies of communities, which spurred research on stratification (Lynd and Lynd 1929 and 1937; Hollingshead 1949). Clark also identifies the untapped potential for comparative study, historical analysis, and research on institutional and system capacities.

His article goes on to provide the conceptual mapping for "a serious sociology of higher education," which he argues gained momentum during the 1960s (1973, p. 6 in this volume). Clark's review includes 52 references, three-quarters of which are books (published by a mix of popular and university presses); only a handful are peer-reviewed journal articles, including two each in the *American Sociological Review* and *Sociology of Education.* There are no references to articles in peer-reviewed higher education journals; most of these were not founded until the 1970s. (See the table in Chapter 12.)

Based on these citations and Clark's own academic orientation, it is clear in retrospect why he characterizes the field as located at a scholarly nexus that reflects a convergence of a sociological concern and a practical problem. We can see this in each of the domains identified. The study of educational inequality reflects a sociological interest in stratification and a political interest in extending postsecondary access to disadvantaged populations. Studying the effects of college on students focuses inquiry into their character, beliefs, and thought, as framed by conceptualizations from various perspectives in social psychology. Given the turbulent sixties, it is no surprise that research on college students subsequently extended into the nature of student life on campus and student attitudes, including the political beliefs that led to student protests.

Of the "smaller" literatures Clark identifies at the time, interest in studying the academic profession gained momentum alongside a growing interest in the sociology of professions. Early work reflected prevailing conceptions of faculty as professional men. His reference to the titles *The Academic Man* (1942) and *The Academic Mind* (1958) reveals the homogeneity of faculty at the time and of the universalizing presumptions as to their "mind," what we most commonly refer to as "mindset." Such writing on the academic profession captured the distinctive mix of professional and bureaucratic authority inherent in academic organizations. Faculty, then referred to as "academic men," were seen as professionals, based on their credentialed expertise, self-regulating norms, and ethos of service, all justifying their autonomy in carrying out their responsibilities. The image from that time starkly contrasts with changes that would occur over subsequent decades. Aside from the gradual demographic diversification of the professoriate, faculty autonomy came to be reframed in a context that defined them as employees in organizations that were growing larger and more complex. Studying the "faculty role" in the singular would be displaced by the plural "faculty roles," connoting more differentiated expectations of faculty work and academic life across faculty ranks, disciplinary specializations, and campus settings.

The awareness of a distinctive mix of professional and bureaucratic authority intermingled with development of the other "smaller" literature Clark identifies, on governance and organization, which examines not only patterns of authority in academic organizations but also such essential activities as decision making and adaptation. Although Clark links "governance" with "organization" in a single category, over time several lines of inquiry developed as divergent streams. Inspired by advances in the sociology of formal organizations and comparative sociology, these studies of higher education found support in literature that conceptualizes colleges and universities as organizations with numerous structural and normative dimensions for analysis, from the campus as a whole and its subunits to beyond the organization, including external levels of state systems and national systems of higher education. Especially as open-systems perspectives came to dominate organizational theory, the study of academic governance extended beyond a focus on internal political interests to examine the broader political dynamics and policymaking that play a defining role in shaping higher education. Some research came to reflect interests central to other domains—such as inequality and access—yet new lines of inquiry were also identified, focusing for example on the contested terrain of academic workplaces; the nature of changes under way in academic missions, resources, and programs; and the complex dynamics between colleges and universities and wider political economic actors, to name a few.

Overall in the early 1970s, Clark sees sociology of higher education as a "relatively young and unformed" field with much to contribute to sociological theory and method as well as to an understanding of higher education's immediate problems (p. 9). He calls for more comparative analysis in each of the field's domains of inquiry and for more historical studies. Considering the field's future, he warns against some potential pitfalls of subsequent development. Addressing researchers oriented to quantitative as well as qualitative methodologies, he notes the tension between depth and breadth: each yields different gains and carries its own dangers. He expresses a specific concern about efforts to measure more intensively the determinants in college effects on students, a field of inquiry that benefited from advances in statistical techniques but was in danger of becoming "an inbred tradition of work" (p. 10), the relative importance of which he questioned, given that it had become "increasingly costly in time and money" (p. 10). Inversely, in spreading across too broad a domain, one risked becoming a "wandering analytical gypsy" (p. 11) who would "leapfrog from one idea to another" (p. 10). Across the board, his message was that researchers risk myopia and insularity, a theme he revisits in Chapter Eleven of this volume.

Also in his 1973 essay, in considering prospects for the future, Clark identifies an ongoing challenge for the field as a whole: "how can the sociology of higher education take cues from, and make returns to, the concerns of educational practitioners without becoming a managerial sociology?" (p. 12 in this volume). He observes that it would be unfortunate if research were co-opted by those in a position to run colleges and universities, framed simply according to the instrumental interests of educational administrators and policymakers: "educational questions not only too easily set the sociological questions, but they also become voiced around the immediate needs of administration and public policy" (p. 12). As a corrective, he advocates critical inquiry into higher education's institutional character and broader social functions. He proposes that researchers adopt a Durkheimian sensibility and focus their analyses on the "values, traditions, and collective identities" (p. 13) that are central to understanding higher education as "social institutions heavy with affect and nonrational involvement" (p. 12).

An illustration of what he has in mind is evident in Clark's own *The Distinctive College* (1970), a sociological inquiry into those expressive characteristics of higher education. Setting them in their historical contexts, he portrays the organizational sagas of three "distinctive colleges" —Reed, Antioch, and Swarthmore—and the affective dimensions that stay with their graduates. Over time this book has been read by many audiences, including those interested in emulating what worked, although the research was not framed to address practitioners at liberal arts colleges. Another example sharply foregrounds higher education's social functions. In *The Open Door College* (1960b), Clark depicts the "cooling-out function," using a case study of a community college to reveal the specific processes whereby students who initially had aspirations for transfer are moved into terminal programs. He observes that this reorientation process from transfer to terminal student is concealed, so as to preserve the wider public's expectations of access and opportunity. Even though Clark's study and core concept of "cooling out" have since been used by those who criticize community colleges for falling short of their transfer mission and could conceivably have been used to guide the behavior of community college practitioners, neither was his explicit intention. In his 1960 article based on the book, which appeared in the *American Journal of Sociology* (Clark 1960a), he frames the study as a sociological inquiry addressing a perennial challenge for institutions in democratic societies as they must deal with the discrepancy between the promise of equal opportunity and the reality of limited abilities. That he framed the study within the context of prior work by sociologists Robert Merton and Erving Goffman also indicates that his inquiry was not intended to meet the instrumental needs of educational practitioners or policymakers, nor was it intended to provide ammunition to critics who subsequently alleged that community colleges were complicit in a system that knowingly reproduces inequality.

This piece raises the question of whether subsequent developments in the field would drift to the other end of the continuum from Clark's concern about a managerial sociology. Although not articulated by Clark at the time, the inverse concern would be whether research in the field need have *any* relevance to practitioners. What if researchers made it their priority to advance sociological theories and methods in the field and dedicated their efforts to publishing academic writing for scholarly audiences? If the sociology of higher education were to come to occupy a secure place as a distinct area of inquiry in sociology, it stands to reason that it would need to be driven primarily by disciplinary interests. In retrospect, Clark could have anticipated this outcome, especially given the weight of the academic reward structure for faculty located in research universities, where peer-reviewed journal articles have become the coin of the realm for tenure and promotion. Curiously, more than thirty years later, it is this concern rather than that of serving higher education practitioners that draws Clark's ire, in part because he grew impatient with scholarly prose. Notably (as will be revealed in Chapter 11 of this volume), he criticizes researchers with this orientation for producing a seemingly endless stream of articles that fall short of overly grand scholarly ambitions and suffer from obtuse writing that is impenetrable to practitioners. Thus much later in his career, while underscoring the need to understand the nature of university change via case study methods, he urges researchers to reorient their questions and conclusions to the needs of practitioners.

The 1973 essay's vivid, direct prose is vintage Clark. His early assessments and admonitions provide several strong starting points for thinking about the sociology of higher education—its foci, scope, and impact—as it developed over the next three decades. The remainder of this chapter reviews some contextual factors that facilitated or constrained developments within that sociology of higher education in the course of those decades. The chapters in Parts II and III of this volume cover in depth the distinct areas of inquiry and foundational contributions within each area. Then, in the final part, Clark and I step back to reconsider some factors that shape the field's future prospects.

Contextual Factors

How specific social conditions shape knowledge is a fundamental concern of sociologists of knowledge. Although it is important to identify the scholarly legacies and the very ideas that have defined a field's canon to date, the basic premise of a sociology of knowledge is that the intellectual currents of a field do not simply flow in a self-propelled intellectual trajectory. Rather, the parameters and momentum of particular research questions and approaches are determined by human interests and the social contexts in which human beings reside. Together they make the very categories of thought thinkable and seen as worthwhile to pursue (Swidler and Arditi 1994). Through this "sociology of knowledge" lens, we can see more clearly how the sociology of higher education has been shaped by its contexts.

As some readers may be uncomfortable with the premise that wider conditions are so powerfully determinative of ideas, it may be more palatable to consider how the epistemological space for ideas is created within particular social and political conditions. For example, the study of educational inequality would not find much traction in a society where egalitarian ideology was fully institutionalized and realized. Research on the impact of college on students would not develop without concern for student development and the availability of information either from or about students themselves. The study of the academic profession would not have formed unless academic positions proliferated and became infused with some degree of professional authority and expertise. For the field as a whole—its past purposes as well as future prospects—it is also instructive to think about the contexts in which researchers work, what fuels their interests, and what professional pressures are brought to bear on them to draw in external research funding or tailor their research to address local problems. (This has particular significance for the sociology of higher education, where researchers to varying degrees straddle distinctly different academic orbits, sociology and higher education—a topic that is addressed more fully in Chapter 12's discussion of professional contexts.)

Two levels of contextual factors—societal and organizational—warrant attention up front, for over these several decades they have generated changes in the practical realities of higher education. Interest in those changes has led researchers to draw on sociological resources to explore these topics, because they were of interest in their own right or because they provided suitable sites to advance sociological ideas. Although thematic interdependencies will be obvious across these levels, I attempt to separate them as analytically distinct contextual elements linked with the ideas that researchers pursued as dominant lines of inquiry in the sociology of higher education. Rather than providing a comprehensive review, this discussion surveys particular dynamics (and associated citations) to illustrate how specific research interests were stimulated by changing conditions.

Societal

By 1970, there was a heightened awareness that societal conditions beyond colleges and universities reshape academic purposes and practices. This coincided with higher education research that called attention to the role of "external forces" in academic change (Hefferlin 1969). Although at the time researchers tended to conceptualize a somewhat arbitrary distinction between internal and external forces, it was readily apparent to researchers and observers alike that wider societal currents were reflected on campuses, and vice versa. As discussed below, interest in particular research topics within the sociology of higher education was fueled by these currents and by mounting pressures on higher education to serve society's diverse needs.

Continued Expansion in the Scale of the Enterprise

By 1970, U.S. society looked to higher education to play roles over and above earlier expectations, most visibly to grant credentials to a wider proportion of the population in an ever-expanding array of fields. Even with continued expansion of the U.S. higher education system, its magnitude and decentralization worked against the public's perception of it as a system. Expansion occurred in many arenas: unprecedented increases in enrollment, increased size of campuses, the founding of new campuses, the dramatic development of research capacity, the increased number of faculty (tripling in the decade of the 1960s alone), knowledge growth across the disciplines and a concomitant increase in library holdings, and increases in expenditures due to increased public funding for student financial assistance and sponsored research.

Given the increased size and complexity of academic organizations, prominent organizational theorists (e.g., Cohen, March, and Olsen 1972) turned their analytical attention to the *internal* workings of colleges and universities. Overall, the study of organizational continuity and change was enhanced by functionalist perspectives from sociology, such as bureaucratic organization (March and Simon 1958), differentiation (Blau 1970; Clark 1983), systems theory (Parsons and Platt 1973), and key works in institutional theory that emphasize the supporting roles of rationalized myth and ceremony in legitimation (Meyer 1977; Meyer and Rowan 1977). Specific foci addressed essential features of academic structures (hierarchy, rules, positions) and practices (leadership, decision making, resource allocation). The *ASHE Reader on Organization and Governance in Higher Education* (Peterson 1983) captured many interests that were central to this period. It is noteworthy that the volume, in its fifth edition by 2006, was part of the ASHE Reader Series, used primarily by faculty and students in higher education programs around the country. (The Association for the Study of Higher Education, ASHE, was founded in 1976, with Burton Clark serving as president from 1979 to 1980 and Marvin Peterson from 1982 to 1983.) Peterson's Chapter Six in this book offers an even more comprehensive overview of these and related developments in the study of academic organizations over several decades prior to and since then, characterizing the major conceptual approaches to organizational studies of colleges and universities.

Over the next two decades it became more commonplace to examine higher education's adaptation. Notable full-length studies also contributed foundational concepts for analyzing higher education's structures, as well as changes and tensions therein, whether as a state system (Smelser 1973) or as a national system (Clark 1983). These last two books deserve special mention because they address the mechanisms for dramatic expansion as higher education continued its transformation in meeting society's expectations, from elite to mass to universal access. They also make explicit how the institutional division of labor serves a range of egalitarian and meritocratic purposes, extending from colleges with open access to very selective campuses that pride themselves on having a concentration of talent and resources to provide excellence in teaching and research. (See also Jencks and Riesman 1968; Trow 1970, 1984; Collins 1979.)

To analyze these and related transformations, scholars have continued to conceptualize the expanding array of key social functions that higher education has been expected to fulfill for society. Higher education is understood as serving the nation-state, with societal forces legitimating higher education's production of social actors, among them colleges and universities as organizational actors (Meyer 1977; Meyer, Ramirez, Frank, and Schofer's Chapter 7 in this volume). As societal expectations change, they have been characterized as a steady accretion of demands for complexity (Clark 1993), and as changes in the social charter between higher education and society, the social charter defined as the implicit understanding of their respective rights and responsibilities.[1] By the close of the twentieth century, the prominence of widely divergent expectations for higher education's priorities prompted higher education analysts to consider whether the social charter was being redefined or reinterpreted (Gumport 2000; Kezar 2004).

Underlying the literature, an implicit question on the minds of some researchers and observers is how well higher education is fulfilling its responsibilities and adapting to changing societal expectations for educating citizens and workers. Yet the companion question must also be asked in the same vein: to what extent society is fulfilling its responsibilities and making an ongoing public investment to sustain higher education's institutional capacity, to trust professional authority, and to protect campuses for their unique societal functions as places that have historically fostered critical thinking and even social dissent.

It is often remarked that higher education has expanded in scale and complexity, and quite reasonably, research in this field has addressed those changes. Research on the expansion of the enterprise and the consequences emanating from that growth and diversification of campuses has been clearly reflected in each of the initial domains in the sociology of higher education, from the study of higher education as a social institution to different types of academic organizations, to faculty, to students, to inequality. In contrast, research on the changing relationships between higher education and society still warrants much more creative thinking about how to conceptualize (let alone frame research designs for) studying such key ideas as the changing dynamics of status attainment and stratification, the needs of the labor market and the economy more broadly, and the many ways that higher education has come into play within political issues, from state to national to transnational levels. Even a cursory look at the topics reveals an interdependence of the social with the political and economic (or the political economic, depending on one's theoretical mindset). Accordingly, since

1. Among other things, colleges and universities of all types expect academic freedom and a certain degree of institutional autonomy. Society writ large in turn expects that higher education will be accessible and affordable for all who seek it, while simultaneously rewarding merit, advancing knowledge, training the workforce, and educating citizens. Moreover, since the 1990s, colleges and universities have faced mounting societal pressure to demonstrate accountability, especially for how they use public funding, within a more widely taken-for-granted "institutional performance" paradigm (Gumport 1997).

1970, sociologists of higher education have looked broadly across disciplines as they develop questions and concepts for their research. This is especially apparent in Part III of this volume, where chapters trace the evolution of key lines of inquiry in studies of higher education as an institution and as a complex organization, studies on diversity and diverse learning environments, and studies linking higher education policy and politics. Thus, societal expectations to expand the enterprise in scale and complexity have been a driving force for many lines of inquiry in the field.

Economic Turbulence

Over the last few decades, recurring economic cycles of recession, abundance, and retrenchment have produced specific challenges that lend themselves to study. Conceptually, as open-systems perspectives developed in the 1970s and came to dominate in the minds of those studying organizations in the 1980s and 1990s, colleges and universities were perfect sites for the analysis of organizational responses to environmental changes, including adaptation and isomorphism. Research questions differed in emphasis, linking environmental forces with changes in organizational structure, planning, or decision making. The nature of the scholarly contributions ranged from developing theory and more sophisticated methods (e.g., modeling) to developing a conceptual framework that shed new light on practical problems. Researchers across sociology departments, business schools, and schools of education developed a massive literature on higher education's responses to changing conditions in different academic settings (Tolbert 1985; Cameron, Sutton, and Whetten 1988). Major foci extended from organizational strategy and the management of change to the challenges entailed in resource dependence and the need for managers to attend to the vulnerabilities therein (Gumport and Sporn 1999).

The 1980s in particular saw extensive conceptual and empirical work on change processes within the context of decline (Cameron, Sutton, and Whetten 1988; Zammuto and Cameron 1985). George Keller's *Academic Strategy* (1983) became a long-running hit among leaders of colleges and universities: the book's implicit use of sociological concepts took a back seat to the author's addressing practical concerns of academic leaders. The tremendous interest in the practical problems of campuses raises the question of which publications should be considered sociology of higher education: whether studies should be considered sociology at all when researchers have borrowed tools from other disciplines (economics, management science, and political science) and whether publications should even be considered scholarship when they at most only implicitly use sociological concepts or when they have little to no empirical grounding. These questions remain unanswered meta-considerations among those interested in defining what constitutes work in this field and identifying the field's contributors.

During these decades, some lines of inquiry among sociologists studying higher education considered the impact of economic turbulence on the scope of the academic enterprise. This interest burgeoned over the years with the increasingly pervasive belief that campuses (especially research universities) should change in direct correspondence to market shifts. The labor market for faculty was initially studied by Theodore Caplow and Reece McGee in *The Academic Marketplace* (1958), specifically revisited by D. L. Burke (1986), and more comprehensively considered by M. J. Finkelstein (1984) and H. R. Bowen and J. H. Schuster (1986). Some research also conceptualized the interdependence between shifting resources, categories, and careers of academic personnel and national science policy. For example, David E. Drew's (1985) study of academic science, which took an instrumental hue, signaled interest in the convergence of faculty careers, graduate education, and wider economic and political forces.

However, it was not until the late 1990s that the presumption of market forces as a legitimate driving force for change came to dominate among practitioners and researchers alike, including examining where and how market forces have come to occupy center stage and how campuses adapt and handle the organizational consequences (Leslie and Fretwell 1996; Gumport 2000; Breneman, Pusser, and Turner 2000). A contributing factor was the crumbling presumption that states would provide sufficient funding for public colleges and universities, as campuses were left to step up their revenue-generating activities and more purposefully cultivate nonstate sources of revenue. These shifts marked possibilities for study at several levels, from more macro dynamics (discussed by John Meyer and colleagues in Chapter 7) to the very local realities of academic units (addressed by James Hearn in Chapter 8) and the effects of these changes on faculty and the academic workplace (as Gary Rhoades considers in Chapter 5).

Politics: Liberal and Neoliberal Interests

Several topics in the sociology of higher education over the last thirty years can be traced to a sustained liberal sensibility that persisted despite eras when conservative political administrations dominated the nation's capital. Many of these topics were reenergized by waves of social movements, including civil rights, free speech, the anti–Vietnam War movement, women's liberation, and gay rights.

Such wider political conditions can be seen as galvanizing the study of educational inequality: both how inequality leads to different patterns of college attendance and how higher education reproduces social inequality and status hierarchies. Research on educational inequality was initially embedded in a larger body of sociological work on status attainment and occupational attainment, where the main interest was to describe and explain the role of education in status differences. The political agenda of the Left and more radical groups provided further impetus to study inequality as a social problem. It is critical to note that many students entering graduate programs in the late 1960s and early 1970s brought a sense of urgency to study if not to solve social problems, or at the very least they were preoccupied by social problems and even helped define the research agenda of those who developed academic careers (Gumport 2002a). Whether framed as an explicit commitment to social justice or as more of an academic interest, from 1970 on, the identification and elaboration of research questions about inequality were a great preoccupation for faculty and graduate students within both sociology and education. Building upon the sociological theory of stratification (e.g., Bendix and Lipset 1953), concepts of class, status, and power provided leverage to study race, class, and gender from several angles (including what came to be known as identity politics). Moreover, as U.S. higher education made the transition to universal access (Trow 1970), the ensuing diversity of student populations reinforced a sense of urgency to study these issues (see Chapters 3, 4, and 9 of this volume) as well as patterns of group membership and social mobility, not only in the United States but worldwide.

A related set of questions spurred further research on the impact of college on students, research that tended to focus on the social-psychological effects of college rather than on students' subsequent status attainment—although in retrospect some research could be seen as both (e.g., the choice of college major and the subsequent destinations of students).

Research on inequality and college effects is an excellent example of how a thematic interest manifests on several levels of higher education, each of which warrants inquiry. Research in these areas also reflects a range of methodological approaches, including examining college student characteristics and pathways through the analysis of large data sets and analyzing social and cultural dynamics on campuses. By the 1990s researchers were also taking phenomenological approaches, extending even into high schools to study college aspirations and college knowledge and linking those with varying rates of persistence (McDonough 1997; see also Chapters 3, 4, and 9 in this volume).

Theoretically, another residual of this political climate is found in renewed enthusiasm for scholarly approaches with explicit intellectual roots in Marxism and the Frankfurt School and for those that aim to characterize, analyze, or explain power, domination, or exploitation in higher education. The basic political sensibility expressed throughout the 1960s questioned the nature and limits of authority and dispelled myths of political neutrality with a critical lens that opened up new scholarly avenues. Although such approaches have not been institutionalized as widely as functionalism in sociology, they have gained visibility in the study of higher education, such as in analyzing organizations (Heydebrand 1990), faculty behavior (Silva and Slaughter 1984), and the spread of technology as a vehicle for advancing the commercialization and corporatization of higher education (Noble 2002).[2]

At the same time, however, we must note the lack of either theoretical or empirical research on the role of the state, as Rhoades (1992) observes. Informed by the views of higher education scholars trained initially in political science, research has focused on mechanisms for statewide coordination of higher education (e.g., Berdahl 1971) and has critically reexamined perennial issues like academic freedom (Slaughter 1988) and university autonomy (Slaughter and Leslie 1997). With regard to these topics, it must be noted that these researchers have developed a critical lens beyond the practical realities of contemporary higher education, and they have contributed analyses of the linkages between particular academic settings (especially universities) and broader political-economic domains, such as university contributions to economic development, national defense, and the commercialization of science. The focus

2. Although his contributions analyze wider social forces at work in higher education, David Noble is regarded more as a critical historian than as a sociologist, a nuance often lost in the controversy over his explicitly political—leftist—agenda.

was on the state as regulator until more recent work examined the state as client, which provides another angle on understanding how the state legitimates particular structures and forms of knowledge. These topics have been elaborated to advance both theory and empirical research in the field by Gary Rhoades and Sheila Slaughter (2004), alongside more sweeping critiques that lament problematic political economic developments in the enterprise (Aronowitz 2000; Readings 1996). Efforts to reexamine the relationship between higher education and the state have laid the groundwork for refocusing the lenses of research to consider higher education's increasingly pivotal role in today's knowledge economy.

Societal Demands for Knowledge

The study of higher education has long emphasized the enterprise's people-processing functions over its role in knowledge production, transmission, and legitimation (Clark 1983). In spite of ever-expanding societal demands for each of these knowledge functions, this nexus between conceptual and practical concerns has not received the attention it deserves, as will be discussed further in Chapter Twelve.

In the 1970s, the biotechnology and computer industries joined the federal and state governments in urging higher education to step up its research capacity, especially to advance knowledge applications. By the 1980s, various government agencies sought to cultivate industry's direct support of academic research, in an attempt to wean research universities off federal funding. The Patent and Trademark Amendments of 1980 (also known as the Bayh-Dole Act) paved the way for this, by allowing universities and their faculty to apply for patents on scientific discoveries emerging from federally funded research projects. Along with legislation, passed in 1984, that further loosened restrictions on commercializing research, the Bayh-Dole Act created new opportunities for collaboration between universities and industry. In reducing legal barriers to commercialization of publicly funded academic research, the act encouraged university administrators and faculty to consider the fruits of academic research as intellectual property with value in the marketplace.

These initiatives and their underlying issues offered several topics ripe for sociological analysis, including analyses that downplay the impact of this legislation (Mowery et al. 2004). Key questions range from what mechanisms support knowledge production processes to how changing research priorities have altered higher education's structures and values, faculty work roles and rewards, and graduate students' professional socialization. Aside from Clark Kerr's definitive proclamation of "the multiversity" as a new organizational form, the study of knowledge production and its consequences for campuses and for faculty as knowledge producers was relatively underdeveloped until the 1990s.

One line of inquiry in this domain can be traced back to Florian Znaniecki's *The Social Role of the Man of Knowledge* (1940) and the resulting subfield of the sociology of intellectuals, popular in the 1960s and 1970s but in subsequent decades losing currency as a specialization within sociology. More contemporary investigations by higher education researchers include John M. Braxton's (1993) study of Mertonian norms and Clark's studies on the research foundations of graduate education (1995), case studies of entrepreneurial universities in Europe (1998), and sequel to the latter on sustaining change (2004).

Against a backdrop of society's expectations that higher education fulfill critical knowledge functions, these studies illustrate how the investigation of both normative and structural dimensions can capture some important transformations within the academy, including faculty roles, academic priorities, and the institutional leadership required to ensure the centrality of higher education to the knowledge economy. The change over time can be marked by the old reference to "academic" as "irrelevant," which has been replaced by a new mandate that academic priorities should reflect a strategic search for opportunities and make the requisite changes in organizational practices and forms. The studies themselves are examples of work in the field that seeks to advance our understanding of practical realities while adding to the field's conceptual foundations.

A related line of inquiry has been pursued by sociologists of science, although more within the scholarly parameters of that subfield—exemplified by studies of laboratories (Latour 1979), networks (Crane 1972), and boundary work in scientific communities (Gieryn 1983)—than in universities per se. This research does underscore the importance of studying knowledge creators themselves, and some researchers in higher education have framed their studies on faculty in university settings with this in mind (Clark 1987a, 1987b; Hackett 1990; Gumport 1990, 2002a). For the most part, unfortunately, the tendency among higher education researchers is to revisit topic-oriented problems that have been well traversed, such as the presumed tension between teaching and research, rather than breaking new ground conceptually or empirically.

One exception is the study of knowledge production in universities by sociologists who have examined universities and their collaboration with industry, building a conceptual and empirical foundation that brings to light some contemporary dynamics in research and patenting relationships, commercialization, and knowledge networks (e.g., Powell 1990; Powell and Owen-Smith 1998).

The transmission of knowledge through the formal curriculum (and through the "informal curriculum" experienced by students outside of class) has offered great potential for sociological analysis, a potential that remains largely untapped. During the 1980s some interest in this area was prompted by tensions in curricular change and enlivened by the "culture wars" debates over core requirements (Nussbaum 1997; D'Souza 1991). The study of knowledge change across the disciplines has been investigated from distinctive angles—for example, through the window of graduate education (Clark 1995). But for the most part, commentaries are far more common than research on a few selected disciplines (Bender and Schorske 1998) or on a cluster of disciplines (Ellis 1997). During the 1980s and 1990s discussions ensued about the relative impact of race, gender, sexual orientation, and class on the curriculum, as students pressured for expanded course offerings reflecting identity-specific subject matter and treating issues of difference and as degree programs and departments were created for ethnic and gender studies. While some research has examined the impact of race or gender on a discipline (J. Scott 1999), it has been rare to see studies of knowledge change at the intersection of changing disciplinary and organizational contexts (Gumport 1990, 2002a; Lattuca 2001; Slaughter 1997). By the 1990s more academic calls were heard for studying power and "positionality" in knowledge (Burbules and Rice 1991), for studying the contextual factors that determine how entire institutional orderings of knowledge are established and changed (Swidler and Arditi 1994; Gumport 2000, 2002b; Gumport and Snydman 2002; Frank and Gabler 2006), and for examining how higher education produces culture together with other institutions like media (Swidler and Arditi 1994). More broadly in the academy, a multiplicity of critical voices emerged with a new vocabulary about postmodernism and cultural studies, deconstructing categories of thought; however, these did not jell as a sustained subfield, given that the scholars themselves juggle multiple identities and affinity groups and often have fractured group politics.

Given the momentum behind wider expectations for higher education to meet societal demands for knowledge, it is no surprise that some observers have oversimplified the issue by characterizing knowledge as higher education's "core business." This is problematic because it presumes a common set of priorities among different types of campuses. Even more profoundly, it belies suspense about the future, for as some researchers note, higher education has no monopoly on knowledge—neither its production nor its transmission. Various possibilities for researchers to penetrate further some complexities of knowledge production, transmission, and legitimation will be discussed in this volume's concluding chapter.

Growing Interest in National Systems and Global Interdependence

Over the past several decades the general U.S. population has become increasingly aware of global interdependence and the ensuing related economic and political changes. The related changes in higher education have occupied less attention, despite dramatic changes in cross-national student mobility, scholarly communication, and institutional collaboration.

The sociology of comparative higher education has for some time had much potential, as Clark (1973) indicated, and yet the area remains underdeveloped. Major contributions in cross-national research on higher education systems have come from sociologists, providing lenses with which to examine national systems. At one end of a continuum can be found work that conceptualizes change at the most macro world-systems level (Meyer et al. 1997; Meyer, Ramirez, and Soysal 1992; Meyer et al., Chapter 7 of this volume). At the other end we can note key studies that have defined how to think about the nature and evolution of academic systems (Ben-David 1977; Clark 1983, 1995). These works have had "big picture" value that has stood the test of time, regardless of substantive changes in higher education in any particular country.

Yet only a small community of scholars in the United States have demonstrated a primary commitment to studying higher education in other countries, such as in Latin America and more recently in Asia. In addition to Burton Clark and John Meyer, these include Philip Altbach, Roger Geiger, D. Bruce Johnstone, Daniel Levy, and Francisco Ramirez. Their research spans the major domains put forward by Clark—the study of inequality and college impact, and research on faculty and academic work, as well as organization and governance.

The growing emphasis on—and opportunities to study—globalization widens out research possibilities to a different scope, prompting us to consider the appropriate levels of analysis. The ascendance of higher education subfields, such as institutional study of academic change and comparative analysis of academic systems, continues to be facilitated by sociological legacies from institutional theory (Meyer 1977; W. Scott et al. 2000; DiMaggio and Powell 1983), systems theory (Parsons 1937, 1951; Parsons and Platt 1973), and the study of organizations (W. Scott 1998).[3] In addition, as sociologist Randall Collins (1999) has argued, the macro level of analysis can provide an illuminating historical context for broader economic and political phenomena. In relation to higher education, the utility of these levels of analysis suggests even greater potential for studying not only national differences but dynamics that are transnational and possibly global. (See Chapter 12 for further discussion of prospects for future inquiry.)

By the 1990s, important scholarship explicitly urged researchers to address understudied conceptual directions and to be more purposeful in determining the theoretical and empirical parameters for study. Whether in cross-national studies or in research solely within the United States, arguments have been made for greater attention to the "meso" or middle level. As Neil J. Smelser (1997) has proposed, scholars can profit from analyzing institutions for the changes in their social functions and dynamics of interdependence. Another provocative suggestion, taking its cue from organizational theory in sociology, is to study higher education

---

3. A critical distinction must be made here between the terms *institution* and *organization*. In higher education the term *institutional* tends to be used casually as synonymous with *organizational*, when one is referring to features that characterize a particular organization, its leaders, its policies, or its autonomy. In contrast, the term *institution* or *institutional* sends a clear signal to those familiar with sociology and institutional theory that the referent includes the organization but also extends to the wider society. Through the lens of institutional theory, colleges and universities as well as the individuals within them can be understood as being subjected to societal imperatives emanating from wider expectations about higher education's social functions. This perspective is a valuable window for examining the redefinition of what activities are or are not recognized as "higher education." Over time there has been an expansion of activities regarded as falling within the legitimate province of higher education, from educating the masses, fostering human development, advancing and credentialing learning, socializing citizens and cultivating political loyalties, promoting scholarly discourse and preserving knowledge to contributing directly to economic development, advancing knowledge through research, and developing industrial applications—all pointing to an increase in higher education's social embeddedness. Over the past two decades, a growing interest in institutional theory among higher education researchers has necessitated greater specificity in the use of these terms. It should further be noted that there are distinct institutional theories, from the sociological work of Meyer and colleagues (Chapter 7 of this volume) to variants in political science and economics.

as an organizational field (McDonough, Ventresca, and Outcalt 2000). Further conceptual and empirical work along these lines needs to examine the differentiation of academic organizations into levels and types, each with distinct sets of environmental expectations. This line of inquiry is all the more salient in a historical period when universities and colleges are confronted with new problems as they visibly engage in partnerships with different types of organizations in commercialization and distance learning—activities that call into question previously established distinctions between internal and external and that redraw boundaries so as to blur distinctions between and among academic and nonacademic organizations, thereby resulting in new organizational forms. Such challenges richly variegate the already complex study of international higher education.

Organizational

In addition to these changes transpiring in the wider society, in the decades from 1970 on, colleges and universities continued to expand and elaborate their structures. From a cross-national perspective, the magnitude of the enterprise and the mission differentiation among U.S. campuses is nothing short of extraordinary. As Peterson notes in Chapter Six, the term *postsecondary* came to be a preferred referent among some observers and analysts for distinguishing between the traditional higher education system and the proliferation of institutional types— differentiation of missions, expansion, and diversification of enrollments and personnel—all dramatic changes further elaborated in the last quarter of the twentieth century. These changes are all the more noteworthy given the cycles of environmental turbulence, which produced formidable challenges to managing resources and finding opportunities for growth amid financial constraints.

Against that backdrop, three sets of organizational transformations after 1970 nurtured scholarly inquiry within the sociology of higher education, specifically in the study of organization and governance but spilling over into research on students and faculty: (1) environmental uncertainty and the concurrent rise of academic management; (2) organizational innovation and integration; and (3) profound changes in the academic workplace. Although these transformations became subjects of distinct lines of inquiry, their interdependence anchored their co-evolution in higher education. In turn these topics achieved easy recognition as worthwhile foci for problem-oriented research in the sociology of higher education, as the forthcoming chapters detail.

The heightened awareness of environmental uncertainty and adaptation challenges opened the door for campus leaders to expand their capacity to plan and manage resources. The growth in the number of administrators may be seen as an attempt to manage internal functions —to coordinate the work of an increasingly complex organization and to report on campus operations as demands for information increased from system and state offices. From 1970 onward, we saw growth in budgets and numbers of administrative positions, accompanied by an increasingly elaborate set of tools and ideology for academic management (Gumport and Pusser 1995; Gumport and Sporn 1999). Increased expenditures for administration during periods of fiscal stringency warranted some explanation. Expanded administrative positions did as well, given calls for streamlining and downsizing. If scholars found Weberian notions of bureaucracy and rationalization apt before, these became all the more revelatory of higher education as administrative tasks and offices proliferated, along with standardized procedures that entitled staff with oversight responsibilities to be informed of decentralized activities. The advent of computers and dramatic advances in information technology and the associated computer hardware enabled staff to manage budgets and personnel, maintain student records, and track hours taught, the production of credit hours, and faculty members' courses taught. For those who study colleges and universities, of course, all this information becomes data.

Both in times of abundant financial resources and sometimes with only symbolic resources available, campuses have increased experimentation with initiatives in academic programs and residential life under the banner of "innovation." With these efforts came the opportunity for researchers to investigate and explain which types of innovation succeed and which fail (Levine 1980). Some of the most visible organizational changes occurred peripheral to instruction; for example, the proliferation of organized research units, the growing number of nonfaculty researchers, and the establishment of new research centers. More central to the educational mission, curricular innovation tended to be additive as well. Both organizationally and intellectually, the curriculum was stretched into numerous fields of specialization, and academic departments splintered off into new majors and degree programs, some of which spanned academic units. This more elaborate curricular scaffold-

ing provided opportunities for researchers to analyze academic change
—the nature of change, resistance to change, and the consequences of
change. Another set of issues ripe for study in the arena of curricular
change relates to the deep-seated tension between divergent aims of
studying knowledge—for its own sake and for its instrumental value.
Particularly in the reform of general education requirements, emphases
have changed among the long-standing rationales for higher education
to develop character, cultivate citizenship, promote cultural literacy, and
prepare the workforce. It has been illuminating to examine these shifts
in light of wider societal pressures and vis-à-vis social movements that
reframe educational priorities. Questions have been posed such as,
Should a core curriculum enlighten people about multiculturalism and
diversity? Is it the place of the university to further practical and vocational skills?

Academic settings became more internally diverse as changing societal demographics were reflected—slowly in student populations and
even more slowly in the changing composition of faculty. One dominant concern among those in charge of academic organizations was
whether individuals from a wider range of backgrounds and interests
would reconstitute the social order on campus; specifically whether they
would create a new pluralism or fragment into semiautonomous units
and groups (Dill 1982). These concerns were readily taken up in the
mid-1980s and early 1990s by those applying the concept of organizational culture to colleges and universities, bolstered by a resurgence of
sociological interest in culture (Pettigrew 1979; Martin 1992) and sensemaking in organizations (Weick 1995).

Although rarely defined or used consistently, the idea of culture was
also invoked as a placeholder for shared norms and understandings that
constitute a way of life, bringing to the fore softer and less tangible
dimensions of social organization than those derived from structuralist
accounts; and as such, cultural differences could be conceived of across
academic disciplines and academic departments. For higher education,
this interest also found a strong legacy in Clark's (1970) concept of saga
and in his highlighting the expressive dimensions and traditions of
organizational identities. Given that many campuses had reached unprecedented levels of diversity by the late 1990s, the spirit of multiculturalism was to embrace "difference" rather than overlook it. This
dovetailed with broader intellectual currents in the social sciences engaging in particularistic inquiry. However, the legal context—affirmative

action and the backlash against it—added new reasons for further study of diversity, not simply for understanding student life but to document the educational benefits of diverse learning environments broadly defined. (See Chapters 4 and 9 of this volume.)

It is no surprise that some higher education researchers studying organizational dynamics adopted interpretive frameworks premised on subjectivity and problematized consensus. (Functionalist approaches to analyzing conflict viewed it as a pathology to be overcome for equilibrium to be restored, as opposed to theoretical approaches that saw conflict as an ongoing organizational dynamic.) Conceptualizing campuses as having distinct cultures also has provided a suitable set of lenses for studying how culture affects students and how students are socialized. Framed by Kenneth Feldman and Theodore Newcomb (1969, p. 5), one major research focus examines the impact of college on undergraduates, "assessing whether and how undergraduates change their beliefs, values and character" as mediated by specific kinds of institutional arrangements. Studies of college impact continued to be central work in higher education, though much of the research favored psychological approaches following the growth of developmental theory in late adolescence (e.g., Chickering, Kohlberg, Perry, Gilligan). Two notable exceptions were the work of Vincent Tinto (1987) and John C. Weidman (1989), whose perspectives emphasize normative values and attitudes, influential membership and reference groups, and more generally, the socializing function of student, faculty, and organizational cultures. Increasing diversity in the student body with respect to race, ethnicity, age, national origin, enrollment status, and residential status (e.g., part time, full time, commuter) prompted researchers to acknowledge the existence of multiple and overlapping college subcultures (Tinto 1997; Hurtado 1992 and Chapter 4 in this volume).

Cultural approaches to understanding student socialization were further enlivened by increased diversity in the late 1980s and 1990s (see Chapter 9). Building on the theoretical and methodological foundations of Burton Clark and Martin Trow's (1972) study of student subcultures and Clark's (1970) analyses of distinctive liberal arts colleges, several researchers conducted ethnographic and case study research on various subpopulations: women (Holland and Eisenhart 1990), gay men (Rhoads 1994), Chicanos (Gonzalez 2000), and others. The development of an increasingly complex mix of subcultures on college campuses raised a more general problem in practice that was ripe for study: how an organization inhabited by multiple—and often contentious—cultural groups creates community across differences (Tierney 1993). This diversity gave rise to comparative studies of race and ethnicity, by the close of the century.

Just as the diversification of student populations signaled changes within the organization, the composition of the faculty came to reflect more women, although at lower ranks and in lower-status institutions (Valian 1998). Faculty of color were slower to be hired and gain visibility on campuses around the country (Milem and Astin 1993), but the juxtaposition of their limited representation alongside unprecedented student diversity placed mounting pressures on institutions for organizational change. From a functionalist perspective, one potential consequence of greater diversification was increased fragmentation among faculty, beyond that resulting from intellectual specialization. This fed the recognition in the late 1980s that the academic profession was not monolithic, neither nationally nor on a given campus (Ruscio 1987). The dramatically different working conditions across stratified institutional types of campuses—and for full-time versus part-time faculty—were critical to examine, along with their consequences for teaching and research.

Disciplinary specialization had become a powerful force for organizing academic life into enclaves that gave further traction to the concept of academic cultures (Clark 1987; Becher 1987). We have come a long way since C. P. Snow's initial characterization of two cultures (1959), and academic organizations can be seen as having dozens of cultures—not only in the disciplines but also locally, as faculty assemble around an ever-growing number of interdisciplinary and multidisciplinary academic programs, majors, and scholarly agendas. A resulting challenge for the organization as a whole—and the academic workplace specifically—for some time now has been how to hold it together. One sociological vantage point for addressing this practical concern is rooted in Durkheim's insights about the division of labor in modern society: in a differentiating system, integrating mechanisms not only can coordinate work but can also reinforce the awareness of interdependence. From a Parsonian perspective, social control dynamics embedded in the structural and normative foundations support continuity in the social order. These are powerful legacies for inquiring into the nature of fragmentation within higher education organizations and within the academic profession.

For example, the orientations of faculty can be considered: political views in the 1970s were understood as a potential basis for solidarity, as E. C. Ladd and S. M. Lipset (1975) report in their national survey data. The tendency toward liberal leanings was well summarized by a newspaper headline at the time, which as I recall read "Professors drive Volvos, turn left." Yet scratching beneath the surface of this characterization, we see a greater mix of beliefs and purposes, including those associated with divergent political commitments and disciplinary loyalties. In fact, Clark's (1987) comprehensive investigation into academic life shows quite vividly how disciplinary specialization fosters fragmentation, such that disciplinary categories organize academic life but do so into small separate worlds. How they can be linked by overlapping membership and values (Clark's metaphor of fish scales) remains an interesting practical and scholarly puzzle from a functionalist perspective, especially given continued increases in the proportion of nontenure line (also referred to as "off-track") fixed-term and part-time faculty appointments and increased demographic diversity.

The fact of fragmentation in academic life has been compounded by further strain in the academic workplace related to ambiguity in the nature of its authority. Amitai Etzioni (1964) diagnosed some modern organizations as having a mix of professional and administrative authority, creating role ambiguity. All of these features have been evident in academic settings. Professionally oriented administrators have an ambiguous basis for authority. Administrator-faculty relations have been fraught with disagreement over unclear jurisdictions of authority, at times temporarily resolved through negotiation over respective rights and responsibilities that is formalized in collective bargaining contracts. Faculty are not of one mind as to whether they are self-regulating professionals (who ostensibly require autonomy to carry out their responsibilities) or employees in large organizations, nor as to the responsibilities and entitlements attendant upon each role.

Researchers have begun to examine several layers of this question, both the nature of the problem and how it plays out in contemporary workplace conditions for faculty, staff, and students. Some definitive work in this domain has sought to examine how rights and responsibilities are altered by the spread of managerialism (Rhoades 1998; Enteman 1993). Further research along these lines can advance the field by drawing on the conceptual foundations within sociological classics in the study of professions (Freidson 1986; Larson 1977; see also Chapter 5 in this volume).

From the twenty-first-century perspective, the nature of authority in academic organizations has reached an unprecedented complexity: bureaucratic authority embedded in organizational structures, professional authority embodied in faculty as academic professionals, and managerial authority enacted by an administrative cadre that gained momentum during the last quarter of the twentieth century. Prior research provides a starting point for examining the conditions wherein these distinct forces are likely to coexist, either in conflict or in harmony, as "shared authority." Conditions of organizational restructuring are revealing of these dynamics, particularly where some academic programs and departments are targeted for elimination or consolidation in times of budget cuts and faculty are concerned about losing faculty lines. The tensions in authority then become evident, as each campus is challenged to identify what knowledge matters most and should be protected, how it should be organized and supported, and what are legitimate decision-making procedures for making these determinations. As will be discussed in Chapter Twelve, this can be analyzed as the ideological underpinnings of a significant trend in restructuring: an industry logic that presumes competition and asks academic organizations to function more like businesses and to establish deeper ties with industry. Ripe for study, then, is not only the changing character of academic organizations but also the fact that new organizational forms entail new roles and rewards, and emerging knowledge areas along with changing personnel structures challenge the disciplinary organization of knowledge—major questions taken up by a few in the field (Abbott 2002; Brint 2005; Gumport 2002b). How and to what extent do such changes displace long-existing conceptions of what higher education is, how it should be organized, and how people are expected to act within it (Gumport 2000)?

In this context, significant changes in the workplace also suggest the efficacy of drawing upon foundational studies to examine academic departments as the intersection of changes in organizations, governance, and the profession (see Chapter 8 this volume). Although departments are widely recognized as self-reproducing in their power, and the expectation of departmental organization in colleges and universities is common, the academic structure has coevolved with academic knowledge such that concomitant changes in the nature of academic work have occurred and new organizational forms have emerged. These realities have made evident a new host of practical problems that lend themselves to study, calling for sociological concepts from adaptation and decision making to legitimation and status hierarchies.

Concern about the changing nature and context of faculty work has increased as campuses have hired greater numbers of fixed-term and part-time faculty, with estimates that non–tenure-line faculty account for up to 40 percent of instruction (Schuster and Finkelstein 2006). As institutional memory is lost with the retirement of an aging member-ship and as salary increases fail to keep pace with the cost of living, low faculty morale is further exacerbated by a declining public trust in them as professionals, with increasing public scrutiny of and accountability required for their work (Gumport 1997). Indeed, organizational trans-formations have brought us to a critical juncture with respect to faculty. We have yet to determine how colleges and universities may be sustained —not only as economic and organizational entities but also as intellec-tually viable and attractive places for academic work.

Changing Contours

These organizational transformations since 1970 have inspired and will continue to inspire inquiry within the sociology of higher education, specifically in what was once simply referred to as the study of organiza-tion and governance. The complexity of the changing realities them-selves have played a role in reshaping the organizing categories for the field, with inquiries that cross categories even within any given research project. For example, research on students or faculty may address ques-tions focused on organizational or governance dynamics, or on wider political, cultural, or ideological forces at work, which in turn play out locally. One result is that lines of inquiry do not necessarily develop linearly or with increased specialization. So while this complicates our work assembling such a volume, it may be interpreted as signifying the field's intellectual vitality.

Such complexities in the development of higher education, while suggesting many fruitful lines of inquiry within the sociology of higher education, also affect the interests and sense of possibilities for research-ers who contribute (or who might contribute) to the field. Researchers are drawn to research opportunities they perceive as worthwhile, but to varying degrees their perceptions are also shaped by their professional contexts, primarily their local university settings and professional associations—two contexts that visibly institutionalize enduring ideas within their academic structures, specializations, and subgroups, thereby signaling the categories of ideas deemed worthy of study and those considered trivial. Moreover, the corpus of work identified as *sociology of higher education* may straddle both worlds in name, but the researchers themselves tend to have a faculty appointment in either a professional school of education or a sociology department, and sometimes a courtesy appointment in one or the other. In each location they face distinct sets of expectations for the form and content of their research contributions and for how these are packaged for peer review. How actual or potential researchers may reconcile these pressures and what their contexts signal about the institutionalization of inquiry in the sociology of higher education are two considerations key to the field's vitality. I raise these themes now to identify contexts perhaps most immediately influencing the lines of inquiry explored in Parts II and III, and I will revisit and explore them more fully in the book's concluding chapter.

References

Abbott, A. 2002. "The Disciplines and the Future." In *The Future of the City of Intellect*, ed. S. Brint. Stanford, CA: Stanford University Press.

Aronowitz, S. 2000. *The Knowledge Factory: Dismantling the Corporate University and Creating True Higher Learning.* Boston: Beacon.

Becher, T. 1987. *Academic Tribes and Territories.* Milton Keynes, UK: Society for Research into Higher Education and Open University Press.

Ben-David, J. 1977. *Centers of Learning.* New York: McGraw-Hill.

Bender, T., and C. E. Schorske, eds. 1998. *American Academic Culture in Transformation: Fifty Years, Four Disciplines.* Princeton, NJ: Princeton University Press.

Bendix, R., and S. M. Lipset, eds. 1953. *Class, Status, and Power.* Glencoe, IL: Free Press.

Berdahl, R. O. 1971. *Statewide Coordination of Higher Education.* Washington, DC: American Council on Education.

Blau, P. M. 1970. "A Formal Theory of Differentiation in Organizations." *American Sociological Review* 35 (2): 201–18.

Bowen, H. R., and J. H. Schuster. 1986. *American Professors: A National Resource Imperiled.* New York: Oxford University Press.

Braxton, J. M. 1993. "Deviancy from the Norms of Science: The Effects of Anomie and Alienation in the Academic Profession." *Research in Higher Education* 34:213–28.

Breneman, D., B. Pusser, and S. Turner. 2000. *The Contemporary Provision of For-Profit Higher Education: Mapping the Competitive Market.* Working Paper SWP-02, For-Profit Higher Education Research Project, Curry School of Education, University of Virginia.

Brint, S. 2005. "Creating the Future: 'New Directions' in American Research Universities." *Minerva* 43:23–50.

Burbules, N. C., and S. Rice. 1991. "Dialogue across Differences: Continuing the Conversation." *Harvard Educational Review* 61:393–416.

Burke, D. L. 1986. "Change in the Academic Marketplace: A Study of Faculty Mobility in the 1980s." Ph.D. dissertation, University of North Carolina at Chapel Hill.

Cameron, K. S., R. I. Sutton, and D. A. Whetten, eds. 1988. *Readings in Organizational Decline.* Cambridge: Ballinger.

Caplow, T. C., and R. J. McGee. 1958. *The Academic Marketplace.* New York: Basic.

Clark, B. R. 1960a. "The 'Cooling Out' Function in Higher Education." *American Journal of Sociology* 65: 569–76.

——. 1960b. *The Open Door College: A Case Study.* New York: McGraw-Hill, 1960.

——. 1970. *The Distinctive College.* Chicago: Aldine.

——. 1973. "Development of the Sociology of Higher Education." *Sociology of Education* 46:2–14.

——. 1983. *The Higher Education System.* Berkeley: University of California Press.

——. 1987a. *The Academic Life: Small Worlds, Different Worlds.* Princeton, NJ: Carnegie Foundation for the Advancement of Teaching.

——, ed. 1987b. *The Academic Profession: National, Disciplinary, and Institutional Settings.* Berkeley: University of California Press.

——. 1993. "The Problem of Complexity in Modern Higher Education." In *The European and American University since 1800: Historical and Sociological Essays,* ed. S. Rothblatt and B. Wittrock, 263–79. Cambridge: Cambridge University Press.

——. 1995. *Places of Inquiry: Research and Advanced Education in Modern Universities.* Berkeley: University of California Press.

——. 1998. *Creating Entrepreneurial Universities.* Oxford: International Association of Universities Press.

——. 2004. *Sustaining Change in Universities: Continuities in Case Studies and Concepts.* Berkshire, UK: Open University Press.

Clark, B. R., and M. Trow. 1972. *Students and Colleges: Interaction and Change.* Berkeley: University of California, Center for Research and Development in Higher Education.

Clifford, G. J., and J. W. Guthrie. 1988. *Ed School: A Brief for Professional Education.* Chicago: University of Chicago Press.

Cohen, M. D., J. G. March, and J. P. Olsen. 1972. "A Garbage Can Model of Organizational Choice." *Administrative Science Quarterly* 17:1–25.

Collins, R. 1979. *The Credential Society.* New York: Academic Press.

———. 1999. *Macrohistory: Essays in Sociology of the Long Run.* Stanford, CA: Stanford University Press.

Crane, D. 1972. *Invisible Colleges: Diffusion of Knowledge in Scientific Communities.* Chicago: University of Chicago Press.

Dill, D. D. 1982. "The Management of Academic Culture: Notes on the Management of Meaning and Social Integration." *Higher Education* 11:303–20.

DiMaggio, P. J., and W. W. Powell. 1983. "The Iron Cage Revisited: Institutional Isomorphism and Collective Rationality in Organizational Fields." *American Sociological Review* 48:147–60.

Drew, D. E. 1985. *Strengthening Academic Science.* New York: Praeger.

D'Souza, D. 1991. *Illiberal Education: The Politics of Race and Sex on Campus.* New York: Free Press.

Ellis, J. M. 1997. *Literature Lost: Social Agendas and the Corruption of the Humanities.* New Haven, CT: Yale University Press.

Enteman, W. F. 1993. *Managerialism: The Emergence of a New Ideology.* Madison: University of Wisconsin Press.

Etzioni, A. 1964. *Modern Organizations.* Englewood Cliffs, NJ: Prentice-Hall.

Feldman, K. A., and T. M. Newcomb. 1969. *The Impact of College on Students.* San Francisco: Jossey-Bass.

Finkelstein, M. J. 1984. *The American Academic Profession.* Columbus: Ohio State University Press.

Frank, D., and J. Gabler. 2006. *Reconstructing the University: Worldwide Shifts in Academia in the 20th Century.* Stanford, CA: Stanford University Press.

Freidson, E. 1986. *Professional Powers: A Study of the Institutionalization of Formal Knowledge.* Chicago: University of Chicago Press.

Gieryn, T. 1983. "Boundary Work and the Demarcation of Science from Nonscience." *American Sociological Review* 48:781–95.

Gonzalez, K. P. 1999. *Campus Culture and the Experiences of Chicano Students in Predominantly White Colleges and Universities.* Paper presented at the annual meeting of the Association for the Study of Higher Education, San Antonio, TX, November.

Gumport, P. J. 1990. "Feminist Scholarship as a Vocation." *Higher Education* 20:231–43.

———. 1997. "Public Universities as Academic Workplaces." *Daedalus* 126 (4): 113–36.

———. 2000. "Academic Restructuring: Organizational Change and Institutional Imperatives." *Higher Education* 39:67–91.

———. 2002a. *Academic Pathfinders: Knowledge Creation and Feminist Scholarship.* Westport, CT: Greenwood.

——. 2002b. "Universities and Knowledge: Restructuring the City of Intellect." In *The Future of the City of Intellect: The Changing American University*, ed. S. Brint. Stanford, CA: Stanford University Press.

Gumport, P. J., and B. Pusser. 1995. "A Case of Bureaucratic Accretion: Context and Consequences." *Journal of Higher Education* 66:493–520.

Gumport, P. J., and S. Snydman. 2002. "The Formal Organization of Knowledge: An Analysis of Academic Structure." *Journal of Higher Education* 73 (3): 375–408.

Gumport, P. J., and B. Sporn. 1999. "Institutional Adaptation: Demands for Management Reform and University Administration." In *Higher Education: Handbook of Theory and Research*, vol. 14, eds. J. C. Smart and W. G. Tierney, 103–45. New York: Agathon.

Hackett, E. J. 1990. "Science as a Vocation in the 1990s: The Changing Organizational Culture of Academic Science." *Journal of Higher Education* 61:241–79.

Hefferlin, J. B. L. 1969. *Dynamics of Academic Reform*. San Francisco: Jossey-Bass.

Heydebrand, W. 1990. "The Technocratic Organization of Work." In *Structures of Power and Constraint: Papers in Honor of Peter M. Blau*, ed. C. J. Calhoun, M. Meyer, and W. R. Scott. Cambridge: Cambridge University Press.

Holland, D. C., and M. A. Eisenhart. 1990. *Educated in Romance: Women, Achievement, and College Culture*. Chicago: University of Chicago Press.

Hollingshead, A. B. 1949. *Elmtown's Youth*. New York: John Wiley.

Hurtado, S. 1992. "The Campus Racial Climate." *Journal of Higher Education* 63 (5): 539–69.

Jencks, C., and D. Riesman. 1968. *The Academic Revolution*. New York: Doubleday.

Keller, G. 1983. *Academic Strategy*. Baltimore: Johns Hopkins University Press.

Kezar, A. 2004. "Obtaining Integrity: Reviewing and Examining the Charter between Higher Education and Society." *Review of Higher Education* 27 (40): 429–59.

Ladd, E. C., and S. M. Lipset. 1975. *The Divided Academy: Professors and Politics*. New York: McGraw-Hill.

Larson, M. S. 1977. *The Rise of Professionalism: A Sociological Analysis*. Berkeley: University of California Press.

Latour, B. 1979. *Laboratory Life: The Social Construction of Scientific Facts*. Beverly Hills, CA: Sage.

Lattuca, L. 2001. *Creating Interdisciplinarity*. Nashville: Vanderbilt University Press.

Lazasfeld, P. F., and W. Thielens Jr. 1958. *The Academic Mind: Social Scientists in a Time of Crisis*. Glencoe, IL: Free Press.

Leslie, D. W., and E. K. Fretwell Jr. 1996. *Wise Moves in Hard Times: Creating and Managing Resilient Colleges and Universities.* San Francisco: Jossey-Bass.

Levine, A. 1980. *Why Innovation Fails.* Albany: State University of New York Press.

Lynd, R. S., and H. M. Lynd. 1929. *Middletown: A Study in Contemporary American Culture.* New York: Harcourt Brace.

———. 1937. *Middletown in Transition: A Study in Cultural Conflicts.* New York: Harcourt Brace.

March, J. G., and H. A. Simon. 1958. *Organizations.* New York: Wiley.

Martin, J. 1992. *Cultures in Organizations.* Oxford: Oxford University Press.

McDonough, P. M. 1997. *Choosing Colleges.* Albany: State University of New York Press.

McDonough, P. M., M. J. Ventresca, and C. Outcalt. 2000. "Field of Dreams: Organization Field Approaches to Understanding the Transformation of College Access, 1965–1995." In *Higher Education: Handbook of Theory and Research*, vol. 14, ed. J. C. Smart and W. G. Tierney, 371–405. New York: Agathon.

Meyer, J. W. 1977. "The Effects of Education as an Institution." *American Journal of Sociology* 83: 55–77.

Meyer, J. W., J. Boli, G. M. Thomas, and F. O. Ramirez. 1997. "World Society and the Nation-State." *American Journal of Sociology* 103:144–81.

Meyer, J. W., F. O. Ramirez, and Y. N. Soysal. 1992. "World Expansion of Mass Education, 1870–1980." *Sociology of Education* 65:128–49.

Meyer, J. W., and B. Rowan. 1977. "Institutionalized Organizations: Formal Structure as Myth and Ceremony." *American Journal of Sociology* 83:340–63.

Milem, J. F., and H. S. Astin. 1993. "The Changing Composition of Faculty: What Does It Really Mean for Diversity?" *Change* 25 (2): 21–27.

Mowery, D. C., R. R. Nelson, B. N. Sampat, and A. Ziedonis. 2004. *Ivory Tower and Industrial Innovation: University-Industry Technology Transfer before and after the Bayh-Dole Act.* Stanford, CA: Stanford University Press.

Noble, D. 2002. *Digital Diploma Mills: The Automation of Higher Education.* New York: Monthly Review Press.

Nussbaum, M. 1997. *Cultivating Humanity: A Classical Defense of Reform in Liberal Education.* Cambridge, MA: Harvard University Press.

Parsons, T. 1937. *The Structure of Social Action.* New York: McGraw-Hill.

———. 1951. *The Social System.* New York: Free Press.

Parsons, T., and G. M. Platt. 1973. *The American University.* Cambridge, MA: Harvard University Press.

Peterson, M. W., ed. 1983. *ASHE Reader on Organization and Governance in Higher Education.* Lexington, MA: Ginn.

Pettigrew, A. 1979. "On Studying Organizational Culture." *Administrative Science Quarterly* 24:570–81.

Powell, W. 1990. "Neither Market Nor Hierarchy: Network Forms of Organization." *Research in Organizational Behavior* 12:295–336.

Powell, W., and J. Owen-Smith. 1998. "Universities as Creators and Retailers of Intellectual Property: Life Sciences Research and Commercial Development." In *To Profit or Not to Profit*, ed. B. Weisbrod, 169–93. Cambridge: Cambridge University Press.

Readings, B. 1996. *The University in Ruins*. Cambridge, MA: Harvard University Press.

Rhoades, G. 1992. "Beyond the State." In *Higher Education: Handbook of Theory and Research*, vol. 13, ed. J. C. Smart, 84–142. New York: Agathon.

———. 1998. *Managed Professionals*. Albany: State University of New York Press.

Rhoades, G., and S. Slaughter. 2004. *Academic Capitalism and the New Economy: Markets, State, and Higher Education*. Baltimore: Johns Hopkins University Press.

Rhoads, R. A. 1994. *Coming Out in College: The Struggle for a Queer Identity*. Westport, CT: Bergin and Garvey.

Ruscio, K. P. 1987. "Many Sectors, Many Professions." In *The Academic Profession: National, Disciplinary, and Institutional Settings*, ed. B. Clark, 331–68. Berkeley: University of California Press.

Schuster, J., and M. Finkelstein. 2006. *The American Faculty: Restructuring Academic Work and Careers*. Baltimore: Johns Hopkins University Press.

Scott, J. W. 1999. *Gender and the Politics of History*. New York: Columbia University Press.

Scott, W. R. 1998. *Organizations: Rational, Natural, and Open Systems*. 4th ed. Upper Saddle River, NJ: Prentice-Hall.

Scott, W. R., et al. 2000. *Institutional Change and Healthcare Organizations: From Professional Dominance to Managed Care*. Chicago: University of Chicago Press.

Silva, E. T., and S. A. Slaughter. 1984. *Serving Power: The Making of the Academic Social Science Expert*. Westport, CT: Greenwood.

Slaughter, S. 1988. "Academic Freedom and the State: Reflections on the Uses of Knowledge." *Journal of Higher Education* 59:241–62.

———. 1997. "Class, Race, and Gender and the Construction of Post-secondary Curricula in the United States: Social Movement, Professionalization, and Political Economic Theories of Curricular Change." *Journal of Curriculum Studies* 29:1–30.

Slaughter, S., and L. L. Leslie. 1997. *Academic Capitalism*. Baltimore: Johns Hopkins University Press.

Smelser, N. J. 1973. "Growth, Structural Change, and Conflict in California Public Higher Education, 1950–1970." In *Public Higher Education in California*, ed. N. J. Smelser and G. Almond, 9–143. Berkeley: University of California Press.

———. 1997. *Problematics of Sociology: The Georg Simmel Lectures, 1995.* Berkeley: University of California Press.

Snow, C. P. 1959. *The Two Cultures and the Scientific Revolution.* Cambridge: Cambridge University Press.

Swidler, A., and J. Arditi. 1994. "The New Sociology of Knowledge." *Annual Review of Sociology* 20:305–29.

Tierney, W. G. 1993. *Building Communities of Difference: Higher Education in the Twenty-first Century.* Westport, CT: Bergin and Garvey.

Tinto, V. 1987. *Leaving College: Rethinking the Causes and Cures of Student Attrition.* Chicago: University of Chicago Press.

———. 1997. "Classrooms as Communities: Exploring the Educational Character of Student Persistence." *Journal of Higher Education* 68:599–623.

Tolbert, P. 1985. "Institutional Environments and Resource Dependence: Sources of Administrative Structure in Institutions of Higher Education." *Administrative Science Quarterly* 30 (March): 1–13.

Trow, M. 1970. "Reflections on the Transition from Mass to Universal Higher Education." *Daedalus* 99:1–42.

———. 1984. "The Analysis of Status." In *Perspectives on Higher Education,* ed. B. Clark, 132–64. Berkeley: University of California Press.

Valian, V. 1998. *Why So Slow? The Advancement of Women.* Cambridge, MA: MIT Press.

Veblen, T. 1918. *The Higher Learning in America.* New York: B. W. Huebsch.

Weber, M. 1918. "Science as a Vocation." In *From Max Weber: Essays in Sociology,* ed. H. H. Gerth and C. W. Mills, 1946. London, UK: Routledge and Kegan Paul.

Weick, K. E. 1995. *Sensemaking in Organizations.* Thousand Oaks, CA: Sage.

Weidman, J. C. 1989. "Undergraduate Socialization: A Conceptual Approach." In *Higher Education: Handbook of Theory and Research,* vol. 5, ed. J. C. Smart, 289–322. New York: Agathon.

Wilson, L. 1942. *The Academic Man: A Study in the Sociology of a Profession.* New York: Oxford University Press.

Zammuto, R. F., and K. S. Cameron. 1985. "Environmental Decline and Organizational Response." In *Research in Organizational Behavior,* ed. L. L. Cummings and B. M. Staw, 223–62. Greenwich, CT: JAI Press.

II FOUR DOMAINS

3　The Study of Inequality

PATRICIA M. MCDONOUGH AND
AMY J. FANN

In 1973, Burton Clark wrote that the sociology of higher education had two major areas of focus, the social psychological impact of college on students and "educational inequality beyond the secondary level" (1973, p. 3 in this volume). Clark specifically identified inequalities related to social class, race, and gender as important units of analysis for studying aspiration and achievement, especially in college admissions. He further suggested the need to explore new research domains that would focus on the values, traditions, and identities of educational social systems, for which he has subsequently provided some of the most influential research (Clark 1986, 1987).

Clark also urged us to look at stratification across higher education institutions, encouraging us to speak to both sides of this tension without "becoming a managerial sociology." He pointed to a great tension between an imperative for the sociological study of inequality and stratification in higher education and an equally pressing imperative to aid and change the profession of higher education practice.

Since that time, the streams of research on college impact and inequality have stayed central to higher education and arguably constitute the foci of a significant proportion of its scholarly research. Moreover, sociological research—with its focus on these intellectual core issues, vibrant conceptual frameworks, and cutting-edge methodological techniques—is integral to a thriving future for the field of higher education.

Our project in this chapter is to focus on inequality research, and specifically on research that addresses access to college, which was Clark's main focus in relation to inequality in his 1973 essay. We do this through a brief analysis of thirty-one years of articles in six major journals, three of which are leaders among higher education peer-reviewed outlets and three are high-prestige sociological venues that focus mainly on education research. Specifically, this chapter reviews 114 articles with direct relevance to college access published in these journals from 1973 (when the Clark essay was published) through 2004.

Using those 114 journal pieces as a starting base and adding other journals, books, conference papers, and policy reports, our second round of analysis updates Clark by sketching the history and progress of the sociological study of inequality. In 1973, studies of inequality nearly exclusively focused on individuals and how they were influenced by their parents and their parents' educational and occupational attainment. In fact, Clark (1960) branched out from this individual-level model by pioneering the exploration of how organizations shape or limit educational opportunities and thus student outcomes: he analyzed tests, counselors, and courses used to "cool out" students' transfer aspirations. Sociology has long been animated by seesaw swings of paradigms and their shifting explanations of causation from individual agency to organizational structure as the fundamental reason for inequality and change. Clark's early research (1960) highlighted the role of organizations in enabling or constraining individual action, thereby helping to shift the balance back to analysis of organizations. However, beyond his work, college access studies only rarely undertook organizational analysis for a long time after 1973.

We organize this review of college access research since 1973 categorizing it by individual, organizational, and field levels. Patricia McDonough, Marc Ventresca, and Charles Outcalt (2000) call for analysis of the field of college access and describe it as a web of opportunities and structural arrangements, including K–12 schools and colleges, aggregates of individuals, the entrepreneurial admissions sectors, and policymakers at all levels. Using organizational and Bourdieuian perspectives, their approach makes visible relationships of culture, power, and stratification within organizational environments, how these organizational arrangements enable or constrain actors, and the interplay between individual agency and organizational structures in shaping educational opportunity.

At the individual level, we have learned much from studies of students and the influences on their preparation for—and actions related to their gaining access to—college, as well as studies of the professionals who assist them. Student studies draw upon status attainment theories and methods as well as Weberian and Bourdieuian analyses of educational structures and other cultural approaches. One thriving tradition continues to exert an important influence: social-psychological analysis of the stages through which students proceed in aspiration development and attainment (Hossler et al. 1989). Of late, individual-level studies have also produced cultural and critical analyses that give us a better understanding of how diverse groups of individuals, families, and communities navigate college access—making us more aware of the role and strengths of families and communities.

Organizational-level studies look at organizational arrangements and processes within institutions *and* the linkages between organizations that mediate individuals' achievements. In contrast to individual-level studies, which emphasize people's attributes as the key determinants of inequalities, organizational-level studies focus on the role of educational organizations in structuring opportunity, shaping aspirations, and providing information. School-level literature posits organizational contexts as critical to understanding the empirical patterns of individual educational outcomes and analyzes schools' organizational structures, resources, constraints, and contingencies (Coleman 1987; Oakes 1989) in order to document how different school environments produce different curricula, administrative supports, and student outcomes. Building on the empirical and conceptual insights of organizational culture and climate research (Martin 1992; Ouchi and Wilkins 1985; Schein 1990), researchers have investigated students' college choice processes as shaped by high schools' structural and cultural arrangements. More recent organizational analyses have drawn upon Weberian bureaucratic approaches toward admissions offices; political organizational analyses of policy development and implementation; econometric analyses of enrollment and marketing; and cultural research, not only on the role of schools in reproducing class structures but also analyzing the internal dynamics of educational systems.

Yet for all that we have learned from individual- and organizational-level research, this accumulated knowledge does not take into account the macro-level changes in the institutions, professions, and technology of admissions in order to reveal how student perceptions and actions grow from, as well as influence, organizational and institutional perceptions and action. Specifically, a field-level analysis increases insight by integrating individual and institutional levels of analysis, by accounting for the reciprocal influence of students and institutions on each other and by illuminating the dynamic interactions of student behavior with professionals' and policymakers' practices.

Finally, field-level analyses direct attention to the individual, organizational, and interorganizational interests and agency at play and call for simultaneous analysis of the reciprocal influence of individuals and institutions. Field-level studies contribute to the study of inequality in higher education by providing strategies for research design and methods as well as by providing integrative research on college access, choice, and stratification. Field approaches employ comparative and historical research designs to examine large-scale changes in all the arenas of college access: individual practices, high schools, colleges, policy environments, and the entrepreneurial admissions sector (McDonough, Ventresca, and Outcalt 2000)

Our approach will be first to review the development of the field of college access since 1973—when Clark urged us to respond to the twin imperatives of aiding the profession and calling attention to inequality, all without descending into a managerial sociology. In a brief overview of more than three decades of research articles, we look at disciplinary differences between sociological and higher educational research on college access and develop a timeline of when specific critical issues (race, class, gender, financial aid, etc.) came under scrutiny by college access researchers. We then use the analytic framework of individual, organizational, and field perspectives to review in more depth the current state of knowledge within college access research.

Journal Reviews

Articles on college access in the *American Journal of Sociology, American Sociological Review, Sociology of Education,* the *Journal of Higher Education, Review of Higher Education,* and *Research in Higher Education* were reviewed from 1973 to 2004. In this 31-year period, a total of 114 articles were identified as related to college access primarily from their titles, a review of their abstracts, and reading the entire article.

Seventy-seven percent of these 114 articles used quantitative methodology, while 19 percent of them consisted of a combination of policy analysis, literature reviews, and/or reviews of institutional documents. Only 4 percent of the articles (6 out of 114) used qualitative methods, and these articles began to show up in the literature only in the mid-1990s. In other words, in spite of Clark's call for new and different analyses of aspiration, achievement, and admission into colleges, quantitative analysis dominated the field for two decades.

Based on a content analysis of the articles, we identified seven major categories for research on college access: financial aid; policy and institutional analysis; student ability and achievement; college choice; family and socioeconomic status (SES); nontraditional students; and students of color (African American, Latino, Asian Pacific Americans, and Native American students). The articles overlapped somewhat in category, so our decisions required identifying the primary focus of each.

The largest grouping of the articles in the higher education journals (40%) focused on financial aid, and only one article on this topic appeared in the sociology journals—this focused on black-white differences in parental expectations of responsibility for funding college. All of the financial aid–related articles were quantitative. The second largest category within the higher education articles was students' college choices, accounting for 29 percent of the articles.

In contrast, the largest grouping of articles in the sociology journals (56%) focused on family socioeconomic status as broadly related to students' educational attainment. K–12 school effects—research on tracking or private versus public school differences—was the second largest category (21%) within the sociological articles; these articles began appearing in the mid-1980s.

In the higher education literature, articles on college access for specific racial groups began to appear only in the 1980s. Higher education has published only seven articles on the college choice processes of ethnic minorities: four on African Americans, two on Latino students (both specifically on financial aid), one on Asian Pacific Americans, and none on Native American students. In the sociology literature, articles on college access for specific racial groups began appearing in 1978, with three on African Americans, one on Latino students, one on Asian Pacific Americans, and none on Native American students. Eight studies were published on multiethnic college choices in the higher education literature, while only one such study was published in the sociological literature. Finally, higher education has published two articles on nontraditional students, while sociology has not published any.

State of the Art of College Access Research

Over the last three decades, college access research has made more evident the constellation of factors that affect the cumulative and complex process of getting to college. We present a macro perspective on college access research that sees the pursuit of education beyond the secondary level as a long-term systemic event where individual opportunity is constrained or enabled by educational structures, the free agency choices of rational, goal-directed individuals, and the complex interplay of those individuals and structures throughout individuals' educational careers. Researchers taking such a long-term, systemic perspective study how aggregate individual actions influence organizations; how institutionalized patterns of racism condition the expectations and actions of both individuals and schools; and how forces such as privatization, free market competition, and legal decisions alter the terms of competition.

In considering college access research, we now describe how the literature has developed from social psychological perspectives on college choice, with studies that treated students' college choices as a technical fit between an individual and a college; to organizational analyses positing organizational contexts as critical to understanding the empirical patterns of individual outcomes; and, later, cultural analyses focused on the role of schools' cultures in reproducing class structures, studies that began to account for a multiplicity of students' cultural identities and how cultural identity affects college access. This body of work has begun to identify specific ways that cultural and geographical differences affect reasons for deciding to prepare for and attend college and the cultural and historical factors influencing parental involvement.

In the following section, we organize our review of college access research according to the following categories with the identified subtopics:

1. *individual-level analyses:* socioeconomic status, race, ethnicity, culture, family, community, traditional/nontraditional student status, peers, communities, geography (especially rural access)
2. *organizational-level analyses:* high school policies and practices, academic preparation, high school agents (counselors and teachers), outreach programs, and postsecondary admissions
3. *field-level analyses:* admissions testing, federal and state policies (financial aid, affirmative action, accountability movements), entrepreneurial admissions sector, professional organizations, and media

Many interconnections cross these arenas, and the factors within them represent the interconnectedness of the myriad complex factors that enable or constrain students' dreams for college—and their structural opportunity.

Individual-Level Analyses

Individual-level studies are microanalyses of student college choice. College choice can be a lengthy process extending back to the earliest inculcation of college aspirations and then passing through predisposition, search, and choice (Hossler, Braxton, and Coopersmith 1989). In students' *search* and *choice* phases, a number of factors have been found to be influential. Parents; the college's size, location, academic program, reputation, prestige, selectivity, and alumni; the student's peers, friends, and guidance counselor; and the availability of financial aid—all have consistently been found to be influential factors (Hossler, Braxton, and Coopersmith 1989; Manski and Wise 1983; Zemsky and Oedel 1983). Students' access to information, the college knowledge of parents, and students' perceptions of their ability to pay all factor into the range of institutions that students consider (Cabrera and La Nasa 2000). Students' opportunities for higher education are further influenced by socioeconomic status, life experiences, culture, family responsibilities, and goals for work and life beyond the degree.

Socioeconomic Status. SES is widely cited in sociological literature as the most influential factor in college access, affecting students' college aspirations, eligibility, and attendance beyond ability or achievement (Jencks et al. 1972; McDonough 1997; Oakes, Rogers, Lipton, and Morrell 2002). Across all achievement levels, students from the lowest-SES groups are less likely to apply for or attend college and much less likely to apply to selective institutions than are the highest-SES students (Astin and Oseguera 2004; Paulsen and St. John 2002; Perna and Titus 2004). Seventy-seven percent of high-income students enroll in a four-year college or university within two years of graduation, while only 33 percent of low-income students do (Gándara 2002). Similarly, among students whose parents are college graduates, 71 percent enroll in a four-year institution, compared to only 26 percent of students whose parents have no more than a high school diploma (Perna and Titus 2004).

Poor and first-generation students tend to develop aspirations for college later than middle-class students, whose parents are more likely to have college knowledge and experience (Hossler, Schmit, and Vesper 1998; McDonough 1997) and having early plans for college is critical for completing university eligibility requirements, such as taking the correct sequence of courses, enrolling in honors or advanced-placement courses, achieving competitive scores on college entrance exams, and participating in the extracurricular activities and community service virtually necessary for admission to selective institutions (Cabrera and La Nasa 2000; McDonough 1997).

Family income dictates residential patterns, which in turn dictate the range of public and private elementary and secondary schools students are able to attend. More affluent families can afford to buy homes in neighborhoods with perceived better schools and even benefit from the tax breaks (Jellison 2002). Schools in more affluent areas tend to have more qualified teachers, as measured by degrees held and test scores (Gándara 2002). McDonough (1997) observes that schools that educate children from affluent families are more likely to have a "college culture," with parents, students, and school personnel expecting students to attend college, whereas in schools serving primarily poor and working-class students, high school graduation and workforce preparation are often emphasized over college preparation. College information in these latter schools, if provided at all, is likely to direct students to community colleges as the only option for higher education after high school.

Competition for access to highly selective and elite colleges and universities is especially palpable in suburbia, where advantaged college applicants and their parents have the capacity to stack the deck in their own favor by improvising admissions management behaviors such as hiring tutors, SAT coaches, and private counselors (McDonough et al. 1998). For highly affluent families, college begins before kindergarten. Private consultants can be hired to help families prep toddlers to improve their odds of getting into elite nursery schools that feed into the right elementary schools, ultimately leading to a place in an elite university (Marbaix 2004).

In the zero-sum game of educational equity and excellence, P. A. Noguera's (2001) study shows, even in urban schools serving two different constituencies, affluent white students and low-income African Americans and Latinos, that a school-within-a-school situation emerges. Instead of seeking a school where educational opportunities are equally distributed between affluent students and low-SES students of color, even well-intentioned white parents tend to perceive efforts to provide more opportunities to low-SES students at the same school as evidence of compromising the educational interests of their own children (Noguera 2001). Because these affluent white parents are able to exercise their considerable cultural capital to secure school resources for their children, at these schools more black and Latino students tend to be found in special and compensatory education classes and more white students in gifted and advanced-placement courses.

Race, Ethnicity, and Culture. In spite of progress made over the last thirty years in the enrollment of minority students in higher education, African Americans, Latinos, Native Americans, and ethnic subgroups of Asian Americans remain underrepresented in college (McDonough 2004). While African Americans and Latinos have been closing the gap in high school graduation compared to their white counterparts, white students are still more than twice as likely to complete college degrees than either African Americans or Latinos. As Patricia Gándara (2002) admonishes, differences in educational attainment result in significant differences in lifetime earning levels and other benefits generally enjoyed by college graduates.

The lower enrollment of students of color in higher education is exacerbated if we consider who goes where to college. African American, Latino, and Native American students are less likely to be eligible for four-year institutions, and Latinos and Native Americans (Gándara 2002; Pavel et al. 1998; Pewewardy and Frey 2004) are more likely to attend two-year colleges. Students who enroll in four-year institutions are more likely to complete degrees than those who enroll in two-year colleges (Astin and Oseguera 2004). Low-income and minority students are less likely than other students to take college admission tests or complete admission procedures even if they are qualified (Hossler, Schmit, and Vesper 1998), tend to aspire to less selective placements than do white students with comparable academic records (McDonough, Korn, and Yamasaki 1997), and are less likely to enroll in their first choice of institution (Hurtado et al. 1997).

Although racial differences tend to correspond closely to class differences with regard to educational attainment (Noguera 2001), in contrast to whites, students of color live in a world dominated by race (Delgado 1988) and must deal with overt and implicit forms of racism, stereotypes, and continual reminders (subtle and otherwise) of their status as people of color—all of which may limit real opportunity (Tate 1997). Research addressing the educational experiences and opportunities to learn for students of color has shown that racist attitudes, assumptions, and practices on the part of teachers and school counselors affect academic achievement and college pathways for students of color (Deyhle

1992, 1995; Oakes 1985; Oakes et al. 2002; McDonough et al. 1998; Solór-zano 1992; Solórzano and Villalpando 1998). According to D. G. Solór-zano and Octavio Villalpando (1998), the low percentages of African American, Latino, and American Indian students who are eligible for university admission can partly be explained by the cumulative effects of inadequate academic preparation, negative teacher expectations, and their disproportionate tracking into nonacademic, vocational courses—such that access to college seems beyond reach to these students.

A promising line of research has looked at the impact of socially constructed statuses like race on college choice (Allen 1988; Ceja 2000; Freeman 1997; McDonough, Korn, and Yamasaki 1997; Teranishi et al. 2004). Robert Teranishi and colleagues examine the extent to which ethnicity and social class affect the college choice process of five Asian American ethnic subgroups: Chinese, Filipino, Japanese, Korean, and Southeast Asians. These authors confirm that Asian Americans from different ethnic subgroups do indeed approach the college choice process differently. Chinese American and Korean American students were shown to attend more selective colleges even after the researchers controlled for other variables, while Southeast Asian students did not attend selective colleges.

Along these same lines of cultural permutations not captured when categories of race alone are used, students from migrant farm families who are predominantly Latino have most often been aggregated as part of the Latino population. However, these students, by the nature of their families' economic and locational legacies, face a different set of circumstances and are armed with a different set of resources from which to exert agency (Tejeda, Espinoza, and Gutierrez 2004). Focusing on their ethnicity alone does not get to the complexity of their college access barriers—and resources.

Analyses of college access using cultural frameworks highlight the interplay between ethnicity and culture. Kassie Freeman conducted a qualitative study (1997, 1999) examining how racial factors influenced the college participation of the African American high school students she interviewed. She found that race-related and cultural issues affected every aspect of their daily life and played a major role in the way these students perceived their decision to go to college. Freeman asserts that culture matters in college going: "Although it could be argued that the influences on students to choose or not to choose college participation are similar across cultures, the depth of meaning (the perception of reality) each culture attaches to those influences differs" (1999, p. 10).

Examining the role of Alaska Native leaders in negotiating not only accessible but relevant higher education programs for Alaska Natives, Michael Jennings (2004) finds that the cultural milieu of students cannot be taken for granted as a variable within a larger set of characteristics. Culture must be explored, as part of a fundamental framework from which Native nations understand everything—from the basis and purposes of the educational endeavor to organizational and individual behavior on behalf of the endeavor (Jennings 2004).

Amy Fann (2002, 2005) has studied the barriers to college access for Native American high school students. American Indian students are the most underrepresented group in higher education, yet virtually no research had previously addressed their college access experiences. In order to inform postsecondary outreach efforts in California, with one of the largest Indian populations in the country, Fann conducted a statewide analysis of barriers to college access from the perspective of American Indian high school students, primarily from reservation communities in rural areas. She found that effectively delivering college information and support to native students with aspirations for college requires understanding what these students think about their opportunities for college access and how their ideas are influenced by families, tribal affiliation, peers, and schools. Fann also focuses on understanding (1) how tribal sovereignty and economic development needs shape the college aspirations and behaviors of tribal citizens from both nongaming and gaming tribes; (2) how tribal needs relate to the college education of tribal citizens; and (3) how this context shapes students' aspirations. Fann's linking college access with Indian gaming issues points to the complex matrix of intrinsic, economic, and occupational motivations for pursuing a higher education. Her research further offers the opportunity to understand the impact of gaming monies on the development and implementation of educational aspirations, achievements, and objectives for some Native American students—potentially revolutionary research, given that individual-level economic motivation is an essential underpinning of college aspirations.

Studies like the above, which take into account unique and varied cultural factors, are borne out by Villalpando and Solórzano (2005), who argue that traditional notions of Bourdieuian cultural capital based on social class need to be reconceptualized based on consideration of the "cultural wealth" of students of color, their families, and their communities. Cultural wealth includes values and the applications of those values through practices that support student academic achievement and college going—values and applications that would not be considered forms of cultural capital within a traditional Bourdieuian framework. In reviewing the role of culture in college preparatory programs, Villalpando and Solórzano describe culture as

> dynamic, cumulative, and an influence of the constant process of identity formation. It is a process of behaviors and values that are learned, shared, and exhibited by a people. For students of color, their culture is frequently represented symbolically through language and can encompass identities around immigration status, gender, phenotype, sexuality, regionality, race and ethnicity. . . . But perhaps the most important dimension of culture for students of color is that it is very often the guide for their thinking, feeling, and behaving—indeed, it is a means of survival. The cultures of students of color can nurture and empower them. (pp. 16–17)

Cultural analyses of college choice, using a variety of methodologies and conceptual frameworks such as critical race theory, cultural wealth, and cultural integrity, offer researchers and practitioners further insight into perceptions of educational opportunity within different cultural groups and identify rich and unique sources of cultural wealth within families and communities, resources that can be used to support student achievement and postsecondary access and success.

Traditional/Nontraditional Status. One of the limitations of college choice and access research to date is its nearly exclusive focus on the transition from high school to college (Adelman 2002; Baker and Vélez 1996); for, as of 2002, almost three-quarters of undergraduates are reported to be in some way "nontraditional" (NCES 2002). Further, the proportion of nontraditional students in postsecondary education varies by institutional type: nontraditional student enrollment is highest in two-year colleges and for-profit private institutions, and lowest in four-year doctorate-granting institutions (Baker and Vélez 1996; NCES 2002).

The traditional undergraduate is characterized by the National Center for Education Statistics (2002) as having a high school diploma, enrolling full time immediately after graduating from high school, and not working during the school year, or working only part time. Traditional students now constitute just 27 percent of all undergraduates, which means that almost two-thirds of all undergraduates delay enrollment after high school, attend part time, work full time, are financially independent of their parents, have dependents other than a spouse, are single parents, or do not have a high school diploma.

Laura J. Horn (1996) defines nontraditional students on a continuum based on the numbers of characteristics present. For example, minimally nontraditional students have one of the above characteristics, while moderately nontraditional students have two or three. Highly nontraditional students are those with four or more characteristics. The undergraduate population now consists of as many highly nontraditional students as traditional students (NCES 2002). Clifford Adelman (2002) suggests that quantitative longitudinal research should include students until at least the age of thirty to give us better information on when nontraditional students enter higher education. College access research has virtually ignored these students, and future research needs to develop a line of inquiry on the college access concerns of nontraditional students.

Parents and Families. Research has shown that parents, regardless of race or socioeconomic status, want the best for their children, value educational achievement, and view higher education as extremely important (Cooper et al. 2002; Gándara and Bial 2001; Immerwahr and Foleno 2000; Solórzano 1992). Parental support and encouragement are the most important influences in the development of students' college aspirations (Gándara and Bial 2001; Hossler, Braxton, and Coopersmith 1989; Hossler, Schmit, and Vesper 1998; McDonough 1997). Students take their cues from their parents about what is reasonable to expect for their educational goals, and they plan their futures accordingly (Attanasi 1989; McDonough 1997; Pérez 1999).

Donald Hossler, Jack Schmit, and Nick Vesper (1998) differentiate between parental encouragement and parental support. "Parental encouragement" refers to parents' expressions for their children's educational aspirations through discussing college and helping children make the connections between college going and future career goals. "Parental support" includes such direct activities as starting a college savings fund and taking students on visits to college campuses.

Parental levels of education play a significant role in parents' college knowledge and the repertoire of traditional resources they have available to help their children prepare for enrollment in higher education (Attanasi 1989; McDonough 1997; Tierney and Auerbach 2005). Unfortunately, parents who have not had opportunities to attend college themselves have neither experience with the process of college preparation and college going nor access to needed information. Structural barriers, language barriers, and unwelcoming school environments make it difficult for low-SES parents of color to help their children prepare for college (Tierney and Auerbach 2005).

Latino parents may experience a number of roadblocks to involvement in their children's college planning process, including communication barriers with schools, negative experiences with teachers and school counselors, and lack of knowledge about standardized exams, college admissions policies and practices, and postsecondary costs and financial aid options (Pérez 1999). Immigrant parents face language and cultural barriers that make it difficult for them to guide their children's college pathways effectively in the United States (Hurh 1998; Siu 1996). Lack of knowledge about the U.S. educational system, coupled with cultural norms of deference for teachers and school authorities, make seeking information from their children's school a formidable process (Hurh 1998; Kim 1999; Pérez 1999). Some African American parents feel that counselors and college admissions officers are "hiding" or purposefully withholding information they need to help get their children into college (Smith 2001).

We must also recognize, again on the cultural capital side, that extended family and kin relationships within indigenous and other communities mean that students can rely not only on their parents but also on other adults, older siblings, and cousins who are significant figures in their lives and may prove important allies in college going (Friedel 1999; Tierney and Auerbach 2005). The challenge for schools and postsecondary institutions is to find meaningful ways to involve families in this process, along with effective and timely ways to disseminate information about college options, preparation, application procedures, and financial aid (McDonough and McClafferty 2001). Furthermore, engaging families and learning about the many unrecognized forms of cultural capital or cultural wealth (Villalpando and Solórzano 2005) that support the academic achievement of children is a way of "affirming students' cultures and building a more holistic college-going culture that pervades students' lives" (Tierney and Auerbach 2005, p. 46).

Peers and Communities. Hossler, Schmit, and Vesper (1998) find that the closer students come to approaching high school graduation, the more relationships with peers who plan to attend college positively influence their own motivation for higher education. The role of peers, say W. G. Tierney and Julia Colyar, is "deceptively simplistic"; they admonish that regardless of how peer groups are defined, students are in fact members of peer groups, which should be engaged as a resource in college preparation (2005).

Communities can be thought of as ecological systems that include families of similar social status, schools, peers, and services. Neighborhood resource theory as laid out by Gándara suggests that the variability of resources across neighborhoods "and the quality of local resources available to families (e.g., parks, libraries, childcare facilities) affects developmental outcomes" (2002, p. 86). Affluent neighborhoods have more of these supportive resources than do neighborhoods in which poor children grow up (Gándara 2002).

Mia Zhou and Carl Bankston (1998) have found that just as families can be connected to the achievements of students, community structures can be instrumental in the explicit attainment of educational advantages. For example, Korean immigrant families are at a disadvantage in preparing their children for college because of language barriers, cultural attitudes of deference to school personnel, and lack of information about how to navigate the U.S. education system and college preparation process (Hurh 1998). However, a variety of community-based components in Los Angeles' Koreatown specifically promote college accessibility for Korean youth (Fann 2001). For example, Korean newspapers and radio regularly offer information regarding higher education and tips for parents to help their children become eligible for entrance into four-year universities. Private Korean tutoring schools or *hagwan* frequently provide college information as part of their service. Some Korean churches offer workshops on preparing for the SAT, and middle and high school students gain information about getting to college through informal social networks with college graduates who attend the same church.

Geography-Rural Access. One lens through which scholarship has been reluctant to engage issues of educational opportunity is the geographic. However, a growing body of literature does take account of geography—specifically, in considering students who come from rural areas (Apostal and Bilden 1991; Haller and Virkler 1993; McDonough and McClafferty 2001; McGrath et al. 2001). Rural students are the least likely to go to college, even when they are otherwise comparable to students from urban areas (Adelman 2002), yet rural college access is not well understood nor adequately addressed as policy (McDonough, McClafferty, and Fann 2002). Black women and Latino men and women from rural areas are enrolled at increasingly lower rates than their metropolitan peers. The NCES (2002) shows that despite graduating students from high school at higher rates than urban high schools, across race/ethnicity and gender, rural high schools still send fewer students on to two- and four-year colleges. This compels us to recognize the particular college access barriers faced by rural students.

Often the primary obstacle preventing rural students from attending four-year institutions is a lack of finances, mediated by students' perceptions of affordability, actual postsecondary costs, cost-benefit analyses that rank local community colleges as less expensive local alternatives, and students' immediate desires to earn a salary (McDonough and McClafferty 2001). Rural communities offer very few employment opportunities for college graduates, thus lowering the desirability of college (Ward 1995).

Lacking opportunity to learn is another significant barrier for rural students, resulting from schools' insufficient resources for attracting well-qualified personnel, providing adequate technology, and offering a full range of college preparatory, advanced placement, and honors courses and outreach programs (McDonough, McClafferty, and Fann 2002; Pavel 1999; Ward 1995). Lacking proximity to four-year institutions also figures significantly. Geographical challenges include physical and social distance as well as anxiety-producing unfamiliarity. Many students do not want to leave home and familiar surroundings because they do not know what other places or college campuses are like (McDonough and McClafferty 2001). Lack of exposure to postsecondary institutions diminishes college aspirations, and for many rural citizens, lack of transportation is a real barrier to attending a community college and an even greater obstacle to attending a four-year institution. Even for students with cars, long travel times between home, work, and college can make attendance prohibitive (McDonough and McClafferty 2001; Ward 1995).

Research projects investigating such issues, in continuing to develop studies of inequality, must further disaggregate by status characteristics, such as racial and ethnic identifications, and geography. And college access research must use new frameworks, like cultural wealth, and integrative frameworks, like community ecology, to provide greater analytic purchase and to capture students' lived experiences more accurately than current frameworks have done.

Organizational-Level Analyses

All of these individual-level factors are mediated or constrained by K–12 school practices and personnel; proximity to colleges and universities; postsecondary institution costs and admission requirements; and political policies based on the notion of who "merits" college education, enacted through financial aid, affirmative action, and accountability plans. We will now review the research on K–12 schools, outreach programs, and postsecondary institutions.

K–12 Schools. Research has consistently shown that academic preparation is the best predictor of students' developing early college aspirations and enrolling in college immediately after high school (Adelman 2002; Cabrera and La Nasa 2000; Hossler et al. 1998; Perna 2005; Stampen and Fenske 1988). Mathematics classes in particular are gateway courses, and completing high-level math courses correlates most strongly with college attendance (Adelman 2002; Perna 2005). High schools serving low-income and minority youth are less likely to focus attention on rigorous, standards-based instruction.

Fifty years ago in *Brown v. Topeka Board of Education,* the United States outlawed segregation in public schools, yet today we have an educational system defined by educational inequality and segregation. K–12 students are educated in highly segregated schools (Kahlenberg 2004; Orfield 1996). Black and Latino students are concentrated in schools with high dropout rates, and these schools lack any significant college preparation capacity (Orfield 1998).

The K–12 school system acts as a gatekeeper to postsecondary access through practices and policies whereby poor and minority students are much more likely to be found in vocational and general education tracks (Oakes 1985; Oakes et al. 2002). The way schools structure curricular offerings, access to information, and college advising sends powerful messages to students about their ability to attend college, and the role of schools is especially critical for poor and first-generation college-bound students, who must rely almost exclusively on the school for information about getting to college (McDonough 1997).

The college enrollment rate of K–12 graduates is not an accountability indicator and is not in any job description. School counselors are the logical source of college access preparation and assistance, yet in most public high schools they are inappropriately trained and structurally constrained from being able to fulfill this role (McDonough 2004).

Research shows that counselors influence students' aspirations, plans, enrollments, and financial aid knowledge. Meeting frequently with a counselor increases a student's chance of enrolling in a four-year college, and if students, parents, and counselors work together and communicate clearly, students' chances of enrolling in college significantly increase. The effect of socioeconomic status on the college enrollment of low-income students is largely explained by a lack of counseling (King 1996; Plank and Jordan 2001).

Counselors have an impact through the following components of the college preparation and advising process: (1) structuring information and organizing activities that foster and support students' college aspirations and their understanding of college and its importance; (2) assisting parents in understanding their role in fostering and supporting college aspirations, setting college expectations, and motivating students; (3) assisting students in academic preparation for college; (4) supporting and influencing students in decision making about college; and (5) organizationally focusing the school on its college mission (Hossler, Schmit, and Vesper 1998; McDonough 2004).

Yet in public school counseling the priority tasks are scheduling, testing, and discipline; then dropout, drug, pregnancy, and suicide prevention; sexuality and personal crisis counseling; tardy sweeps and lunch supervision. A study of how counselors spend their time found that counselors give college guidance only 13 percent of their time (Moles 1991). By way of comparison, private college preparatory schools send the largest proportion of their students on to college, and they provide counselors whose time is devoted exclusively to college counseling.

Lack of access to college counseling in most public schools is greatly exacerbated by the student-to-counselor ratio. According to the National Association for College Admission Counseling, the national average of students to counselors is 490:1 (Hawkins 2003). Some statewide averages are as high as 994:1, and in schools serving large numbers of poor students and students of color, the ratios are 1,056 students to one counselor, or higher (McDonough 2004). In California the average high school student to counselor ratio is 979:1 (CDE 2000). Such ratios clearly do not allow for personal attention, even when the counselor has the best of intentions.

Repeated studies have found that improving counseling would have a significant impact on college access for low-income, rural, and urban students as well as students of color (Gándara and Bial 2001; King 1996; McDonough 2004; Plank and Jordan 2001). Specifically, if counselors actively support students and their families through the college admissions process, as opposed to simply disseminating information, this increases students' chances of enrolling in a four-year college.

Counseling is often tied to the track placement of students. A student who is not in the college track does not receive college information. African American and Latino (and first-generation) college-bound students are significantly more likely than their white counterparts to be in noncollege tracks and to have their college plans influenced by their high school counselors, both positively and negatively (McDonough 2005a; Plank and Jordan 2001). Yet these are the students least likely to have counselors, most likely to have underprepared counselors, and most likely to have counselors pulled away from college counseling to work on other tasks. Further, research has shown that these students often exhibit deep and well-founded distrust of counselors, because of racist and socioeconomic biases in advising (Gándara and Bial 2001).

Student access to college counseling within their school, together with the counselor's role in channeling students into certain courses, determine how much information students receive about college options and how to make themselves eligible for four-year institutions, and whether they choose vocational pathways (Freeman 1997; McDonough 1997, 2004, 2005b). African American and Latino students have consistently received poor counseling because counselors tend to focus on students who fit preconceived notions of who will be successful (Hawkins 1993, p. 14; Smith 2001).

Teachers also play an important role in college access, but although we have research on teacher impacts, it has not been integrated into the study of inequality of college access. Even though the gap in educational achievement between African American and white students was halved between 1970 and 1988, progress in that area stopped in 1988 (Haycock 2001). Kati Haycock provides evidence that much of the "opportunity gap" that low-income and minority students suffer results from poor teacher effectiveness as measured by five indicators. She shows that poor students and students of color are "systematically" taught by teachers who are less effective because they lack content knowledge for their areas of teaching; they have less experience; they teach on emergency credentials; they score lower on standardized tests, teacher licensing tests, assessment of basic skills, and college admissions tests; and they attended noncompetitive undergraduate institutions at much higher rates than did teachers at higher-SES schools (Haycock 2004). Based upon these findings, she identifies two crucial components for improving K–12 education: a challenging curriculum and effective teachers.

Research tells us that high expectations and access to a caring, knowledgeable adult who monitors students' educational success are key precursors to academic achievement in high school and enrollment in college (Gándara and Bial 2001). Teachers can and do affect students' academic preparation, opportunities to learn, self-esteem, and motivation to achieve. Unfortunately, teachers' expectations for children are heavily influenced by their beliefs about race, ethnicity, and social class. Their assumptions in turn affect their assessments of students' ability and motivation to learn, which again affect how teachers interact with and support students, whether and how many opportunities they provide to students to learn and excel, the advice they give students, and their interactions with students' families (George and Aronson 2002; Oakes et al. 2002).

A plethora of educational research and policy reports have documented inequitable conditions in K–12 public education for low-SES and racial and ethnic minority students (Bill and Melinda Gates Foundation 2003; Callan and Finney 2003). Some evidence suggests that the disparities in academic achievement progressively worsen as students advance from elementary to secondary schools (Obidah, Christie, and McDonough 2004). Empirical evidence shows that low-income and immigrant children and children of color are being denied essential opportunities to learn—by schools that shock the conscience, because they deprive students of essentials: books, qualified teachers, and safe places to learn (Oakes 2004).

The current structure of middle and high schools is inadequate to prepare minority, low-income, and first-generation students to attend college (Martinez and Klopott 2003). The Aspen Institute reports that for more than two decades we have known of the U.S. high school's significant shortcomings and that even though we have detailed and well-documented evidence of our failures, the problems and gaps between successful and unsuccessful high schools is growing and "most secondary schools seem impervious to change" (McNeil 2003, p. 5).

Today, educators and policymakers are barraged by calls for reforming K–12 schools, most of which are not designed to increase college access but which do have, at their core, the essential precondition for improving college access—increasing academic performance. Nearly all policy and research reports on the condition of K–12 schools agree that we need comprehensive reform to meet states' statutory obligations to educate all their citizens, to reduce disparities in academic preparation for college, and to raise performance levels to meet standards-based accountability (Callan and Finney 2003; Bill and Melinda Gates Foundation 2003; Oakes 2004).

Monica Martinez and Shayna Klopott (2003) find that the most promising elements of these reform initiatives are a more rigorous academic curriculum for all students, academic and social supports, small learning environments, and the P–16 alignment of curriculum. Aligning curricula and high school graduation requirements with college entrance requirements ensures that students are continually prepared for academic success, are aware of academic expectations, and are prepared for college (Kirst and Venezia 2004; Martinez and Klopott 2003).

Outreach Programs. Too often, low-income and minority students are enrolled in high schools that fail to provide opportunities for preparation for more competitive colleges because of shortages of qualified teachers and college counselors, inadequate honors and advanced placement classes, etc. Precollegiate outreach or intervention programs are designed to supplement schools and communities with resources that are helpful for students preparing for college.

Since the 1960s, higher education leaders, policymakers, advocates, and philanthropists have developed outreach programs to provide select students with the necessary preparation and assistance for college. In 1964, the midst of President Lyndon B. Johnson's War on Poverty, Congress established Upward Bound as the first federal intervention program. The Higher Education Act of 1965 established the TRIO programs and added Talent Search and Student Support Services to Upward Bound, thereby building the foundation of our major federal financial underwriting of intervention programs. TRIO programs were originally developed to provide exposure to college and academic support for low-income and first-generation high school students so that they might prepare for and succeed in college. Although designed to serve these two often overlapping populations, TRIO programs make economically disadvantaged students their first priority.

In subsequent policy directives, more TRIO intervention programs have been added, including the Ronald McNair Postbaccalaureate Program, Veterans Upward Bound, Educational Opportunity Centers, and Upward Bound Math/Science. In 1998, Congress created GEAR-UP (Gaining Early Awareness and Readiness for Undergraduate Programs) a grant program that helps students beginning in the sixth grade to overcome social and cultural barriers to higher education access. Together these programs accounted for a billion dollars in the fiscal year 2002 federal budget.

GEAR-UP represents a new federal model for serving students. GEAR-UP identifies cohorts of students and provides services to these cohorts, working systematically with students, their families, schools, and nonschool partners to build students' and parents' knowledge of college, its potential benefits, and college preparation needs. GEAR-UP is a comprehensive program with several important characteristics: it is organizational and collaborative in requiring partnerships between local education agencies, community groups, families, and colleges and universities; it focuses on students and their families; and it is systemic in its cohort focus. In fact, newer early intervention programs serve students beginning in middle school, since it is well established that the earlier a student develops college aspirations, the more likely it is that she or he will attend college.

In addition to federal efforts, at least 15 states have undertaken their own intervention programs and campaigns. These programs run the gamut of early information and awareness, like California's College: Making It Happen middle school parent campaign, the Georgia Hope Scholarship program, the Minnesota Get Ready Program, Rhode Island's Children's Crusade for Higher Education, and others. Moreover, many private programs provide college preparation intervention. The best known of these programs is probably Eugene Lang's I Have a Dream, which financially supports more than 13,000 low-income students in 26 states (Perna and Swail 2002). Some other programs have been growing significantly, like AVID (Advancement Via Individual Determination) and MESA (Mathematics, Engineering, and Science Achievement).

Federal and state efforts are important, but the major players in college outreach programs are colleges and universities. One in three colleges and universities offers some kind of outreach program to assist students who are low income, first generation, or of color in their college access quest. Most college intervention programs seek to improve opportunities for individual students, rather than changing the structure or functioning of schools, and thus are student-centered rather than school-centered programs. The problem with this is that, as we have seen, access is an institutional, not individual, problem. More-over, outreach programs are inequitable by design, because they target only a small percentage of students and they do not and cannot serve all students consistently. By design also, intervention programs are external to K–12 schools (Gándara and Bial 2001; Kirst and Venezia 2004) and therefore supplement but do not fundamentally change the curriculum or schools' interactions or perceptions of student potential. Patricia Gándara and Deborah Bial find that "students are exposed to the same school practices that have been proved to be unsuccessful for them" (2001, p. xi). Intervention efforts are insufficient without core academic services from K–12 schools (Gándara and Bial 2001; Perna 2005; Perna and Swail 2002).

Thus, not surprisingly, intervention programs have had very little effect on academic achievement. However, intervention programs can double college-going rates for at-risk youth (Horn 1996), can expand students' educational aspirations (Gándara 2002), can increase students' educational and cultural capital assets (Gándara and Bial 2001), and can boost college enrollment and graduation rates. The benefits are often greatest for low-income students with low initial expectations and achievement.

The overriding strength of early intervention programs is how they enhance the awareness of and readiness for college in underrepresented students and their families early enough to have a positive impact. Such programs have become an increasingly important part of institutional strategies at national, state, and local levels, particularly since affirmative action has been reversed in a number of states. However, our outreach intervention efforts are not a systematic solution to a policy problem of equalizing educational access across all populations but merely a system of educational triage. We sort and allocate scarce educational treatment to students, but most estimates suggest that we are reaching approx-imately 10 percent of the eligible or needy populations and that it would take 6 billion dollars to serve all eligible students (McDonough 2004).

Recruitment. University recruiters provide information and encour-agement to students. However, even students ranking at the top of their class in inner-city high schools are less likely to have been visited by college recruiters than students who attend suburban schools. These students are also less likely to have visited a college campus and less likely to have received the most basic information necessary for college eligibility and choice. At the same time, in many inner-city (and rural) schools, military recruiters are likely to have a weekly presence on campus, and they have been effective in making students aware of the future economic benefits of joining the service (McDonough 1999, 2001).

Military recruiters use sophisticated market-based research to entice and convince high school seniors to enter the military instead of going to college. Moreover, recruiters have demonstrated greater success at explaining complicated contracts, are better at guaranteeing money for college, and therefore often are more successful with low-income students than are college recruiters (McDonough 1999). In a policy paper, D. M. Stewart (1988) discusses how a College Board marketing campaign could not compete with the resources of the armed forces in influencing teens' perceived career options. The presence of military recruiters at high schools serving low-income and students of color is on the rise, as recruiters across the country are under orders to help the army increase the ranks of enlisted personnel (Moehringer 2004). In the absence of college counselors in large urban schools, recruiters purposefully position themselves as students' advocates and advisers (McDonough and Calderone 2006).

Postsecondary Institutions. College type matters in investigations of inequality in college access. College access research has focused almost exclusively on entrance into four-year institutions, and often with a concentration on entrance into elite and selective college and universities (Adelman 2002; Baker and Vélez 1996; Kirst and Venezia 2004). Adelman notes that a research emphasis focusing exclusively on entrance to elite universities is "neither wise or kind to those who struggle against considerable odds to reach any level of higher education, let alone the vast majority of students who attend institutions in which the very notion of selectivity is moot" (2002, p. 39). For most community college students, "the choice is not between the community college and the senior residential institution but between the community college and nothing" (Cohen and Brawer 2003, p. 53).

Two-year colleges focusing on specific student populations such as historically black colleges (HBCs), Hispanic-serving institutions (HSIs), tribal colleges (TCs), and women's colleges provide significant points of access for the students attending them (Townsend 1997). For example, tribal colleges have had success at promoting tribal students' academic success, transfer, and four-year degree completion (AIHEC 1999, 2001; Benham and Stein 2003; Stein 1999).

Research shows that students who begin at two-year colleges are 15 percent less likely to complete a bachelor's degree than students who start at four-year colleges, and nationally only 22 percent of students who start at the community college with intentions to transfer actually do so (Cohen and Brawer 2003). Yet two-year colleges remain the most financially, geographically, and academically accessible routes to higher education for women, minority, and rural students (Townsend 1997) and certainly merit study within the field of college access. College access researchers have neglected these institutions, and future studies need to investigate their impact on exacerbating or ameliorating inequality in postsecondary entrance.

Field-Level Analyses

Although individual and organizational research contributes in important ways to understanding college access, scholars who do not look simultaneously and thoroughly across these domains understand only a small part of the field and may misrecognize important interactions and dynamics. Field-level analysis focuses attention on the macro-level changes in the institutions, professions, and technology of admissions in order to understand how student perceptions and actions grow from, as well as influence, organizational and institutional perceptions and action.

Financial Aid. There is no question of the direct relationship between income and going to college (Baker and Vélez 1996; Fitzgerald and Delaney 2002; Heller 1999; Paulsen and St. John 2002; Spencer 2002; Stampen and Fenske 1988). The gap in college going between the lowest- and highest-income families has remained steady since 1970, even for the academically best-prepared students (Fitzgerald and Delaney 2002).

Tuition and other college costs influence access to higher education both directly, as a response to costs and available financial aid, and indirectly, through perceptions and expectations about ability to pay for college costs (Fitzgerald and Delaney 2002; Paulsen and St. John 2002). Having early knowledge of financial aid has been found to increase college going and the number of postsecondary options a student considers.

The straightforward goal of the Higher Education Act of 1965, part of President Johnson's War on Poverty, was expanding access to higher education by directing money to academically prepared students with unmet financial need (Baker and Vélez 1996; Fitzgerald and Delaney 2002; Paulsen and St. John 2002; Spencer 2002; Stampen and Fenske 1988). A secondary purpose was to provide low-income students with a moderate level of choice between public and private institutions (Fitzgerald and Delaney 2002). Having unmet financial need for college is thought to be the central most remediable cause preventing postsecondary enrollment (Spencer 2002). For this reason, within the policy arena, financial aid and college cost are thought to be the sine qua non of college access (McDonough 2004).

Providing increased grant support to lower-income students is a relatively uncomplicated mechanism that has been clearly and repeatedly shown to improve college access (Fitzgerald and Delaney 2002; Heller 1999; Paulsen and St. John 2002; Spencer 2002). However, since 1978, the Middle Income Assistance Act expanded financial aid opportunities for middle-income and more affluent families, a trend that gained momentum in the 1980s and continues today, in the form of decreased grant money and increased dependence on student loans, a policy that effectively limits access for many low-income and students of color (Baker and Vélez 1996; Fitzgerald and Delaney 2002; Heller 1999; Paulsen and St. John 2002; Spencer 2002). This trend in policy and practice effectively privileges the broad middle-class concern with affordability through a tuition tax credit, on which the federal government spends more than on all federal student aid put together (Spencer 2002). At the institutional level, selective colleges and universities are now targeting new money disproportionately to programs aimed at merit, further benefiting middle- and upper-middle-class students with opportunities to learn (Spencer 2002).

Admissions Policies and Practices. Since 1970, a significantly larger number of both public and private colleges are classified as "competitive"—or the most difficult to gain acceptance to—and a larger number of public colleges are now classified as "selective," the intermediate category of selectivity. Students are filing larger numbers of applications to hedge their bets in an uncertain admission environment, and thus colleges' yield rates—the percentage of admitted students who actually enroll—have significantly declined (McDonough 2004).

One popular hedge against declining yield rates is early admission programs, which also help to improve a college's placement in *U.S. News and World Report*'s annual rankings (Avery, Fairbanks, and Zeckhauser 2003). Early decision (ED), which is practiced at about a third of all four-year colleges (primarily the most selective), allows students to apply early and receive their acceptance or rejection early, but binds students to enroll if accepted, before they receive other admission decisions or financial aid offers. Early action features the same early application and quick decisions from the college, but students are not obligated to attend. Critics of early decision note that these programs create tension and anxiety for applicants when making final decisions without competitive offers, privilege white and affluent applicants from resource-rich high schools, and increase competition for the remaining slots in the "regular" application cycle. These programs effectively amount to a doubling of the chances of admission, or the equivalent of a boost of 100 points in SAT scores for early applicants (Avery, Fairbanks, and Zeckhauser 2003). In late 2006, Harvard and Princeton decided to stop using early admissions on a trial basis. It is not clear that many more institutions will follow suit, as long as *U.S. News and World Report* uses ED in its ranking methodology.

A major area of concern related to the school-to-college transition is admissions policies and preferences for certain groups of students. The national media have provided ample coverage over the last few years to calls for doing away with legacy and major-donor admissions preferences. Even the U.S. president and other national leaders who have themselves benefited from legacy admission policies have joined in the chorus of voices calling for their elimination.

The role of affirmative action schemas for diversifying our student bodies is the focus of a never-ending stream of litigation, advocacy, and research. The Supreme Court ruled that colleges and universities can continue to use race-conscious admissions policies, but most legal analysts advise colleges to proceed with caution. Recent analyses show that various state percent plans, as alternatives to affirmative action, have proved to offer very little hope for increasing African American and Latino students' presence on more selective college campuses (Carnevale and Rose 2003). Moreover, because of the low and stagnant numbers of poor students entering college today, other researchers have advocated for socioeconomic diversity to be incorporated into the goals of existing affirmative action plans (Carnevale and Rose 2003). In fact, Anthony Carnevale and Stephen Rose find that even though African

Americans and Latinos together account for 12 percent of students at more selective colleges today, the lowest-quartile SES students are a mere 3 percent (and the bottom half of SES students only 10 percent) of all undergraduates at these institutions.

The research synthesized here has shown that the barriers to college access are primarily financial and academic, with additional needs for earlier information, more and better trained counselors, opportunities and support for families to partner in the college preparation process, and admissions policies that do not exacerbate existing inequalities. However, four of these barriers—the academic, informational, counseling, and family partner needs—are dependent upon K–12 schools, and it is important to understand more about the state of K–12 education in order to understand specifically how to improve these conditions of college access.

Entrepreneurial Admissions Sector. Because competition for access to highly selective and elite colleges and universities is on the rise, socioeconomically advantaged college applicants and their parents—who have the economic, social, and cultural capital to position their children for competitive eligibility—are hiring tutors, SAT coaches, and private counselors to help them manage the admissions process (McDonough 1994; McDonough et al. 1998; McDonough, Ventresca, and Outcault 2000). Three percent of high-SES college-bound students have access to private counselors, who offer highly specialized college admissions knowledge, provide uninterrupted one-on-one college counseling, help with managing the entire college choice process through enrollment, and match student clients to institutions that are a good fit given the students' aspirations and interests and the probability of their acceptance based on their academic record (McDonough 1994, 1997; McDonough, Korn, and Yamasaki 1997).

In a study of the use of newsmagazines that rank colleges, P. M. McDonough, A. L. Antonio, Marybeth Walpole, and L. X. Pérez (1998) find that almost 40,000 first-time first-year students (40%) used these publications, which means that the vast majority of the million-plus first-year students at four-year institutions were not using them. Not surprisingly, the students who use college-rankings magazines are the same high-SES students whose families can marshal other additional resources such as tutoring, SAT preparation, and, as described above, private counselors. Potentially these magazines could serve as an inexpensive resource for students with less access to college counseling through their schools, and thus they could be a source of "democratized knowledge" for college decision making (McDonough et al. 2000). However, these publications are decidedly not used by those students, instead representing the privatization or commodification of college knowledge that has transformed the field of selective college admissions (McDonough, Ventresca, and Outcault 1998). With the purchasing power enjoyed by affluent families, who continue to develop new strategies for ensuring that their children gain access to the "best" colleges, it remains much more difficult for first-generation students with far fewer opportunities to cobble together hard-earned academic capital and enter the competition (McDonough 1994; McDonough et al. 1998; McDonough, Ventresca, and Outcault 2000).

Limitations

In winding up our review of college access research, we must point out two significant limitations of our analysis. First, we focused only on the journal literature and did not analyze books or any other written media. The second limitation is that we focused on only six journals, all of which are high-prestige journals. Often, such journals represent only the dominant ideologies of a field and are highly resistant to new theories and methodologies. Journals—by design or default—serve a gatekeeping function, representing the editors' and reviewers' assessments of rigorous and promising research. Often new theories like critical race theory or new methodologies like ecocultural family interviewing have to prove themselves in lower-tiered journals before breaking into the mainstream. One promising avenue for future investigation would be to analyze this phenomenon to see where the impetus for paradigm shifts comes from and how often new generations of scholars have to utilize lower-tiered journals before their work is accepted by higher-prestige journals.

Conclusion

From the perspective of the new millennium, what do we think the sociology of higher education offers—and needs—in its function of taking on persistent issues of inequality, especially as evidenced in college access? First, the U.S. educational system, including higher education, remains intractably inequitable in advantage and disadvantage, in its stratification of students and resources, in school contexts in which students have access (or not) to educational opportunity, and in the influences of familial and social forces (e.g., families, financial aid policy, and the entrepreneurial admissions sector) on structuring educational opportunity. The impacts of these forces are cumulative and dynamic across students' educational experiences.

Second, the sociology of higher education literature related to access has morphed from social psychological perspectives on college choice, to organizational analyses, to cultural analyses focused on the role of schools' cultures in reproducing class structures. However, we believe these intellectual advances are not enough. We have briefly shown that the field needs to embrace more qualitative and naturalistic methodologies to provide more insight and balance.

Clark (1973) spoke of educational inequality—but in subsequent years, too much of the research on college access has focused on inequality at the *individual* level. As a field we need more research attention to the role of higher education in mitigating *societal* inequality. Frighteningly, despite 40 years of significant policy efforts, the college participation gap between low-income and high-income students today is roughly the same as the participation gap in the 1960s (Gladieux and Swail 1999). We also need to do more research at the organizational and field levels, as we have demonstrated here.

We believe the sociology of higher education needs to engage in integrative inquiry, where we look at the whole system of education, the educational experience of individuals across this system, and the key indicators and transitions that make up equality and inequality in education. We need to shift paradigms more frequently to a field perspective that investigates the interconnectivity and interdependencies of inequalities. Edward St. John's (2003) work is a good example of integrating policy, economics, and social justice frameworks, while Michael Kirst and Andrea Venezia (2004) offer a second example of integrating across educational levels to focus on a P–16 educational system that better aligns K–12 progress with postsecondary entrance.

This review of the literature on persistent inequality suggests that our current state of research ignores students' agency and thus their ability to influence their educational achievement. However, we also are calling into question a system that differentially prepares students for college and the college admissions contest. Inequalities in college access are cumulative manifestations that develop dynamically throughout and across students' educational experiences. Thus, we sociologists of higher education must find ways to bridge the borders of K–12 and higher education, because without incorporating important sociological knowledge of K–12 conditions, we will have inaccurate understandings of the sources of inequality and thus will not advance our theory and practice sufficiently to interrupt this persistent inequality.

We began this chapter by noting Clark's call for sociologists of higher education to be attentive to stratification across higher education institutions. We believe we have shown that the field has been passionately attentive to inequality in college access, across class, race/ethnicity, and culture. Outside the domain of college access, we also have a thriving literature on stratification in terms of resources and student outcomes (Bastedo and Gumport 2003; Walpole 2003).

Also in the beginning of this chapter we repeated Clark's admonition to avoid becoming a "managerial sociology" and instead to engage in a delicate balancing act, addressing issues of inequality and stratification in higher education while attending to the imperative to inform the profession of higher education practice. Yet more than three decades later, criticisms persist within higher education that policymakers and practitioners alike find our research irrelevant (Kezar 2000). The same can be said for the discipline of sociology itself, which has struggled with relevance, as evidenced by the 2005 annual meeting subtitle, "Accounting for the Rising and Declining Significance of Sociology."

Practitioners have been more successful at building bridges to scholars to address the issue of relevance and to make better and more routine connections between research, theory, and practice. Two notable groups recently addressing this issue are the Social Science Research Council and the Pathways to College Network. These advocacy and research organizations have brought together practitioners and scholars through meetings and common databases that share state-of-the-art research and practitioner innovations. These two organizations have created fruitful ways to engage in metasynthesis, identifying crucial knowledge gaps and directing research to much-needed areas. Each organization, separately and together, has also identified potential funding sources for research.

We have two remaining concerns about the state of the art of college access research: privatization and field correctives. We believe that privatization is threatening equality in college access. One form of privatization that has occurred is the entry of private producers into markets that were formerly public monopolies. In college access this has affected counseling, knowledge (guidebooks and other resources), test preparation, and more (McDonough et al. 1998). With privatization, accountability in relation to the public's goals of fair access to social goods, optimal deployment of human talent, and distributive justice is neglected, even eviscerated. With the spread of privatization, resources, information, and cultural capital are accumulated further by those who already have them, admissions criteria become more demanding as wealthy students receive assistance and coaching, and equality of college opportunities becomes further out of reach.

In order to push the field to attend to unconsidered or underconsidered issues, we need to think about field correctives. Fields are fundamentally shaped by individual preferences (the accumulated choices of individual scholars pursuing the issues they choose in the theoretical and methodological ways they wish) as well as journal choices and tenure imperatives. However, periodically fields need to reassess and identify the gaps that its scholars need to fill in. One way, as we have mentioned, is to further disaggregate status characteristics, such as racial and ethnic groups, rural and migrant students, nontraditional students, students in foster care, and other groups that have been neglected.

College access has been studied as a piece of the equality of the educational opportunity pipeline for the last 50 years; our democracy prides itself on an equal educational opportunity for college as a cornerstone of American public policy. Yet by default we have retreated from our commitment to equal college opportunities—through marketing and recruitment imperatives and federal and state accountability imperatives that ignore school disparities and have shifted student aid to the middle classes (McDonough 2004). It is our hope and our intention that further research will have an impact on these trends.

References

Adelman, C. 2002. "The Relationship between Urbanicity and Educational Outcomes." In *Increasing Access to College: Extending Possibilities for all Students*, ed. W. G. Tierney and L S. Hagedorn, 15–34. Albany: State University of New York Press.

AIHEC (American Indian Higher Education Association). 1999. *Tribal Colleges: An Introduction*. Washington, DC: AIHEC.

——. 2001. *Tribal College Contribution to Local Economic Development*. Washington, DC: AIHEC.

Allen, W. R. 1988. "Black Students in U.S. Higher Education: Toward Improved Access, Adjustment, and Achievement." *Urban Review* 20 (3): 165–88.

Allen, W. R., M. Bonous-Hammarth, and R. Teranishi. 2002. "Stony the Road We Trod: The Black Struggle for Higher Education in California." Research report, Choices: Access, Equity, and Diversity in Higher Education. Los Angeles: University of California–Los Angeles.

Apostal, R., and J. Bilden. 1991. "Educational and Occupational Aspirations of Rural High School Students. *Journal of Career Development* 18 (2): 153–60.

Astin, A., and L. Oseguera. 2004. "The Declining Equity of American Higher Education." *Review of Higher Education* 27 (3): 321–41.

Atkinson, R. C., and P. A. Pelfrey. 2004. *Rethinking Admissions: US Public Universities in the Post–Affirmative Action Age.* Center for the Study of Higher Education Research and Occasional Paper Series CSHE.8.04. Berkeley: University of California. Available at http://ishi.lib.berkeley.edu/cshe/.

Attanasi, L. C. 1989. "Getting In: Mexican Americans' Perceptions of University Attendance and the Implications for Freshman Year Persistence." *Journal of Higher Education* 60:247–77.

Avery, C., A. Fairbanks, and R. Zeckhauser. 2003. *The Early Admissions Game: Joining the Elite.* Cambridge, MA: Harvard University Press.

Baker, T. L., and W. Vélez. 1996. "Access to and Opportunity in Postsecondary Education in the United States: A Review." *Sociology of Education* 69 (extra issue): 82–101.

Bastedo, M. N., and P. J. Gumport. 2003. "Access to What? Mission Differentiation and Academic Stratification in U.S. Public Higher Education." *Higher Education* 46:341–59.

Benham, M. K. P., and W. J. Stein, eds. 2003. *The Renaissance of American Indian Higher Education.* Mahwah, NJ: Lawrence Erlbaum Associates.

Bill and Melinda Gates Foundation. 2003. *High Schools in the Millennium: Imagine the Possibilities.* Seattle: Bill and Melinda Gates Foundation.

Cabrera, A. F., and S. M. La Nasa. 2000. "Understanding the College Choice Process." In *Understanding the College Choice of Disadvantaged Student,* eds. A. F. Cabrera and S. M. La Nasa. New Directions for Institutional Research 107. San Francisco: Jossey-Bass.

Callan, P. M., and J. E. Finney. 2003. *Multiple Pathways and State Policy: Toward Education and Training beyond High School.* Boston: Jobs for the Future.

Carnevale, A., and S. Rose. 2003. *Socioeconomic Status, Race/Ethnicity, and Selective College Admissions.* New York: Century Foundation.

Castillo, E. 1999. "Foreword." In *Exterminate Them! Written Accounts of the Murder, Rape, and Enslavement of Native Americans during the California Gold Rush, 1848–1868,* ed. C. E. Trafzer and J. R. Hyer. East Lansing: Michigan State University Press.

CDE (California Department of Education, California Basic Educational Data). 2002. "Student Counselor Ratios in California, 1992–2002." Available at www.cede.ca.gov/ds/sd/index.asp.

Ceja, M. 2000. "Understanding Chicana College Choice: An Exploratory Study of First-Generation Chicana Students." Ph.D. dissertation, University of California, Los Angeles.

Clark, B. 1960. *The Open Door College.* New York: McGraw-Hill.

———. 1973. "Development of the Sociology of Higher Education." *Sociology of Education* 46 (Winter): 2–14.

———. 1983. *The Higher Education System : Academic Organization In Cross-National Perspective.* Berkeley, CA : University of California Press.

———. 1989. "The Academic Life: Small Worlds, Different Worlds." *Educational Researcher* 18 (5): 4–8.

Cohen, A. M., and F. Brawer. 2003. *The American Community College.* San Francisco: Jossey-Bass.

Coleman, J. S. 1987. *Public and Private High Schools: The Impact of Communities.* New York: Basic Books.

Cooper, C., R. Cooper, M. Azmitia, G. Chavira, and Y. Gullat. 2002. "Bridging Multiple Worlds: How African American and Latino Youth in Academic Outreach Programs Navigate Math Pathways to College." *Applied Developmental Science* 6 (2): 73–87.

Delgado, R. 1988. "Critical Legal Studies and the Realities of Race: Does the Fundamental Contradiction Have a Corollary?" *Harvard Civil Rights–Civil Liberties Law Review* 23:407–13.

Deyhle, D. 1992. "Constricting Failure and Maintaining Cultural Identity: Navajo and Ute School Leavers." *Journal of American Indian Education* 31 (2).

———. "Navajo Youth and Anglo Racism: Cultural Integrity and Resistance." *Harvard Educational Review* 65 (3): 403–44.

Fann, A. J. 2001. "College Pathways for Korean Immigrant Youth in Koreatown: Community Support Networks." Paper presented to the annual meeting of Asian Pacific Americans in Higher Education, San Francisco.

———. 2002. "Native College Pathways in California: A Look at College Access for American Indian Students." Paper presented at the annual meeting of the Association for the Study of Higher Education, Sacramento, CA, November.

———. 2005. "Forgotten Students: American Indian High School Student Narratives on College Access." Ph.D. dissertation, University of California–Los Angeles.

Fann, A. J., D. Wilson., W. Teeter, C. Alvitre, and D. Champagne. 2003. "Tribal Partnership in Higher Education: Bridging Academic and Cultural Scholarship." Paper presented at the annual meeting of the Association for the Study of Higher Education, Sacramento, CA.

Fitzgerald, B. K., and J. A. Delaney. 2002. "Educational Opportunity in America." In *Conditions of Access: Higher Education for Lower-Income Students*, ed. D. Heller. Westport, CT: American Council on Education, Praeger Series on Higher Education.

Freeman, K. 1997. "Increasing African Americans' Participation in Higher Education." *Journal of Higher Education* 68 (5): 523–50.

———. 1999. "The Race Factor in African Americans' College Choice." *Urban Education* 34 (1): 4–25.

Friedel, T. L. 1999. "The Role of Aboriginal Parents in Public Education: Barriers to Change in an Urban Setting." *Canadian Journal of Native Education* 23 (20): 139–58.

Gándara, P. 2002. "Meeting Common Goals: Linking K–12 and College Interventions." In *Increasing Access to College: Extending Possibilities for all Students*, ed. W. G. Tierney and L. S. Hagedorn, 81–104. Albany: State University of New York.

Gándara, P., and D. Bial. 2001. *Paving the Way to Higher Education: K–12 Intervention Programs for Underrepresented Youth*. Washington, DC: National Postsecondary Education Cooperative.

George, P. and R. Aronson, R. 2002. *How Do Educators' Cultural Beliefs Systems Affect Underserved Students' Pursuit of Postsecondary Education?* White paper sponsored by National Association of Secondary School Principals (NASSP) and Pathways to College Network. Boston: Pathways to College Network.

Gladieux, L., and W. S. Swail. 1999. "Financial Aid Is Not Enough: Improving the Odds for Minority and Low-Income Students." In *Financing a College Education: How It Works and How It's Changing*, ed. J. E. King. Phoenix: Oryx.

Haller, E. J., and S. J. Virkler. 1993. "Another Look at Rural-Nonrural Differences in Students' Educational Aspirations." *Journal of Research in Rural Education* 9 (3): 170–78.

Hawkins, D. 1993. "Pre-college Counselors Challenged for Misadvising Minorities: Full Array of Options Not Always Explained." *Black Issues in Higher Education*, July, 14–15.

———. 2003. *The State of College Admissions*. Alexandria, VA: National Association for College Admission Counseling.

Haycock, K. 2001. "Closing the Achievement Gap." *Educational Leadership* 58 (6): 6–11.

———. 2004. "The Opportunity Gap: No Matter How You Look at It, Low-Income and Minority Students Get Fewer Good Teachers." *Thinking K-16* 8 (1): 36–42.

Heller, D. E. 1999. "The Effects of Tuition and State Financial Aid on Public College Enrollment." *Review of Higher Education* 23 (1): 65–90.

Horn, L. 1996. *Nontraditional Undergraduates Trends in Enrollment from 1986 to 1992 and Persistence and Attainment among 1989–90 Beginning Postsecondary Students.* Washington, DC : U.S. Department of Education, National Center for Education Statistics.

Hossler, D., J. Braxton, and G. Coopersmith. 1989. "Understanding Student College Choice." In *Higher Education: Handbook of Theory and Research,* vol. 5, ed. J. Smart, 231–38. New York: Agathon.

Hossler, D., J. Schmit, and N. Vesper. 1998. *Going to College: How Social, Economic, and Educational Factors Influence the Decisions Students Make.* Baltimore: Johns Hopkins University Press.

Hurh, W. M. 1998. "The Korean Americans." In *The New Americans,* ed. R. Bayor. Westport, CT: Greenwood.

Hurtado, A. 2005. "Toward a More Equitable Society: Moving Forward in the Struggle for Affirmative Action." *Review of Higher Education* 28 (2): 273–84.

Hurtado, S., K. K. Inkelas, C. Briggs, and B. S. Rhee. 1997. "Difference in College Access and Choice among Racial/Ethnic Groups: Identifying Continuing Barriers." *Research in Higher Education* 38:43–74.

Immerwahr, J., and T. Foleno. 2000. *Great Expectations: How the Public and Parents—White, African American, and Hispanic—View Higher Education.* National Center Report 00-2. San Jose, CA: National Center for Public Policy and Higher Education and Public Agenda.

Jellison, H. J. 2002. "Buying Homes, Buying Schools: School Choice and the Social Construction of School Quality." *Harvard Educational Review* 71 (2): 177–205.

Jencks, C., M. Smith, H. Acland, M. Bane, D. Cohen, H. Gintis, B. Heyns, and S. Michelson. 1972. *Inequality: A Reassessment of the Effect of Family and Schooling in America.* New York: Basic Books.

Jennings, M. 2004. *Alaska Native Political Leadership and Higher Education: One University, Two Universes.* Walnut Creek, CA: Altamira.

Kahlenberg, R. 2004. *America's Untapped Resource: Low-Income Students in Higher Education.* New York: Century Foundation.

Kezar, A. 2000. "Still Trees without Fruit? Higher Education Research at the Millennium." *Review of Higher Education* 23 (4): 443–68.

Kim, K. S. 1999. "A Statist Political Economy and High Demand for Education in South Korea." *Education Policy Analysis Archives* 7 (19): 1–25.

King, J. 1996. *The Decision to Go to College. Attitudes and Experiences Associated with College Attendance among Low-Income Students.* New York: College Board.

Kirst, M. W., and A. Venezia, eds. 2004. *From High School to College: Improving Opportunities for Success in Postsecondary Education.* San Francisco: Jossey-Bass.

Manski, C. F., and D. A. Wise. 1983. *College Choice in America.* Cambridge, MA: Harvard University Press.

Marbaix, J. R. 2004. "The Pivotal Decision." *Robb Worth Report: Wealth in Perspective*, May, 58–60.

Martin, J. 1992. *Cultures in Organizations: Three Perspectives.* Oxford: Oxford University Press.

Martinez, M., and S. Klopott. 2003. *Improving College Access for Minority, Low-Income, and First Generation Students.* Boston, MA: Pathways to College Network.

McDonough, P. M. 1994. "Buying and Selling Higher Education: The Social Construction of the College Applicant." *Journal of Higher Education* 65 (4): 427–46.

———. 1997. *Choosing Colleges: How Social Class and Schools Structure Opportunity.* Albany: State University of New York Press.

———. 1999. *Doing Whatever It Takes: Conflict-Based College Admissions in the Post–Affirmative Action Era.* Paper presented at the annual conference of the American Educational Research Association, Montreal, Canada, April.

———. 2001. Testimony for California State Senate, Select Committee on College and University Admissions and Outreach, November 8.

———. 2004. *The School-to-College Transition: Challenges and Prospects.* Washington, DC: American Council on Education, Center for Policy Analysis.

———. 2005a. "Counseling and College Counseling in America's High Schools." In *The 2005–05 State of College Admission*, ed. David Hawkins. Washington, DC: National Association for College Admission Counseling.

———. 2005b. "Counseling Matters: Knowledge, Assistance, and Organizational Commitment in College Preparation." In *Preparing for College: Nine Elements of Effective Outreach*, ed. W. G. Tierney, Z. B. Corwin, and J. E. Colyar, 69–88. Albany: State University of New York Press.

McDonough, P. M., A. L. Antonio, M. Walpole, and L. X. Pérez. 1998. "College Rankings: Democratized Knowledge for Whom?" *Research in Higher Education* 39 (5): 513–37.

McDonough, P. M., and S. Calderone. 2006. "The Meaning of Money: Perceptual Differences between College Counselors and Low-Income Families about College Costs and Financial Aid." *American Behavioral Scientist* 49 (12): 1703–18.

McDonough, P. M., and R. E. Gildersleeve. 2005. "All Else Is Never Equal: Opportunity Lost and Found on the P–16 Path to College Access." In *The SAGE Handbook for Research in Education: Engaging Ideas and Enriching Inquiry*, ed. C. Conrad and R. Serlin. Thousand Oaks, CA: Sage.

McDonough, P. M., J. Korn, and E. Yamasaki. 1997. "Access, Equity, and the Privatization of College Counseling." *Review of Higher Education* 20 (3): 297–317.

McDonough, P. M., and K. A. McClafferty. 2001. *Rural College Opportunity: A Shasta and Siskiyou County Perspective.* Technical report to the University of California, Office of the President, and McConnell Foundation.

McDonough, P. M., K. A. McClafferty, and A. Fann. 2002. "Rural College Opportunities and Challenges." Paper presented at the annual meeting of the American Educational Research Association, New Orleans, April.

McDonough, P. M., M. Ventresca, and C. Outcault. 2000. "Field of Dreams: Organization Field Approaches to Understanding Transforming College Access, 1965–1995." In *Higher Education: Handbook of Theory and Research*, vol. 14, ed. J. C. Smart and W. G. Tierney, 371–405. New York: Agathon.

McGrath, D. J., R. R. Swisher, G. H. Elder Jr., and R. D. Conger. 2001. "Breaking New Ground: Diverse Routes to College in Rural America." *Rural Sociology* 66 (2): 244–67.

McNeil, P. W. 2003. *Rethinking High School: The Next Frontier for State Policymakers*. Aspen, CO: Aspen Institute.

Moehringer, J. R. 2004. "Tough Boots to Fill: Army Recruiters Take Orders to Boost Ranks Personally." *Los Angeles Times*, November 21, A1.

Moles, O. C. 1991. "Guidance Programs in American High Schools: A Descriptive Portrait." *School Counselor* 38 (3): 163–77.

NCES (National Center for Education Statistics). 2002. *Nontraditional Undergraduates: Findings from the Condition of Education 2002*. NCES 2002–012. Washington, DC: U.S. Department of Education. Available at http://nces.ed .gov/programs/coe/2002/analyses/nonraditional/index.asp.

Noguera, P. A. 2001. "Racial Politics and the Elusive Quest for Excellence and Equity in Education." *Education and Urban Society* 34 (1): 18–41.

Oakes, J. 1985. *Keeping Track: How Schools Structure Inequality*. New Haven: CT: Yale University Press.

———. 1989. "What Educational Indicators? The Case for Assessing the School Context." *Educational Evaluation and Policy Analysis* 11:181–99.

———. 2004. "Investigating the Claims in *Williams v. State of California*: An Unconstitutional Denial of Education's Basic Tools?" *Teachers College Record* 106 (10): 1889–906.

Oakes, J., J. Rogers, M. Lipton, and E. Morrell. 2002. "The Social Construction of College Access: Confronting the Technical, Cultural, and Political Barriers to Low-Income Students of Color." In *Increasing Access to College: Extending Possibilities for All Students*, ed. W. G. Tierney and L. S. Hagedorn, 105–22. Albany: State University of New York Press.

Oakes, J., A. S. Wells, S. Yonezawa, and K. Ray. 1997. "Equity Lessons from Detracking Schools: Change Agentry and the Quest for Equity." In *Rethinking Educational Change with Heart and Mind*, ed. A. Hargreaves, 43–71. Alexandria, VA: Association for Supervision and Curriculum Development.

Obidah, J., T. Christie, and P. McDonough. 2004. "Less Tests, More Redress: Improving Minority and Low Income Students' Academic Achievement." *Penn GSE Perspectives on Urban Education*.

Orfield, G. 1996. *Dismantling Segregation: The Quiet Reversal of "Brown v. the Board of Education."* New York: New Press.

——. 1998. "Exclusions of the Majority: Shrinking Public Access and Public Policy in Metropolitan Los Angeles." *Urban Review* 20 (3): 147–63.

Ouchi, W., and A. L. Wilkins. 1985. "Organizational Culture." *Annual Review of Sociology* 11:457–83.

Paulsen, M. B., and E. St. John. 2002. "Social Class and College Costs: Examining the Financial Nexus between College Choice and Persistence." *Journal of Higher Education* 73 (2): 189–236.

Pavel, D. J. 1999. "American Indians and Alaska Natives in Postsecondary Education: Promoting Access and Achievement." In *Next Steps: Research and Practice to Advance Indian Education*, ed. K. G. Swisher and J. W. Tippeconnic, 239–58. Charles, WV: Educational Resources Information Center (ERIC) Clearinghouse on Rural Education and Small Schools.

Pavel, D. M., R. R. Skinner, E. Farris, M. Calahan, and J. Tippeconnic. 1998. *American Indians and Alaska Natives in Postsecondary Education.* NCES 98–291. Washington, DC: U.S. Department of Education, National Center for Education Statistics.

Pérez, L. X. 1999. "In Search of the Road to an Open College Door: The Interface of Individual, Structural, and Cultural Constructs in Latino Parents' Efforts to Support Their Children in Planning for College." Ph.D. dissertation, University of California–Los Angeles.

Perna, L. 2005. "The Key to College Access: Rigorous Academic Preparation." In *Preparing for College: Nine Elements of Effective Outreach*, ed. W. G. Tierney, Z. B. Corwin, and J. E. Colyar, 13–28. Albany: State University of New York Press.

Perna, L., and W. S. Swail. 2002. "Pre-college Outreach and Early Intervention Programs." In *Conditions of Access: Higher Education for Lower-Income Students*, ed. D. Heller. Westport, CT: American Council on Education, Praeger Series on Higher Education.

Perna, L. W., and M. Titus. 2004. "Understanding the Differences in the Choice of College Attended: The Roles of State Public Policy." *Review of Higher Education* 27 (4): 501–25.

Pewewardy, C., and B. Frey. 2004. "American Indian Students' Perceptions of Racial Climate, Multicultural Support Services, and Ethnic Fraud at a Predominantly White University." *American Indian Journal of Education* 43 (1): 32–60.

Plank, S. B., and W. J. Jordan. 2001. "Effects of Information, Guidance, and Actions on Postsecondary Destinations: A Study of Talent Loss." *American Educational Research Journal* 38 (4): 947–79.

Schein, E. 1990. "Organizational Culture." *American Psychologist* 45 (2): 109–19.

Siu, S. 1996. *Asian-American Students at Risk: A Literature Review*. Report 8. Baltimore: Center for Research on the Education of Students Placed at Risk, Johns Hopkins University and Howard University.

Smith, M. J. 2001. "Low SES Black College Choice: Playing on an Un-level Playing Field." *Journal of College Admission* 71:16–21.

Solórzano, D. G. 1992. "An Exploratory Analysis on the Effects of Race, Class, and Gender on Student and Parent Mobility Aspirations." *Journal of Negro Education* 61:30–44.

———. 1995. "The Chicano Educational Experience: Empirical and Theoretical Perspectives." In *Class, Culture, and Race in American Schools*, ed. S. W. Rothstein. Westport, CT: Greenwood.

Solórzano, D. G., and O. Villalpando. 1998. "Critical Race Theory, Marginality, and the Experience of Students of Color in Higher Education." In *Sociology of Education: Emerging Perspectives*, ed. C. A. Torres and T. R. Mitchell. Albany: State University of New York Press.

Spencer, C. 2002. "Policy Priorities and Political Realities." In *Conditions of Access: Higher Education for Lower-Income Students*, ed. D. Heller. Westport, CT: American Council on Education, Praeger Series on Higher Education.

Stampen, J. O., and R. H. Fenske. 1988. "The Impact of Financial Aid on Ethnic Minorities." *Review of Higher Education* 11 (4): 337–52.

Stein, W. J. 1999. "Tribal Colleges, 1968–1998." In *Next Steps: Research and Practice to Advance Indian Education*, ed. K. G. Swisher and J. W. Tippeconnic. Charleston, WV: ERIC Clearinghouse on Rural and Small Schools.

Stewart, D. M. 1988. "Overcoming Barriers to Successful Participation by Minorities." *Review of Higher Education* 11 (4): 329–36.

St. John, E. 2003. *Refinancing the College Dream: Access, Opportunity, and Justice for Taxpayers*. Baltimore: Johns Hopkins University Press.

Swail, W. S., and L. W. Perna. 2002. "Pre-college Outreach Programs: A National Perspective." In *Increasing Access to College: Extending Possibilities for All Students*, ed. W. G. Tierney and L. S. Hagedorn, 15–34. Albany: State University of New York Press.

Tate, W. 1997. "Critical Race Theory and Education: History, Theory, and Implications." *Review of Research in Education* 22:195–247.

Tejeda, C., M. Espinoza, and K. Gutierrez. 2004. "Toward a Decolonizing Pedagogy: Social Justice Reconsidered." In *Pedagogy of Difference*, ed. P. Trifonas. New York: Routledge.

Teranishi, R., M. Ceja, W. Allen, S. Suh, and P. McDonough. 2004. "Examining College Opportunities for Asian Americans: Ethnicity and Social Class at the Crossroads." *Review of Higher Education* 27 (4): 527–51.

Tierney, W. G. 1992. *Official Encouragement, Institutional Discouragement: Minorities in Academe, the Native American Experience*. Norwood, NJ: Ablex.

——. 1997. "The Parameters of Higher Education: Equity and Excellence in the Academy." *Review of Educational Research* 67 (2): 165–96.

——. 1999. "Models of Minority College-Going and Retention: Cultural Integrity versus Cultural Suicide." *Journal of Negro Education* 68 (1): 80–91.

——. 2001. "A University Helps Prepare Low Income Youths for College." *Journal of Higher Education* 72 (2): 205–25.

Tierney, W. G., and S. Auerbach. 2005. "Toward Developing an Untapped Resource: The Role of Families in College Preparation." In *Preparing for College: Nine Elements of Effective Outreach*, ed. W. G. Tierney, Z. B. Corwin, and J. E. Colyar, 13–28. Albany: State University of New York Press.

Tierney, W. G., and J. Colyar. 2005. "The Role of Peer Groups in College Preparation Programs." In *Preparing for College: Nine Elements of Effective Outreach*, ed. W. G. Tierney, Z. B. Corwin, and J. E. Colyar, 49–68. Albany: State University of New York Press.

Tippeconnic, J. W. 1999. "Tribal Control of American Indian Education: Observation Since the 1960s with Implications for the Future." In *Next Steps: Research and Practice to Advance Indian Education*, ed. K. Swisher and J. Tippeconnic. Charleston, WV: ERIC Clearinghouse on Rural Education and Small Schools.

——. 2000. "Reflecting on the Past: Some Important Aspects of Indian Education to Consider as We Look toward the Future." *Journal of American Indian Education* 39 (2): 39–47.

Townsend, B. 1997. *Two-Year Colleges for Women and Minorities: Enabling Access to the Baccalaureate*. New York: Falmer.

Villalpando, O., and D. G. Solórzano. 2005. "The Role of Culture in College Preparatory Programs: A Review of the Research Literature." In *Preparing for College: Nine Elements of Effective Outreach*, ed. W. G. Tierney, Z. B. Corwin, and J. E. Colyar, 13–28. Albany: State University of New York Press.

Walpole, M. 2003. "Socioeconomic Status and College: How SES Affects College Experiences and Outcomes." *Review of Higher Education* 27 (1): 45–73.

Ward, C. 1995. "American Indian High School Completion in Rural Southeast Montana." *Rural Sociology* 60:416–34.

Zemsky, R., and P. Oedel. 1983. *The Structure of College Choice*. New York: College Entrance Examination Board.

Zhou, M., and C. L. Bankston. 1998. *Growing Up American: How Vietnamese Children Adapt to Life in the United States*. New York: Russell Sage Foundation.

4 The Study of College Impact

SYLVIA HURTADO

Although educational research, particularly efforts toward understanding student learning and development, has traditionally been dominated by psychologists, much of the research on students at the postsecondary level has focused on college outcomes as a function of the characteristics of institutions and of their educational programs (Pascarella and Terenzini 1991, 2005). One could therefore argue that the majority of premises foundational to research on the impact of college on students are sociological in nature. This is primarily because college impact research assumes that institutions shape the development of individuals (their values, skills, and knowledge) in preparation for work and leadership in society. Indeed, historically, the earliest work defining college impact research drew heavily from social psychology and sociology (Feldman and Newcomb 1969). Since the field's inception, researchers have focused on the effects of formal structural features of institutions and of social normative environments, and on the social nature of students' behavior that reinforces or undermines "college effects." That is, college impact researchers take for granted that varying rates of development among college students occur, and they attempt to link such variation to college environmental differences and opportunities within the formal structures of institutions (their characteristics and programs) and social normative environments. This line of research is intended to inform educational practice and policies, in order to produce desired effects on students and positive outcomes for society, as well as to justify continued state and private investment in postsecondary education. The purpose of this chapter is to identify and review sociological thinking commonly used in the study of college impact, to highlight some major contributions made and conclusions drawn by researchers, and to point to some promising new directions opened up by sociological developments in the field.

Sociological Premises within Frameworks in the Field

Though sociologists have differed in their conceptualization of *social structure*, it is generally defined as persisting patterns of behavior and interaction among people or social positions (Blau 1975; House 1981). James House (1981) argues that the study of social structure and its effect on individuals or personality (as defined by beliefs, motivations, and behaviors) has roots in classic sociology. Karl Marx's concept of alienation itself can be understood as a social response in the relationship between societal structure (capitalism) and its institutions, on the one hand, and individual beliefs and motivations on the other. According to House, "Marx was centrally concerned with (1) the nature and consequences of the 'fit' between social structure and the characteristics of individuals, and (2) with how position in the socioeconomic structure shaped values, beliefs, and motives" (1981, p. 529). Max Weber (1958) was also concerned with social structure, which he argues is shaped by beliefs, and which, once established, shapes successive generations' attitudes, values, and beliefs. Émile Durkheim's concept of "anomie" in his study *Suicide* (1951) focuses on social systems, individual states of mind, and the maintenance of the social order. Moreover, Alex Inkeles's (1960) "convergence thesis" places strong emphasis on the impact of social structure through institutions: "institutions with similar structures tend to induce common psychic structures or regularities in the personalities of their participants. This is especially true if, as in the case of schools and the work place, the individual spends time in the institutions and they control powerful rewards and punishments" (quoted in House 1981). The study of social structure and personality is an essential area, for it looks at how macrosocial phenomena, proximate social stimuli, and interactions or the interpersonal environment of individuals are linked as mediating processes (Elder 1973), and how each of them affects individual psychology (changes in individual behaviors, beliefs, and attitudes). While the prevailing view is that social structure and its institutions shape individuals, House posits that personality (collective beliefs and behaviors) can also influence the social structure, although he notes that such phenomena are understudied.

Thus, the study of social structure in relation to personality is the sociological root of college impact research. These roots become clearer in investigating well-regarded frameworks in the field that posit how the college environment shapes student interactions (interpersonal environments) and subsequent behaviors, beliefs, lifestyle preferences, cognition, and attitudes. The theoretical student retention frameworks posited by Vincent Tinto (1993, 1975) and William G. Spady (1970, 1971) and John C. Weidman's (1989) model of undergraduate socialization all borrow directly from sociological concepts, and subsequent research based on these models has extended the initial sociological premises.

Retention Models

Tinto's (1975, 1993) theoretical model of voluntary student departure and Spady's theoretical model of the undergraduate dropout process (1970, 1971) make liberal use of Durkheim's (1951) theory of suicide: the likelihood of suicide increases when individuals are not fully integrated into the normative social and intellectual structure of society. Spady posits that students' responses to the college environment parallel this process when the "lack of consistent, intimate interaction with others, holding values and orientations that are dissimilar from those of the general social collectivity, and lacking a sense of compatibility with the immediate social system" result in a student's dropping out from an institution (1970, p. 78). According to Tinto, student background characteristics, initial intentions, goals, and commitments influence and are further shaped by students' interactions within the formal and informal academic and social structures of a college environment. These student interactions, in turn, produce personal or normative integration (academic and social), which influences subsequent intentions and commitments that can result in a departure decision. Tinto notes that *interaction* in the social and academic systems (or social communities) in the college environment does not guarantee persistence; rather, some degree of "social and intellectual *integration* must exist as a condition for continued persistence" (p. 119, emphasis added). This latter point suggests that interactions required for participation in the academic and social systems (social structure) of a college may operate independently from an individual's psychological sense of integration. The psychological sense referred to here functions as an independent construct in the model, labeled *personal/normative integration.*

At the same time that these frameworks are widely used in empirical studies and have become part of the language in institutional practice, several criticisms have been raised about their concept of integration and their assumption of "normative congruence" with the dominant values and expectations of the college environment. Scholars have argued that normative congruence in social and value orientation implies the acculturation of historically marginalized groups—for it is nontraditional students who are least likely to conform to dominant modes of thinking and acting—and that this construct ignores the way students make meaning of their role in large college campuses where it is not possible to have face-to-face contact with or know everyone (Attinasi 1989, 1992; Tierney 1992; Hurtado and Carter 1997; Braxton, Sullivan, and Johnson 1997). Both Spady (1970) and Tinto (1993, in response to criticism) concede that conformity can also be incomplete and cultural dissimilarities accommodated, and that forms of "normative incongruence" can coexist within college environments. Spady suggests that students with nonmainstream value orientations can establish close relationships with other "deviants" and find subgroup support that can override the "diffuse influence of the general system" (1970, p. 78). He states that students may find faculty support for their divergent views and specifies the importance of *friendship support* in his theoretical model, to highlight the affiliative aspects that are key to integration. Tinto's response to the criticisms mentioned above is that conformity is not always associated with integration and that the "concept of 'membership' is more useful than 'integration' because it implies a greater diversity of participation" within the college environment (1993, p. 106). Different group memberships can be formed around a diverse set of activities and opinions. However, group membership remained unspecified in the reformulation of Tinto's model over the years and has received scant attention from higher education researchers (Hurtado and Carter 1997). More research is needed to determine how student memberships, in producing varying levels of students' sense of social cohesion, link to the overall campus environment.

Empirical studies of college students and student retention in college have enthusiastically adopted elements of frameworks for which the concept of *integration* is central. However, much like studies of social cohesion in sociology (Bollen and Hoyle 1990), empirical studies attempting to capture integration have used such variant measures that the results have served to obfuscate the central sociological premises. To clarify such empirically based research processes, studies that address the basic sociological premises underlying these models should aim to capture the following:

- aspects of the formal and normative structure (academic and social environments)
- interpersonal environments or the substance and quality of interactions
- students' own psychological sense of social cohesion or integration
- subsequent outcomes (e.g., dropping out, changing attitudes)

Measures used in these studies can be classified in at least four domains:

- *characteristics* (features of formal structure and programs) and *characterizations* of the environment (perceptions) that capture the social and academic systems
- social *interactions*—behavioral measures of the quality of academic and social engagement in college
- *membership*—group affiliations, which can vary depending on how a group determines entry and confers privileges on its members
- *perceived social cohesion*—the students' psychological sense of belonging to a college community

In attempting to draw these distinctions, my previous research has shown how, for Latino students in college, different group memberships, different types of interaction with other students or faculty, and differences in characterization of their college (perceptions of the climate) have resulted in variant levels of perceived social cohesion (Hurtado and Carter 1997). Subsequent work has further revealed that even in a mobile community college population where sustained levels of interaction are not possible, students' sense of belonging to the college community (perceived social cohesion) is related to student retention (Allison 1999). Thus, as in the original Tinto and Spady models, personal/normative integration (or one's sense of being part of the larger campus community) is distinct from interactions within the college academic and social structures, and subsequent empirical work has shown that not all types of activities or group membership in which diverse students engage elicit strong feelings of affiliation with the overall college community (Hurtado and Carter 1997). Moreover, college structures or opportunities are key, for recent work has revealed that academic support programs influence not only confidence in academic skills but also a student's sense of belonging in college (Oseguera and Hurtado 2004; Hurtado and Ponjuan 2005; Nunez 2005). Unfortunately, in many empirical studies, such distinctions for capturing personal/ normative integration apart from student interactions have been lost (Braxton et al. 1997).

Instead, many studies have used student interactions as proxies for integration (Braxton et al. 1997), and subsequent work on student engagement in college shows results on numerous college outcomes after controlling for student characteristics (Pascarella and Terenzini 1991, 2005; Astin 1993). From a sociological viewpoint, however, studies of student engagement in college are incomplete if they do not take account of the opportunity structure or elements of the college environment that shape student interaction on campus, in addition to assessing students' psychological sense of integration. Campuses vary in their levels of overall social cohesion, which is related to the normative structure as well as to structural features (e.g., size, residence halls) that shape student interaction. Many of these structural features of the college environment have been mainstays of college impact studies and are detailed in a subsequent section.

The Undergraduate Socialization Model

Weidman's model of undergraduate socialization (acquiring the knowledge, language, skills, and attitudes valued by society for particular roles) stands alone in the field as the most comprehensive and explicit specification of social structure as normative contexts that shape student career choices, lifestyle preferences, aspirations, and values (Weidman 1989). Weidman's work gives emphasis to both the informal and formal aspects of the academic and social features of the college environment in relation to socialization processes and normative pressures (precollege and in college), and it acknowledges the continuing socializing influences that parents and noncollege reference groups (e.g., peers, employers, community organizations) exert on student outcomes. The formal academic context consists of such things as institutional quality, institutional mission, and major or department, whereas the informal academic environment consists of the hidden curriculum or implicit rules that govern academic life. The formal social context involves the structural features of a college such as institutional size, residences, and organizations, while the informal involves student peer groups.

Although the model gives concrete examples of normative structure, some of the elements may be difficult to measure (e.g., the hidden curriculum, institutional mission), and the model's complexity may contribute to its lack of widespread empirical testing. Still, researchers have adopted some aspects of the model to show the effect of peer normative influences on student outcomes. For example, Anthony L. Antonio (2004) has studied the effect of the characteristics of a student's immediate peer group and has found that peer group degree aspirations raise, but peer group SAT scores depress, intellectual self-confidence among individual white students. In contrast, the SAT scores of the immediate peer group have no significant effect on the intellectual self-confidence of students of color. However, a racially/ethnically diverse friendship group and a high level of intellectual self-confidence in the immediate peer group are associated with increases in intellectual self-confidence among individual students of color.

The study establishes that normative peer contexts or proximal interpersonal environments are more influential than are general measures of student interactions in college. The mechanisms by which these peer groups have influence are still theoretical and beg further examination. It may well be that such proximal interpersonal environments are where normative pressures are the greatest. The potential for extending sociological theory using this undergraduate socialization model is great in terms of capturing a range of phenomena that constitute normative structure. Moreover, the model's inclusion of socializing influences outside of college may best capture the experience of those students who juggle multiple roles and are subject to multiple influences. That is, this college impact model takes account of alternative sources of social influence that may be competing with or reinforcing college goals and expectations. Overall, these sociological frameworks have done much to advance our thinking about student experiences within institutions. The next section addresses more macro-level influences that produce variation both within and between institutions in the higher education system.

Structural Features of the Environment and Their Impact on College Students

Embedded in our educational institutions are the basic elements of social structure that differentiate individual experience within institutions, but structural features also differentiate colleges in terms of resources, opportunities, and training for specific occupations and roles. Scholars have studied the varied structural features of college environments, features related to student educational outcomes (e.g., size, type, homogeneity/heterogeneity, and selectivity). In a sociological sense, the structural properties of the environment are central to shaping social interaction and the individual's attitude or behavior within it (Kiecolt 1988). These structural properties or features are often studied through the use of "objective" measures that describe the characteristics of a college. These features have also been referred to as "contextual variables" (Kiecolt 1988) or "distal characteristics" (Jessor 1979) to distinguish them from more proximal interpersonal environments.

In college impact research, these features are referred to as institutional characteristics that distinguish college environments, and they are often used to determine "between college effects" (Pascarella and Terenzini 1991, 2005). In order to assess differentiation in college effects, studies have required multi-institutional samples, with a sufficient number of students in each context. Many of these are therefore large-scale studies, assessing institutional quality in terms of selectivity and resources; institutional type and classification (e.g., two-year versus four-year, university, liberal arts college); racial composition; gender composition; urban-rural distinctions; and institutional size. This approach thus looks at the impact of different types of colleges on different types of students. However, while many of the listed institutional characteristics are unquestionably influential in shaping the experience of students and the life of the academic organization, it is very difficult to change such features as urban location, college racial composition, and private or public control for the purposes of improving practices within institutions. These distinctions among structural features continue to be studied, because they provide insight into how the overall system of higher education is stratified in terms of structure, resources, and outcomes. Yet these college characteristics are not considered as relevant to daily practice and are at times excluded from studies altogether. Depending on the study, these features may be considered more policy relevant, in that they can serve to inform the public about differentiation and about corrections needed in particular types of institutions or in the higher education system overall. Moreover, it could be argued that it is just as difficult to change a college's normative structure, shaped over time by collective beliefs, practices, and ideology. I will return to this issue at the end of the chapter, as there are ways—at least in theory—that normative structure can be examined through college impact research over time.

While many areas of work on the structural characteristics of institutions can be analyzed for their impact and sociological relevance, much of this work is already summarized elsewhere (Pascarella and Terenzini 1991, 2005). I will focus on only three areas of research regarding the formal structural features of institutions, areas that bear upon other elements critical to studying social structure and personality. These structural features do affect and shape interaction and interpersonal environments, perceptions, and behavior—all of which are relevant to educational outcomes. I will look more closely at studies on institutional size, selectivity, and racial composition.

Institutional Size

Within college impact research on institutional structural features, perhaps one of the most important sociological influences has been Peter Blau's (1973) theoretical and empirical work, *The Organization of Academic Work*—most notably his findings on institutional size. Blau found that institutional size correlates with many conceptually distinct features in colleges and universities, including revenues, vertical and horizontal differentiation in administrative units or bureaucracy, specialization of academic departments in new fields, average faculty salaries, the level of clerical support faculty receive, faculty allegiance to the institution, presidential span of control, and a college's ability to attract able students. He essentially demonstrated how the structural feature of size shapes the nature and level of individuals' interactions and experiences within the college environment. Institutional size subsequently was regularly examined in college impact studies, especially since this one feature affects many aspects that figure significantly in an institution's carrying out its educational mission, as well as in the development of student outcomes.

As documented by college impact researchers, institutional size shapes interaction patterns in several ways. Studies demonstrate that college students enrolled at large institutions are less likely to interact with faculty, get involved in student government, participate in athletics or honors programs, or have opportunities to speak up during class; and as a result, they are also much less satisfied with faculty relationships and classroom instruction than are students attending smaller campuses (Astin 1979). However, students on large campuses are more satisfied than are students on smaller campuses with the social life, the quality of science programs, and the variety within the curriculum. Although students who attend small colleges typically have good records of educational attainment and positive self-images relative to students attending large campuses, successful students at the larger campuses have relatively higher long-term earnings and occupational status (Pascarella and Terenzini 1991). These latter findings have been deemed strong, positive independent effects of institutional size on long-term outcomes.

Also, some evidence suggests that students on large campuses are able to adjust (socially, academically, and emotionally) to college, once they learn to navigate the social and physical geography of a campus (Hurtado, Carter, and Spuler 1996). L. C. Attinasi (1989) uses ethnomethodology to understand how students make sense of large college environments. He explains that they engage in cognitive mapping and locate themselves in a niche, breaking down large environments into manageable small communities where they pursue their own interests and form peer groups. Students' ability to make these adjustments successfully suggests that colleges can employ a similar strategy by formally organizing proximal environments that facilitate students' closer connections with their institutions. This (along with interest in improving student retention rates) has been the impetus behind many specialized learning communities recently developed on college campuses.

Overall, these results would indicate significantly different types of educational experiences for students on large compared to small campuses. Yet many of the beneficial outcomes that accrue to students at the larger schools may be due to the presence of formal structures and informal patterns of behavior that counter some of the negative effects of large institutional size. Further research is needed about these activities, as well as about the mechanisms by which students gain in long-term earnings and occupational status as a result of attending large institutions.

College Selectivity

Almost 90 percent of high school seniors indicate that they expect to attend some type of postsecondary institution in the future (Hurtado, Inkelas, Briggs, and Rhee 1997), and the U.S. system is considered to have universal access relative to other countries. Yet one of the U.S. higher education system's most obvious features is its differentiation in terms of access. In other words, institutions vary substantially in the level of access afforded to students, as determined by established admissions practices. To apply this distinction to questions of college impact: what difference does college selectivity make, generally, in college outcomes? There is some disagreement in the literature, although no scholar of college impact would neglect to include this institutional characteristic in her study. E. T. Pascarella and P. T. Terenzini (1991) refer to institutional selectivity as an indicator of college quality when, in fact, it refers to the quality of students entering a college, not the process of education or the available programs. Selectivity tends to be highly correlated with institutional resources (Astin 1985), though many studies also evaluate the impact of these resources independent of college selectivity. From a social stratification perspective, college selectivity can also be thought of as the embedded structure of unequal distribution of resources and the institutional stratification process through which only a few students have access to the best resources. College selectivity is set by the tradition of the institution and carried out in its admissions policies. In some cases, state policy dictates the selectivity of public institutions; for example, the California Master Plan for Higher Education assigns to the state's public institutions different levels of selectivity, and only the most selective institutions can award the most advanced graduate and professional degrees. In a nutshell: college selectivity ensures differential access, preparation, and outcomes—all of which lead to different occupational statuses in society. This is not a view, however, that predominates in education, as most institutional leaders believe they are doing their best with the students who arrive at their doorstep; they tend to value college selectivity, and faculty work both to introduce it and to maintain it.

In many college impact studies comparing educational effects, the average SAT/ACT score of students entering an institution serves as the measure for selectivity. In part this has been influenced by the early work of Alexander Astin (1965), in which he defines selectivity as a college's ability to recruit high-aptitude students, and uses the average SAT scores of entering freshmen. In citing Astin's work in his study of academic organizations, P. M. Blau prefers to use the rejection rate as the measure of the "actual degree of selectivity among a college's pool of applicants" (1973, p. 132), so that student aptitude is a separate measure and can be evaluated independently. Thus, for Blau, the popularity of the college and institutional flexibility in choosing among the best applicants become the focus, but few researchers have actually used this measure of selectivity in subsequent college impact studies.

The impact of college selectivity is broad, but college impact researchers find—as the stratification viewpoint might predict—that the effects of selectivity are strongest on student educational aspirations, educational attainment, occupational status, and long-term earnings (Pascarella and Terenzini 1991). Given this evidence, the clamor among the growing number of college applicants to be accepted at a selective institution is not unwarranted. Moderate effects of attending a selective college have also been observable in career mobility and success, entrance into sex-atypical careers, and political and social liberalism. Still, after introducing many measures of peer norms (aggregated across institutions), Astin (1993) concludes that selectivity has few direct effects; much is accounted for by the socioeconomic status of the college student body (peer SES), which after four years of college has a direct effect on students' cognitive, affective, and behavioral outcomes. Indeed, peer SES has more effects than does any other measure of the peer group or faculty. In effect, then, Astin identifies the mechanism through which college selectivity has such a broad and significant impact. Selective institutions provide the normative influence of a talented or high-SES peer group, opportunities for interaction, and ample resources.

College Racial Composition

The process of colleges' developing such that they differ substantially from each other in racial composition is a function of several factors: a history of exclusion and racial segregation in education; regional differences in employment of demographic groups in specific industries (such as agriculture or manufacturing); differential resources for schools that serve different racial groups; and funding sources based on private philanthropy and on legislative initiatives. In the case of the latter, the Morrill Act and the Second Morrill Act served the "separate but equal" doctrine that dictated social relations in the South until it was contested in 1954. Racial stratification continues to the present in the higher education system in terms of access, college student experiences, and outcomes. For example, even though today's black undergraduates are more likely to enroll in a predominantly white institution, colleges and universities that are historically black have continued to attract more low-income black first-year students than have predominantly white institutions for the past 30 years (Allen et al. 2005). Across the nation, black students also attain bachelor's degrees most often at historically black institutions.

Sociologist Walter Allen undertook studies of black students in both predominantly black and predominantly white institutions and found marked distinctions in their college experiences. Among black college students attending historically black institutions, he found greater contact with faculty, a stronger sense of support, and a more positive academic self-concept (1988, 1992). Though black students were more satisfied with the resources offered at predominantly white institutions, they tended to characterize the climate at such institutions as more hostile to racial issues (Allen 1992). Further review of the college impact research evidence in this area indicates that black colleges appear to have a moderate impact on the cognitive development and educational attainment of black students and a small positive effect on black women's occupational status and on black students' social and academic self-image (Pascarella and Terenzini 1991). The normative structures of institutions developed for the advancement of black people appear to achieve their goals, though more study is needed to tie aspects of the normative structure embedded in practices (at both predominantly black and predominantly white institutions) to effects, to explore whether normative structures actually make a difference for interpersonal environments and social mobility.

One area where related normative structures may be studied in the features of institutions is in the changing racial composition of predominantly white institutions. This area is gaining some traction among college impact researchers examining issues of climate (or perceptions based on group standpoints), integration, and outcomes. Some sociologists have theorized that discrimination and conflict increase in environments where minority numbers rapidly increase, because different racial groups are in competition for resources (Blalock 1967) or because the dominant ideology or worldview comes into competition with others (Giroux 1983). These theories seem to support further some of the early work in this area. In 1971, Astin collaborated with sociologist Alan Bayer to study campus protest and conflict. They found such events to be associated with the absolute number of black students on campuses—a finding that contributed to the development of the notion of the importance of a "critical mass." They documented some of the early impacts of the civil rights and other student movements on college campuses, indicating a clash of normative structure with the values and beliefs of a changing student body, a conflict that was heightened by the historical and social conditions of the period. M. W. Peterson et al. (1978) also documented institutional responses resulting from new increases in black enrollment, some of which indicate that campuses were relatively unprepared for the changes these enrollments brought.

These few examples turn college impact research on its head: not only do institutions influence the development of students, but institutions are also influenced by the types of students they recruit. Moreover, students have historically urged institutions to become engaged in social change. Thus the study of social structure in relation to personality reflects a dynamic relationship, as House (1981) suggests, one that can be documented in higher education research—although in the field one would be hard pressed to call these research efforts college impact studies, unless the changes are related to differences in student outcomes. In terms of college impact, a body of work regarding the impact of the racial/ethnic diversification of predominantly white institutions on individual student outcomes and the long-term benefits to society is emerging (see Chapter 9 in this volume on the sociology of diversity).

These research areas of college size, selectivity, and college racial composition are illustrative of just a few structural features of institutions that have been examined in college impact studies, and study of them is extending the early sociological premises. More elaborate models today, however, do not limit their assessments to these structural features, as many researchers choose measures of the college environment that may be more relevant to policy (particularly those that document variation in resources and opportunities) given their impact on students. Furthermore, these structural features simply provide the context for interactions in more proximal environments, so it may well be that their impact is actually indirect. Future research may consider modeling these contextual effects to show more directly how students' interactions and sociopsychological responses change in different environments. Many other future directions are possible to extend the sociology of college impact; some areas for new directions are discussed in the next section.

New Directions for the Sociology of College Impact

The study of college impact is extensive enough to have warranted several volumes of research that attest to the importance and value of a postsecondary education over time (Feldman and Newcomb 1969; Pascarella and Terenzini 1991, 2005). Though this research has not given substantial attention to political and state budget agendas, the premise about the broad and significant impact of college is not contested. This volume of work on a wide variety of college outcomes, which has surveyed various student populations at different historic points, suggests at least two important new directions for extending the sociology of college impact.

First, given the volume of empirical work, it seems there is substantial room for a generation of new theory that will extend or replace existing frameworks. Syntheses of specific models have already begun to confirm that only particular aspects of the theories have been supported by consistent findings (Braxton, Sullivan, and Johnson 1997), and critics have begun to question the underpinnings of established frameworks (Hurtado and Carter 1997). Some fresh thinking about institutions in relation to students and their development is called for—approaches that consider how macro social forces and institutions influence the microprocesses identified in student behavior that result in both intended and unintended outcomes. For example, scholars can ask whether institutions with consistently low retention rates have become the "revolving doors" of higher education (intended as way stations) or students' stepping stones on the way to other destinations and goals (i.e., essentially serving a transfer function even though they offer four-year degrees). What mechanisms of formal and informal structure make this a fairly constant outcome over time for particular institutions, and what roles do faculty play in these normative contexts? These questions suggest a new theory of voluntary student departure outside of the dominant perspective regarding student integration frameworks.

Second, the volume of empirical work in college impact over time is ideal for identifying "period effects." D. F. Alwin, R. L. Cohen, and T. M. Newcomb (1992) define period effects as the intersection of biological and historical time—effects that may be due to national or societal events that affect particular cohorts of students as they develop. We know, for example, that students' political attitudes have shifted dramatically over time and that they are likely influenced by historical periods—the civil rights era, the Reagan era, or now, the post-9/11 world. Thus the effects of college on specific outcomes may not be the same, nor as significant, in all historical periods. College impact researchers do not always acknowledge the wider social and historical contexts in which they conduct their work, but these contexts are probably affecting the results of their studies. One way to determine this is to review studies across the various periods (with the more than 30 years of college impact research that makes this possible) and encourage the replication of studies in new historical periods. What makes replication difficult is that both students and institutions are changing, and taking account of these changes is essential if we wish to make definitive statements about the impact of college or of particular features of a college.

Another accounting of the larger social forces that affect institutional dynamics and student outcomes would be to study the changing demographics in higher education. For example, demographic changes coupled with variations of admissions policies have led to the development of Hispanic-serving institutions (institutions that serve a population that is at least 25% Hispanic) and institutions that enroll large numbers of Asian students. These may be ideal sites for studying how normative structures and changing student demographics coexist or clash, with differential student outcomes (though Hispanics and Asians often attend very different types of institutions in terms of selectivity). Recent studies of Latino students have revealed that students report less hostility and more inclusive climates at four-year institutions with higher Latino enrollments (Hurtado 1994). This is in contrast to H. M. Blalock's theory of increased conflict, but it remains to be seen if the normative structures of these formerly predominantly white institutions have undergone transformation so as to contribute to the success of Latino students in the same way that historically black institutions have supported the advancement of black students. In addition, if changing peer group norms are the basis for college effects on many outcomes, we as yet know very little about increases among Asian and Latino students and the effect of these new peer groups on other students.

Working at the micro level is also important, to gain a better understanding of these processes and to identify links with macro-level contexts. Research can be extended into how students jointly construct meaning regarding performance, effort, and involvement in particular college programs. New investigations can examine their uses of technology, their accepted routines and habits, the role of specific types of memberships that students seek, and their use of social networks; these areas may reveal more about how individual student responses are influenced by collective expectations and practices that may undermine or reinforce intended outcomes for college. New modes of college going are emerging, for students are participating in higher education as time, resources, institutional structures, and life plans allow. For example, even among the traditional-age college students, the number expecting to work full time while attending college has doubled in the last 20 years (Sax et al. 2004). College impact research has yet to tap into this emerging variation, which may work against the expectations of existing institutional structures. In addition, it is appropriate to delineate more aspects of college environments' formal and informal systems, aspects that are responsive to changes in student population and that achieve desired outcomes. Borrowing from new developments in sociology—and thereby extending sociological thinking—remains natural to the study of college impact, for the field essentially studies institutions and individuals, their responses in various contexts, and variation in the college outcomes that are essential to our society.

References

Allen, W. R. 1988. "Black Students in U.S. Higher Education: Toward Improved Access, Adjustment, and Achievement." *Urban Review* 20 (3): 165–87.

———. 1992. "The Color of Success: African American Student Outcomes at Predominantly White and Historically Black Public Colleges and Universities." *Harvard Educational Review* 62 (1): 26–44.

Allen, W. R., U. M. Jayakumar, K. A. Griffin, W. S. Korn, and S. Hurtado. 2005. *Black Undergraduates from Bakke to Grutter: Freshmen Status, Trends, and Prospects, 1971–2004.* Los Angeles: Higher Education Research Institute, University of California–Los Angeles.

Allison, L. 1999. "Integrating Experiences and Retention of Nontraditional Students." Ph.D. dissertation, University of Michigan.

Alwin, D. F., R. L. Cohen, and T. M. Newcomb. 1992. *Political Attitudes over the Life Span: The Bennington Women after Fifty Years.* Madison: University of Wisconsin Press.

Antonio, A. L. 2004. "The Influence of Friendship Groups on Intellectual Self-Confidence and Educational Aspirations in College." *Journal of Higher Education* 75:446–71.

Astin, A. W. 1965. *Who Goes Where to College?* Chicago: Science Research Associates.

——. 1979. *Four Critical Years.* San Francisco: Jossey-Bass.

——. 1985. *Achieving Educational Excellence.* San Francisco: Jossey-Bass.

——. 1993. *What Matters in College: Four Critical Years Revisited.* San Francisco: Jossey-Bass.

Astin, A. W., and A. E. Bayer. 1971. "Antecedents and Consequents of Disruptive Campus Protests." *Measurement and Evaluation in Guidance* 4 (1): 18–30.

Attinasi, L. C. 1989. " 'Getting In': Mexican Americans' Perceptions of University Attendance and the Implications for Freshman Year Persistence." *Journal of Higher Education* 60:247–77.

——. 1992. "Rethinking the Study of Outcomes of College Attendance." *Journal of College Student Development* 33:61–70.

Blau, P. M. 1973. *The Organization of Academic Work.* New York: John Wiley and Sons.

——. 1975. *Approaches to the Study of Social Structure.* New York: Free Press.

Blalock, H. M., Jr. 1967. *Toward a Theory of Minority-Group Relations.* New York: Wiley.

Bollen, K. A., and R. H. Hoyle. 1990. "Perceived Cohesion: A Conceptual and Empirical Investigation." *Social Forces* 69:479–504.

Braxton, J. M., A. V. Sullivan, and R. M. Johnson. 1997. "Appraising Tinto's Theory of College Student Departure." In *Higher Education Handbook of Theory and Research*, vol. 12, ed. J. C. Smart, 107–64. New York: Agathon.

Durkheim, E. 1951. *Suicide.* Glencoe, IL: Free Press.

Elder, G. H. 1973. "On Linking Social Structure and Personality." *American Behavioral Scientist* 16:785–800.

Feldman, K. A., and T. M. Newcomb. 1969. *The Impact of College on Students.* San Francisco: Jossey-Bass.

Giroux, H. A. 1983. "Theories of Reproduction and Resistance in the New Sociology of Education: A Critical Analysis." *Harvard Educational Review* 53 (3): 257–93.

House, J. S. 1981. "Social Structure and Personality." In *Social Psychology: Sociological Perspectives*, ed. M. Rosenberg and R. H. Turner, 525–61. New York: Basic Books.

Hurtado, S. 1994. "The Institutional Climate for Talented Latino Students." *Research in Higher Education* 35 (1): 21–41.

Hurtado, S., and D. F. Carter. 1997. "Effects of College Transition and Perceptions of Campus Racial Climate on Latinos' Sense of Belonging." *Sociology of Education* 70 (4): 324–45.

Hurtado, S., D. F. Carter, and A. Spuler. 1996. "Latino Student Transition to College: Assessing Difficulties and Factors in Successful Adjustment." *Research in Higher Education* 37 (2): 135–57.

Hurtado, S., K. Kurotsuchi Inkelas, C. U. Briggs, and B. S. Rhee. 1997. "Differences in College Access and Choice among Racial/Ethnic Groups: Identifying Continuing Barriers." *Research in Higher Education* 38 (1): 43–75.

Hurtado, S., and L. Ponjuan. 2005. "Latino Educational Outcomes and the Campus Climate." *Journal of Hispanic Higher Education* 4 (3): 235–51.

Inkeles, A. 1960. "Industrial Man: The Relation of Status to Experience, Perception, and Value." *American Journal of Sociology* 66:1–31.

Jessor, R. 1979. "The Perceived Environment and the Study of Adolescent Problem Behavior." Paper presented at the Symposium of the Situation in Psychological Theory and Research at LOVIK, Stockholm.

Kiecolt, K. J. 1988. "Recent Developments in Attitudes and Social Structure." *Annual Review of Sociology* 14:381–403.

Kuh, G. D., J. H. Shuh, E. J. Whitt, and Associates. 1991. *Involving Colleges.* San Francisco: Jossey-Bass.

Nunez, A. "Modeling College Transitions of Latino Students." Ph.D. dissertation, University of California–Los Angeles.

Oseguera, L., and S. Hurtado. 2004. "Linking Diversity and Transition to College." Paper presented at the International First Year Experience Conference, Maui, Hawaii.

Pascarella, E. T., and P. T. Terenzini. 1991. *How College Affects Students: Findings and Insights from Twenty Years of Research.* San Francisco: Jossey-Bass.

———. 2005. *How College Affects Students: A Third Decade of Research*, vol. 2. San Francisco: Jossey-Bass.

Peterson, M. W., R. T. Blackburn, Z. F. Gamson, C. H. Arce, R. W. Davenport, and J. R. Mingle. 1978. *Black Students on White Campuses: The Impacts of Increased Black Enrollments.* Ann Arbor, MI: Institute for Social Research.

Sax, L., S. Hurtado, J. Lindholm, A. W. Astin, W. S. Korn, and K. M. Mahoney. 2004. *The American Freshman: National Norms for Fall 2004.* Los Angeles: Higher Education Research Institute.

Spady, W. G. 1970. "Dropouts from Higher Education: An Interdisciplinary Review and Synthesis." *Interchange* 1:64–85.

———. 1971. "Dropouts from Higher Education: Toward an Empirical Model." *Interchange* 2:38–62.

Tierney, W. G. 1992. "An Anthropological Analysis of Student Participation in College." *Journal of Higher Education* 63:603–7.

Tinto, V. 1975. "Dropouts from Higher Education: A Theoretical Synthesis of Recent Research." *Review of Educational Research* 45:89–125.

———. 1993. *Leaving College: Rethinking the Causes and Cures of Student Attrition.* 2nd ed. Chicago: University of Chicago Press.

Weber, M. 1958. *The Protestant Ethic and the Spirit of Capitalism.* New York: Scribner.

Weidman, J. 1989. "Undergraduate Socialization." In *Higher Education Handbook of Theory and Research*, vol. 5, ed. J. C. Smart, 289–322. New York: Agathon.

5 The Study of the Academic Profession

GARY RHOADES

In 1973, the year that Burton Clark's "Development of the Sociology of Higher Education" appeared, I was a sophomore at the University of California–Los Angeles and had just declared sociology as my major field of study. One of my first classes was a primer in sociological theory, an introduction to the trinity of Durkheim, Marx, and Weber, whose analytical influences Clark traced in the unfolding sociological study of higher education. Within three years I was beginning a Ph.D. in sociology, still at UCLA. My initial interests were social psychology and collective behavior, in part reflecting the strengths of UCLA's department. Soon after, I concentrated more on political sociology and social movements and revolutions, in part reflecting the tenor of the times and the prominence of various contemporary social movements and political struggles: from civil rights and the women's movement to the consumer and environmental movements and Watergate, all of which challenged the basic institutions and professions of the day. Within eight years of when Clark wrote his essay, I was working for him as a postdoctoral research scholar, observing firsthand the defining contributor to the comparative study of faculty and of higher education, at a time of intensified globalization. The dual and interrelated dimensions of preeminent contributors to social science theory and research, on the one hand, and prevailing societal trends, on the other, define my discussion of the sociology of academic professions.

From the mid-1970s to the present, the evolving sociological study of academic professions has been shaped not only by enduring turn-of-the-twentieth-century sociologists but also by emergent mid- and late-twentieth-century scholars of professions and of higher education. It has also been shaped by powerful societal and institutional developments of the 1970s, 1980s, and 1990s, in the United States and throughout the world. This chapter looks at developments since 1973, synthesizing the work and identifying emerging lines of inquiry. With a bow to Clark's modus operandi of parsimoniously creating a few key concepts to capture major analytical points, I organize the main body of my discussion around a few key concepts that capture important lines of inquiry for the future. Each speaks to gaps in the literature. First, I consider the changing power relations between academic managers and professors, who are increasingly "managed professionals" (Rhoades 1998a). Second, I discuss the rise of nonfaculty professions on campus, what I have called "managerial professionals" (Rhoades 1998a, 1998b; Rhoades and Sporn 2002). Third, I invoke three concepts reflecting major developments both in society and in social science theory—feminism, marketization, and globalization—that challenge us to go beyond traditional boundaries in studying faculty. Before exploring these concepts, I open with a consideration of past developments in the study of the academic profession, and Clark's central contributions to such scholarship.

Past Developments in the Study of the Academic Profession

A great deal has been written about the academic profession in the more than 30 years since Clark's essay. Much of that work can be described in terms of the dominant social science theories and scholars—the Marxian, Weberian, and Durkheimian traditions identified by Clark. It has also reflected important external trends, such as the growing and changing academic labor market.

Clark's analysis traced several important potential lines of inquiry that were not addressed until the 1980s. These revolved around three dominant influences on social science theory, work that addressed: power and control in higher education; bureaucracy and rationalization; and normative and cultural dimensions in higher education and the academic profession. With the exception of some classic studies in knowledge and power by Thorstein Veblen (1918) and H. P. Beck (1947), this potential had been largely untapped. That is no longer the case.

A limited number of studies of academics adopt an explicitly neo-Marxist perspective. In the early 1980s, following the rise of a sociology of professions informed by Marx and Weber (e.g., Larson 1977), Edward Silva and Sheila Slaughter (1984) traced the rise and professionalization of the social sciences in the United States, showing how members of national associations in these fields gained power by "serving power." Subsequently, with an explicit bow in her title to Veblen, Slaughter in *The Higher Learning and High Technology* (1990)—as well as Clyde Barrow in *Universities and the Capitalist State* (1990)—traced the academy's domination by corporate business interests. Similarly, but with a focus on faculty, Slaughter and L. L. Leslie (1997) detailed the rise of "academic capitalism," the academy's participation in the private marketplace. And Slaughter and Rhoades (2004) have detailed the rise of "academic capitalism and the new economy," addressing the aggressive pursuit of "new economy" economic opportunities by faculty members and academic managers. Indeed, in the last several years, the commercial activities of the academy and of academics have become the subject of much empirical study and commentary (Readings 1996), including from a non-neo-Marxist perspective (e.g., Bok 2003; Geiger 2004; Kirp 2003).

A line of research on bureaucracy has also emerged, largely focused on academic decision making. However, in contrast to the studies identified above, this work takes an internalist approach. Patterns of decision making, for example, are not connected to patterns of rationalization or industrialization in society, as was done by Weber. Not long after Clark's essay, Kenneth Mortimer and T. R. McConnell wrote their now-classic study *Sharing Authority Effectively* (1978), the title of which reveals less a Weberian analysis of bureaucracy than a functionalist analysis of "effective" decision making, in some sense looking to identify best practices. In this same vein, a literature emerging in the 1990s identifies mechanisms and processes for faculty members and academic managers to participate more effectively in strategic decision making. Thus J. H. Schuster et al. (1994) detail in several case studies "how to make big decisions better," and David Leslie (1996) discusses mechanisms for making "wise moves" in "hard times." However, the overwhelming focus of this work is on central committees and structures such as faculty senates, more than on faculty generally or on conditions of work in an increasingly bureaucratized academy.

A considerably larger body of work has developed around Durkheimian concerns about faculty norms and socialization. A good deal of that work also addresses not just faculty attitudes but faculty's allocation of time among various activities—in part as an indicator of their preferences for teaching and research. Two now-classic studies emerged shortly after Clark's essay. As part of the Carnegie Commission studies of higher education in the United States, E. C. Ladd and S. M. Lipset

(1975) explored various dimensions of "the divided academy," including the political opinions of faculty members. Martin Trow (1975) contributed to the ongoing exploration of how much time faculty members spend teaching and in research activities. In the 1980s, Martin Finkelstein's *The American Academic Profession* (1984) definitively traced faculty members' activities and their preferences in teaching and research, and Howard Bowen and Jack Schuster (1986) described various characteristics and activities of academics. In the 1990s, E. L. Boyer (1990) spoke to redefining the "priorities of the professoriate," and James Fairweather (1996) portrayed the dominance of research in the academic reward system. By contrast, J. M. Braxton and A. E. Bayer (1999) concentrated on teaching norms among faculty members. And D. H. Wulff and A. E. Austin (2004) and W. G. Tierney and E. M. Bensimon (1996) have examined "pathways to the professoriate" and new faculty members' socialization into the academy.

Like the work on decision making, the majority of this work has an internalist focus. But if often functionalist in perspective, such work does not develop a Durkheimian connection between norms of the academic profession and the changing moral order of (in this case) postindustrial society. Two analyses of academe in the McCarthy era, by Lionel Lewis (1988) and Ellen Schrecker (1986), are important exceptions to that pattern. And recently, a few studies have begun to link the above patterns of time allocation and faculty attitudes to the increasingly close connection between the academy and the private-sector economy (Blumenthal et al. 1986; Campbell and Slaughter 1999; Louis et al. 1989).

Scholarship on faculty has also developed along a focus on the academic marketplace, as Clark (1973) suggested, based on classic studies of this phenomenon (Caplow and McGee 1958; Wilson 1942). Shortly after Clark's essay, Lewis wrote an insightful analysis, in *Scaling the Ivory Tower* (1975), of embedded social norms that come into play in academic hiring. Allan M. Cartter, for whom Clark's endowed chair at UCLA would be named, then published his classic study *PhD's and the Academic Labor Market* (1976). Toward the end of the 1980s, David Breneman and Ted Youn (1988) examined academic labor markets and careers, detailing segmented labor markets in an academy divided among various institutional sectors. Toward the end of the 1990s, Martin Finkelstein, Robert Seal, and Jack Schuster's *The New Academic Generation* (1999) traced trends in new cohorts of faculty members and charted the growing prominence of non–tenure-track positions in the academy.

Since the 1970s, a significant body of work has also emerged that details life outside the full-time, tenure-track academic mainstream and outside of research universities. D. W. Leslie, S. E. Kellams, and G. M. Gunne (1982) and J. M. Gappa and D. W. Leslie (1993) have analyzed "the invisible faculty," providing various classifications for considering part-time faculty and their experiences. Adopting similar language, W. N. Grubb (1999) has explored the lives of the "honored but invisible" faculty in community colleges, as have other major studies, including those by Howard London (1978), Lois Weis (1985), and Earl Seidman (1985). And R. G. Baldwin and J. L. Chronister (2001) have detailed various aspects of the working conditions and lives of so-called contingent faculty.

Each of the above developments in the study of the U.S. academic profession was foreshadowed in Clark's essay. As I have suggested throughout, each of these lines of work is characterized by a largely internal focus on academe and academic organizations. Far less attention has been devoted to the connection between these internal characteristics of the academic profession and the academy, on the one hand, and the broader society on the other. This internalist approach to academe also characterizes Clark's own work, which has helped to shape the ways in which higher education scholars think about and study higher education in the United States and abroad.

Clark's Contributions to the Study of the Academic Profession

In some important regards, Clark's 1973 essay foreshadowed his own central contribution to the emerging comparative study of core academic faculty's basic values and collective identities, as well as their involvement in governance at the level of individual organizations and national systems of higher education. Analytically, Clark's work has been characterized by a focus on clarifying case studies that capture significant functions and structures of academic work. Moreover, that work—and relatedly Clark's career—has coincided with patterns of intensified marketization and globalization in the past twenty-five years. From its inception, higher education has been an activity that included accumulating prestige and resources and circulating people and ideas across political borders. Nevertheless, in the last quarter of the twentieth century, the pace and proliferation of policies, practices, and exchanges that generate revenue and that cut across national boundaries have accelerated. Clark's work has addressed these trends, providing us with a language for thinking about and analyzing them.

In contrast to most higher education scholars' work on faculty, Clark's work has discussed not only the full range of structural settings in which faculty work but also the full scope of the basic functions and characteristics of academic work. His concepts and conceptualizations continue to define the field.

If most scholars have concentrated on faculty in one type of institutional setting, Clark has considered faculty in several different contexts, both in the United States and globally. His first book, *The Open Door College* (1960), focused on community colleges; his understanding of a key "cooling out function" performed by these organizations has shaped the ways that subsequent researchers have compared faculty (and students) in academic and vocational fields within these postsecondary institutions. In later years, much of Clark's work dealt with professors at research universities, concentrating on the critical "research/teaching nexus," among other subjects. Resisting the trend to separate these activities and even to counterpose them against one another, Clark saw them as essentially integrated functions in universities, which he characterized as "places of inquiry" (1995). In the years between, Clark addressed two other major sectors of four-year institutions, private liberal arts colleges and public comprehensive, masters-granting institutions. For example, his national study of faculty life in different types of institutions, *The Academic Life: Small Worlds, Different Worlds* (1987a)—which earned an award from the American Educational Research Association—framed for future scholars the defining influence of discipline and institutional type on the worldviews and local practices of academics.

Analytically, Clark's work has focused on the authority, work, and values of academics. This is most evident in his detailing the "different worlds" of academe. For professors in different fields and different institutional types, he mapped out different patterns: of authority in the organization; of work in teaching and research responsibilities; and of values in faculty perspectives on the norms of the national profession and how those norms are locally defined. These issues still constitute the major and enduring focus of attention for all sorts of scholars studying academics—their authority in the workplace at the level of the department and the organization, their teaching and research responsibilities and how those are interrelated, and the ways they think about and define key professional values in their work. And Clark's work has ensured that scholars must disaggregate their analyses of academics by field and institutional type, if they are truly to understand the daily lives, professional activities, and beliefs of members of the academic profession.

Clark's greatest analytical contribution has been to foster and shape fundamentally the comparative study of higher education in the United States and western Europe. Like his work on U.S. academic organizations and faculty members, Clark's comparative work has studied the patterns of academics' authority, their teaching and research, and their basic values. First, in a case study of academic power in a national system (Italy), Clark (1977) traced the mechanisms of professors' oligarchic authority, which in some systems reaches to the national level. Subsequently, in *The Higher Education System* (1983), Clark provided what came to be known as the "triangle model" for studying higher education systems cross-nationally, in terms of the significance of the state, the market, and the profession in shaping higher education. Central to such comparisons was an exploration of the bases of authority in the academy. Further, Clark comparatively pursued studies of the organization of academic work, of teaching and research, and of academic values (1987b, 1995).

Although arguably Clark is first and foremost a scholar of academic organizations and, as the subtitle of his seminal comparative book puts it, of academic organization in cross-national perspective, faculty and academic functions are always front and center in his understanding and characterization of these institutions. Scholars of organizational culture continue to grapple with the question of the relationship between the influence of the organization itself and that of the academic discipline and department (Tierney 1991). For Clark, at their core, colleges and universities are bundles of knowledge shaped and defined by academics. Similarly, in providing a schema for higher education scholars to talk about "organizational sagas" (1970), Clark goes beyond merely attributing organizational change to charismatic leaders. He provides a sociologically informed understanding of the institutionalization and routinization of a charismatic leader's agenda. Central roles in this process are played by senior academics who adopt the saga and embed it in the curriculum of the college. More recently, Clark has examined the marketization of European universities in case studies that map their "organizational transformation" toward "entrepreneurial universities" (1998). Rather than simply attributing such change to presidential leadership, Clark features faculty members' agency in the "steering core" and in embedding entrepreneurialism in the "academic heartland" of basic organizational structures of academic work. In following up on this work (2000, 2004), Clark has emphasized the importance of an entrepreneurialism that is collegial more than managerial and that is sustainable—again, centering on the key role of faculty members.

Yet there are significant gaps in the literature, and in Clark's own work. I connect my discussion of these to key analytical concepts and societal developments. Critical sociological scholarship on professions has concentrated on the relationship between professions on the one hand and, on the other hand, groups and changes in the larger political economy—evident, for example, in the rise of unionization in higher education. Moreover, scholarship on professions has increasingly addressed relations among professions and the spread of professions, but higher education scholars have not extended these perspectives to the study of professions in academe. Further, scholarship and societal developments have taken social science scholars beyond traditional boundaries in studying professions. Researchers attend to issues of gender and social movements in the professions, intersections between the world of professions and that of the increasingly neoliberal broader political economy, along with international activities and patterns of professions in an increasingly globalized context. In the ensuing sections of the chapter, I elaborate on each of the above points to map out future directions for the study of professions in academe.

Managed Professionals

Most higher education scholars and many faculty members in the United States would juxtapose faculty professionals with unionized employees to contrast the two, seeing them as fundamentally different. In continental Europe, most professors are civil servants, employees of the state (Neave and Rhoades 1987), whereas in the United States and the United Kingdom, professors have historically been conceptualized as professionals independent of the state, despite the fact that U.S. public college and university professors are part of municipal or state government. Like other so-called liberal professions, higher education scholarship and teaching are considered a profession because they are characterized by advanced education and a specialized body of knowledge over which they have a monopoly; a normative structure of codes of ethics and the rule of meritocracy; a level of autonomy embedded in peer review and considerable professional self-regulation; and, in the case of professors, concepts like academic freedom and shared governance (Goode 1957; Parsons 1954). From such a functionalist vantage point (Durkheim 1957), wherein professions are seen as functional in organizing work to serve clients and society, unions are seen as anathema, as a threat to professions (Metzger 1987b).

Yet such a perspective overlooks the realities of the workplace and ignores another vantage point for considering the professions. Even in the case of the most elite U.S. liberal professions, most doctors and lawyers—and essentially all professors—work in large organizations, where the scope of their autonomy is delimited by various sorts of managers. Moreover, for doctors (some of whom actually unionized in the 1990s) and lawyers, their associations (the American Medical Association and the American Bar Association) arguably act like strong unions, lobbying for the interests of the members. Indeed, 1970s professionalization scholars (Larson 1977) advanced just such a perspective, detailing ways in which professions are groups that aim to establish and maintain monopolies of expertise over certain domains of work, in the interest of the members of the profession. Finally, the current workplace reality is that many professions are, in fact, heavily unionized.

Sociologists of labor have characterized the last quarter of the twentieth century in terms of the rise of "the new unionism" (Troy 1994). As the economy shifted from industrial to postindustrial, the United States saw a major transformation in the types of jobs that expanded and, correspondingly, a fundamental transformation in the sorts of employees who became unionized. As technical occupations grew enormously, as noted in the previous section, the services sector of the economy also proliferated. Corresponding to the declining manufacturing sector, the site of largely blue-collar unions, the most growth in union employment in the past twenty-five years has been in the white-collar public sector. The most heavily unionized occupations in the current U.S. workforce now include public school teachers, nurses, and college and university faculty.

As the location of unionized employees changes, so do the basis and focus of the unions themselves. In their negotiations with employers, public sector and white-collar unions have increasingly appealed to quality-of-service issues, seeking to win public support for their cause through demonstrating a connection between their conditions of employment and the service they can provide. Nurses, for instance, focus on understaffing and the threat it poses to patients' health; public school teachers focus on class size and its relation to educational quality.

The entire process of negotiation between management and labor takes on important new dimensions in this context. Generally, the bargaining is not simply between employees and managers of large private companies. Instead, municipal and state governments are implicated in that they provide public services to the population. Some scholars have argued that this shift may well affect the process of negotiation: it enables employees to defend the legitimacy of their position and demands as more clearly grounded in the public interest, beyond economic leverage and the bread-and-butter issues of wages and benefits that came to characterize most blue-collar unions (Johnston 1994).

For the most part, such developments in unionization have eluded higher education scholars. As discussed above, to the extent that studies have concentrated on issues of power and authority on campus, they have largely addressed delimited structures such as faculty senates and faculty and administrative participation in setting the strategic direction of the institution (Keller 1983). A very limited literature on collective bargaining in higher education emerged shortly after higher education faculty began unionizing, the principal focus of which was on either the conditions that contributed to unionization or the salaries of faculty members in unionized settings (see Rhoades 1998a). And a few studies focused on the impact of unionization on faculty senates (Kemerer and Baldridge 1975; Baldridge and Kemerer 1976).

It was within this context that I wrote about faculty as increasingly becoming "managed professionals" (1998a). My intent was both to feature unionized faculty and to identify a pattern applicable to all academic labor; hence the subtitle, *Unionized Faculty and Restructuring Academic Labor*. In looking at collective bargaining agreements of unionized faculty members, I tracked conditions and changes in salaries, retrenchment, part-time faculty employment, instructional technology, and intellectual property. In short, I went well beyond the prevailing analyses of authority on campus and of relations between professors and administrators. My focus was not on discrete decisions but on the larger negotiation of working conditions as related to professional autonomy and managerial discretion. That larger negotiation, I argued, applied to faculty members in general and revealed a general pattern of increased managerial discretion in each of the realms analyzed.

From the perspective I advanced, grounded more in a sociology of the professions than in an organizational analysis of decision making, various lines of investigation emerge. As we conceptualize and approach the study of faculty in terms of the negotiation between professional autonomy and managerial discretion, our attention is drawn to professors' *collective* exercise of power—locally and nationally (as well as internationally). This collective wielding may be carried out through formal and informal campus-based channels of influence or through professional associations and other such mechanisms. For all that we know about the field in terms of activities and time allocations of individual faculty members, we know very little about how faculty collectively wield—and resist the exercise of—power, at the level of departments, colleges, universities, and municipal or state systems of higher education institutions. We also have very little understanding of the influence that faculty members have on state and federal agencies and policies. Clark (1977) has provided an example of such work internationally, but studies of higher education policy in the United States essentially leave out faculty and their organizations and associations (see Hutcheson 2000 for an exception). Some might argue that such oversight is due to the relative lack of influence that professors have over public policy. But professors and their associations play key roles in science and technology policy, and they also have heavily contributed to the ways that we think about student aid and higher education marketplaces. Whether the perspective is that faculty are unmanageable—that managing them is like herding cats—or that faculty are increasingly managed, such that managerial efforts impinge on professional autonomy in important ways, or whether the interest is in how they manage to resist such efforts and exercise influence of their own—from any of these angles, we need to understand better how professional power and influence are exercised in the concrete daily lives of faculty members, the organizations in which they work, and the policies that they influence.

Another line of research to develop would focus on the working conditions and experiences of faculty members. We lack any national study of institutional policies that define the parameters of faculty lives. We also lack sufficient case studies to help us better understand the concrete working conditions and experiences of faculty members in a higher education system that by all accounts is changing dramatically. In short, we have an incomplete, insufficient understanding of faculty life.

Part of the everyday experience of faculty lives is that professors' work is increasingly interconnected with that of other professionals on campus, as noted in the previous section of this chapter. The restructuring of academic labor is related to the restructuring of professional labor and to the increase among managerial professionals on campus. The rise of these other professionals also needs to be understood in the context of the changing balance between faculty autonomy and managerial discretion.

In focusing on unionized faculty and in conceiving of faculty as increasingly managed professionals, our attention is particularly drawn to faculty in nonelite institutions, not only community colleges but also large state systems of comprehensive, master's, and doctoral institutions that often get overlooked in our research. Although there is a dearth of research in these areas, some important exceptions must be noted. For instance, in the case of community colleges, some studies have either revealed important dimensions of faculty life through organizational case studies (e.g., London 1978; Weis 1985) or have provided various case analyses of types of faculty members (Grubb 1999; Seidman 1985). But our understanding of the complex and various types of faculty members in community colleges is woefully incomplete, even in the case of full-time faculty. This is all the more true for faculty members in the largely unstudied middle sectors of public comprehensive colleges and universities and nonselective private liberal arts colleges and universities. With the exception of Clark's 1987 study and work by Dot Finnegan, higher education scholars largely overlook the nonelite four-year sector.

Such gaps are problematic not just substantively but also analytically. Our conception of the faculty condition—and of the roles of faculty in higher education—is largely shaded, or perhaps more accurately, clouded, by the conditions of research university professors. This means that we fundamentally fail to understand fully and represent accurately various dimensions of faculty that play out in institutional contexts other than research universities. In the case of the balance of authority between faculty and administration and the mechanisms through which that authority is exercised, the literature focuses overwhelmingly on a structure (academic or faculty senate) that is less likely to be found in less prestigious institutions. In such settings, authority is exercised in other contexts and through other mechanisms.

Similarly, in the case of social relations with students, literature has tended to focus quantitatively on time allocation to various dimensions of the instructional process. Thus the qualitative and comparative extent and meaningfulness of contact between faculty and students are far too little understood. Given the significance the literature attributes to contact with faculty as a positive contributor to persistence, the nature of the contact is key, yet we really do not understand it. Virtually no literature addresses the question, for example, of faculty members' commitment to providing access for historically underrepresented student populations. In my consulting work with unionized faculty members in community colleges and comprehensive state universities, the depth of that commitment is frequently quite evident. How does that play out in the ways in which faculty interact with students generally, and with certain students in particular? Do faculty interact in different ways, quantitatively and qualitatively, with different types of students? We simply do not as yet have answers to these questions.

Similarly, we lack insight into the extent of faculty members' engagement in the community, the range of their service activities. Again, the literature seems to be largely guided by the conviction that in research universities service is not emphasized and that what is performed serves mainly the profession and not the community. We concentrate on time allocation with a kind of production mentality or in terms of impact on career, suggesting that service is inequitably distributed among types of faculty members, with women and minority faculty disproportionately involved. We have few examples of scholars' exploring the nature, quality, and effect of engagement in various social service activities and the impact these have on the community, the employing institution, and the employee (for an exception, see Baez 2000, who examines the role of race-related service in effecting institutional change).

In short, the higher education literature has not heeded a fundamental principle in the sociology of professions, set forth by one of the progenitors of that field, Everett Hughes. Hughes (1958) put forth the proposition that much is to be gained in understanding professions by studying their less prestigious occupations and segments. There, certain dimensions of professional life may appear in a less complicated or different form. The field of higher education has done just the opposite, concentrating disproportionately on the most prestigious sectors of the academy. In my view, that has led to oversimplifying and distorting the major share of the academic profession.

Managerial Professionals

Sociologists of occupations and professions have characterized the turn of the twentieth century as a time when a culture of professionalism emerged (Bledstein 1976). In Weberian terms, they have traced the ascendance of the specialist over the generalist and the organization of full-time, lifelong careers around this specialization, specialists who replaced those who practiced the occupation on the side, for a period of time, as "amateurs." As sociologists have detailed, the emergence and eventual dominance of professionals over others who performed much the same type of work meant the reorganization of these areas of activity. Various other paths into practice, such as apprenticeship and learning on the job, were replaced by developing a path into the profession that required extended education, through an undergraduate college and often a graduate/professional education, to learn a specialized body of knowledge and technical expertise. Part of professionalizing a realm of work was that preparation for and admission into the profession were channeled through higher education.

That pattern is perhaps most evident in the case of what is arguably the most prestigious profession in the United States, that of physicians. Indeed, most sociology of the professions has concentrated on the elite, so-called liberal professions of medicine and law. Prior to the 1900s, there were many different sorts of practitioners in the medical field and many different paths into such practice. Most deliveries were done by midwives. Most doctors went into practice through a path of apprenticeship, with little standardization in terms of a rigorous regimen of specialized professional education. That changed dramatically with the Flexner Report of 1918, which decried the state of learning and preparation in the medical field. In our current landscape, at a relatively select number of medical schools, future physicians are introduced to their practice through an extended and rigorous period of undergraduate education and then medical school education, followed by internship and residency. This pattern, established nearly 100 years ago, fundamentally reshaped and restricted who could practice medicine. The field became professionalized (Starr 1982).

The academy also came to be professionalized around this time, as universities transformed into serving as the gatekeepers and preparatory path for all the professions. Walter Metzger has traced this path of professionalization of the college teacher, noting that a key part of its development was the "secularization of faculty training" (1987a, p. 134), with the Ph.D. increasingly required in a range of specialized subjects, whereas as late as 1870, a substantial proportion of college professors underwent theological training and held bachelor of divinity degrees. Silva and Slaughter (1984) have traced this professionalization in the case of various social sciences. In a detailed historical analysis of professional associations that emerged in economics, history, sociology, and political science, they contrasted the conceptions and political positions held by emergent professionals regarding their educational roles with those held by the "amateurs" who were college teachers at the time. As did other sociologists of professions, they traced the contest and struggle between the emergent specialists and the generalists as to who would control the occupation of college teaching. And they connected the success of the professionalizing social scientists to their relationship of providing service, with their expertise, to rising corporate industrialists and the imperialist nation-state.

Eventually, the proliferation of professions—and of so-called semi-professions and paraprofessions (Etzioni 1969)—was such that some sociologists wrote about the "professionalization of everyone" (Wilensky 1964). It seemed that virtually every occupation in large organizations was seeking the status of "profession" by taking on the external characteristics of professionals, and requiring more extended periods of formal education. The pattern was such that sociologists began to characterize our society as "the credential society" (Collins 1979).

Despite this proliferation of professionalization throughout the twentieth century, in the eyes of academics, they were the only professionals on campus. Everyone else was either an "administrator" or a clerical or janitorial service employee, with no claim to professional status. Some might suggest that faculty members believed they *were* the university. If such a view of (professional) status was ever justified, it is no longer.

Sociologists of professions and organizations have come to recognize that often in the domain of a large organization, more than one professional group operates. In order to fully understand large, complex organizations, one must understand the relationship and interaction among their multiple professions. In the instance of health care, it has long been the case that the relationship between physicians and nurses is key to an understanding of hospitals and patient care. As more and more advanced technologies come into play in medicine, and as various occupations in the health care field professionalize, it is also increasingly evident that in order to understand the experience of patients and the operation of health care organizations, we must equally take into account the interaction between physicians and various medical technicians who operate the advanced machinery of medicine (Barley 1986).

Further, it follows that in any large, complex organization, its multiple professions compete for jurisdiction over a particular realm of activity. Two major contributions to the sociology of professions in the 1990s highlighted the significance of negotiations of professional "jurisdiction" (Abbott 1988): the control over a specific arena of work and the stratification of professionals by their market position between and within large organizations (Brint 1994). J. R. Sutton and Frank Dobbin (1996) offer an excellent study demonstrating how those conceptual insights inform our understanding of organizational practice. They provide a detailed analysis of changes in employment policies and practices in large, private-sector firms, adjustments that have accompanied changes in employment law at the federal (and state) level. To understand those changing policies and practices, they argue, we must understand the differing and competing interpretations of employment law by two sets of professionals who have some jurisdiction and claim to expertise in the arena—lawyers and human resource professionals.

The same professionals help define employment policies in colleges and universities. Most large universities have in-house legal staffs, and all colleges and universities have human resource professionals who interpret employment law and influence recruitment, appointment, review, reduction, and retirement policies and practices.

Moreover, on college and university campuses, a wide range of represented occupations have increasingly professionalized. The members of these occupations have advanced degrees but are neither professors nor administrators. In the national data, they constitute a category called "support professional" or "nonfaculty professional." Perhaps most apparent are those who provide various services to students—admissions and financial aid personnel, career placement and academic services (advising and tutoring) professionals. In short, they are literally an ancillary or residual category. Yet over the last 30 years, this group has become the fastest-growing category of professional employment in higher education. Just from 1975 to 1985, the numbers of administrative, managerial, and executive positions grew at three times the pace of faculty. But the number of support professionals increased more than three times that of administrators.

This is not simply a matter of a category growing at a fast rate because its numbers are small. By 2000, faculty accounted for 53 percent of all professional employees in higher education, far reduced from the percentage of nearly two-thirds three decades earlier. Support professionals accounted for nearly 30 percent of the professional positions on campus and more than three times the number of administrative positions (Rhoades 1998b).

Simply put, though they may neither realize nor acknowledge it, professors are not the only professionals on campus. Various non-academic professions also populate the academy. And higher education literature has yet to catch up with this significant empirical development. Few scholars attend to this sector of employees (for an exception see Linda Johnsrud's work—e.g., Johnsrud, Heck, and Rosser 2000). And campuses mirror what studies have revealed about the broader workforce. As Stephen Barley (1996) and others have pointed out, the sociology of work literature largely accepts and continues to base analyses on the simple distinction between white- and blue-collar work. Yet the growth areas of employment are in occupations with elements of both white- and blue-collar labor and employment. The national classification system poses this same problem, remaining overdeveloped in the declining blue-collar category and vastly underdeveloped in the growth area of technicians and professionals. Similarly, the distinctive and disaggregated character of support professionals in higher education is not reflected in the national data.

I have coined the term *managerial professionals* to designate these so-called support professionals (Rhoades 1998a, 1998b). The term is intended to capture these occupations' essential bridging in the academy: of the categories of professional (academic) and manager (administrator). These occupations have many characteristics of professions: they require advanced education and technical bodies of knowledge; they have associations and annual conferences, journals with advanced research in their areas of practice, and codes of ethics. Yet they lack many essential features of the professional autonomy enjoyed by tenure-track faculty members; their members have neither academic freedom nor intellectual property rights, for example, as their employment falls under the category of "work for hire." As a result, they are much more connected to management, and their patterns of employment are more tied to the patterns of managers than to those of faculty. These professionals are generally on an 11-month fiscal year rather than an academic-year contract. They are far more likely to work a nine-to-five day than are faculty. They are hired, fired, and reviewed by supervisors, not by professional peers in the ways that faculty members are. They are managerial professionals.

Who are these folks? In an article with Barbara Sporn (Rhoades and Sporn 2002a), I have identified three types of managerial professionals. The most long-standing such professions on college campuses are in the area of providing services to the increasing masses of students gaining access to higher education. As noted above, they are professionals in the various arenas of student services, from admissions and financial aid to residence life and recreation, advising, student programming, cultural centers, computer support, and career services and placement. These professionals largely receive their advanced education in college student personnel and higher education programs.

We can understand the continued growth of this category of managerial professionals on college campuses in terms of three dynamics. First is the continued expansion of access to higher education in the United States, which in Europe has been characterized as "massification," accommodating burgeoning numbers of students amid the massive demand for higher education. A second dynamic is the changing demographic of that growing student population, in terms of gender, ethnicity, attendance status (part or full time), and age, among other factors. Due to distinctive new student populations, new sorts of student services have been developed and expanded. The third dynamic that accounts for the continued expansion of these managerial professionals is the increasing competition to recruit students, such that all sorts of institutions emphasize the range of services and support they can provide students, as they seek to persuade them to apply to and attend their campus.

A second category of managerial professional has developed in part as a more recent phenomenon: the group engaged in a wide range of on-campus activities surrounding professional development and assessment. Their work is aimed at enhancing, monitoring, and demonstrating the quality of higher education's work, particularly with students. Within this category, institutional researchers, a long-standing but expanding occupation, gather data on their college's productivity and quality, and increasingly on patterns of student satisfaction and success. In addition, various assessment personnel directly gauge student progress and academic programs. Further, professional employees work for the professional development of faculty. Perhaps the most visible of these are located in teaching centers, often working with faculty members to incorporate instructional technologies into the classrooms. And perhaps most recently, an emergent category includes occupations surrounding the increased use of information technologies on college and university campuses, often connected to monitoring and enhancing quality and productivity. At the central administrative level, such personnel often fall under the domain of the most recently emergent administrative title, chief information officer (CIO), a position and portfolio increasingly found on campuses.

The growth of these quality assurance managerial professionals can be understood as responsive largely to two dynamics. One is the dramatically increased demand for accountability from multiple external sources, whether state boards and legislatures, trustees, employers, or simply "the public." More and more, the demand is heard that colleges and universities demonstrate their effectiveness and efficiency. That has led to greater attention to various dimensions of quality improvement, particularly in instruction. A second, related dynamic is the technological revolution that has hit college campuses. Often the use of technology is conflated with quality. For example, instructional improvement is often taken to mean increased use of instructional technologies, at least as a baseline.

The third category of managerial professionals is entrepreneurial. Perhaps the clearest example is so-called development or advancement professionals, known to the rest of the world as fundraisers. Such personnel have been common on most private college and university campuses for some decades. But staffs have expanded, in independent higher education and in public higher education as well. In addition, over the last twenty years, research universities, along with other institutions, have expanded their hiring of a range of technology transfer professionals, whose role is to help faculty translate their work and discoveries into products that are marketable in the private sector. Relatedly, campuses have expanded their hiring of various economic development professionals, who are focused more broadly on making connections with powerful economic groups in the community and region and on establishing various sorts of partnerships with corporations, business groups, and municipal and state economic development personnel.

The growth of these entrepreneurial managerial professionals is closely tied to the emergence and expansion of entrepreneurial colleges and universities in the United States. Over the past three decades, colleges and universities have increasingly worked to generate more and more of their own revenues, to become more self-supporting. This pattern is very much in keeping with the ascension of neoliberal policies internationally, deemphasizing public sector subsidies of higher education and encouraging institutions to become more like independent corporations. It is also aligned with the ascension of neoconservative policies within the United States, which have called for reducing public support for education and other human services at the same time that they have encouraged heightened monitoring and delimitation of those services.

These managerial professionals merit investigation for a variety of reasons. From a purely economic standpoint, for example, they account for an increasing proportion of the workforce and thus of the labor costs. Any analysis of productivity in higher education should pay attention to the particular productivity of these managerial professionals in their own realms and also to their contributions to institutional productivity in other realms. Most obviously, and economically, entrepreneurial professionals are focused on generating revenue, which raises the question, how successful are these professionals in advancement, economic development, and technology transfer?

From a sociological standpoint, managerial professionals are increasingly active in the basic production processes of higher education—in teaching, research, and service. They are part of the changing mode of production in higher education (Rhoades and Sporn 2002a). Therefore it is increasingly important to understand the interaction and competition among them and with academics in specific professional jurisdictions. For instance, how effectively do teaching center, professional development, and assessment professionals work with professors in reforming and improving instruction? Similarly, as we invest in more and more professionals to provide an ever larger range of services to students, how effectively do they recruit and move students through colleges and universities, in conjunction with, in competition with, or sometimes running counter to the efforts of faculty members? In what ways, if at all, does interaction with managerial professionals substantially enhance the experience of undergraduate and graduate students? And in what ways, if at all, are these professionals directly challenging and actively changing colleges and universities?

From a feminist standpoint, the managerial professions are the only category of professional employment in higher education in which the majority are women (library professionals are a good example of this). This fact raises a number of interesting questions about the routes and strategies by which these occupations have attained professional status (see Witz 1992 for such a discussion in the case of the health professions). It raises further questions about social relations between the managerial professions and the academic profession, and between these and the often largely male-dominated occupations they liaison with outside the academy (e.g., in the case of technology transfer professionals). Questions arise about stratification among—and differing institutional investment in—various managerial professions (e.g., in entrepreneurial more than in social service professionals). And it raises interesting and important questions about the ideologies of these professions, their conceptions of themselves, and the ways in which they enact their public roles and private lives.

From a comparative higher education standpoint, managerial professionals pose important questions about how certain functions are performed within the academy. If the United States has seen a tendency to spin off new professions around each new function, in other national systems we may find a pattern of academics circulating in and out of these roles without developing new, specialized professions. Or we may find that as more Anglo-American models of university management are adopted, we observe at the same time a marked increase in managerial professional hires.

At present, the above lines of research are virtually unexplored territory. I would argue that managerial professionals represent one of the key post-1973-era developments in the organization of professional work, particularly in U.S. higher education. Our full understanding of academic organizations is contingent on beginning to analyze the roles and activities of these campus employees.

Beyond Boundaries

Sociologists of work have characterized the turn of the twenty-first century in terms of the rise of a new economy marked by the increased predominance of casual, contingent, and part-time labor and of labor markets that cut across national boundaries in a global economy. Some scholars have also emphasized the heightened stratification and inequities that attach to women and minorities in this new economy (Sassen 2001). Despite these changing boundaries of employment, most research on faculty that has been conducted in the decades since Clark's 1973 essay has been delimited by the conventional boundaries that have attached to the literature on work. Yet key patterns in society, corresponding to key developments in social science theory, offer important directions for future scholarship. Three particularly important ones are feminism, marketization, and globalization. Each challenges higher education scholars to go beyond the traditional boundaries that have largely defined the study of faculty.

One of the most significant social movements in American society, and in U.S. social science developments over the past 30 years, has been the women's movement, with the rise of feminist analyses of all sorts of phenomena. The effects on academic fields in the social sciences, humanities, arts—and even the elite professional schools of law and medicine —have been profound. Not only have subfields of scholars studying women and women's issues emerged. In order to be credible, scholars in a range of fields must increasingly address the perspectives of women and the scholarship of feminists. That is a significant change. The women's movement and feminist analysis have had an impact on higher education scholarship as well, though to a lesser extent than in the social sciences. However, in the leading higher education journals, explicitly feminist analyses that go beyond simply treating gender as a variable are relatively rare (Hart 2006). No less important—but unfortunately, considerably less evident in higher education scholarship—is critical race theory and the effects of the civil rights movement in the ways that we conduct our scholarship.

Some of the exceptions to this omission point the way for future research on professions in higher education. Historical analyses of women scientists (Keller 1983; Rossiter 1995) have provided some examples of the ways in which scholars could increasingly incorporate the "femaleness" of leading academic women into biographies and histories, how their distinctive perspectives on and conceptualizations of the world are connected to their gender. Some higher education scholars have explored distinctive "leadership styles" enacted by women (Bensimon 1991). Other work has addressed how women came with their gender and feminist lenses into disciplines such as history, sociology, and philosophy, developing new lines of inquiry that fundamentally reshaped these fields (see Gumport 2002). And some work on the gendered enactment of the faculty role (Perna 2001a; Ward and Wolf-Wendel 2004) pushes beyond the boundaries of focusing solely on faculty members' public lives and connects women faculty's public roles to their "private" ones.

But more than identifying social-psychological differences, scholars of academic women could follow the lead of Sharon Traweek (1988) in tracing the ways in which gendered professional politics track women in academe and the ways in which women resist and challenge—and can overcome—that process. Ethnicity and social class—as well as gender—and the intersections among them also play out in the narratives of scholars' lives in ways that have been traced by some scholars (Jacobs, Cintrón, and Canton 2002; Padilla and Chávez 1995; Sackrey and Ryan 1984; Tokarczyk and Fay 1993). They play out as well in the salaries of faculty (Perna 2001b; Toutkoushian and Bellas 2003). M. L. Bellas (1997) has offered a particularly sophisticated understanding of the structural dimensions of gender's impact on salaries, examining the relation between the feminization of a field and the depression of its salaries for all faculty members in the field.

Another line of work pursued by scholars has focused on the influence of the women's movement in the academy. In other words, it is important not only to connect gender to stratified position in the new economy but also to recognize and examine the role of social movements organized around gender, as well as around other characteristics of faculty, in reshaping the academy (Glazer-Raymo 1999). It makes sense, then, to begin to focus more on activist organizations formed and participated in by women faculty (Hart 2002). In short, the sociology of professions in academe would benefit from an exploration of the role of professionals in relationship to social stratification and institutional and social change.

One of the key changes defining the turn of the twenty-first century is the heightened intersection between public and private sectors of the economy, a reduction—and in some cases, a collapse—of the boundaries between them. That intersection, an explicit part of neoliberal policy and practice, has led to the development of various hybrid organizational forms. These are particularly evident in the academy: scholars have written about entrepreneurial universities and the commercialization of academe.

The changing relationship between public and private sectors has meant the increased involvement of faculty in market behaviors, in the marketplace. As noted earlier, several studies have explored faculty engagement in entrepreneurial activities. Such studies have concentrated on faculty members in the natural sciences, especially the life sciences, where such engagement is most evident. But we lack a fuller understanding of faculty members in general and the ways they are engaged in market behaviors.

An understanding of these intersections is essential to developing a fuller understanding of social relations between faculty and students. Changing boundaries of norms and work as they apply to faculty, in gaining private-sector funding and in focusing faculty work on generating commercializable products (often in companies in which faculty members have a financial interest) almost necessarily affect boundaries between students and their faculty members. A few publications examine this "renorming" of social relations in the academy (Slaughter and Rhoades 1990; Slaughter et al. 2002). But much more work is needed on the complex interconnections among faculty members, students, and private-sector markets and employers.

Even more than on the level of individual faculty and students, it is important to explore larger patterns of change in academic employment, which in many ways mirror what is happening in the larger economy. Just as the general workforce is increasingly characterized by part-time and contingent labor, so has academia experienced a dramatic increase in the proportion of part-time faculty. If that trend has largely been recognized, nevertheless we still lack a full understanding of the lives of part-time and contingent faculty and of their relations with other faculty and with students.

Existing scholarship tends to address part-time employees from the standpoint of categorizing them or developing principles and practices for effectively managing them. What we lack is the perspective of these faculty members themselves, not just individually but collectively. The categories of part-time and contingent employees are at the center of a revitalization of the labor movement nationally. This is no less true in academe. The growth area of unionization in academe is in emerging part-time and contingent faculty associations working to gain collective bargaining, and an increasing number of celebrated cases are winning that right. The current struggle between management and labor is over the definition of basic employment rights and conditions of work. As a growing proportion of the faculty—particularly the new cohorts—are in these contingent categories of employment, higher education scholars must address how such faculty are collectively defining academic employment.

Similarly, unionization has grown among graduate student employees, particularly teaching assistants. As noted earlier, some higher education scholars have studied pathways into the academic profession, focusing on how graduate students are recruited and how new recruits are socialized into the profession. But we lack an understanding of the unionization phenomenon per se and of the ways in which this wave of unionization, and the conditions of work it responds to, are shaping the perspectives and practices of new professors. Despite some examples of studies of these new unions (Julius and Gumport 2003; Rhoades and Rhoads 2003; Schmid and Herman 2003), much work remains to be done, for these particular employees challenge and break down basic boundaries that we have traditionally adopted in defining students and professors. In resisting unionization, many universities have argued that graduate employees are apprentices in the profession, emphasizing their role as students. Yet at the same time, the universities categorize students as employees for the purposes of policies having to do with intellectual property rights, which institutions increasingly seek to capitalize on. In general in the new economy, the clean boundaries surrounding academic jobs and careers are breaking down. In addition to graduate employees, this is true for various categories of contingent academic employees, who often work for more than one college or university and in more than one capacity.

In a variety of ways, the casualization of the economy, accompanying the rise of a service sector economy, is being played out in academe. The provision of services, including educational services, is in the process of being redefined. If higher education scholars are to understand adequately the range of academic employees' experiences, especially in the contingent categories of employment, their work needs to be located within the context of more general changes in patterns of employment, which are redefining the boundaries between employee and organization.

Another set of boundaries increasingly breached in recent decades is that of nation-states. Much has been written about globalization (Appadurai 1996; Burbules and Torres 2000; Castells 1996; Marginson and Rhoades 2002; Ritzer 1998), and it is hard to find a discussion of the strategic orientation and future of academic organizations without some mention of internationalization and globalization. But we lack an understanding of the international networks, associations, and organizations that influence and are influenced by academe.

The scholarship available at present largely takes a cross-national approach, comparing professors in one country to those in another. Even such comparisons do not offer a very well developed understanding of the daily lives and activities of professors from one country to the next. Nor have we begun to explore sufficiently the more subtle and profound differences that attach to different patterns of organization and work in different countries, although Clark's work (1983, 1987) certainly provides a roadmap here.

However, such country-based case comparisons do not afford us a view of the regional, international, and global dimensions of professions in higher education. Globally, professions and professors are powerful purveyors of ideas. In what ways do regional and international networks of professionals shape patterns of higher education policy and practice—indeed, of knowledge—from one country to the next? In the advanced industrial nations, key mechanisms may lie in networks of professionals, in their associations, publications, and global circulation, and their use as consultants (Rhoades and Sporn 2002b). In developing countries, the operative mechanisms may be quite different, such as the intersection between international organizations like the World Bank and national policymaking centers in higher education (Maldonado Maldonado 2004).

Thus there is much work to be done on the regional, international, and global dimensions of professors' professional activities, which in a daily way, by virtue of advanced information technologies, crisscross the globe. The individual dimension to this consists of the daily lives of professors as they come into contact with colleagues, students, and others from all over the world. But also, the collective dynamics in this—the networks and invisible colleges of professors and students that emerge internationally—may well influence patterns of employment and success in academic careers. For example, a reasonable working hypothesis might contend that involvement in international networks of professionals positively contributes to the upward mobility of individual academics, who can leverage those networks for opportunities and resources that enable them to advance in their careers. Such leveraging of international networks may even be particularly important for certain categories of academics, such as women. In the face of relatively restricted opportunities within oligarchic national systems, women academics may be able to use international networks and connections to jump national barriers to career growth. They may gain resources and positions internationally that enable them to later enhance their advancement opportunities within their home country. A regional or global academic marketplace that extends beyond national borders now opens up all sorts of possibilities for research on academic labor markets and careers.

Conclusion

In the thirty-plus years since Burton Clark wrote his 1973 essay mapping and suggesting lines of research for the sociology of higher education, much has been written about faculty—and much of it was shaped by Clark's own work in the field. Yet work remains to be done.

In this chapter, I have provided three sets of concepts that could guide that future work on professions in academe. These concepts are grounded both in key scholarly contributions to the sociology of the professions and in key societal developments in the organization of work. The concept of managed professionals points to the value of considering the balance between professional autonomy and managerial discretion in defining the configuration and future of colleges and universities; it also points to the value of focusing on faculty members' working conditions and the restructuring of academic labor. The concept of different types of managerial professionals points to the significance of emergent professions on college and university campuses. Finally, the concepts of feminism, marketization, and globalization point us to the value of going beyond various conventional boundaries of research on faculty to attend to gendered relations and connections between the public and private dimensions of work; the increasing interconnection between the academy and the private sector (including within forms of casual and contingent academic employment); and global dimensions, variations, and organization of professional work in the knowledge economy.

In closing, I wish to offer a few thoughts about the sociology of the professions in higher education, drawing upon the concern identified by Clark in closing his analysis. Concerning the delimited range of questions being pursued in the sociology of higher education by higher education scholars, Clark offers this cautionary note: "How can the sociology of higher education take cues from, and make returns to, the concerns of educational practitioners without becoming a managerial sociology? It is not that we are so easily bought but that we are so much involved" (1973, p. 12 in this volume). He went on to note that too often the questions that guide our work "become voiced around immediate needs of administration and public policy" and that "even when our attitude is critical of present practice, we are still in the stance of defining the ends of educational work and arranging practices to be effective means to those ends" (p. 12).

Clark's words remain highly relevant to the study of professionals in higher education, particularly to the study of professors. The most commonly collected data and most commonly posed questions about faculty members have to do with their time allocation between research and teaching. It would be hard to argue that such a focus had nothing to do with immediate managerial and public policy concerns. Our questions about the activities of faculty have been heavily influenced by the questions of managers, policymakers, and the so-called (and invoked) "public" as to just what faculty members do with their time.

Yet even in these narrowly defined terms, our understandings are woefully incomplete. For example, in terms of faculty's service to and engagement in their communities, to remain focused primarily on these narrow concerns is a disservice, for it inhibits our understanding of the influence of professors on the communities in which they are located. And in order to address even general policy concerns about productivity in higher education, it is necessary to go well beyond the confines of our current studies, to understand the role of managerial professionals and a range of contingent academic employees in productivity (Rhoades 2001).

Let me close then, as Clark did, by suggesting that we tap into the insights of social science, refracted through and influenced by various societal developments. If we are to understand more fully the changing landscape of professions in academic organizations, the future influence of those professions on the configuration of academic organizations, and their influence on students and society as well as on each other, we would do well to go beyond the confines of our current conceptual blinders. I believe the scholars, the practitioners, and the field will be well served by a literature that asks a wider range of questions about academic professions and professionals.

References

Abbott, A. 1988. *The System of Professions: An Essay on the Division of Expert Labor.* Chicago: University of Chicago Press.

Appadurai, A. 1996. *Modernity at Large: Cultural Dimensions of Globalization.* Minneapolis: University of Minnesota Press.

Baez, B. 2000. "Race-Related Service and Faculty of Color: Conceptualizing Critical Agency in Academe." *Higher Education* 39 (3): 363–91.

Baldridge, J. V., and F. Kemerer. 1976. "Academic Senates and Faculty Collective Bargaining." *Journal of Higher Education* 47:391–441.

Baldwin, R. G., and J. L. Chronister. 2001. *Teaching without Tenure: Policies and Practices for a New Era.* Baltimore: Johns Hopkins University Press.

Barley, S. 1986. "Technology as an Occasion for Structuring: Evidence of Observations of CT Scanners and the Social Order of Radiology Departments." *Administrative Science Quarterly* 31:78–108.

——. 1996. "Technicians in the Workplace: Ethnographic Evidence for Bringing Work into Organization Studies." *Administrative Science Quarterly* 41 (3): 404–41.

Barrow, C. 1990. *Universities and the Capitalist State: Corporate Liberalism and the Reconstruction of American Higher Education, 1894–1928.* Madison: University of Wisconsin Press.

Beck, H. P. 1947. *Men Who Control Our Universities.* New York: King's Crown.

Bellas, M. L. 1997. "Disciplinary Differences in Faculty Salaries: Does Gender Bias Play a Role?" *Journal of Higher Education* 68 (3): 299–321.

Bensimon, E. 1991. "A Feminist Reinterpretation of Presidents' Definitions of Leadership." *Peabody Journal of Education* 66 (3): 143–56.

Bledstein, B. 1976. *The Culture of Professionalism: The Middle Class and the Development of Higher Education in America.* New York: W. W. Norton.

Blumenthal, D., M. Gluck, K. S. Louis, M. Soto, and D. Wise. 1986. "University-Industry Research Relationships in Biotechnology: Implications for the University." *Science* 232:1361–66.

Bok, D. 2003. *Universities in the Marketplace: The Commercialization of Higher Education.* Princeton, NJ: Princeton University Press.

Bowen, H. R., and J. H. Schuster. 1986. *American Professors: A National Resource Imperiled.* New York: Oxford University Press.

Boyer, E. L. 1990. *Scholarship Reconsidered: Priorities of the Professoriate.* Princeton, NJ: Carnegie Foundation for the Advancement of Teaching.

Braxton, J. M., and A. E. Bayer. 1999. *Faculty Misconduct in Collegiate Teaching.* Baltimore: Johns Hopkins University Press.

Breneman, D., and T. Youn, eds. 1988. *Academic Labor Markets and Careers.* New York: Falmer.

Brint, S. 1994. *In an Age of Expert: The Changing Role of Professionals in Politics and Public Life.* Princeton, NJ: Princeton University Press.

Burbules, N. C., and C. A. Torres, eds. 2000. *Globalization and Education: Critical Perspectives.* New York: Routledge.

Campbell, T. D., and S. Slaughter 1999. "Faculty and Administrators' Attitudes toward Potential Conflicts of Interest, Commitment, and Equity in University-Industry Relations." *Journal of Higher Education* 70 (3): 309–32.

Caplow, T., and R. McGee. 1958. *The Academic Marketplace.* New York: Basic Books.

Cartter, A. M. 1976. *PhD's and the Academic Labor Market.* New York: McGraw-Hill.

Castells, M. 1996. *The Rise of the Network Society.* Oxford: Blackwell.

Clark, B. R. 1960. *The Open Door College: A Case Study.* New York: McGraw-Hill.

———. 1973. "Development of the Sociology of Higher Education." *Sociology of Education* 46 (1): 2–14.

———. 1977. *Academic Power in Italy: Bureaucracy and Oligarchy in a National University System.* Chicago: University of Chicago Press.

———. 1983. *The Higher Education System: Academic Organization in Cross-National Perspective.* Los Angeles: University of California Press.

———. 1987a. *The Academic Life: Small Worlds, Different Worlds.* Princeton, NJ: Carnegie Foundation for the Advancement of Teaching.

———, ed. 1987b. *The Academic Profession: National, Disciplinary, and Institutional Settings.* Los Angeles: University of California Press.

———. 1995. *Places of Inquiry: Research and Advanced Education in Modern Universities.* Los Angeles: University of California Press.

———. 1998. *Creating Entrepreneurial Universities: Organizational Pathways of Transformation.* Oxford: International Association of Universities Press and Pergamon.

———. 2000. "Collegial Entrepreneurialism in Proactive Universities: Lessons from Europe." *Change* 32 (1): 10–19.

———. 2004. *Sustaining Change in Universities: Continuities in Case Studies and Concepts.* New York: Society for Research into Higher Education and Open University Press.

Collins, R. 1979. *The Credential Society: An Historical Sociology of Education and Stratification.* New York: Academic.

Durkheim, E. 1957. *Professional Ethics and Civic Morals.* London: Routledge and Kegan Paul.

Etzioni, A. 1969. *The Semi-professions and Their Organization: Teachers, Nurses, and Social Workers.* New York: Free Press.

Fairweather, J. 1996. *Faculty Work and Public Trust: Restoring the Value of Teaching and Public Service in American Academic Life.* Boston: Allyn and Bacon.

Finkelstein, M. J. 1984. *The American Academic Profession.* Columbus: Ohio State University Press.

Finkelstein, M. J., R. Seal, and J. H. Schuster. 1998. *The New Academic Generation: A Profession in Transformation.* Baltimore: Johns Hopkins University Press.

Gappa, J. M., and D. W. Leslie. 1993. *The Invisible Faculty: Improving the Status of Part-Timers in Higher Education.* San Francisco: Jossey-Bass.

Geiger, R. 2004. *Knowledge and Money: Research Universities and the Paradox of the Marketplace.* Stanford, CA: Stanford University Press.

Glazer-Raymo, J. 1999. *Shattering the Myths: Women in Academe.* Baltimore: Johns Hopkins University Press.

Goode, W. W. J. 1957. "Community within a Community: The Professions." *American Sociological Review* 22:194–200.

Grubb, W. N. 1999. *Honored but Invisible: An Inside Look at Teaching in Community Colleges.* New York: Routledge.

Gumport, P. 2002. *Academic Pathfinders: Knowledge Creation and Feminist Scholarship.* Westport, CT: Greenwood.

Hart, J. L. 2002. "Activism among Feminist Academics: Professionalized Activism and Activist Professionals." Ph.D. dissertation, Center for the Study of Higher Education, University of Arizona.

———. 2006. "Women and Feminism in Higher Education Scholarship: An Analysis of Three Core Journals." *Journal of Higher Education* 77 (1): 40–61.

Hughes, E. C. 1958. *Men and Their Work.* Glencoe, IL: Free Press.

Hutcheson, P. 2000. *A Professional Professoriate: Unionization, Bureaucratization, and the AAUP.* Nashville: Vanderbilt University Press.

Jacobs, L., J. Cintrón, and C. E. Canton, eds. 2002. *The Politics of Survival in Academia: Narratives of Inequity, Resilience, and Success.* Boulder: Rowman and Littlefield.

Johnsrud, L. K., R. H. Heck, and V. J. Rosser. 2000. "Morale Matters: Midlevel Administrators and Their Intent to Leave." *Journal of Higher Education* 71 (1): 340–59.

Johnston, P. 1994. *Success While Others Fail: Social Movement Unionism and the Public Workplace.* Cornell, NY: ILR Press.

Julius, D., and P. Gumport. 2003. "Graduate Student Unionization: Catalysts and Consequences." *Review of Higher Education* 26 (2): 187–216.

Keller, E. F. 1983. *A Feeling for the Organism: The Life and Work of Barbara McClintock.* San Francisco: W. H. Freeman.

Keller, G. 1983. *Academic Strategy: The Management Revolution in American Higher Education.* Baltimore: Johns Hopkins University Press.

Kemerer, F., and J. V. Baldridge. 1975. "Senates and Unions: Unexpected Peaceful Coexistence." *Journal of Higher Education* 52:256–64.

Kirp, D. 2003. *Shakespeare, Einstein, and the Bottom Line: The Marketing of Higher Education.* Cambridge, MA: Harvard University Press.

Ladd, E. C., and S. M. Lipset. 1975. *The Divided Academy: Professors and Politics.* New York: McGraw-Hill.

Larson, M. S. 1977. *The Rise of Professionalism: A Sociological Analysis.* Berkeley: University of California Press.

Leslie, D. W. 1996. *Wise Moves in Hard Times: Creating and Managing Resilient Colleges and Universities.* San Francisco: Jossey-Bass.

Leslie, D. W., S. E. Kellams, and G. M. Gunne. 1982. *Part-Time Faculty in American Higher Education.* New York: Praeger.

Lewis, L. 1975. *Scaling the Ivory Tower: Merit and Its Limits in Academic Careers.* Baltimore: Johns Hopkins University Press.

———. 1988. *Cold War on Campus: A Study of the Politics of Organizational Control.* New Brunswick, NJ: Transaction.

London, H. 1978. *The Culture of a Community College.* New York: Praeger.

Louis, K. S., D. Blumenthal, M. Gluck, and M. Soto. 1989. "Entrepreneurs in Academe: An Exploration of Behaviors among Life Scientists." *Administrative Science Quarterly* 34:110–31.

Maldonado Maldonado, A. 2004. "The Influence of International Organizations in the Field of Higher Education in Mexico." Ph.D. dissertation, Boston College.

Marginson, S., and G. Rhoades. 2002. "Beyond Nation States, Markets, and Systems of Higher Education: A Glonacal Agency Heuristic." *Higher Education* 43 (3): 281–309.

Metzger, W. 1987a. "The Academic Profession in the United States." In *The Academic Profession: National, Disciplinary, and Institutional Settings,* ed. B. R. Clark, 123–208. Los Angeles: University of California Press.

———. 1987b. "A Spectre Haunts the Professions." *Educational Researcher* 16 (6): 10–19.

Mortimer, K., and T. R. McConnell. 1978. *Sharing Authority Effectively.* San Francisco: Jossey-Bass.

Neave, G., and G. Rhoades. 1987. "The Academic Estate in Western Europe." In *The Academic Profession: National, Disciplinary, and Institutional Settings,* ed. B. R. Clark. Los Angeles: University of California Press.

Padilla, R. V., and R. C. Chávez. 1995. *The Leaning Ivory Tower: Latino Professors in the Academy.* Albany: State University of New York Press.

Parsons, T., ed. 1954. *Essays in Sociological Theory.* New York: Free Press.

Perna, L. 2001a. "The Relationship between Family Responsibilities and Employment Status among College and University Faculty." *Journal of Higher Education* 72 (5): 584–611.

———. 2001b. "Sex Differences in Faculty Salaries: A Cohort Analysis." *Review of Higher Education* 24 (3): 283–307.

Readings, B. 1996. *The University in Ruins.* Cambridge, MA: Harvard University Press.

Rhoades, G. 1998a. *Managed Professionals: Unionized Faculty and Restructuring Academic Labor.* Albany: State University of New York Press.

——. 1998b. "Reviewing and Rethinking Administrative Costs." In *Higher Education: Handbook of Theory and Research,* vol. 13, ed. J. C. Smart, 111–47. New York: Agathon.

——. 2001. "Managing Productivity in an Academic Institution: Rethinking the Whom, Which, What, and Whose of Productivity." *Research in Higher Education* 42 (5): 619–32.

Rhoades, G., and R. A. Rhoades. 2003. "The Public Discourse of U.S. Graduate Employee Unions: Social Movement Identities, Ideologies, and Strategies." *Review of Higher Education* 26 (2): 163–86.

Rhoades, G., and B. Sporn. 2002a. "New Models of Management and Shifting Modes and Costs of Production: Europe and the United States." *Tertiary Higher Education and Management* 8:3–28.

——. 2002b. "Quality Assurance in Europe and the U.S.: Professional and Political Economic Framing of Higher Education Policy." *Higher Education* 43 (3): 355–90.

Ritzer, G. 1998. *The McDonaldization Thesis.* London: Sage.

Rossiter, M. W. 1995. *Women Scientists in America: Before Affirmative Action, 1940–1972.* Baltimore: Johns Hopkins University Press.

Sackrey, C., and J. Ryan. 1984. *Strangers in Paradise: Academics from the Working Class.* Boston: South End.

Sassen, S. 2001. *The Global City: New York, London, Tokyo.* 2nd ed. Princeton, NJ: Princeton University Press.

Schmid, J. M., and D. M. Herman. 2003. *Cogs in the Classroom Factory: The Changing Identity of Academic Labor.* Westport, CT: Praeger.

Schrecker, E. 1986. *No Ivory Tower: Mccarthyism and the Universities.* New York: Oxford University Press.

Schuster, J. H., D. G. Smith, K. A. Corak, and M. M. Yamada. 1994. *Strategic Governance: How to Make Big Decisions Better.* Phoenix: Oryx.

Seidman, E. 1985. *In the Words of the Faculty: Perspectives on Improving Teaching and Educational Quality in Community Colleges.* San Francisco: Jossey-Bass.

Silva, E., and S. Slaughter. 1984. *Serving Power: The Making of the Social Science Expert.* Westport, CT: Greenwood.

Slaughter, S. 1990. *The Higher Learning and High Technology: Dynamics of Higher Education Policy Formation.* Albany: State University of New York Press.

Slaughter, S., T. Campbell, M. Holleman, and E. Morgan. 2002. "The 'Traffic' in Graduate Students: Graduate Students as Tokens of Exchange between Academe and Industry." *Science, Technology, and Human Values* 27:282–312.

Slaughter, S., and L. L. Leslie. 1997. *Academic Capitalism: Politics, Policies, and the Entrepreneurial University.* Baltimore: Johns Hopkins University Press.

Slaughter, S., and G. Rhoades. 1990. "Renorming the Social Relations of Academic Science." *Educational Policy* 4 (4): 341–61.

———. 2004. *Academic Capitalism and the New Economy: States, Markets, and Higher Education.* Baltimore: Johns Hopkins University Press.

Starr. P. 1982. *The Social Transformation of American Medicine.* New York: Basic Books.

Sutton, J. R., and F. Dobbin. 1996. "The Two Faces of Governance: Responses to Legal Uncertainty in U.S. Firms, 1955 to 1985." *American Sociological Review* 61 (5): 794–811.

Tierney, W. G., ed. 1991. *Culture and Ideology in Higher Education: Advancing a Critical Agenda.* New York: Praeger.

Tierney, W. G., and E. M. Bensimon. 1996. *Promotion and Tenure: Community and Socialization in Academe.* Albany: State University of New York Press.

Tokarczyk, M. M., and E. A. Fay. 1993. *Working Class Women in the Academy: Laborers in the Knowledge Factory.* Amherst: University of Massachusetts Press.

Toutkoushian, R. K., and M. L. Bellas. 2003. "The Effects of Part-Time Employment and Gender on Faculty Earnings and Satisfaction: Evidence from the NSOPF:93." *Journal of Higher Education* 74 (2): 172–95.

Traweek, S. 1988. *Beamtimes and Lifetimes: The World of High Energy Physicists.* Cambridge, MA: Harvard University Press.

Trow, M., ed. 1975. *Teachers and Students: Aspects of American Higher Education.* New York: McGraw-Hill.

Troy, L. 1994. *The New Unionism in the New Society: Public Sector Unions in the Redistributive State.* Fairfax, VA: George Mason University Press.

Veblen, T. 1918 (1954). *The Higher Learning in America.* Stanford, CA: Academic Reprints.

Ward, K., and L. Wolf-Wendel. 2004. "Academic Motherhood: Managing Complex Roles in Research Universities." *Review of Higher Education* 27 (2): 233–58.

Weis, L. 1985. *Between Two Worlds: Black Students in an Urban Community College.* Boston: Routledge and Kegan Paul.

Wilensky, H. L. 1964. "The Professionalization of Everyone?" *American Journal of Sociology* 70:137–58.

Wilson, L. 1942. *The Academic Man.* New York: Oxford University Press.

Witz, A. 1992. *Professions and Patriarchy.* London: Routledge.

Wulff, D. H., A. E. Austin, and Associates, eds. 2004. *Pathways to the Professoriate: Strategies for Enriching the Preparation of Future Faculty.* San Francisco: Jossey-Bass.

6 The Study of Colleges and Universities as Organizations

MARVIN W. PETERSON

This chapter examines the various organizational approaches to the study of colleges and universities, lines of analysis that developed and became prominent in the second half of the twentieth century, especially the last four decades. The rationale for focusing on models of colleges and universities as organizations is determined by feasibility and by relevance. First, research on the many characteristics and dynamics of college and university structures, processes, functions, and relationships (both internal and external, or with their environment) is far too extensive to be covered in a brief chapter. The focus on models is central to understanding how colleges and universities are structured and behave as *organizations*, distinct from dynamics in suborganizational units (departments, offices, etc.), groups of participants within them (faculty, students, administration, etc.), and interinstitutional arrangements among them (associations, consortia, systems, etc.). Second, the organizational nature of groups in society is at the heart of sociology as a discipline. Understanding how particular organizational models have emerged—both as applied to and as contributing to higher education— yields significant insight into higher education's social functions. Further, as we shall see, this is decidedly an interdisciplinary arena—not just a sociological province.

By *model* I refer to more than just the approach one uses to study organizations. *Model* here refers to scholars' conceptual attempts to understand or explain the structure and dynamics of colleges and universities in which academic life occurs. A model provides a set of concepts or constructs and of relationships among them that can be defined and systematically examined. A model can be examined as to whether it fits real organizational behavior and whether, in comparison to other models, it contributes best to understanding the phenomenon.

Within this context, this chapter has three primary purposes. The first is to trace emerging models of colleges and universities as organizations since the 1950s, focusing particularly on developments since Clark's 1973 assessment. Prior to then, little formal research or conceptual development considered the organizational characteristics of colleges and universities. They were examined mostly in descriptions of various types. We have since gone through periods of growth and constraint, crises and challenges that have reshaped higher education. In the process we have developed an extensive array of models to try to explain or help us understand how they function.

The second purpose is to examine what factors influence the development of these organizational models and to suggest a conceptual framework to aid in understanding the development of this large array. The expansion of higher education from 1950 to 1970 attracted an initial group of researchers and scholars—largely from the social science disciplines—who developed early models of these critical societal organizations. But new, more complex models emerged after 1970. Even as the rate of growth slowed, colleges and universities came to face new challenges.

The final purpose of this chapter is to examine the contribution of sociology alongside other disciplines and offer some insights gained from this analysis. These varied approaches to colleges and universities as organizations, as we shall see, have produced a highly eclectic, diverse, and interdisciplinary set of contributions. Indeed, it is often difficult to separate the contributions of sociology from those of other disciplines.

A Focus on Organizational Research

A brief historical perspective on colleges and universities as organizations is informative regarding the need for organizational research. By the end of the nineteenth century, most institutional types had emerged —public land grant universities, the complex public university, private sectarian colleges, military institutions, technical universities, and numerous variations of the private university. The first half of the twentieth century would see junior or community colleges introduced. Yet despite the development of these varying types of higher educational institutions by that time, colleges and universities were portrayed mainly descriptively as structural types and were not the subject of much research, conceptual development (except for institutional histories), or scholarly efforts to examine them as organizations.

Subsequently, comments from astute observers pinpointed the need for systematic research focusing on the organizational patterns and dynamics of colleges and universities. As early as 1928, Alfred North Whitehead observes that in universities "the heart of the matter was beyond regulation" (Whitehead 1928, p. 638). Well into the second half of the century, Frederick Rudolph, in his history *The American College and University*, characterizes change in higher education as characterized by "drift, reluctant accommodation and belated recognition that, while no one was looking, change had in fact taken place" (Rudolph 1962, p. 491). As of 1965, Kingman Brewster, a respected president at Yale, suggests that "the real trouble with attempting to devise a strategy, let alone a plan, for a university is that basically we [faculty] are all anarchists—significant thought, art, and action must have creativity. Creativity by definition defies prediction's plan" (Brewster 1965, p. 45). Any researcher addressing these institutions has been amply forewarned of the complex nature of change in the organizations themselves.

Despite the warnings, research on colleges and universities as organizations eventually began to flourish. Two early scholars' observations on the growth of such research after 1950 provide a rationale for focusing this chapter on higher education's organizational dynamics. In separate publications, T. R. McConnell, then director of the Center for the Study of Higher Education at the University of California–Berkeley, and Algo Henderson, director of a similar center at the University of Michigan, both noted the lack of conceptual literature and research about the organization and administration of colleges and universities (McConnell 1963; Henderson 1963).

A little over a decade later, a comprehensive review of literature on "organization and administration in higher education" for volume 2 of the *Review of Research in Education* (Peterson 1974) yielded an initial list of more than 500 publications, mostly post-1950, of which only about 200 were research based. Although limited in number, the quality of the research in this area seemed to be increasing, and the area was attracting scholars from several social science disciplines, including sociology. A decade later, in a review titled "Emerging Developments in Organizational Research" (1985), I noted that research-based studies of this area exceeded 1,000. Examining the development of an increasingly sophisticated theoretical and research base, I characterized the studies described by McConnell and Henderson, which were prior to 1963, as a stage of "early childhood"; those by 1974 as "pre-adolescence"; and those by 1985 as "advanced adolescence." A literature search of organizational research in higher education today would be well beyond the scope of this chapter. Thus, the focus is on the theoretical or conceptual models of higher and postsecondary institutions as organizations—not on research into all the dynamics of colleges and universities as organizations.

Organizational Models and the Environment: A Contingency Perspective

More than a decade ago, looking back over his career—including his oversight of the Carnegie Commission's comprehensive examination of higher education—Clark Kerr (1993) observed that change in the environment of higher education had been revolutionary rather than evolutionary. In the late 1960s, scholars of organizational behavior had begun adopting an open-system, as opposed to a closed-system, perspective in their study of organizations (Katz and Kahn 1966). After 1970, higher education scholars were to adopt that perspective as well in their organizational approaches to studying higher education. As we begin the twenty-first century, few would question that change in the environment is still ubiquitous and that institutions are still being reshaped by or adapting to those external forces.

Reflecting this perspective about the critical role of the environment in influencing and shaping higher educational institutions, the framework guiding this chapter adopts a contingency perspective. The ensuing development of organizational theories can be seen as a means of understanding and explaining how colleges and universities have sought to respond to those environmentally generated challenges.

The principal components of the contingency framework make explicit the open-systems premise. External societal forces are conceived as changing environmental conditions. These affect or shape college and university dynamics—directly, through the institutional management challenges they present, and indirectly, by changing the nature of our industry and its competitive domain. The impact on colleges and universities and their response to institutional challenges, both from the environment directly and from the changing nature of the industry indirectly, give rise to a new organizational model to explain those impacts and responses. (For a more extended discussion of this framework and the construct of industry, see Peterson, Dill, and Mets 1997.)

The construct of *industry* in this framework merits some explanation. Industry is well understood in the general organizational litera-ture. It is typically defined as a set of organizations that use or require similar resources or attract similar clients and that produce similar products and services. The construct of industry is useful in defining an organization's market and competitive domain (or some segment of it) and in identifying the patterns of governmental control or regulation to which the industry is subjected. The industry and the intensity of com-petition among its member organizations can be characterized as being shaped by five factors (Porter 1980): (1) the threat of new organizational entrants to the industry, (2) the bargaining power or control of suppliers of key resources, (3) the bargaining power of customers who purchase products or services, (4) the threat of substitute products or services from new organizations, and (5) innovations in the core technology of the organizations in the industry. Clearly we can conceive of higher or postsecondary education as an industry.

The discussion that follows identifies the primary environmental conditions operating during different time periods since 1950. How these conditions influenced—or redefined—the industry is also exam-ined. The discussion then considers the primary institutional challenges that resulted directly from these environmental conditions, as well as those resulting from changes in the industry. In response to these in-stitutional challenges, in various periods new organizational models have emerged or become popular, structures that have helped us to understand these processes of transformation in our colleges and uni-versities. The chapter concludes by discussing the evolution and nature of these models.

Traditional to Mass Higher Education: From Stability to Expansion, 1950–1972

While the focus of this chapter is primarily on developments after 1970, it is also important to recall the period prior to 1950, when we had what we now refer to as the traditional higher education system or industry. This consisted of public and private four-year, comprehensive, and university-level institutions. Two-year junior and community colleges were few in number and not serious competitors with the other institu-tions. The concept of traditional higher education provides the context for the next expansion of organizational research after 1970.

Environmental conditions during this period after World War II

Table 6.1. Evolution of Organizational Models

	Dominant Environment Pressures	Primary Institutional Challenges	Emerging Organization Models	Exemplary Source and Author
	*From Traditional to Mass Higher Education (1950–1972)*			
1950–1964	Growth and expansion	Direction and accountability	Community	Clark (1960) Goodman (1962) Millett (1962)
			Rational or bureaucratic	Corson (1960) Stroup (1966)
	*The Postsecondary Era (1972–1995)*			
1965–1972	Disruption and minority demands	Order, control, and access	Saga Political Conglomerate	Clark (1970) Baldridge (1971 a&b) Lee and Bowen (1971)
			Loose coupling Organized anarchy	Weick (1974) Cohen and March (1974)
1972–1985	Declining demand, economic recession and constraint	Market pressure, efficiency, and productivity	Market Institutional theory Resource dependence Techno-managerial	Kotler (1975) Meyer and Rowan (1977) Pfeffer and Salancik (1978) Lawrence and Service (1977) Hopkins and Massy (1981)
			Strategic	Peterson (1980) Keller (1983) Chaffee (1985)
1985–1995	Quality, access, and equity	Effectiveness, complexity, restructuring, and reengineering	Cultural	Masland (1985) Tierney (1990) Berquist (1992) Peterson and Spencer (1993) Simsik and Louis (1994)
			Matrix Cybernetic	Alpert (1985) Birnbaum (1988)

Table 6.1. Continued

Dominant Environment Pressures	Primary Institutional Challenges	Emerging Organization Models	Exemplary Source and Author
The Emerging Postsecondary Knowledge Industry (1995–2005)			
Rapid change, turbulent, high expectations, unpredictable	Institutional redesign	Adaptive	Gumport and Sporn (1998) Sporn (1999) Gumport and Pusser (1999)
	Redefinition, redirection, reorganization, and renewal	Contextual	Peterson (1997)
Diversity, telematics, new learning markets, quality, economic productivity, globalization, and resource constraint		Entrepreneurial	Slaughter and Leslie (1997) Clark (1998)
		Virtual	Carchidi and Peterson (1999)
		Alliances, partnerships, joint ventures, networks cross-national	Needed: new models

started an enrollment expansion that would continue during the latter half of the century. While these conditions affected the institutions, they did not promote extensive change in the nature of the industry, and the institutional challenges did not change the character of the institutions and how they were managed in any substantial way. Since research on colleges and universities as organizations was almost nonexistent, most of the literature from that period consists of descriptive portrayals of different types of colleges and universities. (See Table 6.1 for each time period characterized below.)

1950–1965: An Era of Growth and Expansion

Environmental Conditions and Industry Change. In the period from 1950 to the late 1960s, two actions by the U.S. federal government created an environment fostering growth of enrollments, expansion of the number and type of public institutions, and an increase in institutional size, especially among public institutions. Both the continued success of the G.I. Bill and the publication of the 1950 *Truman Commission Report on Higher Education*, which promoted higher education for all high school graduates, spawned this expanding enrollment demand in the four-year college and university sector and triggered the founding of hundreds of community colleges. It was clearly a period when growth, while challenging, was predictable and policymakers and the public were supportive. Resources were forthcoming, if always a bit late. Thus, two industry-shaping factors—increased demand by customers (student enrollments) and the addition of new organizational entrants (more institutions and community colleges)—were moving us from an industry of traditional higher education to what would become known as the period of mass higher education after 1970—an industry that would be larger, more institutionally diverse, and more competitive (at least for the resources to support growth).

Institutional Management Challenge. During this period of environmental pressure for growth and expansion and the shift toward a mass higher education industry, the primary management challenges were to clarify institutional *direction* or *purpose* in the midst of that expansion and to assure greater *accountability* for the increased resources for which they were responsible. New institutions struggled with issues of purpose and direction, and existing ones struggled with how to organize and manage themselves amid rapid growth and how to be accountable—to provide better information on enrollments, faculty, space, facilities, and financial resource needs.

Internal Organizational Models. In order to analyze how colleges and universities as organizations responded to these challenges, three early theoretical or conceptual models emerged prior to 1970. Two authors used sociological models to probe the problems of managing institutional growth and accountability. John Corson's *Governance of Colleges and Universities* (1960) and H. H. Stroup's *Bureaucracy in Higher Education* (1966) drew on the work of Weber to characterize the dynamics of colleges and universities as formally organized *bureaucracies*. Two other authors also drew on sociology to suggest that colleges and universities were in fact better understood as *communities*. Paul Goodman's *The Community of Scholars* (1962) developed an egalitarian notion of colleges as a community of learners, including faculty, students, and administrators as equals in the enterprise. John Millett's *The Academic Community* (1962) suggested a more restrictive notion of a community of academic professionals—the faculty. These two variations on the community or collegial model seemed to fit better the small private college sector that did not experience the same growth as the public sector and that harked back to the traditional higher education era—ignoring the purpose of accounting for growth and expansion that was implicit in the bureaucratic model. Burton Clark, meanwhile, chose to examine the rapidly growing community college sector. His study *The Open Door College* (1960) used an intensive case-study approach drawing on sociological and anthropological concepts.

There are two common threads to these works. First, all the authors drew directly or indirectly on sociology for their work—bureaucracy, community, and an intensive case-study approach to develop a model of a new institutional type. But they also all viewed colleges and universities as purposive and developed largely internally oriented models of organization. These preceded the open-system perspective that would come to predominate in the years to follow.

1965–1975: A Decade of Conflict

Environmental Conditions. The rapid growth and expansion in higher education and the shift to a system of mass higher education would continue during this decade. However, during this period environmental conditions changed markedly. It was an era marked by extensive unrest in the nation, which spilled over onto college and university campuses with disruptions and minority demands. There were three primary interacting sources of unrest. First, the free speech movement in the early 1960s sparked organized student disruptions on many campuses, such as the one led by Mario Savio at Berkeley. Second, the Vietnam War, which met with widespread national debate, raised great political turmoil in the country and led to many violent confrontations like those orchestrated by the Chicago Seven at the 1968 Democratic National convention. The war was also a key issue on college campuses and catalyzed events like the founding of Students for a Democratic Society (SDS) at the University of Michigan, the police shooting of students protesting at Kent State University, and many violent incidents on other campuses. Finally, across the country in the mid-1960s, the civil rights movement gained widespread nonviolent activist support from students and faculty on college campuses. However, the assassination of Martin Luther King in 1968 foreshadowed the decline of his nonviolent approach to civil rights and the rise of Black Power, led by people like Stokely Carmichael, who took the movement in a decidedly different direction. Not unrelatedly, in the late 1960s and early 1970s, many predominantly white institutions began efforts to increase their African American enrollments. While often small in terms of percentage of the student body, this change provided a critical mass in terms of numbers on many campuses (Peterson et al. 1978). These three issues were intermingled and spawned many activist groups with which administrators and faculty had to contend.

Institutional Challenges. The institutional management challenge during this period consisted of two slightly different pressures. On the one hand, pressures rose both on campus and outside from governmental and policy groups to increase access of black and other minority students. This was a position that many institutions and faculty endorsed. However, the very presence of newly admitted black students provided the critical mass for demonstrations and protests regarding their treatment, curricular and faculty indifference, lack of services, and charges of racism and indifference against faculty and administrators— many of whom had supported minority enrollment and thought of themselves as supporters of civil rights. The minority students' disruptions added to those emanating from issues relating to free speech and the Vietnam War.

On the other hand, pressures emanated from politicians, parents, and some students and faculty to maintain order and control on campus and to ensure that students could continue their academic studies undisrupted. The threat was always the imposition of external force by police or the National Guard, an idea that was abhorrent to most university faculty, students, and administrators.

Models of Organization. In addressing these challenges, many researchers studied the conflicts and institutional responses but failed to develop a new organizational model. It was clear that higher education's organizational researchers needed to adopt a new stance—the open-system perspective that would take account of the role of external changes and of conflict in shaping responses and new organizational dynamics. This perspective was already being used by organizational scholars to examine non–higher education organizations (Katz and Kahn 1966). Although not addressing the external conflict issues directly, during this period five scholars of higher education would develop models that were based on an open-system perspective (as were most of the succeeding models).

Burton Clark (1970), although not directly addressing the pressure for order, control, and access, once again drew on his sociological and anthropological approach when he introduced the notion of an organizational *saga* to deal with conflicting campus dynamics, in his intensive comparative study *The Distinctive College*. While his work focused on the saga that changes an organization's culture, it also employed an open-system perspective that recognized the role of external forces in shaping the saga and treated conflicting perspectives as important for understanding how changes are enacted.

J. Victor Baldridge drew on both sociology and political interest group theory to introduce the *political* model of organization to higher education. His model draws attention to the manner in which issues arise, lead to interest group formation, and dominate the decision process in universities. He originally applied it to the internal dynamics of an institution in his landmark study *Power and Conflict in the University* (1971b). He then expanded it to incorporate both internal and external dynamics in *Academic Governance: Research on Institutional Politics and Decision Making* (1971a).

Three other models introduced during this era reflected the need to understand the influence of the environment as well as the dynamics of large complex institutions that were not easily captured by earlier bureaucratic or community models. Karl Weick, a social psychologist, introduced the notion of universities as *loosely coupled* organizations, in an attempt to capture their more fluid, decentralized character (1976). As a model this does not have the fullness of some of the others, but it is a conceptual notion that has become widely accepted as an important contribution to understanding how universities function. Concurrently, Michael Cohen and James March, using their sociological and political science perspectives, conducted a study of university presidents and proposed a model of decision making that turned the rational paradigm (problem-analysis-solution) upside down, and they instead suggested that much university decision making involved the garbage-can approach (solutions in search of problems). In their classic book *Leadership and Ambiguity* (1974), they argued that this process occurred because large complex universities were *organized anarchies*—an amalgamation of highly decentralized units requiring only limited coordination. In the final model, Eugene Lee and Frank Bowen (1971) employed a business construct, arguing that universities should be viewed with a corporate model, as *conglomerates,* to take account of their complexity.

So this era of viewing colleges and universities as open systems led to five new models: colleges and universities as sagas, political entities, loosely coupled organizations, organized anarchies, and conglomerates. These researchers all had some sociological grounding for their work but also drew upon other disciplines. Clark used sociology and anthropology, Baldridge political interest theory, Weick social and organizational psychology, Cohen and March both sociology and political science, and Lee and Bowen business management. During this period a more interdisciplinary approach to the study of colleges and universities as organizations can be seen to emerge. In the next decade, scholars of higher education—identifying themselves as members of the interdisciplinary field of organizational behavior—also began to emerge. The research and models that followed still grew from sociological roots, but they became interwoven with theories and concepts from other disciplines, so the contribution of sociology is less apparent.

The Emerging Postsecondary Education Industry: An Era of Institutional Change, 1972–1995

Defining a New Industry

The 1972 Higher Education Amendments enacted by Congress almost immediately created a new conception of industry—postsecondary education (see Table 6.1). These 1972 amendments included two key changes from the prior ones. First, the distribution of federal student aid was changed. Previously financial aid funds had been distributed to institutions, which then gave it to the qualified students they had admitted. Under the 1972 amendments, funds were to be distributed by the federal government directly to qualified students, who were free to use them to attend any qualified institution to which they were admitted. This reduced institutional control and increased student choice—essentially increasing the extent to which institutions had to compete for students. Second, the amendments also inserted the word *postsecondary* in place of *higher education*, without clearly defining it. It was later interpreted to include degree-granting proprietary institutions. In effect, this added almost 7,000 new institutions to our mass higher education industry, more than doubling the number of students who were potentially eligible for federal student aid (Carnegie Commission 1973). As in the transition from traditional to mass higher education, these amendments redefined the industry by changing two of the five factors shaping competition in an industry. It added new organizations (proprietary) to the industry and increased the number and bargaining power of the clients (students), who became not only more numerous and diverse but also agents of institutional choice. A far more competitive industry would emerge.

1972–1985: Adjusting to the Postsecondary Industry

Environmental Conditions and Industry Change. During this period, four different environmental dynamics predominated: increased *competition* among institutions, *declining student demand* patterns, an *economic recession*, and the long-term prospect of *resource constraints*. As already noted, the primary impact of the 1972 amendments was the redefinition of higher education as a postsecondary industry, which created more competition for students among a far greater number of institutions. The proportion of high school graduates attending college had increased from around 20 percent after World War II to almost 50 percent by 1980. Mass higher education had succeeded. While enrollment at traditional public institutions continued to grow through 1980, it did so at a diminished rate. So with more institutions and a slowing rate of growth in attendance, institutions experienced what appeared to be a declining demand.

The late 1970s and early 1980s also witnessed a substantial economic recession. Inflation rates soared to 15–18 percent, and unemployment increased substantially. This pattern was especially critical in colleges and universities: the Higher Education Price Index (HEPI) increased to an even higher level, since costs of the goods and services they had to purchase were increasing more rapidly. These conditions thus not only made it more difficult for students to afford higher and postsecondary education but also placed severe financial strain on most college and university budgets.

With greater competition among more institutions, a leveling of enrollment attendance rates, and a projection of economic recovery that was at best long term, colleges and universities began to plan for long-term constraint—both in enrollment growth and in financial support.

Institutional Challenge. As the conflicts of the late 1960s and early 1970s subsided and these new environmental challenges increased, not surprisingly, colleges and universities began to focus on market pressures—how to market their institution more effectively to attract students in this more competitive postsecondary industry. The consequences of the economic recession and the prospect of long-term resource constraint challenged institutions to increase and improve their efficiency and productivity. These issues, previously not of major concern in the higher and postsecondary education literature, now became the central focus at most professional and scholarly conferences and led to new models of organization.

Organizational Models. Five new models emerged during this period, each with an explicit open-system perspective—in fact, four of the five would focus primarily on the relation of the institution with its environment. Phillip Kotler's *Marketing Management* (1976) drew on his business administration perspective and was widely quoted in college and university circles. Although not focused explicitly on higher or postsecondary education, it captured the new competitive nature of the postsecondary industry and presented a model of how to view organizations as market oriented. Although not a clear organizational model nor one that would lead to extensive application in the higher and postsecondary education literature, it attracted much attention at our professional conferences, as institutional leaders attempted to be more market oriented or "market smart," as Robert Zemsky would refer to them two decades later (NCPI 2001).

In 1978, the *resource dependency* model of organizations was introduced by two sociologists (Pfeffer and Salancik 1978). Like Kotler's work, theirs initially was not focused specifically on higher and postsecondary education. However, the model of colleges and universities as *resource-dependent* institutions has been widely embraced and has shaped a great deal of our organizational research.

In the early 1980s, colleges and universities began to be viewed as *strategic organizations* that were attempting to find their market niche—to balance their internal structures, processes, priorities, and decisions with a complex changing environment. Three authors, using an interdisciplinary organizational behavior perspective, attempted to define this model. In 1980 I summarized the organizational literature on the varying approaches to strategy (Peterson 1980). In his classic and widely read work *Academic Strategy* (1983), George Keller gave substance to this perspective in an intensive study that probed the emerging nature of colleges and universities as strategic organizations. Ellen Chaffee's research further elaborated this perspective as a conceptual model in her "Three Models of Strategy" (1985a and 1985b). Conceptions of colleges and universities as strategic organizations have continued to evolve and are still commonplace in our literature, in works like Hearn 1988, Gumport and Pusser 1995, Peterson et al. 1997, and Presley and Leslie 1999.

From a different perspective, in the late 1970s, a more internally focused view of colleges and universities as *technomanagerial* organizations addressed the pressures for efficiency and productivity, thereby gaining attention. This perspective grew out of a merger of the notion of colleges and universities as resource dependent with earlier notions of them as bureaucracies or formal organizations. The technomanagerial model focused on defining units to measure resource flows of all types in colleges and universities and then on building rational computer-based models to examine the implications of management decisions on costs and productivity. This approach, reflecting the application of operations research principles to the task, was championed and led by researchers at the National Center for Higher Education Management Systems (NCHEMS) in this decade. G. B. Lawrence and A. L. Service's *Quantitative Approaches to Higher Education Management* (1977) synthesized this approach. An institution-specific application of this technomanagerial approach was presented in D. S. P. Hopkins and W. F. Massy's *Planning Models For Colleges and Universities* (1981), which combined information theory, operations research, and the formal rational approach to college and university management. Much of this technical and formal rational approach to college and university planning and management is now reflected in analytic studies that are commonplace in supporting management decision making.

Yet another approach that emerged during this period also focused on the role of the environment—John Meyer and Brian Rowan addressed *institutional theory* in their classic article "The Structure of Educational Organizations" (1978). Although their article was not about higher and postsecondary education, as sociologists studying organization, they addressed the limitations of earlier internally oriented formal rational models and of the emerging environment-organization models (market, resource dependence, and strategic). This work provided the foundation for institutional theory as a new perspective that merged formal organizational structure and environment theories. Structure was seen not as the result of an organization's encounter with specific aspects of the environment but as derived from and legitimized by the broader social environment. This notion of institutional theory was applied to the study of higher and postsecondary education organizations only sparingly until the last decade. It is now reflected most directly in the works of scholars like Patricia Gumport (Gumport and Sporn 1999), Burton Clark (1998, 2005), Hassan Simsek (1997), and Barbara Sporn (1999) and will be discussed later.

The authors developing models in this period used backgrounds in sociology, information theory, operations research, business, and organizational behavior. All examined colleges and universities as holistic organizations. They incorporated the varying organizational models to look at structural patterns and strategies and drew upon the organization-environment models to understand both explicit formal responses and patterns of relationships between internal and external dynamics.

1985–1995: Constraint, Quality, and Equity

New Conditions: Focus on Academics. While our redefinition of higher education as a postsecondary industry was still unformed during the decade from 1985 to 1995, the term *postsecondary* gradually came to be accepted as (nontraditional) proprietary institutions came to be identified and legitimized. During this time, associations representing these organizations were becoming active—for example, by establishing standards and regulations regarding the use of financial aid, which were then clarified and became incorporated. Through these and similar developments, the institutional terrain and the competitive arena among all the postsecondary institutions became more clearly formulated and thereby better understood.

However, changes in certain environmental conditions were occurring that would provide colleges and universities with new institutional challenges. These would differ from the earlier, primarily managerial challenges, being more academic in character. During this period, college and university attendance rates were exceeding 60 percent for high school graduates, but minority rates lagged by over 10 percent for African American and Hispanic students (the figures were even more extreme if we take into account age cohorts due to minority students' much lower high school graduation rates). The dual issue of *access and equity* for underrepresented groups—originally raised in the 1960s—became a critical challenge for public policy as well as for college and university leaders.

Following up on the highly critical but politically popular report on K–12 education *A Nation at Risk* (National Commission on Excellence 1983), the Director of the National Institute for Education appointed a Study Group on the Conditions of Excellence in American Higher Education. Charged with examining the state of undergraduate education and making recommendations for improvement, these eminent scholars and leaders of higher and postsecondary education issued the report *Involvement in Learning* (Study Group 1984). The report highlighted a number of problems, raised questions about the quality of undergraduate education, and made recommendations for policy, management, and teaching and learning to all participants—policy leaders, administrators, faculty, and students. Three primary foci of the report were active learning, setting higher expectations, and improving feedback and assessment. Not knowing how to address the first two, policymakers seized on assessment, and a movement was on.

Academic Management Challenges. While environmental conditions had previously reshaped the industry by influencing the number and type of organizations and industry clientele, which presented the institutions primarily with managerial challenges, these new conditions addressed the core academic functions of learning, teaching, and research. While the Study Group report stressed academic topics and issues, policy groups, minority coalitions, and legislators simultaneously pressed their concerns for access and equity. Beginning in 1985, demands for assessment would grow—assessment of student involvement and learning outcomes, of faculty roles and teaching performance, of the quality of programs and instruction, and even of the academic performance of institutions and states or systems. This call for addressing academic quality, access, and equity simultaneously was daunting.

Thus it was a period when, for the first time, institutional leaders and faculty were called upon to address the academic purposes and performance of the institution, not just managerial performance as in previous decades. This was reflected in concerns about educational effectiveness (not just efficiency and productivity). These conflicting pressures also required examining the complexity of an institution's academic purposes, programs, and processes. Restructuring and reengineering of academic—as well as administrative—processes and functions would be required.

New Models. The press for effectiveness and the need to understand the academic complexity of postsecondary institutions along with their structures and approaches to improving access, quality, and equity simultaneously—this constellation of demands resulted in three new organizational models: the cultural, matrix, and cybernetic. While not using institutional theory directly, all three envision colleges and universities holistically, seek to reflect the complexity of the organization-environment interface, and combine managerial and academic perspectives on the organization.

The most prominent model to gain popularity during this decade viewed colleges and universities as *cultural organizations*. Andrew Masland's succinct article "Organizational Culture in the Study of Higher Education" (1985) drew on extant work in the study of organizations outside of higher and postsecondary education but also recognized the earlier contributions of Burton Clark (1960, 1970) and David Dill (1981). Identifying the primary elements of and approach to studying organizational culture, he argued the case for emphasizing it. George D. Kuh and Elizabeth J. Whitt's *Invisible Tapestry* (1988) expanded Masland's presentation, and William Tierney's *Assessing Academic Culture and Climate* (1990) explored that model and its applications. William H. Bergquist's *Four Cultures of the Academy* (1992) linked the concept of organizational culture in higher and postsecondary education to the other models of organizations and reflected Lee Bolman and Terrence Deal's classic work on *Reframing Organizations* (1991). Melinda Spencer and I (Peterson and Spencer 1993) further clarified the distinction between culture and climate, the dimensions of culture, and the difference between qualitative and quantitative approaches to studying organizational culture. In the intervening years studies, articles, and books too numerous to mention have used the cultural model to examine colleges and universities as organizations.

In an attempt to understand the complex relationship between academic and research structures in the research university, Daniel Alpert's "Performance and Paralysis" (1985) introduced and applied the *matrix* model of organizations to them. He used it to explain the influence of different external resource environments on the formation of research units, academic departments, and interdisciplinary structures designed to bridge those two primary and often conflicting structures for teaching and research. Interestingly, Alpert is a physicist—adding to the array of academic backgrounds of contributors to research on higher and postsecondary education organizations.

The third organizational model during the decade attempts to analyze the complexity of colleges and universities as organizations and show how to make them more effective. Robert Birnbaum's *How Colleges Work* (1988) uses a *cybernetic* model drawn from information and systems theory to examine institutional decision making and organizational dynamics. Like Bergquist, he attempted to integrate his approach with other existing organizational models (collegial, bureaucratic, loose coupling, contingency, political, and anarchy). His is probably the most recent work that attempts to present a comprehensive and integrated model of colleges and universities as organizations.

Interestingly, the authors writing during the 1985–1995 decade continued the trend to broaden and incorporate interdisciplinary influences in our study of colleges and universities as organizations. The cultural approach draws mainly on anthropological roots, the matrix on business administration, and cybernetics on information and system theory. They all also reflect the trend to understand colleges and universities holistically and as complex entities in terms of size, structure, decision making, and environmental interaction. The cultural and cybernetics models even attempt to link to or incorporate our previous organization and organization-environment models.

The Postsecondary Knowledge Industry: An Era of Transformation, 1995 and Beyond

The construct of a postsecondary knowledge industry (PSKI) reflects an attempt to interpret what was happening to the postsecondary industry as it was being reconfigured by the information era or knowledge age (see Table 6.1). However, the transformations in question are more complex than just technological advancements' making information ubiquitous and affecting our institutions' delivery capacity. Several other environmental dynamics or changing conditions have emerged during this past decade, trends likely to continue to reshape the postsecondary knowledge industry and affect our individual colleges and universities in significant ways.

Environmental Conditions

Seven environmental dynamics or conditions at work in our postsecondary world can be traced, and most observers will acknowledge them: the press for diversity, revolution in telematics, interest in academic quality, concern about economic productivity, search for new learning markets, expansion of globalization, and continued resource constraint. Space does not allow for an extensive elaboration of each of these conditions; a brief overview must suffice. But their significance is unquestionable; each has impact on virtually all five of the factors previously identified as conditions reshaping an industry (threat of new organizational entrants, bargaining power of clients, bargaining power of customers, availability of substitute services, and innovation in industry core technology).

Diversity refers to the pressure to increase service to underrepresented groups—to admit, educate, and graduate students of different racial, ethnic, social, and economic backgrounds. The list of dimensions for defining diversity is constantly increasing. New minority-serving institutions, new enrollment demands, new educational needs and approaches, and new minority professional associations and political pressure groups are all emerging—and influencing and changing our industry.

Telematics refers to the rapid innovation in and expansion of interacting developments in computing, telecommunications, and information databases. This not only affects our core teaching, learning, and research processes but can reshape our delivery systems, lead to new virtual institutions or delivery systems, and allow for global linkages in teaching and research. This can reach new learners who want different delivery modes and can require new skills from faculty as educational designers who use the technology. New organizations from other industries like telecommunications, computing, and even entertainment firms are participating in the design and delivery of postsecondary educational and learning opportunities.

Quality refers to increased pressure for academic assessment and accountability for student learning, instructional and curricular design, faculty productivity, and program and institutional performance. This has influenced our delivery of teaching and learning and our patterns of accreditation. It has led to the development of special campus units to administer this function, has altered state government relations with public universities, and is often used for planning and resource allocation. And this pressure shows no signs of abating.

New learning markets refers to the increasing need and demand for postsecondary learning opportunities for older students and for continuing education for those seeking advanced degrees as well as for occupational upgrading or training. These markets consist largely of nontraditional students with special program interests and new learning requirements, often provided through new delivery modes. It is a large market that attracts many proprietary institutions, training and development firms, and training programs in business and governmental organizations. The providers may be either competitors to institution-based continuing and professional education or potential customers or partners.

Economic productivity refers to the pressure on institutions not only to train students for gainful employment and provide research findings for others to use but also to contribute more directly through research and service to the economic well-being of the region, state, or nation. This demand has challenged institutions and faculty to link their teaching and research more closely to the productive demands of industry. It has led to the creation or institutional expansion of research parks and technology transfer capacity and has even incubated new enterprises. It has stimulated new partnerships among postsecondary institutions and with government agencies and private firms. Such activities have become a source of funding for more entrepreneurial institutions.

Globalization refers not just to the exchange of students and faculty and the focus of instruction and research on international and global issues but also to the growing array of cross-national and international arrangements. Some institutions have expanded overseas; some engage in international partnerships with foreign institutions of higher education. The advent of telematics makes it possible to deliver educational material and form research ventures on an international basis without ever leaving one's own institution. We have also seen a growing pattern of what one author called "civil societies"—ventures that electronically bring together university faculty, governmental policymakers, and business representatives to work on global problems and issues.

Resource constraint refers to the fact that in most higher and postsecondary institutions, the confluence of institutional costs to maintain programs and activities with demands for new programs and quality engenders a continuous need to find new funding. In the face of rising institutional costs; declining federal and state support; limits on student and family ability to pay; and increased competition for foundation gifts, private giving, and contracts and grants, most institutions struggle with resource shortages and a continuing need to generate new sources of revenue.

The Emerging Postsecondary Knowledge Industry

Reshaping an Industry. The impact of these environmental pressures clearly changes all five factors reshaping an industry. The picture is seen only "through a glass darkly" (Dill and Sporn 1995). The potential student pool (customers) includes more minority students with special needs and interests and older relearning students who are even more diverse and who have special program needs and delivery preferences. Our sources of financial support and key resources (suppliers) are strained and more likely to demand specific programs, services, or delivery modes. With the advent of the information age and its new clientele and new educational modes of delivery, non–higher education organizations are entering the industry (new organizations or substitute services) to provide postsecondary education and services either as competitors or as potential partners. And the availability of the new telematics technology (core technology) allows potential changes in our educational delivery to meet the demands of current and new student learners, in researcher partnerships as well as our own virtual learning and research capacity.

During each previous transition, from traditional to mass higher education and from mass to postsecondary education, only two of the five factors reshaping our industry were activated, unlike our current situation as of 2006. The postsecondary knowledge industry is populated not just by traditional higher and proprietary educational institutions but also by training programs from business and government; virtual institutions and delivery systems; new institutions for particular populations; some telecommunications, computing, information, and entertainment firms that provide postsecondary education services; and new institutional partnership patterns, joint ventures, and even cross-national or international arrangements for postsecondary research and teaching. The postsecondary knowledge industry is a highly competitive arena that challenges our traditional higher education and proprietary institutions to compete, coordinate, or cooperate in new ventures and in new ways.

Institutional Challenge. As we entered the mass higher education era, the primary institutional challenges were to manage growth and expansion and then disruption and new minority demands. In the transition to the postsecondary era, organizations were called upon first to manage declining demand, recession, and constraint and then to respond to issues of quality, access, and equity. As we enter the postsecondary knowledge industry era, the demands are far greater. First, colleges and universities must seek to understand and redefine the very nature of their industry—the changing marketplace, shifting consumer and support patterns for postsecondary knowledge, new delivery modes for teaching and research, new organizations providing postsecondary services, and the competitive dynamics of this industry. They need to consider redirecting their mission and their relationships with postsecondary and other non–higher educational organizations that can provide postsecondary knowledge, learning experiences, and research support. In the process they need to consider reorganizing their academic and administrative structures to coincide more coherently with their changing mission, external environment, and interorganizational relationships. They also may need to reform their academic and faculty roles and create a new culture for doing academic work.

In effect, they may need to consider redesigning their institution—undertaking a macro or transformational organizational change. This is a comprehensive and substantial challenge—one that will probably not be accomplished in a short time. Such a move will depend on the character of the new postsecondary knowledge industry and its development. (For a more comprehensive discussion of the emerging postsecondary knowledge industry and its institutional challenges, see Peterson, Dill, and Mets 1997.)

Comprehensive Models

Not surprisingly, in the face of these extensive environmental pressures —the still emerging PSKI and its complex challenges to institutions— four new organizational models or modifications of earlier ones are being introduced. Three of these models, the *adaptive, contextual,* and *entrepreneurial,* are elaborations of the strategic choice model of the 1980s and 1990s. All three focus on comprehensive institutional change patterns. However, they differ from the strategic model in which institutions are seen as rationally examining the environment, identifying a market niche, and developing a response strategy to adapt to it with a series of selective rationalized choices (purpose, priorities, programs, and resources). These newer models have taken an analytic approach that reflects the influence of institutional theory in order to understand college and university responses. They reflect situations that, in the face of a newly turbulent environment, took a more proactive stance by actively engaging it (or even attempting to change it), or else they undertook what seem to be macro or transformational changes. All these models are based on a holistic perspective on the college or university as organization and its environment, use an approach that draws on institutional theory, and often incorporate aspects of the earlier models.

Gumport and Sporn, in their "Institutional Adaptation: Demands for Management Reform and University Administration" (1999), examine the role of the environment and university management's adaptation to it. They focus on the relationship between forces in the environment, the demands on the institution from that environment, and the impact on and response of the university as organization. They use the study to synthesize and present their model of organizational *adaptation*. They draw on and interpret several organization-environment models (population ecology, institutional theory or isomorphism, contingency, resource dependence, and strategic choice) to understand how an organization adapts to and then legitimizes those changes. In Sporn's book *Adaptive University Structures* (1999), which examines six U.S. and European universities that made extensive changes in response to new environmental changes, she uses the adaptive perspective and incorporates or integrates various other models. Drawing on her work with Gumport and this study, Sporn expands the theory of organizational adaptation, specifying propositions and conditions that support large-scale adaptation to dynamic or turbulent environments.

The *contextual* model (Peterson 1997) is a strategy to address the need for more radical institutional change or transformation in the face of the emerging PSKI, which is ill-defined, rapidly changing, and unpredictable. This model has parallels to Gumport and Sporn's work on adaptation, also drawing on an institutional theory perspective. The contextual approach, however, stresses the notion of industry as an intermediary between the larger societal environment and institutional management challenges. The contextual model suggests that the nature of the seven societal forces already discussed and the emerging postsecondary knowledge industry may require radical institutional change. In this environment and period of industry change, colleges and universities may be faced with four challenges—redefining their industry and their role in it; redirecting or modifying their mission and external organizational relationships; reorganizing academic and administrative structures, functions, and processes; and renewing or recreating their academic workplace and culture. To accomplish these changes, a less rational process of planning or change is proposed, one based on examining institutions that have undergone extensive or transformational change. The process includes the following six activities: gaining insight into or envisioning new possibilities in the postsecondary knowledge industry, promoting initiatives or general directions for change, investing in infrastructure to support the initiatives, providing incentives to encourage faculty and staff involvement in the change initiatives, using information and communications both internally and externally to monitor and support the changes, and finally, integrating the changes that have been successful into the institution.

In a variant of the adaptive and contextual model, Clark's *Creating Entrepreneurial Universities* (1998) provides a model of the *entrepreneurial* university and its approach to transforming itself in the new PSKI. Based on case studies of five European universities that underwent radical transformation, he proposes five elements or characteristics of such a university: a strengthened core, enhanced development of peripheral units, a discretionary fund base (or autonomy to pursue and distribute resources), a stimulation of the heartland (selective development of academic units in response to their environments), and an enhanced entrepreneurial belief or set of values for the institution. Although focused on European universities, Clark's perspective might well apply to some of the universities examined by Gumport and Sporn.

In a study of how academic units behave in a research university, Sheila Slaughter and Larry Leslie's *Academic Capitalism* (1997) portrays how such units are driven by entrepreneurial, capitalistic decisions. While this is not an organizational model per se, it is an excellent example of employing multiple models to portray behavior. The researchers view academic units as residing in institutions characterized as loosely coupled organized anarchies. They draw on resource dependency to examine the relationship of these units to their research support environment, and they invoke institutional theory to help explain beliefs about what legitimizes academic reputation and the importance of resource acquisition to maintaining and enhancing status.

A fourth model, that of the *virtual* college or university, has yet to be fully elaborated. D. M. Carchidi and I (Carchidi and Peterson 2000), in examining the nature of these new organizations, make an important structural distinction between those with a virtual delivery system, those with a virtual organizational and administrative pattern, and those with both. We identify six archetypes of such organizations. Carchidi (1997) elaborates on this distinction in a study of differing types of virtual organizations. Using an open-system perspective and an institutional theory approach, and drawing on the adaptive and resource dependence models, he examines managerial patterns that have emerged. However, the model of the virtual university as organization is not well developed as of yet.

In this era, scholars and their work once again reflect the role of sociology and of other disciplines. Clark and Gumport are sociologists, Sporn's background is in business, Leslie is an economist, Slaughter is a political scientist, and Carchidi and Peterson come from an organizational-behavior perspective. Yet each now uses various organizational perspectives and models. The study of colleges and universities as organizations has become decidedly interdisciplinary.

A Contingency Perspective: Shaping Organizational Models

This chapter has provided the basis for a model that may help explain the emergence of our various organizational models and could guide us in thinking about future model development. Clearly the environment of colleges and universities has changed drastically over the past fifty years and affected them directly—but so has the industry within which they function. Figure 6.1 depicts a general framework for understanding how the conceptual nature of organizational models has changed in direct response to environmental conditions and changing conceptions of our primary industry.

Internal Models, Pre-1972

While our focus is primarily post-1970, organizational models had begun to emerge in the two previous generations. The societal environment of this era was relatively stable, predictable, and supportive. During the 1950s and 1960s, resources (enrollments, funding) were increasing at a rapid but steady rate and were also largely predictable—indeed, forecasting was the primary mode of planning during this time (Peterson 1986). There was strong public sentiment and public policy support for higher education, and states supported new and expanding institutions and operating funds for growing enrollments.

Our notions of a traditional higher education industry prior to 1950 and of mass higher education that emerged during this period were well understood. Colleges and universities were largely separated into subgroups by institutional type (research universities, comprehensive colleges, liberal arts colleges, and community colleges, with some distinction between

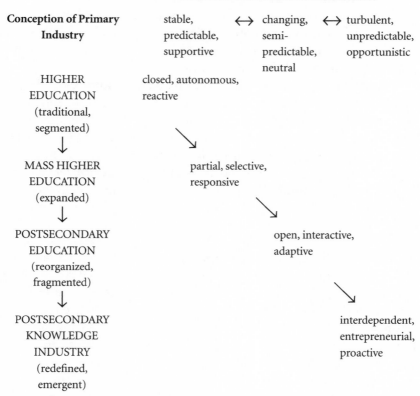

Environmental Condition and Pressures

Conception of Primary Industry

stable, predictable, supportive ⟷ changing, semi-predictable, neutral ⟷ turbulent, unpredictable, opportunistic

HIGHER EDUCATION (traditional, segmented) — closed, autonomous, reactive

MASS HIGHER EDUCATION (expanded) — partial, selective, responsive

POSTSECONDARY EDUCATION (reorganized, fragmented) — open, interactive, adaptive

POSTSECONDARY KNOWLEDGE INDUSTRY (redefined, emergent) — interdependent, entrepreneurial, proactive

Figure 6.1. A contingency perspective: primary industry and environmental conditions shaping emerging organizational models.

public and private) or by segments of the industry with which they identified and which were viewed as their primary competition.

In such an environment, our early models of organization (bureaucracy and community or collegial) treated colleges and universities as basically closed systems with a good deal of autonomy and were only reactive to external changes. There was substantial enrollment growth, and institutions expanded—especially in the community college sector. Growing institutions added administrative bureaucracy as well as faculty to accommodate student needs.

In the late 1960s and early 1970s, the various disruptions in society (the Vietnam War, free speech, and civil rights) made it clear that our higher education institutions were not immune to external events. The environment became more intrusive and less predictable. Public sentiment was less effusive, and public policymakers demanded more order and control on the part of institutions in exchange for continued support for mass higher education's expansion and minority groups' access.

Our organizational models were only partially responsive—and only in selective ways—to this environmental and industry shift. Although the saga and early political models acknowledged that colleges and universities are open systems and not immune to external changes, initially they focused primarily on internal dynamics. The loose coupling and organized anarchy models also recognized the influence of external conditions but mostly focused on the complexity of universities as increasingly large organizations with diverse academic and professional units.

External Models, 1972–1995

By 1972, following the mass higher education period, the environment was already changing as large cohorts of students attended college, minority groups pressed for access, and economic recession constrained institutional finances. The 1972 amendments, which launched the postsecondary era by adding proprietary institutions and changing the patterns of student aid distribution, made the industry more fragmented and more competitive (see Figure 6.1). The industry had come to include unprecedented numbers of community colleges and proprietary institutions. The increased competition for students led institutions to define more specifically the student clientele they were trying to attract and the other institutions that were competing for them. They were becoming more market oriented. During the 1980s, additional pressures for quality and equity and conditions of economic constraint were added to the mix. The institutional challenges also took on a more decidedly academic—as opposed to a strictly managerial—character and were more concerned with effectiveness than with efficiency and productivity, concerns that had dominated during previous times. Not only was the environment changing, but predictions for enrollments and resources were less certain. Public policy support for higher education shifted to a more neutral stance.

The models of organization that emerged recognized the changing institutional challenges and were now clearly all open-system models focused heavily on organization-environment relations. The market, resource dependence, strategic, matrix, and cultural models—and the reintroduction of an institutional theory approach to organizational analysis—all emphasized the interactive nature of this interface and began to recognize that institutions were adapting (not just reacting) to new industry patterns and to the external forces and the challenges they presented.

Adaptive and Proactive Models, 1995–2005

The environment during this decade, as already discussed, was the source of a broad array of changing conditions and pressures on institutions. These changing conditions would also give rise to an emerging notion of a postsecondary knowledge industry with its own implications and challenges to colleges and universities. This environment could only be characterized as turbulent. Both financial and enrollment patterns became a major unpredictable factor for institutional management. The nature of the industry, its participants, and its patterns of competition or cooperation—all were changing in ways not yet completely clear. Increased public expectations for higher education coupled with declining resource support made acquiring new resources and launching new ventures and initiatives critical for institutions. It required them to be much more opportunistic as well as market driven. Institutional redesign and macro or transformational change, not just strategic responses, became necessities for some.

In this milieu, another array of organizational models was called for, and several closely related ones have emerged. The adaptive, contextual, and entrepreneurial models all reflect the growing dominance of our understanding of the role of the environment in shaping colleges and universities as organizations. The models differ from those of the previous decade in their changing stance toward the environment. Previously institutions were viewed as interacting with and adapting to their environment. These new models emphasize a more interdependent and proactive stance toward the environment— institutions either transform themselves or seek to engage with or change elements of the environment to their advantage. Today's models also place greater stress on entrepreneurial behavior.

Needed: Future Models

Perhaps we can use this framework of environment-industry influence on our organizational models (see Table 6.1) to anticipate what will or should emerge next. Past the midpoint of this first decade in the twenty-first century, the next models to be developed in this highly volatile and emerging postsecondary knowledge industry are not clearly apparent. However, among the patterns we already see, several new possibilities deserve conceptual and research attention. The model of a college or university as a virtual organization, as already noted, is not fully developed. Colleges and universities are now engaging in a variety of new alliances, partnerships, and joint ventures, not only with other colleges and universities but also with other governmental and business firms. These may be new interorganizational models or may merely represent one of Clark's elements of the entrepreneurial organization—its enhanced periphery. The organizational nature of cross-national and international postsecondary colleges and universities, with that of partnerships or ventures operating in different countries with different systems, deserve our attention. How are we to understand such organizations, which include partnerships or joint ventures with new, non–higher education, other governmental, or commercial enterprises? New networks of individuals loosely organized as civil societies—with or without college and university sponsorship for learning and research on complex societal problems and issues—merit attention. The idea of a network organization might serve as a useful way of understanding the reach of many of these new interorganizational arrangements. Clearly, we still need to develop better ways of understanding our changing institutions, as they engage the ever-changing environment and the emerging postsecondary knowledge industry.

Some Evolutionary Insights

Over the past decades, many organizational models for higher education have been developed. In tracing this evolution of our organizational models and the forces shaping them, a number of insights emerge.

The Borrowed and Cumulative Nature of Models

Two characteristics of these models in higher education are apparent. First, most all of the models are borrowed. Not only do they derive from theories and concepts in various disciplines, but they have often been developed or refined in studies of non–higher education organizations before being applied here. In fact, while Cohen and March's theoretical base draws on decision-making concepts from other disciplines, their organized anarchy model may be the only model that qualifies as developed primarily in the context of higher education.

Second, models are not replaced. While most models have emerged as separate or fairly distinct models to characterize the organizational behavior of colleges and universities, their uses and effects have been cumulative. None of the models have been discredited or dropped from our arsenal of conceptual models. The bureaucratic model has evolved and expanded into the current and commonly used notion of the formal-rational model (in fact, I consider it an extension and did not even mention it). The collegial and community models are still widely used. The same can be said of almost all the models. When they were developed, they captured an institutional response to one set of challenges, and they are still useful now. Also, our models have moved from a focus on specific aspects of an organization to a more holistic focus on the entire organization or on the organization and the environment. Many of these most recent models incorporate or accommodate other models (e.g., Birnbaum's cybernetic model, 1988; Gumport and Sporn's adaptive model, 1999).

The Role of Sociology and the Rise of Interdisciplinary Studies

It is obvious that the early organizational models, bureaucracy and community, were direct derivatives of sociology. In the intervening years, many of the models have had a sociological influence or, some would argue, qualify as such because they are studies of organization—a province of sociology. However, the study of colleges and universities as organizations has drawn heavily on many other disciplines: anthropology, organizational and social psychology, political science and public administration, business administration and management, operations research, information sciences, and biology. Perhaps more important, what this interdisciplinary set of sources reflects is the emergence of the field of organizational behavior—an interdisciplinary field of scholars interested in the study of organizations. While many of the early researchers and scholars who studied organizations in higher education were from individual disciplines, most of the more recent ones, especially those trained in higher education programs, come from this background. So it is increasingly difficult to identify work or models as clearly based in sociology.

Internal-External-Holistic Models

It is clear that our early models of organization, such as the bureaucratic and collegial, represented college and university organization from an internally oriented and closed-system perspective. However, in the early 1970s, theorists began to adopt the open-system perspective that was gaining popularity in the broader field of organizational studies. In fact, from 1975 forward, virtually all the models have either explicitly or implicitly taken the open-system perspective. The most recent have encompassed both organization and environment models, explicitly recognizing the legitimacy and importance of both these domains.

In addition to this transition from internal to external focus, our organizational models have changed from an early focus on the specific aspects or dynamics of an organization to a much broader or holistic perspective. For example, the bureaucratic model focused on rational processes and structures, while the later saga, organized anarchy, and cultural models attempted to look at certain other aspects or dynamics of the organization. Even the organization-environment models were initially focused on specific dynamics of that relationship, while later ones included many different aspects of it. For example, the resource-dependence model focused on a specific organizational relationship with the environment through the flow of resources. Later the strategic and matrix models attempted to broaden that relationship but within a rational set of organizational dynamics. The more recent adaptive, contextual, and entrepreneurial models attempt to examine both the environment and the organization from a holistic perspective.

Institutional Theory, Postmodernism, and
Holistic Integrated Frameworks

This chapter has mentioned these three major influences on the analysis of organizational behavior in higher education—institutional theory, postmodernism, and holistic frameworks—but did not portray them as organizational models. While they are widely drawn upon and used today, the argument is that they are not really models of how organizations are structured or how they function. Rather, each is an approach to analyzing colleges and universities as organizations.

Institutional theory looks holistically at the societal context and examines how forces in that environment lead to isomorphic or new legitimized patterns of structure or process. It primarily focuses on a qualitative approach, often incorporating other models to help understand the legitimizing process. Michael Bastedo's recent work on governing boards (2005) and Gumport and Sporn's examination of changing management patterns (1999) are good examples that also incorporate other models into their analyses to explain what is happening. Institutional theory is a very useful analytic approach but lacks the specificity of constructs or concepts of our other models of the organizational behavior itself.

To use holistic integrated frameworks such as that presented in Bolman and Deal's updated *Reframing Organizations* (2003) is an integrative approach to organizational analysis that draws on other models but is not itself a model. For example, the structural (bureaucratic or rational), human resource (people), and political and symbolic (cultural) models are presented as different perspectives or frames that contribute to an integrated mode of analysis to understand organizational dynamics, but they do not present a particular model. Others, such as Bergquist (1992), attempt to integrate several different models to provide a more holistic approach to the cultural model. But this does not develop a well-defined model.

Postmodern theory is a perspective that is not new to sociologists, to other social scientists, nor to organizational scholars in several related professions, including those identified with organizational behavior as a field of study (Gergen 1993). Postmodernism stresses a less rational and formal approach to understanding organizations, focusing on discursive analysis to elicit the meanings and relationships that emerge in organizational life. It has not yet been discussed in the organizational scholarship on higher education to the extent that it has been in other applied professional fields. It often overlaps with, and is implicit in, some approaches to the cultural model. To date it has been the focus of some thoughtful discussions, like Harland G. Bloland's "Postmodernism and Higher Education" (1995), and has had some implicit use in higher education research on certain specific organizational dynamics, such as leadership and decision making (Tierney 1993) and the nature of power (Simsek 1997). However, there is a void in translating postmodern theory to the organizational nature of higher education. And it may even be antithetical to the postmodern perspective to suggest it could become a model!

Thoughts on a Contingency Approach to Organizational Models

This chapter has presented a framework for attempting to understand the development of these multiple and varied models of organization over the past five decades. This contingency framework argues that broad environmental forces and conditions reshape not just our institutions but also our industry. These two sources, environmental conditions and the changing nature of the industry, both present colleges and universities with major academic and management challenges. It is suggested that these challenges—and the ways institutions are shaped by and respond to them with new structures, processes, and other dynamics—provide the impetus for new organizational models to help explain or understand the institutional changes and their new dynamics. Sociology, while not the only contributor to our organizational models, undergirds many of them. Thus it has served as the basis for this contingency examination of our many models of colleges and universities as organizations.

References

Alpert, D. 1985. "Performance and Paralysis: The Organizational Context of the American Research University." *Journal of Higher Education* 56 (3): 241–81.

Baldridge, J. V. 1971a. *Academic Governance: Research on Institutional Politics and Decision Making.* Berkeley, CA: McCutchan.

———. 1971b. *Power and Conflict in the University: Research in the Sociology of Complex Organizations.* New York: Wiley.

Bastedo, M. 2005. "The Making of an Activist Governing Board." *Review of Higher Education* 28 (4): 551–70.

Bergquist, W. H. 1992. *The Four Cultures of the Academy: Insights and Strategies for Improving Leadership in Collegiate Organizations.* San Francisco: Jossey-Bass.

Birnbaum, R. 1988. *How Colleges Work: The Cybernetics of Academic Organization and Leadership.* 1st ed. San Francisco: Jossey-Bass.

Bloland, H. 1995. "Postmodernism and Higher Education." *Journal of Higher Education* 66 (5): 522–59.

Bolman, L. G., and T. E. Deal. 1991. *Reframing Organizations: Artistry, Choice, and Leadership.* San Francisco: Jossey-Bass.

Brewster, K., Jr. 1965. "Future Strategy of the Private University." *Princeton Alumni Weekly*, 45–46.

Carchidi, D. M. 1997. "Virtual Postsecondary Educational Organizations."

Ph.D. dissertation, Center for the Study of Higher and Postsecondary Education, University of Michigan, Ann Arbor.

Carchidi, D. M., and M. W. Peterson. 2000. "Emerging Organizational Structures." *Planning for Higher Education* 28 (3).

Carnegie Commission on Higher Education. 1973. *The Purposes and Performance of Higher Education in the United States.* New York: McGraw Hill.

Chaffee, E. E. 1985a. "The Concept of Strategy: From Business to Higher Education." In *Higher Education: Handbook of Theory and Research,* vol. 1, ed. J. C. Smart, 133–72. New York: Agathon.

———. 1985b. "Three Models of Strategy." *Academic Management Review* 10 (1).

Clark, B. R. 1960. *The Open Door College: A Case Study.* New York: McGraw-Hill.

———. 1970. *The Distinctive College: Antioch, Reed, and Swarthmore.* Chicago: Aldine.

———. 1998. *Creating Entrepreneurial Universities: Organizational Pathways of Transformation.* 1st ed. New York: Pergamon.

———. 2005. *Sustaining Change in Universities.* Maidenhead, UK: Open University Press, McGraw Hill Education.

Cohen, M. D., and J. G. March. 1974. *Leadership and Ambiguity: The American College President.* New York: McGraw-Hill.

Corson, J. J. 1960. *Governance of Colleges and Universities.* New York: McGraw-Hill.

Dill, D. 1981. "The Management of Academic Culture: Notes on the Management of Meaning and Social Integration." In *Organizational Governance in Higher Education,* ed. M. W. Peterson. ASHPE Reader Series 5. Needham Heights, MA: Ginn.

Dill, D. D., and B. Sporn. 1995. *Emerging Patterns of Social Demand and University Reform: Through a Glass Darkly.* 1st ed. Tarrytown, NY: Pergamon.

Gergen, K. J. 1993. "Organization Theory in the Postmodern Era." In *Rethinking Organization: New Directions in Organizational Theory and Analysis,* ed. M. Reed and M. Hughes. London: Sage.

Goodman, P. 1962. *The Community of Scholars.* New York: Random House.

Gumport, P. J., and B. Pusser. 1995. "A Case of Bureaucratic Accretion." *Journal of Higher Education* 66 (5): 493–520.

———. 1999. "University Restructuring: The Role of Economic and Political Contexts." In *Higher Education: Handbook of Theory and Research,* vol. 14, ed. J. C. Smart. New York: Agathon.

Gumport, P. J., and B. Sporn. 1999. "Institutional Adaptation." In *Higher Education: Handbook of Theory and Research,* vol. 14, ed. J. C. Smart. New York: Agathon.

Hearn, J. C. 1988. "Strategy and Resources." In *Higher Education: Handbook of Theory and Research,* vol. 4, ed. J. C. Smart. New York: Agathon.

Henderson, A. 1963. "Improving Decision Making through Research." In *Current Issues in Higher Education*, ed. G. Smith. Washington, DC: American Association of Higher Education.

Hopkins, D. S. P., and W. F. Massy. 1981. *Planning Models for Colleges and Universities*. Stanford, CA: Stanford University Press.

Katz, D., and R. Kahn. 1966. *The Social Psychology of Organizations*. New York: John Wiley and Sons.

Keller, G. 1983. *Academic Strategy: The Management Revolution in American Higher Education*. Baltimore: Johns Hopkins University Press.

Kerr, C. 1993. "Universal Issues in the Development of Higher Education." In *Higher Education in Indonesia: Education and Reform*, ed. J. B. Balderston and F. Balderston. Berkeley: Center for Studies in Higher Education, University of California.

Kotler, P. 1976. *Marketing Management*. Englewood Cliffs, NJ: Prentice-Hall.

Kuh, G. D., and E. J. Whitt. 1988. *The Invisible Tapestry: Culture in American Colleges and Universities*. College Station, TX: Association for the Study of Higher Education.

Lawrence, G. B., and A. L. Service. 1977. *Quantitative Approaches to Higher Education Management: Potential, Limits, and Challenge*. AAHE-ERIC Research Report 4. Washington, DC: American Association of Higher Education.

Lee, E. C., and F. M. Bowen. 1971. *The Multicampus University: A Study of Academic Governance*. New York: McGraw-Hill.

Masland, A. T. 1985. "Organizational Culture in the Study of Higher Education." *Review of Higher Education* 8 (2).

McConnell, T. R. 1963. "Needed Research in College and University Organization and Administration." In *The Study of Academic Organizations*, ed. T. Lunsford. Boulder: Western Interstate Commission for Higher Education.

Meyer, J. W., and B. Rowan. 1978. "The Structure of Educational Organizations." In *Environments and Organizations*, ed. M. W. Meyer and associates. San Francisco: Jossey-Bass.

Millett, J. D. 1962. *The Academic Community: An Essay on Organization*. New York: McGraw-Hill.

National Commission on Excellence in Education. 1983. *A Nation at Risk: The Imperative for Educational Reform; A Report to the Nation and the Secretary of Education, United States Department of Education*. Washington, DC: National Commission on Excellence in Education.

NCPI (National Center for Postsecondary Improvement). 2001. "Resurveying the Terrain: Refining the Taxonomy for the Postsecondary Market." *Change Magazine*, March/April. Written as part of the Landscape series, without attribution, by Robert Zemsky.

Peterson, M. W. 1974. "Organization and Administration in Higher Education:

Sociological and Social-Psychological Perspectives." In *Review of Research in Education,* ed. F. Kerlinger. Itasca, IL: Peacock.

———. 1980. "Analyzing Alternative Approaches to Planning." In *Improving Academic Management: Handbook of Planning and Institutional Research,* ed. P. Jedamus and M. W. Peterson and associates. San Francisco: Jossey-Bass.

———. 1985. "Emerging Developments in Postsecondary Organization Theory and Research: Fragmentation or Integration." *Educational Researcher,* March.

———. 1986. "Continuity, Challenge, and Change." *Planning for Higher Education* 14 (3).

———. 1997. "Using Contextual Planning to Transform Universities." In *Planning and Management for a Changing Environment,* ed. M. W. Peterson, D. D. Dill, L. A. Mets, and associates. San Francisco: Jossey-Bass.

Peterson, M. W., and D. D. Dill. 1997. "Understanding the Competitive Environment of the Postsecondary Knowledge Industry." In *Planning and Management for a Changing Environment,* ed. M. W. Peterson, D. D. Dill, L. A. Mets, and associates. San Francisco: Jossey-Bass.

Peterson, M. W., D. D. Dill, L. A. Mets, and associates, eds. 1997. *Planning and Management for a Changing Environment: A Handbook on Redesigning Postsecondary Institutions.* 1st ed. San Francisco: Jossey-Bass.

Peterson, M. W., and M. Spencer. 1993. "Qualitative and Quantitative Approaches to Academic Culture." In *Higher Education: Handbook of Theory and Research,* vol. 9, ed. J. C. Smart, 344–88. New York: Agathon.

Peterson, M. W., et al. 1978. *Black Students on White Campuses: The Impacts of Increased Black Enrollments.* Ann Arbor, MI: Institute for Social Research.

Pfeffer, J., and G. R. Salancik. 1978. *The External Control of Organizations: A Resource Dependence Perspective.* New York: Harper and Row.

Porter, M. E. 1980. *Competitive Strategy.* New York: Free Press.

Presley, J. B., and D. W. Leslie. 1999. "Understanding Strategy: An Assessment of Theory and Practice." In *Higher Education: Handbook of Theory and Research,* vol. 14, ed. J. C. Smart. New York: Agathon.

Rudolph, F. 1962. *The American College and University.* New York: Vintage.

Simsek, H. 1997. "The Power of Symbolic Constructs in Reading Change in Higher Education." *Higher Education* 33 (3).

Simsek, H., and K. S. Louis. 1994. "Organizational Change as Paradigm Shift." *Journal of Higher Education* 65 (5).

Slaughter, S., and L. L. Leslie. 1997. *Academic Capitalism: Politics, Policies, and the Entrepreneurial University.* Baltimore: Johns Hopkins University Press.

Sporn, B. 1999. *Adaptive University Structures.* London: Jessica Kingsley.

Stroup, H. H. 1966. *Bureaucracy in Higher Education.* New York: Free Press.

Study Group on the Conditions of Excellence in American Higher Education, National Institute of Education. 1984. *Involvement in Learning: Realizing the*

Potential of American Higher Education. Washington, DC: National Institute of Education, U.S. Department of Education.

Tierney, W. G. 1990. *Assessing Academic Climates and Cultures.* San Francisco: Jossey-Bass.

———. 1993. *Building Communities of Difference: Higher Education in the Twenty-first Century.* Westport, CT: Bergin and Garvey.

Weick, K. E. 1976. "Educational Organizations as Loosely Coupled Systems." *Administrative Science Quarterly* 21 (1): 1–19.

Whitehead, A. N. 1928. "Universities and Their Functions." *Atlantic Monthly* 141 (5).

III EMERGING LINES OF INQUIRY

7 Higher Education as an Institution

JOHN W. MEYER, FRANCISCO O. RAMIREZ,

DAVID JOHN FRANK, AND

EVAN SCHOFER

It is common to analyze higher education in concrete terms, as a set of specific and local organizations, roles, interactions, and economic transactions. Such analyses may start with particular individual students, as persons, sitting in classrooms with particular teachers and peers, studying specific topics, in a specific organizational context. Or they may situate the university and students within the context of an immediate labor market and economy, with associated individual and collective demands and interests. But in the alternative sociological institutionalist perspective of this chapter, one can view higher education as deeply affected by—indeed, something of an enactment of—structures whose nature and meaning have been institutionalized over many centuries and now apply throughout the world. The meaning of categories such as student, professor, university, or graduate, or of topics such as physics or literature, may be locally shaped in minor ways but at the same time have very substantial historical and global standing. These wider meanings obviously have pervasive impacts on the content and character of local settings, and they help explain many of the features and effects of higher education that seem problematic from other analytical purchases.

In this chapter, we consider how viewing higher education as an institution helps explain many of its characteristics and its effects in modern society. Sociological institutional theory in part arose from studies in the sociology of education (Meyer 1970, 1977; Meyer and Rowan 1977), and it turns out to have considerable leverage vis-à-vis the

The ideas presented here reflect collaborative work carried out over a good many years, as referenced in the text. Work on the paper itself was supported by grants (to Francisco Ramirez and John Meyer) from the Freeman Spogli Institute of Stanford University and from the Spencer Foundation (20060003).

analysis of higher education in the modern world. In general, institutional views stress the dependence of local social organization on wider environmental meanings, definitions, rules, and models. The dependence involved goes well beyond what is normally thought of as causal influence in the social sciences: in institutional thinking, environments *constitute* local situations—establishing and defining their core entities, purposes, and relations.

This line of thought is exceptionally useful in analyzing higher education for two reasons. First, in contrast to particularizing views, an institutional perspective supports the realization that local higher-educational arrangements are very heavily dependent on broader institutions—even more than most local work organizations are. This means, on the one hand, that it is difficult to create a university if the concept "university" is not available in the wider cultural and organizational environments. On the other hand, if the environment does contain a blueprint or model, then the whole founding process turns out to be easy. And in fact—as Figure 7.1 illustrates—thousands of universities have appeared over recent decades, with enormous and ever-growing numbers of students.

Second, in contrast to conventional views, seeing higher education as an institution directs one's attention to the cultural scripts and organizational rules built into the wider national and world environments that establish the main features of local situations. In its central "university" form, higher education has a history of almost a millennium, and throughout the whole period it has nearly monopolized some very central steps in the implementation of Western and now world cognitive models of progress and justice, models now echoing and circulating through the excellence (progress) and equity (justice) themes so prevalent in higher education. Universities and colleges, together with their disciplinary fields and academic roles, are defined, measured, and instantiated in essentially every country in explicitly global terms and are so reported to international institutions like UNESCO (United Nations Educational, Social, and Cultural Organization). They are thus sharply attuned to transnational ratings and world standards, which contain heroic accounts of fair and equitable universities to be emulated everywhere. Even rather recent university creations such as "professors of sociology" enjoy global and practically universal status (analogous to that of rabbis or priests), and occupants of such positions can travel the world interacting with reciprocally recognized peers. Moreover, a proliferation of world conferences and international associations reflect a

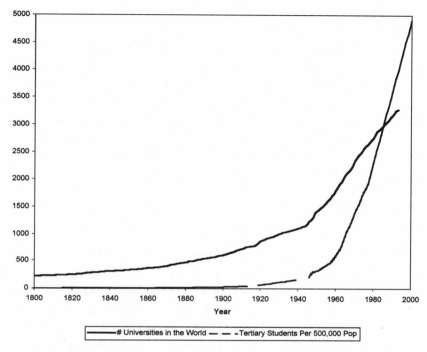

Figure 7.1. Worldwide expansion of universities and postsecondary enrollments, 1800–2000. *Sources:* Banks 2001; Schofer and Meyer 2005; UNESCO
2000, 2004.

broad array of disciplines, interdisciplinarities, professions, theories,
and research applications that presuppose common models of progress
and justice as they further their higher-educational reach. Conferences
and associations—indeed, universities themselves—are carriers of wider
environmental models, sites for their theoretical elaboration, and ultimately they depend on these cultural models for their legitimacy.

It thus makes good sense to look at higher education as an institution
and to consider the consequences of its extensive and intensive institutionalization. We do this in several steps. First, we briefly review the
emergent tradition of sociological institutionalism, emphasizing its core
ideas. Then, in the main body of the chapter, we discuss the explanatory
ideas that this line of theory has contributed to the sociological analysis
of higher education.

Sociological Institutional Theory

Institutional theory arose in reaction both to functionalism and to the various strands of Marxist/conflict theory that dominated American sociology in the 1970s. These sociological perspectives sought to explain the production of social structures in terms of the functional needs or the power and interests of actors operating in local situations. In contrast, institutional theory emphasizes that local organizations arise in good measure independent of local circumstances—deriving from wider sociocultural environments that support and even require local structuration around exogenous models and meanings. Three main ideas elucidate this perspective (for more extensive reviews, see Thomas et al. 1987; Meyer et al. 1997; Jepperson 2002; Hasse and Kruecken 2005).

Institutional Environments Constitute Local Structures

A first central theme of institutional theory—that environments supply the blueprints and building blocks of local structures—has been explored both generally and in the context of higher education at the levels of persons, organizations, and societies. These analytical levels themselves are elaborately institutionalized in a set of cultural assumptions and organizational rules that establish the framework of modern societies.

At the level of persons, the modern life course or career is heavily patterned on exogenous models and definitions—including those that define virtually all contemporary persons as "individuals" (Meyer 1977; Meyer and Jepperson 2000). By law, individuals must attend primary schools in countries worldwide (Ramirez and Ventresca 1992), and advanced educational certificates are commonly required to gain entry into desirable occupational and training arenas (Brint 1998; Brown 2001). The education-occupation link encompasses a thick layer of institutional definitions, which have rather distant relations to actual role performance. In the modern world, it does one little good to possess the skills of a university graduate if one lacks proper certification from a properly accredited university. Conversely, if an individual does carry the right documentation, his or her actual abilities are often treated as secondary matters (Collins 1971).

Organizationally, the existence and legitimation capacity of rulelike external models are crucial to the creation and stabilization of all sorts of everyday structures (Meyer and Rowan 1977). Firms, hospitals, and government agencies do not generally spring from local soils if their forms are not prefabricated and available in the institutional environment (Scott 2002). The dependence on external cultural models is even more extreme for schools and universities, given their cultural centrality (despite task ambiguity and goal complexity). Yet when higher-educational organizational models are globally institutionalized, specific instances can—and do—arise, essentially everywhere.

At the societal level, taken-for-granted cultural and organizational models contribute greatly to the apparatus of the nation-state (Anderson 1991; Meyer et al. 1997), including the content and scope of citizenship (Ramirez, Soysal, and Shanahan 1997). At the same time, world scripts define the features of proper social organization—for example, regarding health (Inoue 2003) and the natural environment (Frank, Hironaka, and Schofer 2000). Of course, education is central in all these models, and not surprisingly, schooling arrangements in particular countries dramatically reflect wider world patterns, as discussed below.

Institutionalized Models Reflect Collective and Cultural Processes

A generation of research has provided powerful support for the first proposition above. But this raises forcefully the following research question: if external cultural models drive local social organization, where do these models come from? Some sociologies argue that dominant models (a) reflect the interests and powers of the strongest actors in the environment or (b) emerge from evolutionary selection or functional adaptation.

Both lines of argument fall short in the modern system. Neither easily explains many of the world's most dynamic movements. Powerful nation-states and dominant corporations did little to spur the massive environmental protection (Frank et al. 1999) and human rights movements (Ramirez and Meyer 2002). Nor did they, in reality, lead modern world movements for scientific expansion (Drori et al. 2003; Schofer 1999) or organizational rationalization (Drori, Meyer, and Hwang 2006). Nor did they fuel various worldwide movements around education, such as Education for All (Chabbott 2002) or higher education's enrollment explosion (Schofer and Meyer 2005). And while ex post facto accounts can attribute functional qualities to environmental protection, human rights, etc., empirical evidence of their supposed benefits is often fleeting (see, e.g., Schofer, Ramirez, and Meyer 2000 on the science-development tie).

Institutional arguments point out that all these broad social movements are shaped by highly institutionalized collective authorities—many associated with the university. These authorities eschew sectarian interests and instead putatively represent common goods and universal truths (Meyer and Jepperson 2000). In all the cases listed above, professionals imbued with authority from the knowledge system and the sciences play agenda-setting roles. So do the widest variety of nongovernmental associations (Boli and Thomas 1999), operating on both national and global scales. And so do social movements operating in the same ways. Professionals, associations, and social movements—in the name of collective interests—function as creators and carriers of national and world models in the modern system. And finally, institutionalists call attention to the ways the world's stratification system upholds successful cases operating as admired models, rather than as simply working through power and dominance.

Enacted Institutional Models Are Likely to be Disconnected from Local Practice and Realities

As emphasized above, institutional theories envision local structures as embodying wider models. Such models facilitate and direct local organizing, and local situations gain meaning, authority, and legitimacy by conforming. If a local business gains stability by organizing according to standard legal and professional models, it is even truer that a local university—lacking production or profit as guide—lives and dies by its formal conformity to wider rules.

A powerful implication of the institutional perspective here is obvious: it is often more important to embody exogenously legitimated proprieties than it is to adapt these forms to local possibilities and demands. In institutional theory, the gap between the legitimated model and its immediate enactment is referred to as "loose coupling" or "decoupling" (Meyer and Rowan 1977; Meyer and Scott 1983; Weick 1976). Vis-à-vis higher education, it is clear that universities must observe proper standards formally, whether or not they can be maintained in practice. Thus, for example, a formal commitment to faculty research must be made even by a resource-starved university. Likewise, high admissions standards can have loopholes that distort outcomes without overtly challenging meritocratic ideals. Even when the gap is noted, the formally compliant university gets credit for at least playing by the rules of the game.

Institutional Explanations in Higher Education

Having reviewed some core ideas of institutional theory in sociology, we turn to the lines of argument and research these ideas put forward. A good deal of empirical research is involved, but also much reinterpretation of existing findings.

Explaining Global Isomorphism and Isomorphic Change

The University Is a World Institution. Given the enormous variation in social, cultural, and economic conditions within countries and (even more) across the world, most lines of sociological theory would predict extreme variation in the character of educational institutions in different national or regional locales and very different trajectories of growth and change. Institutional theories, fairly uniquely, predict isomorphism and isomorphic change.

This is perhaps the single most important implication arising from institutional theory. If higher educational structures, like universities and colleges, reflect common models in national or world environments, they should show unexpected similarities across diverse settings and change in similar ways over time. And by all accounts, the university is indeed a central historic global institution, core to the distinctive trajectory of Western and now world society (see, e.g., Eisenstadt 1986, 1987 on the heteronomy of intellectuals).

The empirical literature provides clear evidence on this issue. Educational systems are remarkably similar around the world, and increasingly so over time. Historically, higher education, taking the form of the university, spread around the world with a great deal of isomorphism in aspiration and content (Riddle 1989, 1993). The university's medieval roots were cosmopolitan and universal, and it spread wherever the Western system spread, retaining universalistic aspirations (Rashdall 1895/1987); Thorndike 1944; Altbach 1998). The same isomorphism holds in research on the diffusion and cross-national expansion of the university in the contemporary period. Paul Windolf (1997) shows that similar patterns of higher-educational expansion characterize several different Western countries. Evan Schofer and John W. Meyer (2005), meanwhile, find consistent patterns of enrollment growth worldwide over the twentieth century, especially the last half-century.

Second, studies that attend to the curricular content of the university show the same patterns. The university evolved as a global institution, retaining much of its medieval cultural character through most of the eighteenth century, then shifting into a more modern and scientific mode in the nineteenth century and into an even broader rationalism in the twentieth century. David Frank and Joy Gabler (2006; Gabler and Frank 2005) analyze changes in faculty composition across a set of universities worldwide through most of the twentieth century and show consistent global trends and increasing isomorphism over time, which yielded dramatically expanded emphasis on the social sciences, sharply contracted attention to the humanities, and slightly weakened focus on the natural sciences. Across the branches of learning, the so-called applied fields outperform their so-called basic counterparts (Brint 2002b). Gili S. Drori and Hyeyoung Moon (2006) and Francisco Ramirez and C. Min Wotipka (2001) show the same patterns in analyzing student enrollments by field for the last third of the century. Even when examining prestigious outliers like Oxford, one finds that the curricular trends therein parallel world trends (Ramirez 2006a).

Third, the global character of the institution is indicated by its own self-referential conceptions. Schools identify themselves with the category "university" and vigorously seek to be accredited as such, enhancing their longevity in doing so. As Clark Kerr famously notes (1987 and elsewhere), most of the really long-lived organizations in the world are universities. Phyllis Riddle (1989) furthermore notes that higher-educational institutions go to great lengths to portray themselves as universities, often parading unrealistic institutional histories or self-portraits with much of the "invention of tradition" typical of nation-states themselves (Hobsbawm and Ranger 1983).

The University as a National Institution and Organizational Form. With the breakdown of integrated medieval Christendom and the rise of the Westphalian Europe of nation-states, the university tended to become disconnected from the church and empire and closely linked to the emergent national (and subnational) states. In terms of cultural content and the nature of academic authority, it retained its global and universalistic forms and aspirations. But organizationally, the nineteenth-century universities generally became more nationalized, leading to their depiction as "laboratories of nationalism" (Reisner 1922) and supporters of the national project (Readings 1996).

So studies that attend to the organizational form of the university tend to emphasize a very different pattern from the culturally globalized one noted above. If the university is, in terms of cultural content, surprisingly homogeneous around the world—and tends to be isomorphic in change trajectories—it is organizationally quite variable across national boundaries, and sometimes across strata or category within national states. For instance, countries differ dramatically on how much their higher education is public or private (Levy 1986). They differ greatly and systematically on patterns of organizational structure and control: the landmark studies undertaken by Burton Clark and his many colleagues provide very dramatic evidence on the extreme organizational differences in variables like degree of university (or professorial) autonomy and differentiation (Clark 1983, 1987, or even 1998; see also Schriewer 2004).

Studies in this tradition also suggest some qualifications on overall generalizations about isomorphism. These studies see cross-national variations in organizational structure as also affecting variations in the cultural content carried and transmitted by the university. Some university systems are relatively closed to change and to broad linkages to changing societies, while others are strikingly open (Ben-David and Zlockzower 1962; see the detailed contrast between German and U.S. universities in Lenhardt 2005). Ramirez (2002, 2006a, 2006b) also emphasizes these differences, contrasting the American tendency to celebrate university linkages with society (e.g., in the land-grant universities) with European traditions that create sharp boundaries against society (as in Germanic cases).

Ramirez's observation calls attention to a central distinction. The university, practically everywhere, claims an intimate tie to a universal and global or cosmopolitan knowledge system. But in the whole modern period, it brings this knowledge to bear within the frame of a particular (commonly national) polity (this is also a central point made by Riddle 1989). And its organizational structure, as opposed to its cultural content and authority, reflects the organization of that particular polity or state. Thus, U.S. universities often develop as private formal organizations, with a good deal of embeddedness in both the "civil society" and market structure, while continental universities operate more directly under the authority of the bureaucratic state.

In a sense, the organizational structures of higher education reflect political institutional frames rather than educational ones. In more centralized polities, universities tend to be more centrally authorized and funded, and professors are more likely to be national civil servants (Ramirez and Rubinson 1979). One main implication of this difference is that in more centralized polities, perceived success or failure in higher education is more likely to be attributed to the state or to a national educational ministry than to an entrepreneurial university president or a friendly benefactor. And thus reforms to repair perceived failure are likely to occur through more centralist routes. But this difference in the locus of the perceived success or failure account is not likely to correlate strongly with differences in the actual content of instruction and research. For this reason, few empirical studies find tight linkages between the organizational structures of higher education and the actual content of instruction and research (but see Lenhardt 2005 for examples of exceptions). For instance, the centrality of the study of social inequality in our own field of sociology holds true across national systems of higher education, despite well-known organizational differences.

Moreover, what nation-state-based variations have occurred in university contents appear to have waned over time. Cross-national differences among overall academic profiles declined over the twentieth century (Frank and Gabler 2006), and across a broad sample of universities worldwide, the field of history became increasingly less oriented to particular nation-states (Frank et al. 2000).

This increased homogeneity now seems to extend even to the organizational structures of higher education. Ironically, the European countries that led the breakdown of the more cosmopolitan medieval university system and tied the university closely to the emergent national state now experience a concerted effort at organizational isomorphism. The "Bologna Process," reflecting recent agreements at standardization, is having great impacts on university systems throughout the continent (see, e.g., Kruecken and Meier 2006, Teichler 2002).

Overall, higher-educational systems exhibit even more isomorphism nationally than globally—topics, fields, and credentials tend to have many commonalities (for a comparison of trends in the history curricula at Harvard and Wisconsin over the twentieth century, see Frank, Schofer, and Torres 1994). For example, the contents of syllabi in the sociology of education field exhibit little dependence on the legal status of the university, its overall prestige, or the extent of federal grants awarded to its faculty (see the American Sociological Association's website for a collection of sociology of education syllabi). Successful innovations are copied throughout national systems (Kraatz and Zajac 1996; Soule 1997 and forthcoming). This is especially notable in U.S. higher education. The U.S. system (a) is very weakly controlled by integrated political authorities, (b) has very diverse constituency bases, and (c) has widely varying levels of resources. Nevertheless, there is surprising homogeneity in definitions, content areas, degrees, and the like. Students in all sorts of schools are seen as "college students," and graduates have surprisingly similar rights and opportunities (but see Karabel 2005; Dougherty 1994). And many analyses of the individual effects of higher education show very weak effects of school characteristics, in comparison to the background properties of the individual students themselves.

In countries in which higher education is more centrally controlled, schools are sometimes structured in clearly distinct categories with sharply different status and rights. Here, national-level institutions yield distinctive charters that sharply differentiate among schools and students (Meyer 1970, 1977). Formal differentiation can occur along axes of stratification (as between universities and polytechnics in some countries) or along disciplinary boundaries (e.g., special universities of engineering or science). In some such instances, very substantial distinctions between the opportunities available to students follow.

Expanded Higher Education as Support for the Nation-State of High Modernity

Clearly, there are worldwide models for higher education, and these models render higher education essential to the successful nation-state. And in fact, higher education spreads in rather standardized forms wherever the nation-state system spreads. This means that universities typically emerge concomitant with independent national identities and state organizations.

But none of the models involved are static, nor are their real-world embodiments. With the consolidation of the nation-state system around the turn of the nineteenth century, and then its spread to the New World and diffusion worldwide, the globally institutionalized model of higher education expanded and changed. Thus, countries were dealing with moving targets. Institutional theory, as discussed above, helps explain why higher education around the world reflects common models. It also helps explain why these common models promoted almost universal higher-educational expansion in the period from around 1800 to World War II.

Higher Education and Modernity. During the nineteenth century, the competitive nation-state moved rapidly to claim authority over and responsibility for governing domestic and international public life. The nation-state's goals, increasingly, were rationalized under the rubrics of "progress" and "justice," and its competence to produce these goals was rooted in a newly emerging knowledge system (Toulmin 1989; Schofer 2001, 2003). The imagined powers of science and rationality took on mythic status during this period, as did notions of a national or civilizational high culture descending variously from Athens, Rome, or Jerusalem.

Higher education, increasingly through the century, became the institutional locus of this new knowledge system. The old university of the early modern period—training a very few priests, lawyers, doctors, and teachers—came to life. More rapid expansion began—in the sheer number of universities, in the number of countries with universities, in student enrollments, and in the range of scholarly topics. Higher education, which had grown slowly and steadily through previous centuries, embarked on a rapid upward trajectory (Riddle 1989). Because higher education was expanding as a model-driven institution—growing to produce a progressive and equitable future rather than to manage a stable society—it expanded on a very widespread basis. Growth occurred not simply in areas with industrial or commercial development but everywhere the new model of national society spread. Higher education expanded both in developed Europe and in rural America, for instance. Later, much of this expansion would be justified in terms of human capital (as progress) and of citizenship and human rights (as justice).

Modernity and the Survival and Growth of the University. One core problem in the study of the historical development of higher education is the survival and growth of the university as its key locus. Over the last two centuries, there have been many clear practical and theoretical reasons why it should have lost out in the long-term expansion of higher education. Around the turn of the nineteenth century, critics accused the university of being archaic, linked to the old regime and its culture, and in need of replacement by specialized education in emergent sciences and technologies. Thus late into the nineteenth century, Andrew Carnegie lamented that the worst thing that could happen to a young man was to get a college education. It was thought that a new system was needed, attuned to the specializations required by a more complex and differentiated economy, state, and society.

In more radical countries, the university was indeed partially replaced. In France, a set of specialized institutions for state service appeared. The United States, through the Jacksonian destruction of core elite monopolies (Hofstadter 1963), witnessed the rise of a college system. In other countries such as Germany and Spain, a wave of university deaths also occurred (Riddle 1989, 1993). By the end of the nineteenth century, however, the university was back everywhere.

The explanatory question is why the modernizing differentiating society did not, as many expected and sought (or feared), generate specialized training institutions linked to its structural needs but rather returned to—and expanded—the university. By the end of the twentieth century, the process had gone so far that in many countries, even business had found a home in universities (Moon 2002), as had ethnic and women's studies programs, influenced by multiculturalism and other innovations in inclusiveness (Brint 2005).

To understand this, it is important to look at the institutionalized cultural base underlying nineteenth-century modernity's extensive claims to technical sophistication. Taken at face value, these might indeed have required a good deal of specialized higher-educational training. But these claims, more than reflecting functional realities of society at the time, constituted rather a myth of the unified authority, power, and sovereignty of the growing nation-state. The university may have been an inefficient producer of actual governing capabilities at the individual level, but it was an excellent locus of expanded governmentality at the collective level (Foucault 1991). It supported a claim to unified knowledge and authority, rooted in the most universal principles. In other words, the university supported the production of a whole system of knowledge together with assumptions about the world, more than it supported the installation of knowledge itself. The university qua institution, in short, was more important (and efficient) than the university as organization.

Any realistic examination of the curriculum of the nineteenth-century university, in practically any country, makes the situation clear (Frank and Meyer 2006). At that time, the university was sustaining a high rationalistic (and national or civilizational) culture, more than training people for positions in the differentiated society. At the supposedly land-grant University of Wisconsin in 1879, for example, fully 32 percent of the students were studying the Ancient Classical curriculum, built around Latin and Greek, and another 39 were studying the Modern Classical curriculum, in which French or German replaced Greek. The rise of our own field of sociology, at the end of the century, furthermore illustrates the point: in the complete absence of useful knowledge or technical sophistication, sociology arose on the claim that a whole arena of human life could be analyzed and managed in light of scientific principles—principles that were as yet unknown but were to be created in the future (Hamilton and Sutton 1989).

The unity of the university survived, thus, as a core cultural base of high modernity, not as an effective training system for the human parts of the new machine. Newman, Humboldt, and Hutchins live on in the history of the university as core enactors of the "city of intellect" (Brint 2002), not as successful organizational leaders or managers.

Globalization and the Postnational University

Parallel to the explanatory points about the expansion (and survival) of the university in the period of high national modernity, similar issues have developed for the period since World War II.

Explaining Global Expansion. A key elucidating question is why higher education expanded so explosively beginning about 1955. The facts of the matter are not in dispute. In 1900, less than 1 percent of a global cohort could be found in higher education. In 1950, the number was up to perhaps 2–3 percent. Now, it is around 20 percent (Schofer and Meyer 2005). A country like Kazakhstan now has about as many university students as the whole world had in 1900. Note that this expansion was based on opening the doors to various segments of the population that had been historically excluded from the university just about everywhere—most prominently, women. After World War II, the number of women in higher education increased both as a proportion of the age cohort and as a share of total tertiary enrollments (Bradley and Ramirez 1996). The expansion took place across curricular domains (Ramirez and Wotipka 2001). Women's share of university places increased even at the most elite institutions, including Oxford (Soares 1999) and in the Ivy League (Karabel 2005). Also during this period, the university's curricular coverage expanded greatly, bringing all sorts of matters into university focus that had for centuries been excluded. The rise of the social sciences, undoubtedly, is the most striking such change. Absent world models of progress and justice and their national and local enactments, it is difficult to make sense of these ongoing world trends.

Classic functionalist explanations (left or right) fail to explain the university's extraordinary recent expansion: there is simply no evidence whatsoever that the growth was mainly driven by the integrative needs of the social order or by the requirements of class reproduction. In terms of role training, the occupational structures of developed countries shifted steadily over the whole century, with no dramatic or discontinuous leap in professionalization after World War II that would account for intensified growth (see also Windolf 1997). Moreover, university expansion characterized the poor or developing countries almost as much as the developed ones.

Competition and conflict explanations are often employed (Collins 1971, 1979; Boudon 1973; Bourdieu and Passeron 1977; and others). The idea is that with mass educational expansion, status-competition and group-competition processes shift to the higher educational level, and inflationary expansion results. It is generally argued that this process occurs in weak or decentralized states, which are unable to stop it. (This is one classic explanation of rapid and early American expansion.) But this explanatory story has limits. First, it does not explain why education becomes, worldwide, the legitimated principal basis of status competition. Second, it does not explain why elites powerful enough to control success educationally would keep expanding education rather than simply restricting access for their lower-status competitors (Rubinson 1986). And third, it does not explain why modern societies and their elites generally proclaim the value of university expansion rather than worrying about the overeducation involved. Indeed in previous periods, much elite concern about overexpanded higher education could be found (Shils 1971; Dore 1976; Freeman 1976). For one thing, it was seen as inefficient; for another, it was seen as generating excessive social aspirations and expectations, and thus anomie. Such ideas now seem to have lost legitimacy and almost disappeared: the World Bank, in supporting expanded and improved higher education for the whole developing world, does not mention them (World Bank 2000).

Concerns about the putative inefficiencies and anomie-generating consequences of "overeducation" can still be found in some elite quarters, perhaps especially in Europe. But elites and political forces have been completely ineffective in actually constraining the explosive current expansion of higher education (Schofer and Meyer 2005). And the current European "Bologna Process" in fact involves a number of pressures for continued rapid expansion. Interestingly, the only elites in the postwar world that had the will and power to slow or block expansion were the communist parties. Concerned to match education with national needs, and even more concerned to block the rise of schooled elites that would weaken the proletariat and its party, Eastern country after country in fact slowed higher educational expansion in the 1970s and 1980s. The story is told in detail by Gero Lenhardt and Manfred Stock (2000 and elsewhere).

The decline of the idea of overeducation assessed in relation to the needs of national society turns out to be a key to the expansion question. In the prewar period of high modernity, nation-state society was the clear locus of higher education. This society was seen as a bounded corporate body with a limited set of available roles: education was supposed to produce people in numbers appropriate to this relatively fixed role structure. World War II, a depression, human-rights disasters, a cold war, decolonization, and the emergent nuclear age all undercut the legitimacy of this brand of nationalist and corporatist imagery (Djelic 1998). The dominance of the United States in the post–World War II period—much more liberal and vastly less corporatist than the former European powers—furthered the shift. The emergent model of society was more conceptually fluid and increasingly oriented toward an expanding world society. Thus the fashionable notion of "globalization" points to fundamental changes not only in production and exchange systems and governance structures but also in cognitive models of society (Robertson 1992), changes increasingly extending to all humanity (Boli 2005).

According to the new and resolutely optimistic model of society, individual and social progress could be achieved everywhere. Development theories became widespread, guiding the main world policies of dominant countries and institutions like the World Bank and the United Nations. Individual development—meaning education—would produce (practically by definition) social progress, and with it a more just and equitable order. Thus in the new cultural and organizational blueprints, education was by no means treated as a training ground for a fixed set of roles in a stable national social order. It was rather the root source of human, social, cultural, and economic capital. In the new model, there could never be too much—more education was always better. Thus educational expansion acquired the highest legitimacy in terms of both individual and collective good. In this way, a new globally institutionalized model of society generated a new and expanded model of higher education, and explosive growth resulted worldwide (Schofer and Meyer 2005).

Explaining the Success of the University in the Context of Globalization. The huge contemporary expansion of higher education occurs mainly in integrated institutions claiming university-equivalent academic status. But despite the striking success of the university—multiplication in its numbers, explosion in its enrollments, proliferation in its direct objects of study, etc.—an elaborate popular and academic literature bemoans crisis and breakdown in the present context. On the research side, the core of the university is seen as fragmenting in the face of funding and pressures from a variety of applied interests in society (Slaughter and Leslie 1997; Kirp 2003). On the teaching side, the university's core is thought to be breaking down under the joint pressures of extreme modern specialization, applied and vocational training, competition from the nonacademic world, and the loss of central academic values (Gumport 2000). Mostly these changes are depicted fearfully, as cultural destruction (Readings 1996; Aronowitz 2000). Sometimes they are accepted—and even lauded—as the necessary triumph of organizational rationality and efficiency, as in the celebration of entrepreneurial universities (Clark 1998; Branscomb and Keller 1998).

The university's present triumph and success as a global institution, in other words, is also one in which fragmentation and breakdown are envisioned. In this sense, the present period parallels the nineteenth century, which was rife with fears and hopes about the university's breakdown.

The explanatory task is simply to understand, much as in the previous era, why the complex and differentiated postnational society does not create a completely differentiated set of research and training institutions to support its elaborated and specialized role structure. The core answer is that the postnational society, like the earlier modern one, rests on a bed of cultural assumptions involving universalistic values, human empowerment, scientific knowledge, and rationality. The university—while inefficient at preparing people for specialized roles, in comparison to direct role-training arrangements—is extremely well positioned to support precisely such generalized notions. Students learn—and society itself learns—that all the specialized and professionalized roles of contemporary society are fundamentally based on universal scientific knowledge and rationality and that with schooling ordinary persons can be transformed to possess the relevant competencies. Actual role training is not the point—if it were, the university would indeed weaken and fragment, and more efficient competitors would win out. In an odd way, this emphasis on a schooled consciousness in the modern system reflects or reactivates an older notion of natural law to which modern doctrines of rationality and scientific knowledge are subordinated. The issue is beyond the aims of this paper but is worth analysis.

The institutional point is that postnational society, much like its national counterpart, ultimately rests on faith in science, rationality, and human capability, much like religious understandings. The unified university, no matter how inefficient at teaching specific occupational roles, is ideally set up to celebrate the unity of knowledge and cultural authority and to affirm the extraordinary human capacity for agency in acting in the newly global world.

The University and the Global "Knowledge Society." The comments above suggest that the much-heralded "knowledge society" is more important and realistic as a set of assumptions and cultural claims than it is as an actual depiction of a mundane social order. Only a very few countries could even plausibly be described as possessing a "knowledge economy." And even in these, as we detail below, links between the university and the role system prove surprisingly weak. Indeed, many headliners in the technology industry, including Bill Gates and Steve Jobs, do not possess a university degree.

Yet the myth of the "knowledge society" is very much at the heart of the university's centrality in the postnational and increasingly global world. The present-day liberal world polity places great demands on social actors—nation-states, organizations, and individuals—to act in behalf of a variety of private and public ends. The global knowledge-society myth empowers these actors and provides the basis for coordination among them—resulting in much more action (collective and otherwise) than one might expect (Olson 1971; Drori et al. 2003; Drori, Meyer, and Hwang 2006). The university, science, and rationalized knowledge together supply a symbolic infrastructure that sustains the status of individuals and states as what are now called "actors" and provides the basis for order in a globalized but stateless world. In this sense, the postmodern world bears some similarities to nineteenth-century America, as analyzed by Alexis de Tocqueville. Bringing order into their stateless world, the Americans then celebrated—precisely as the global system now does—individual empowerment and capacity, scientific and metascientific principles, and the benefits of organizational rationalization. At the center of all these, the Americans placed a rapidly expanding system of education, precisely as the whole world does now.

The myth of the knowledge society makes it seem reasonable to suppose that our world can be held together by expanded and competent persons schooled in a common objective culture of science and rationality. The supposition is only partly unrealistic. As Yehudi Cohen (1970) presciently noted some decades ago, our world is now criss-crossed by university-educated elites who share a great deal of cultural material (Nussbaum 1997). The elites of many countries, it seems, communicate more easily with elites elsewhere than with the parochial populations of their own citizenries.

Indeed, scientific and university elites play a central role in global society, bolstered by the knowledge-society myth. Scientists and expert knowledge form the basis for much international mobilization and coordination. University-trained experts carry policy models around the world, acting as diffusers and receivers of innovations (Frank et al. 2000). For instance, university-trained economists played a key role in establishing neoliberalism in Latin America (Fourcade-Gourinchas and Babb 2002). Likewise, scientists have played a critical role in spreading global environmentalism (Frank et al. 2000; Hironaka 2003). Indeed, much contemporary social change—on issues such as the environment, human rights, indigenous people's movements, economic policy, and the like—can be traced in some significant part to a global web of "knowledge society" participants. (See, e.g., Suarez 2005 on human rights–education professionals.)

Globalization and the associated powerful myths of a knowledge society not only drive university expansion around the world but also produce major changes in organizational structures. World society has no regulating and sheltering Ministry of Education under whose dictates a traditionally academic university could operate. It is an open and competitive place, much like the American society of de Tocqueville's time (and our own). This produces a worldwide wave of managerialism in university structure, as in many other kinds of organizations (Drori, Meyer, and Hwang 2006; Moon 2002). The managed and administered university competes on an increasingly global scale, with a rapidly expanding set of regional or global schemes for rating and ranking and accrediting universities on standardized bases. The impact is strongest in Europe and is pressed by the Bologna Process, but the effects are worldwide. Thus in far-off Korea, Hanyang University (a respected private school) announces a strategic plan (2005). "Hanyang's recent 'HYU Project 2010' [with a] vision of fostering global leaders incorporates a plan to educate leaders, who can actively deal with issues relating to the global environment. . . . The result of this development is to be Han-yang's ranking as one of the most renowned universities in Korea. Fur-thermore, consequent of this domestic success, Hanyang plans to prog-ress further in order to join the world's top 100 universities by 2039." Typical of the new and rationalized system coming into place world-wide, Hanyang reports its ratings on 16 different dimensions evaluating its research, the success of its alumni, and its overall university status.

Thus, the modern university functions as a purposive actor in a world that is globalized and rationalized. In this world of imagined homogeneity, standardized dimensions of ranking, certification, and accreditation make sense. Universities around the world can be com-pared and rated on standard scales. And if they are effectively and pur-posively managed organizations, perhaps they can improve their rank-ings vis-à-vis all the other universities of the world.

The Effects of Higher Education as an Institution

Traditional perspectives on higher education take the view that particu-lar higher-educational programs produce knowledge and skill that tan-gibly affect individual role performance and social progress. The idea is that this occurs through research and innovation, certainly, but also through the productivity of trained individual graduates. To those who see higher education as a potentially efficient training machine, this is the core justification for proliferation and growth.

It is thus interesting to observe (a) how little evidence consistently supports this core point over the last century of massive expansion of higher education (Rubinson and Browne 1994) and (b) how little differ-ence the absence of evidence seems to have made in slowing the univer-sity's trajectory (Chabbott and Ramirez 2000).

To be sure, individuals with university degrees earn more than those without such credentials. But it has been difficult to show that university-trained individuals create more productivity (Boudon 1973) or even that they outperform their less-well-educated peers (Berg 1970). Moreover, studies have failed to observe any aggregate effect of overall tertiary expansion on economic development, whereas strong beneficial effects of secondary education are routinely observed (Benavot 1992; Barro 1991; Levine and Renelt 1992; Schofer, Ramirez, and Meyer 2000). This situa-tion makes more sense if one conceives of higher education as an institu-tion, i.e., if the university exists more to link the role structure of society to universalized cultural knowledge than to efficiently prepare graduates to fill these roles. Role learning, after all, is best produced by proximately located training—situations of practice, apprenticeship, and technical training. And more practical programs of this sort routinely do assess role-relevant learning and capacity. This is precisely what the university does not do; it has been criticized for this lapse for centuries. Rather than carrying on such criticism, perhaps it is better to consider why immediate outcome assessment is so consistently avoided in the university.

The Legitimization of Personnel and Knowledge for the Postmodern Society. Conceived as an institution, rather than as an organization for producing trained individual outputs, the university serves a highly collective function. It defines certain types of knowledge as authoritative in society, and authoritative on the basis of the highest cultural principles (e.g., science, rationality, natural law). Situating relevant knowledge in the context of general academic principles is a basic strategy for building authority throughout modern history. And organizing this knowledge as having, by social definition, been installed in a clearly demarcated category of certified persons is crucial (Collins 1979). Discussions of professionalization routinely note the importance of locating professional schooling near to the cultural center, and thus the university (e.g., Abbott 1988).

The historical success of these authority-building projects appears dramatically in the main research literatures on modern social stratification. In essentially all modern countries, the single most powerful predictor of the social status of an occupation is the education required for it and held by its incumbents. The effect here is very clearly an institutional one—defined in cultural terms at the collective level. Often the rules giving preference to the educated are organized in the law, directly or indirectly. Specified levels of education are commonly required for occupational positions, and in any case assigning important positions on the basis of educational credentials is very highly legitimated. Discrimination on the basis of education—in stark contrast to discrimination on most other bases—is typically not illicit. Note that these requirements and legitimations do not usually rest on any actual inspection of the individuals being certified or any direct assessment of the knowledge thought to be salient. The legitimizations of personnel and knowledge are institutional and collective, not individual. They arise over long periods of time, and they hold more or less constant worldwide.

Many concrete instances are discussed in the research literatures. D. A. Barrett (1995), for instance, ties the cross-national distribution of demographers to the rise of national population-control policies. Moon (2002) shows links between the rise of managerialism in business and the development of business schools and MBA programs. C. M. Wotipka and Francisco Ramirez (2004) find that the numbers of women in higher education correlate with the earlier establishment of women's studies courses. The causal relations, here, are obviously bidirectional. The rise of certified academic knowledge props up the expansion and authority of corresponding roles in modern society, and in turn, roles that gain importance root their success in academicized knowledge (Abbott 2005). Thus expertise in population, management, and gender issues is bolstered by the consolidation of academic specializations in these domains.

All these more institutional connections are strengthened precisely because of the relative absence of individual- and activity-level linkages between training and work. If individuals were in fact allocated positions on the basis of skills, and if implicated knowledge were indeed closely linked to organizational performance, the authority of higher education would be greatly weakened. And the legitimacy of the linkage claims between occupational activity and the highest cultural knowledge would be lowered. In short, the decoupling of concrete skills and individual capacities from the system that provides abstract certification maintains the university's collective cultural authority and capacity.

Institutionalized Higher Education and Social Stratification. The decoupling of local and practical and individual experience from the institutional linkages between higher education and society has strong effects on individual educational experience and outcomes. At every phase, the roles of the "student" and the "graduate" are organized in terms of very general institutionalized rules. And so they are experienced: The individual knows he or she is a student, acquiring credentials and therefore possessing certified knowledge and capacity. Others know it, too. Under these conditions, it is less relevant whether the knowledge actually exists or is possessed by the student.

These insights provide the bases for a general explanation of one of the most central, but also most intellectually problematic, empirical observations in the sociology of American higher education. This is the finding that the extreme variations in resources and quality among higher-educational organizations often yield surprisingly modest differences in many social outcomes, with individual properties (abilities, intentions, and the like) held constant. The finding has a long history (Jacob 1957; Feldman and Newcomb 1969). It is constantly contested (see the reviews in Pascarella and Terenzini 1991). Many of the studies that do find positive "effects" fail to control for student selection (contrast Useem and Karabel 1986, and Bowen and Bok 1998, with Kruger and Berg 2002).

The finding seems very unreasonable to those analysts who see educational effects as resulting from the interactions and experiences students have in immediate circumstances. From an institutional point of view, however, the finding makes sense. The student has a role and an identity in what is really a national and global institution. The role and the identity thus have transcendent meanings: they are known by the student and everyone around the student, including all sorts of gatekeepers in society. An individual's opportunities and expectations are substantially transformed by his or her becoming a college graduate, and this transformation is largely independent of the particular college or particular student experiences involved. The student acquires the generalized charter or status of a graduate (Meyer 1970). So over and above the individual properties (prominently including intentions, plans, and the whole apparatus of individual choice) that affect outcomes, the formal rules of the game matter greatly.

Thus, the particulars of one's university experience may show modest effects on one's life chances, but becoming a "graduate" generates very large effects on one's future life and is known by everyone to do so. Naturally, a wide variety of intellectual and psychological effects follow. An individual who will experience all of his or her subsequent life course as a graduate is clearly a very different person from one who will experience life as a nongraduate.

Where effects can be found on individual life outcomes is where higher education is itself stratified and categorically demarcated. American community colleges, for instance, have weaker positive effects on their graduates than do four-year schools (Dougherty 1994; Brint and Karabel 1989). In some countries, the opportunities available to polytechnic graduates are more limited—sometimes by law—than those available to university graduates, such that life outcomes differ sharply. The same effects occur in secondary education: for instance, students who attend secondary schools that do not confer access to higher education are obviously unlikely to attend. Similar effects can be found in comparing substantive educational programs. Specializing in a given subject, even with individual properties held constant, can open doors if doing so is required, and known to be required, for entry into particular roles.

All these kinds of effects are built into the institutional structure of modern societies. They are cultural and organizational rules, whose implications and consequences affect individual life courses independent of the properties of the individuals involved. Naturally, as individuals become aware of the rules that govern their lives and opportunities, they acquire appropriate consciousness, abilities, and orientations.

Conclusions and Directions

Higher education is, and has been, the central cultural institution of the modern system. Over many centuries, it links an ever-expanding set of specific activities, roles, and organizations to a universal and unified cultural core. And it defines categories of certified persons as carrying these linkages and as possessing both the relevant cultural core and the specific authority and capacity to carry out the roles.

Several important things can be learned from thinking about higher education as an institution. First, attention can be more sharply directed to the world and national frames that provide higher education, and especially the university, with a compelling rationale. From their medieval origins to their postnational incarnation, universities are not mainly local organizations justified by specific economic and political functions or shaped by particular historical legacies or power struggles. A much broader cultural and civilizational mission has always informed higher education. Its legitimacy and development throughout history have been linked to enacting this broader mission, which today includes the idea that universities are sites for developments that lead to social progress.

This first point leads to a second one: universities (in contrast to other higher educational possibilities) have not merely endured but have prevailed, despite all sorts of local inefficiencies, disjunctures, and criticisms. Town and gown tension—in the most general sense—has a well-established pedigree, but this legacy has not stopped country after country from expanding its system of higher education and organizing it around a university base. Everywhere universities play a central role in this expansion; efforts to kill the university have repeatedly failed. Theories that emphasize distinctive local or even distinctive national features cannot account for the global explosion of higher education after World War II. This unanticipated growth is clearly attuned to worldwide directives and transnational celebrations of the broadly accessible, socially useful, and organizationally flexible university. These directives and celebrations are found in international conferences and associations, and much transnational expertise mobilizes itself in support of the learning society and its university roots and ties.

A third point logically follows: higher education not only expands but is increasingly standardized around the world. While communities and countries vary with respect to resources and traditions, universities nevertheless grow more similar with respect to goals and programs for meeting these goals. Broad accessibility translates itself into more diverse student bodies in higher education cross-nationally. University curricula change and change in similar directions across higher education cross-nationally. Social progress goals lead to and are embellished in what are imagined to be more socially useful curricula: canonical gods embodied in the humanities give way to more rationalized and people-centered social-science curricula. Lastly, profound organizational differences reflecting local and national "path dependencies" are undercut by transnational standardization processes (Teichler 2002; Lenhardt 2005; Kruecken and Meier 2006). The latter ever more firmly situate universities in a global field, within which comparisons increase along multiple dimensions. Protestations of distinctiveness seem feeble; the Bologna declaration regarding higher education and the Shanghai world ratings of universities both penetrate deeply.

These inferences seem to be at odds with much of the comparative education literature, which continues to emphasize distinctive national systems of higher education. This literature needs to be modified in three important ways. First, we need to recognize that universities emerged and developed before the age of nationalism. These universities were cosmopolitan and global in outlook; they became more nationalized in the eighteenth and nineteenth centuries. Second, much of this nationalist flavor was evident at the level of formal organization and as regards the cultural account of the university, its charter, and its saga. But there were deeper commonalities among curricula than is generally recognized. Last, we are once again in a transnational or global era, and this should lead to a narrowing of organizational differences across universities within and between countries. This is evident in the spread of business schools, for example, but it is important to recognize that other less industry-linked programs of study, such as women's studies, are also diffusing. Much of this diffusion is positively theorized, evoking frames of excellence and equity.

Taken as a whole, these developments suggest that the mantra "no salvation outside higher education" is more deeply institutionalized today than at any earlier time. The World Bank used to have qualms about higher education growth in less-developed countries, but the manpower-planning inclination the Bank once shared with more centralized economies (e.g., Lenhardt and Stock 2000) is no more. Furthermore, the profile of the "best" systems of higher education or "best" universities is more likely to be known worldwide due to the rise and activity of a cadre of transnational higher education experts. Translocal comparisons and their implications are not new. But in a more integrated world we should find a plethora of higher education reforms holding up successful systems or universities as exemplars. All sorts of sober instrumental goals will be articulated, but the overriding process will continue to be one of proper identity enactment. We will see greater awareness of whether the right goals were articulated and less knowledge of whether these are realized. Universities will continue to be model driven, and the models will be worldwide in character and influence.

What further research directions are suggested by thinking about higher education as an institution? First—and perhaps obviously—we would predict that, net of other factors, more isolated countries are less likely to experience higher educational growth. The case of Maoist China illustrates this point, as does the whole episode of communist resistance to expansion (Lenhardt and Stock 2000). A parallel prediction is that more isolated cases will also be less standardized with respect to curricula, goals, and educational certification itself. Within Maoist China and the communist world in general, "red" could trump "expert." Isolation here means limited or no contact with world educational conferences and associations as well as with universities and educational authorities from the main world centers. The research direction basically consists in creating a set of indicators of the degree of nations' educational linkage to world and regional educational models. A second and related avenue of inquiry is based on the idea that the probability of a country's or a university's adopting an educational program, reform, or objective is influenced by regional or world rates of similar adoptions. For example, universities are more likely to offer courses on human rights in their law schools or to launch environmental studies programs in a country or region where many other universities are already doing so.

Comparing across eras instead of across regions or countries can reveal whether the current period indeed instances more world and regional educational conferences and associations and whether higher rates of participation in these conferences and memberships in these associations are also peculiarly characteristic of the current era. An institutional perspective would expect to find these differences across time. That is, one would expect to find in place today a world with relatively thick educational networking and in which network ties are relatively strong predictors of educational outcomes, such as growth and standardization.

Lastly, more qualitative research is needed to study world model constructions and their enactment in local sites. We have contended that world models of progress and justice give rise to excellence and equity frames in higher education. We have further contended that many changes in higher education are rationalized around these frames. How this transformation plays out in specific systems of higher education or universities is an important question. We assume that the older and more prestigious universities are more able to resist change, especially if they are located in the older and relatively wealthier countries. But even these establishments have changed with the times—admitting women, developing nontraditional programs of study, differentiating between professors and managers in the universities, etc. Still, it would be interesting to see which emphases of the world educational regime—accessibility or usefulness or flexibility—are more resisted, for what reasons, and with what consequences.

The institutionalized character of higher education—which supports the organizational and role structures of contemporary society through highly cultural and collective processes—creates a web of tautological relations among central cultural knowledge, authority, and the widest variety of particular roles and activities. Higher education creates the presumption of legitimate knowledge and of the authoritative personnel carrying this knowledge. As a result, the concrete social inspection of the knowledge and personnel is often weakened or eliminated. The schooled individual, in part by social definition, carries the credential. And the schooled knowledge is part of it. In itself, this produces some strikingly standardized individual effects of higher education.

References

Abbott, A. 1988. *The System of Professions: An Essay on the Division of Expert Labor.* Chicago: University of Chicago Press.

——. 2005. "Linked Ecologies: States and Universities as Environments for Professions." *Sociological Theory* 23 (3): 245–74.

Altbach, P. G. 1998. *Comparative Higher Education: Knowledge, the University, and Development.* Greenwich, CT: Ablex.

Anderson, B. 1991. *Imagined Communities: Reflections on the Origin and Spread of Nationalism.* London: Verso.

Aronowitz, S. 2000. *The Knowledge Factory: Dismantling the Corporate University and Creating True Higher Learning.* Boston: Beacon.

Banks, A. S. 2001. *Cross-National Time-Series Data Archive.* Dataset. Binghamton, NY: Computer Systems Unlimited.

Barrett, D. A. 1995. "Reproducing Persons and a Global Concern: The Making of an Institution." Ph.D. dissertation, Stanford University.

Barro, R. J. 1991. "Economic Growth in a Cross Section of Countries." *Quarterly Journal of Economics* 106 (2): 407–43.

Benavot, A. 1992. "Educational Expansion and Economic Growth in the Modern World, 1913–1985." In *The Political Construction of Education*, ed. B. Fuller and R. Rubinson. New York: Praeger.

Ben-David, J., and A. Zloczower. 1962. "Universities and Academic Systems in Modern Societies." *European Journal of Sociology* 3:45–85.

Berg, I. E. 1970. *Education and Jobs: The Great Training Robbery.* New York: Praeger.

Boli, J. 2005. "Contemporary Developments in World Culture." *International Journal of Comparative Sociology* 46 (5–6): 383–404.

Boli, J., and G. M. Thomas, eds. 1999. *Constructing World Culture: International Nongovernmental Organizations since 1875.* Stanford, CA: Stanford University Press.

Boudon, R. 1973. *Education, Opportunity, and Social Inequality.* New York: John Wiley.

Bourdieu, P., and J. C. Passeron. 1977. *Reproduction in Education, Society, and Culture.* London: Sage.

Bowen, W., and D. Bok. 1998. *The Shape of the River: Long-Term Consequences of Considering Race in College and University Admissions.* Princeton, NJ: Princeton University Press.

Bradley, K., and F. O. Ramirez. 1996. "World Polity and Gender Parity: Women's Share of Higher Education, 1965–1985." *Research in Sociology of Education and Socialization* 11:63–91.

Branscomb, L. M., and J. Keller. 1998. *Investing in Innovation: Creating a Research and Innovation Policy That Works.* Cambridge, MA: MIT Press.

Brint, S. 1998. *Schools and Societies.* Thousand Oaks, CA: Pine Forge.

———, ed. 2002a. *The Future of the City of Intellect: The Changing American University.* Stanford, CA: Stanford University Press.

———. 2002b. "The Rise of the 'Practical Arts.'" In *The Future of the City of Intellect*, ed. S. Brint, 231–59. Stanford, CA: Stanford University Press.

———. 2005. "Creating the Future: New Directions in American Research Universities." *Minerva* 43:23–50.

Brint, S., and J. Karabel. 1989. *The Diverted Dream: Community Colleges and the Promise of Educational Opportunity in America, 1900–1985.* Oxford: Oxford University Press.

Brown, D. K. 2001. "The Social Sources of Educational Credentialism: Status Cultures, Labor Markets, and Organizations." *Sociology of Education*, extra issue, 19–34.

Chabbott, C. 2002. *Constructing Education for Development: International Organizations and Education for All.* London: Taylor and Francis.

Chabbott, C., and F. O. Ramirez. 2000. "Development and Education." In *Handbook of the Sociology of Education*, ed. M. T. Hallinan, 163–87. New York: Plenum.

Clark, B. 1983. *The Higher Education System: Academic Organization in Cross-National Perspective.* Berkeley: University of California Press.

———, ed. 1987. *The Academic Profession: National, Disciplinary, and Institutional Settings.* Berkeley: University of California Press.

———. 1998. *Creating Entrepreneurial Universities: Organizational Pathways of Transformation.* Oxford: Pergamon.

Cohen, Y. 1970. "Schools and Civilization States." In *The Social Sciences and the Comparative Study of Education*, ed. J. Fischer. Scranton, NY: Industrial Textbook.

Collins, R. 1971. "Functional and Conflict Theories of Educational Stratification." *American Sociological Review* 36:1002–19.

———. 1979. *The Credential Society. An Historical Sociology of Education and Stratification.* New York: Academic.

Djelic, M-L. 1998. *Exporting the American Model: The Postwar Transformation of European Business.* Oxford: Oxford University Press.

Dore, R. 1976. *The Diploma Disease.* Berkeley: University of California Press.

Dougherty, K. 1994. *The Contradictory College. The Conflicting Origins, Impacts, and Futures of the Community College.* Albany: State University of New York Press.

Drori, G., J. W. Meyer, F. O. Ramirez, and E. Schofer. 2003. *Science in the Modern World Polity: Institutionalization and Globalization.* Stanford, CA: Stanford University Press.

Drori, G., J. W. Meyer, and H. Hwang, eds. 2006. *Globalization and Organization.* Oxford: Oxford University Press.

Drori, G., and H. Moon. 2006. "The Changing Nature of Tertiary Education: Neo-institutional Perspective on Cross-National Trends in Disciplinary Enrollment, 1965–1995." In *The Impact of Comparative Education Research on Institutional Theory*, ed. D. P. Baker and A. W. Wiseman, 163–92. Boston: Elsevier JAI.

Eisenstadt, S. 1986. *The Origins and Diversity of Axial Age Civilizations*. Albany: State University of New York Press.

———. 1987. *European Civilization in Comparative Perspective*. Oslo: Norwegian University Press.

Feldman, K. A., and T. M. Newcomb. 1969. *The Impact of College on Students*. San Francisco: Jossey-Bass.

Foucault, M. 1991. "Governmentality." In *The Foucault Effect*, ed. G. Burchell, C. Gordon, and P. Miller. Chicago: University of Chicago Press.

Fourcade-Gourinchas, M., and S. L. Babb. 2002. "The Rebirth of the Liberal Creed: Paths to Neoliberalism in Four Countries." *American Journal of Sociology* 108:533–79.

Frank, D. J., and J. Gabler. 2006. *Reconstructing the University: Worldwide Changes in Academic Emphases over the Twentieth Century*. Stanford, CA: Stanford University Press.

Frank, D. J., A. Hironaka, J. W. Meyer, E. Schofer, and N. B. Tuma. 1999. "The Rationalization and Organization of Nature in World Culture." In *Constructing World Culture*, ed. J. Boli and G. M. Thomas, 81–99. Stanford, CA: Stanford University Press.

Frank, D. J., A. Hironaka, and E. Schofer. 2000. "The Nation-State and the Natural Environment over the Twentieth Century." *American Sociological Review* 65:96–116.

Frank, D. J., and J. W. Meyer. 2006. "The University: Worldwide Expansion and Change." Manuscript, Department of Sociology, University of California–Irvine.

Frank, D. J., E. Schofer, and J. C. Torres. 1994. "Rethinking History: Change in the University Curriculum, 1910–90." *Sociology of Education* 67:231–42.

Frank, D. J., S. Y. Wong, J. W. Meyer, and F. O. Ramirez. 2000. "What Counts as History: A Cross-National and Longitudinal Study of University Curricula." *Comparative Education Review* 44:29–53.

Freeman, R. 1976. *The Overeducated American*. New York: Academic.

Gabler, J., and D. J. Frank. 2005. "The Natural Sciences in the University: Change and Variation over the Twentieth Century." *Sociology of Education* 78:183–206.

Gumport, P. J. 2000. "Academic Restructuring: Organizational Change and Institutional Imperatives." *Higher Education* 39:67–91.

Hamilton, G., and J. R. Sutton. 1989. "The Problem of Control in the Weak State: Domination in the United States, 1880–1920." *Theory and Society* 18:1–46.

Hanyang University. 2005. *University Development Plan*. Seoul: Hanyang University.

Hasse, R., and G. Kruecken. 2005. *Neo-institutionalismus*. Rev. ed. Bielefeld, Germany: Transcript-Verlag.

Hironaka, A. 2003. "Science and the Environment." In *Science in the Modern World Polity*, ed. G. Drori, J. W. Meyer, F. O. Ramirez, and E. Schofer, 249–64. Stanford, CA: Stanford University Press.

Hobsbawm, E., and T. Ranger, eds. 1983. *The Invention of Tradition*. Cambridge: Cambridge University Press.

Hofstadter, R. 1963. *Anti-intellectualism in American Life*. New York: Alfred A. Knopf.

Inoue, K. 2003. "*Vive la patiente!* Discourse Analysis of the Global Expansion of Health as Human Right." Ed.D. dissertation, Stanford University.

Jacob, P. E. 1957. *Changing Values in College. An Exploratory Study of the Impact of College Teaching*. New York: Harper.

Jepperson, R. L. 2002. "The Development and Application of Sociological Neoinstitutionalism." In *New Directions in Contemporary Sociological Theory*, ed. J. Berger and M. Zelditch Jr., 229–66. Lanham, MD: Rowman and Littlefield.

Karabel, J. 2005. *The Chosen: The Hidden History of Exclusion and Admission at Harvard, Yale, and Princeton*. Boston: Houghton Mifflin.

Kerr, C. 1987. "A Critical Age in the University World." *European Journal of Education* 22 (2): 183–93.

Kirp, D. L. 2003. *Shakespeare, Einstein, and the Bottom Line: The Marketing of Higher Education*. Cambridge, MA; Harvard University Press.

Kraatz, M. S., and E. J. Zajak. 1996. "Exploring the Limits of the New Institutionalism: The Causes and Consequences of Illegitimate Organizational Change." *American Sociological Review* 61:812–36.

Kruecken, G., and F. Meier. 2006. "Turning the University into an Organizational Actor." In *Globalization and Organization*, ed. G. Drori, J. Meyer, and H. Hwang, chap. 10. Oxford: Oxford University Press.

Kruger, A., and S. Berg. 2002. "Estimating the Payoff to Attending a More Selective College: An Application of Selection on Observables and Unobservables." *Quarterly Journal of Economics* 4:1491–527.

Lenhardt, G. 2005. *Hochschulen in Deutschland und in den U.S.A.: Deutsche Hochschulpolitic in der Isolation*. Wiesbaden, Germany: VS Verlan fuer Sozialwissenschaften.

Lenhardt, G., and M. Stock. 2000. "Hochschulentwicklung und Bürgerrechte in der BRD und der DDR." *Kölner Zeitschrift für Soziologie und Sozialpsychologie* 52:520–40.

Levine, R., and D. Renelt. 1992. "A Sensitivity Analysis of Cross-Country Growth Regressions." *American Economic Review* 82 (4): 942–63.

Levy, D. 1986. *Higher Education and the State in Latin America.* Chicago: University of Chicago Press.

Meyer, J. W. 1970. "The Charter: Conditions of Diffuse Socialization in Schools." In *Social Processes and Social Structures*, ed. W. R. Scott, 564–78. New York: Holt, Rinehart, and Winston.

———. 1977. "The Effects of Education as an Institution." *American Journal of Sociology* 83:55–77.

Meyer, J. W., J. Boli, G. Thomas, and F. O. Ramirez. 1997. "World Society and the Nation-State." *American Journal of Sociology* 103:144–81.

Meyer, J. W., and R. L. Jepperson. 2000. "The 'Actors' of Modern Society: The Cultural Construction of Social Agency." *Sociological Theory* 18:100–20.

Meyer, J. W., D. Kamens, A. Benavot, and Y. K. Cha. 1992a. *School Knowledge for the Masses: World Models and National Primary Curricular Categories in the Twentieth Century.* Washington, DC: Falmer.

Meyer, J. W., F. O. Ramirez, and Y. N. Soysal. 1992b. "World Expansion of Mass Education, 1870–1980." *Sociology of Education* 65:128–49.

Meyer, J. W., and B. Rowan. 1977. "Institutionalized Organizations: Formal Structure as Myth and Ceremony." *American Journal of Sociology* 83:340–63.

Meyer, J. W., and W. R. Scott. 1983. *Organizational Environments.* Beverly Hills, CA: Sage.

Moon, H. 2002. "The Globalization of Professional Management Education, 1881–2000." Ph.D. dissertation, Stanford University.

Nussbaum, M. C. 1997. *Cultivating Humanity: A Classical Defense of Reform in Liberal Education.* Cambridge, MA: Harvard University Press.

Olson, M. 1971. *The Logic of Collective Action.* Cambridge, MA: Harvard University Press.

Pascarella, E. T., and P. T. Terenzini. 1991. *How College Affects Students: Findings and Insights from Twenty Years of Research.* San Francisco: Jossey-Bass.

Ralph, J. H., and R. Rubinson. 1980. "Immigration and the Expansion of Schooling in the United States, 1890–1970." *American Sociological Review* 46:943–54.

Ramirez, F. O. 2002. "Eyes Wide Shut: University, State, and Society." *European Educational Research Journal* 1:255–71.

———. 2006a. "Growing Commonalities and Persistent Differences in Higher Education: Universities between Globalization and National Tradition." In *The New Institutionalism in Education: Advancing Research and Policy*, ed. H-D. Meyer and B. Rowan. Albany: State University of New York Press.

———. 2006b. "The Rationalization of Universities." In *Transnational Governance: Institutional Dynamics of Regulation*, ed. M-L. Djelic and K. Shalin-Andersson. Cambridge: Cambridge University Press.

Ramirez, F. O., and J. W. Meyer. 2002. "Expansion and Impact of the World Human Rights Regime: Longitudinal and Cross-National Analyses over the

Twentieth Century." Funded proposal, National Science Foundation, Sociology Program.

Ramirez, F. O., and R. Rubinson. 1979. "Creating Members: The National Incorporation of Education." In *National Development and the World System: Educational, Economic, and Political change, 1950–1970*, ed. J. W. Meyer and M. T. Hannan, chap. 5. Chicago: University of Chicago Press.

Ramirez, F. O., Y. Soysal, and S. Shanahan. 1997. "The Changing Logic of Political Citizenship: Cross-National Acquisition of Women's Suffrage Rights, 1890 to 1990." *American Sociological Review* 62 (5): 735–45.

Ramirez, F. O., and M. Ventresca. 1992. "Building the Institution of Mass Schooling: Isomorphism in the Modern World." In *The Political Construction of Education*, ed. B. Fuller and R. Rubinson, 47–59. New York: Praeger.

Ramirez, F. O., and C. Min Wotipka. 2001. "Slowly but Surely? The Global Expansion of Women's Participation in Science and Engineering Fields of Study, 1972–1992." *Sociology of Education* 74:231–51.

Rashdall, H. 1895/1987. *The Universities of Europe in the Middle Ages.* Oxford: Clarendon.

Readings, B. 1996. *The University in Ruins.* Cambridge, MA: Harvard University Press.

Reisner, E. H. 1922. *Nationalism and Education since 1789: A Social and Political History of Modern Education.* New York: Macmillan.

Riddle, P. 1989. "University and State: Political Competition and the Rise of Universities, 1200–1985." Ed.D. dissertation, Stanford University.

———. 1993. "Political Authority and University Formation in Europe, 1200–1800." *Sociological Perspectives* 36:45–62.

Robertson, R. 1992. *Globalization: Social Theory and Global Culture.* London: Sage.

Rubinson, R. 1986. "Class Formation, Politics, and Institutions: Schooling in the United States." *American Journal of Sociology* 92:519–48.

Rubinson, R., and I. Brown. 1994. "Education and the Economy." In *The Handbook of Economic Sociology*, ed. N. Smelser and R. Swedberg, 583–99. Princeton, NJ: Princeton University Press.

Schofer, E. 1999. "The Rationalization of Science and the Scientization of Society: International Science Organizations, 1870–1995." In *Constructing World Culture*, ed. J. Boli and G. M. Thomas. Stanford, CA: Stanford University Press.

Schofer, E. 2001. "The State and the Expansion of European Science, 1750–1990." Paper presented at the annual meetings of the Pacific Sociological Association Meetings.

———. 2003. "The Global Institutionalization of Geological Science, 1800–1990." *American Sociological Review* 68:730–59.

Schofer, E., and J. W. Meyer. 2005. "The World-wide Expansion of Higher Education in the Twentieth Century." *American Sociological Review* 70:898–920.

Schofer, E., F. O. Ramirez, and J. W. Meyer. 2000. "The Effects of Science on National Economic Development, 1970–1990." *American Sociological Review* 65:877–98.

Schriewer, J. 2004. "Multiple Internationalities: The Emergence of a World Level Ideology and the Persistence of Idiosyncratic World-View." In *Transnational Intellectual Networks*, ed. C. Charle, J. Schriewer, and P. Wagner, 473–534. Frankfurt: Campus Verlag.

Scott, W. R. 2002. *Organizations: Rational, Natural, and Open Systems*. 5th ed. Englewood Cliffs, NJ: Prentice-Hall.

Shils, E. 1971. "No Salvation outside Higher Education." *Minerva* 6:313–21.

Slaughter, S., and L. Leslie. 1997. *Academic Capitalism: Politics, Policies, and the Entrepreneurial University*. Baltimore: Johns Hopkins University Press.

Soares, J. 1999. *The Decline of Privilege: The Modernization of Oxford University*. Stanford, CA: Stanford University Press.

Soule, S. 1997. "The Student Divestment Movement in the United States and the Shantytown: Diffusion of a Protest Tactic." *Social Forces* 75:855–83.

———. Forthcoming. "Divestment by Colleges and Universities in the United States. Institutional Pressures toward Isomorphism." In *How Institutions Change*, ed. W. Powell and D. Jones. Chicago: University of Chicago Press.

Suarez, D. 2005. "Education Professionals and the Construction of Human Rights Education." Paper presented at the 49th annual conference of the Comparative International Education Society, School of Education, Stanford University, Stanford, CA, March 22.

Teichler, U. 2002. *Towards a "European Higher Education Area": Visions and Realities*. Centre for Research on Higher Education and Work. Kassel, Germany: University of Kassel.

Thomas, G. M., J. W. Meyer, F. O. Ramirez, and J. Boli. 1987. *Institutional Structure: Constituting State, Society, and Individual*. Newbury Park, CA: Sage.

Thorndike, L. 1944. *University Records and Life in the Middle Ages*. New York: Columbia University Press.

Toulmin, S. 1989. *Cosmopolis: The Hidden Agenda of Modernity*. New York: Free Press.

UNESCO (United Nations Educational, Social, and Cultural Organization). 2000. *Statistical Yearbook*. Paris: UNESCO.

———. 2004. UNESCO Online Database. Paris: UNESCO Institute for Statistics.

Useem, M., and J. Karabel. 1986. "Pathways to Top Corporate Management." *American Sociological Review* 51:184–200.

Weick, K. 1976. "Educational Organization as Loosely Coupled System." *Administrative Science Quarterly* 21:1–19.

Windolf, P. 1997. *Expansion and Structural Change: Higher Education in Germany, the United States, and Japan.* Boulder: Westview.

World Bank. 2000. *Higher Education in Developing Countries: Peril and Promise.* Published for the Task Force on Higher Education and Society. Washington, DC: World Bank.

Wotipka, C. M., and F. O. Ramirez. 2004. "A Cross-National Analysis of the Emergence and Institutionalization of Women's Studies Curricula." Paper presented at the annual meetings of the American Sociological Association, San Francisco, August.

8 Sociological Studies of Academic Departments

JAMES C. HEARN

Academic departments are the foundational unit of U.S. colleges and universities. Curricula, degree programs, grading practices, and research initiatives, as well as faculty norms, values, and careers, are shaped there, and it is there that the notion of shared academic governance is most developed (Peterson 1976; Trow 1976). Departments provide the most publicly visible organizational manifestation of the various academic disciplines, as of the academic profession as a whole (Clark 1983, 1987b). Given this, the structuring and functioning of these units have long attracted sociological attention.

Indeed, the breadth of sociological work potentially relevant to the study of departments is striking. The sociologically informed literature on intradepartmental resource allocations is extraordinarily rich, as is the literature on the sociology of faculty roles, performance, and expectations (e.g., see Finkelstein 1984; Bayer 1991; Fox 1996). Fortunately, other authors in this volume (notably, Gumport, Rhoades, and Meyer et al.) deal extensively with such literatures. Therefore these topics are covered here only as they relate to internal departmental structures and processes. This chapter focuses its attention as exclusively as possible on the academic department as a social organization.[1]

The chapter also focuses almost solely on work that takes an explicitly sociological approach. Much valuable work on departments has been

Patricia Gumport provided many excellent suggestions on an earlier draft of this chapter. The author also gratefully acknowledges the able research assistance of Alexander Gorbunov and Ying Liu.

1. Peterson (1976) accurately reminds us that departments are not the only major academic subunit—institutions also have divisions, centers, institutes, all of which vie for faculty effort, attention, and resources. To the extent that other units have functions distinctive from departments, they are not considered here. Likewise, Gumport and Snydman

produced by scholars working from the perspectives of economics, management science, operations research, psychology, and higher education studies (e.g., see James and Neuberger 1981; Manns and March 1978; Massy and Zemsky 1994; Hackman 1985; Biglan 1973; Baird 1986). Sometimes, work by non-sociologists employs concepts closely linked to the field. For example, W. F. Massy and colleagues (Massy, Wilger, and Colbeck 1994) coined the term *hollowed collegiality* to capture aspects of the normative climate in departments in which faculty collegially discuss certain issues (especially those relating to facilitating research) while regularly avoiding collegial discussion of other issues (especially those relating to improving teaching and learning). Their work provides propositions regarding the organizational conditions likely to produce the "hollowed collegiality" behavioral pattern. Distinguishing work that suggests or employs ideas resonant of sociology from work that is *foundationally* sociological requires extraordinary discernment. A standard for making the call is elusive, to say the least. Thus, this chapter's effort to target and report upon foundational work is surely flawed. The ideal reader will be forgiving.

All that said, one can still identify several domains of relevant sociological inquiry. This essay will review in turn the contributions of those domains, then conclude with thoughts on lacunae and theoretical and policy questions emerging from the literature as a whole.

The interconnections in the sociological work on departments are enough to frustrate any aspiring typologist. Nevertheless, six reasonably distinct strands of inquiry may be identified: the structuring of academic work; competition, conflict, and change within departments; resource dependencies and power relations; organizational implications of disciplinary differences; compositional patterns; and departments as contexts for student development and socialization. Because many studies cross the six domains,[2] judgments had to be made on where best to place a study in the typology, and those judgments are inevitably debatable. Also debatable is the ordering of the strands in the presentation

---

(2002) remind us that academic structure features two primary dimensions—departments and degree programs—and these dimensions are not the same thing. Again, to the extent that programs are distinct from departments, they are not considered here.

2. For example, research on resources, power relations, and competition among departments on campuses has often highlighted disciplinary differences, e.g., the consistent advantages of certain disciplines over others with different kinds of knowledge bases (e.g., see Salancik and Pfeffer 1974; Salancik, Staw, and Pondy 1980).

below. Nevertheless, the typology does provide a useful framework for addressing the varied sociological perspectives on departments.

The Structuring of Academic Work

The organizational significance of academic departments has been rising steadily since their inception in the United States in the late 1800s. Now, the nation's two- and four-year institutions are estimated to house more than 40,000 departments averaging about 20 faculty members each.[3] These units are arguably the most salient organizational aspect of higher education for thousands of faculty and millions of students. Whether one focuses on teaching, research, service, or the connections among them, the department is the focal point of academic work. Not surprisingly, the structuring of that work in departments has been addressed by many sociologists.

One of these, Burton Clark, has observed that departments are at the forefront of the bottom-heavy organizational form of colleges and universities, in that each department "has self-evident primacy in a front-line task, each possesses the authority of its own field, and each takes its behavioral cues from peers, departmental and individual, located elsewhere in the country and the world" (1987a, p. 381). The department thus represents an intriguing organizational convergence of discipline and institution. Because of this, Clark suggests, faculty have increasingly been able to use the department to their own advantage:

> The department [is] *the* building block of faculty hegemony, even as it serves as the main operating component of a bureaucratic structure. One of the more curious creations of professionals in organizations, the academic department is much reviled by all those who want to tame the impulses of specialists. But it is so essential to the work, culture, and authority of American academics that it simply grows stronger with each passing decade. It solves many problems in ways congenial to the self-defined interests of academics. National systems that do not have it seem to evolve

3. More precisely, findings from the 1988 National Survey of Postsecondary Faculty (see Russell et al. 1990) suggest that there were at that time 41,000 academic departments, with 31,000 of those in four-year institutions. There is no reason to suggest shrinkage in these figures. In doctoral institutions, the average departmental size in 1987–1988 was 28 faculty, but the average was only 18 in public nondoctoral four-year institutions and 10 in private nondoctoral four-year institutions. Overall, the average department in four-year institutions was home to 18 faculty members, of whom 12 were full-time regular faculty, 2 were part-time regular faculty, and 4 were in temporary positions.

toward it in order to tame the more narrow inclinations of individual specialists and to bring collegial principles to the fore. (1987a, pp. 154–55)

Peter Blau (1973) has also noted the advantages of the departmental form for professors. As he suggests, increased academic specialization and bureaucratization have expanded the organizational capacity for autonomy and authority among high-ranking faculty. Granted that autonomy and authority, faculty have achieved some insulation from central actions.

One can thus see the department as a vehicle through which faculty leverage their authority. In Clark's view, professors "use the department as a tool to mediate between the realities of a particular university context and the demands and desires of their own discipline. . . . Forming the base of the structure of faculty power, the department has undergirded the development of a dual authority structure within universities and colleges. . . . The department is the local rock on which the power of voice is based in academia, the organized base for the capacity of academics to exercise influence within the organization to which they belong and to branch out into larger circles" (1987a, pp. 64–65).

Inevitably, such a system generates tensions between the individual and the organization. A department serves as a sympathetic base for individual productivity within the discipline's research arena and in the classroom. At the same time, it must produce the services desired by its internal and external constituencies. Clark notes that "within the basic operating unit, the problem is how to balance the personal and the collegial, the rights and powers of the individual against those of the collectivity. A strong tilt toward the personal produces barons—or in guild terminology, masters who have complete control over journeymen and apprentices in their individual domains. A strong tilt toward the collegial produces a collective stifling of individual initiative . . . and hence an irrational constraint on the performances and creations to which that initiative might lead" (1987a, p. 153). Units therefore devise multiple cross-checks on individual power, via multiperson thesis committees, student evaluations of faculty teaching, and the like.

While the departmental form may grant power regardless of discipline, it is rooted fundamentally in difference. Talcott Parsons and Gerald Platt (1974) note that the differentiated disciplinary organization of knowledge is an expression of the institution's shared value of cognitive rationality. Departments provide both vertical and horizontal differentiation for institutions, distinguishing fields of study and research and providing distinct professional homes within larger colleges. In a similar vein, Blau (1973) suggests that university departments illustrate a familiar organizational imperative: increasing demands for an organization's products or services generate differentiation, and because differentiation requires expanded coordination, new administrative components arise. In the context of the university, Blau observes, growth in enrollments and research funding have fueled growth in the size and range of academic departments.

Of course, structural differentiation reflects not only how knowledge is organized in the institution but also what is valued there (Gumport and Snydman 2002). What is valued can change over time. That is, departments change over time, as does the array of departments on a campus. Structure not only legitimates knowledge but also shapes the ways institutions respond to external pressures and expectations for perseverance or change. Interestingly, the structure (that is, the departmental array) rarely shrinks: Patricia Gumport and S. K. Snydman's (2002) research suggests that universities tend to respond to knowledge change by *adding* units, not removing them. Reforms must be accommodated within existing systems, and the usual result is slow accretion rather than substitution.[4]

Andrew Abbott (2002) notes that the roster of disciplines on campuses tends to be stable or to grow only slowly because academic disciplines are deeply rooted social structures that institutionalize both the macrostructure of the faculty labor market and the microstructure of each individual university. Three forces maintain departmental stability on campuses, Abbott argues: forces that prevent individual fields from growing larger, forces that keep them from shrinking, and forces that limit the power of other providers. Together, these preserve a *disciplinary division of labor*. This is strongest in the sciences, which have a "natural hierarchy of generality" (p. 217), while social sciences and humanities tend to overlap in many ways (e.g., in their concern with culture). Overall, given the stability of the disciplinary structure, Abbott notes, interdisciplinarity is a difficult unresolved issue on most campuses.

---

4. It is important to note, as Gumport and Snydman (2002) stress, that departments and their home colleges represent only one dimension of structure, the bureaucratic. The other primary dimension is the programmatic (i.e., the curricula and degree programs offered). That dimension is closely related to the bureaucratic, but multidisciplinarity and other factors ensure some distinctions.

Change may be slow in the roster of departments, but that does not necessarily imply that the departments themselves are slow to change internally. Indeed, the loosely coupled nature of academic systems may allow departments to be especially adaptive and flexible (Weick 1976). Clark notes: "Despite the belief of many observers that academic systems change significantly only when pressured by external forces . . . invention and diffusion are institutionalized in the work of departments and counterpart units that embody the disciplines and professions. . . . Such change is widely overlooked. . . . In a bottom-heavy knowledge institution, grassroots innovation is a crucial form of change" (1983, pp. 234–35). In a similar vein, Clark suggests that even the most bureaucratically constrained departmental systems can occasionally be open to innovations pursued out of personal, even charismatic, authority (1984, p. 124).

Of course, generalizations like the above are tempered by the pervasive organizational differences among the various sectors of U.S. higher education. The structuring of academic work varies in particular with a campus's place in the institutional stratification system. Importantly, the context of faculty work appears to be more collegial and less managerial or bureaucratic in institutions high in prestige, such as research universities. Janice Beyer Lodahl and Gerald Gordon (1973a) found that national reputation is even more important than the specific field in explaining the level of collegiality in an academic unit. That is, collegiality is driven less by whether a department is in accounting or English than by whether it is in a high- or low-ranked institution. In high-prestige institutions, Clark argues, "ambiguity is seen as functional, allowing the administration to adapt to the disaggregated, intense professionalism of the faculty, with everyone then praising the dominance of 'community' over bureaucracy" (1987a, p. 152). In contrast, Clark notes, community college faculty experience greater institutional "managerialism" and in some cases union-imposed bureaucratic coordination as well. In those settings, departmental collegiality and autonomy can be constrained by institutional oversight.

These across-sector differences are important, but also important are within-sector stratification (witness the attention to the *U.S. News and World Report*'s various sector-specific annual rankings for undergraduate programs) and within-discipline and across-departments stratification (witness the attention to the *U.S. News and World Report*'s various discipline-specific annual rankings for graduate programs). Stratification systems may overlap in intriguing ways. Within the research university sector, for example, the quality of individual departments undoubtedly contributes to institutional prestige, but institutional characteristics, including national prestige, may also contribute to departments' own rankings on national prestige and research productivity. Indeed, departmental rankings may be driven largely by institutional "halos." The two facts that Harvard is a highly rated institution and has a highly rated chemistry department may be causally connected in both directions.

A variety of sociological works have touched on this question. In a traditionally framed analysis, W. O. Hagstrom (1971) found that specific departments' national prestige in the sciences was associated with departmental size, faculty backgrounds, student characteristics, research opportunities and production, and faculty awards and disciplinary offices. D. H. Kamens (1972) criticized Hagstrom's work, however, on the grounds that he inappropriately assumed that departments within universities operate in relatively autonomous labor markets, so that determinants of the attractiveness, and hence recruitment success, of one department is independent of those for others. Using the earlier data and findings of Allan Cartter (1966), Kamens argued that universities significantly govern departmental development by controlling resources, traditions, and relations with certain external constituencies of universities. Kamens concluded that more attention should be paid to the political economy of universities and how this affects institutions' and departments' internal operations.

Thus, a question of special sociological interest is the relative importance for faculty productivity of departmental contexts—as opposed to societal, other organizational, and individual factors. Jeffrey Pfeffer, Anthony Leong, and Katherine Strehl (1976) found no evidence that publication of departments' national prestige ratings affected subsequent research publication levels in departments, once previous publication levels were taken into account. P. D. Allison and S. J. Long (1990) investigated whether it was departmental or individual factors that prompted differences in productivity (publications and citation rates) among academic scientists. Their results, somewhat in contrast to those of Pfeffer, Leong, and Strehl, suggest that the effect of department affiliation on individual productivity may be more important than the effect of individual productivity on departmental affiliation. That is, although superior faculty are recruited to positions in superior institutions, the nature of the institutions themselves (especially the department recruiting) may supersede selection effects in explaining individual productivity. These results echo earlier analyses by J. M. Braxton (1983), whose work revealed especially strong departmental effects on faculty with weaker prior research records.

Bruce Keith (1999) focused explicitly on the role of one institutional factor: prestige. On the basis of an analysis of national prestige ratings for five disciplinary areas (the social and behavioral sciences, humanities, biological sciences, physical and mathematical sciences, and engineering), he argued that departmental ratings for doctoral programs largely reflect a contextual attribute (mainly eminence) representative of their universities, not performance-based departmental attributes. As a result, academic departments across a given institution are similar with respect to external raters' perceptions of their quality. "Departments operate within a stable institutional context, one in which the perceived reputation of the department is a function of its affiliated university" (Keith 1999, p. 411). Keith's approach and supporting evidence call into question the assumption of numerous studies that departmental ratings are performance based.

Differences in prestige can have important everyday implications for faculty. Stephan Cole and Jonathan Cole (1967) found that departmental reward systems do not operate uniformly across departments of physics. In departments ranked lower in national prestige, sheer publication quantity is more likely to be used as a criterion for promotion, while research quality is more often rewarded when it is produced by physicists in high-ranking departments. On issues such as this, it is important to bear in mind that national prestige may not entirely correspond with internal campus prestige, either within or across fields. For example, a highly rated education school may command little respect on its own campus, while a low-rated physics department may be quite high on prestige hierarchies on its own campus.

One would think that differences in national prestige might shape communication patterns in academic fields, but there is no supporting evidence for that proposition. For example, Cole and Cole (1968) found that the national rank of one's department did not greatly influence physicists' communication patterns. Instead, analysts have found specialization a factor in research communication within and across departments. For example, in a study of communications among physical scientists across various departments in an elite research university, N. E. Friedkin (1978) found that the communication network of a *diversely*

specialized population of physical scientists is more structurally cohesive (i.e., more aware of each other's activities and in contact with each
other) than a network composed of more *homogeneously* specialized
scientists such as an academic department. On this evidence, Friedkin
argued that academic departments are not appropriate units for describing the patterns of research communication among university faculty, at least in the physical sciences.

Still, departments can be significant influences on faculty behavior.
D. H. Kamens and Gian Sarup (1980) empirically examined two models
of organizational impact on faculty sentiments toward collective bargaining and strikes. The "stratification model" focused on discontent
based in the organizational stratification of units on campus. The "consistency model" focused on alienation resulting from discrepancies between stated departmental goals and actual reward policies. Kamens and
Sarup's results provided support for both propositions. Departmental
variation within universities thus did notably influence faculty attitudes.

A persistent theme in the sociological literature on departments considers the extent to which the departmental form serves equity. From
one perspective, equity may be functional for departmental success. For
example, Clark highlights the market for talent as a powerful weapon
for equity: "Department organization tends to break up . . . individual
centered fiefdoms, distributing power locally among a number of full
professors all equal in formal power, and in lesser amounts to associate
and assistant professors on a gradient of rank and responsibility. . . .
Under organization by department individuals are more on their own.
And in the competitive race for status in which American university
departments engage, the recruitment and retention of talent becomes
pressing. Inbreeding is suspect, a weakness to be guarded against, since
the odds are normally high that the best person is not one's own" (1987b,
p. 383). In another essay, Clark notes of the departmental form that "this
powerful instrument has been relatively democratic in its internal operation. . . . Administrative heads rotate; each member has the opportunity that others possess to engage in autonomous teaching and research; all have access to whatever supports are available in the form of
teaching assistants, research assistants, research funds, and sabbatical
leaves" (1987a, pp. 64–65).

Some analysts are not so sanguine, however. In a study of faculty's
work hours, research productivity, and time allocation among teaching,
research, and service, for example, M. L. Bellas and R. K. Toutkoushian

(1999) found that variations in teaching and service loads within and across academic units tend to be distinctly inequitable for women and faculty of color.

Competition, Conflict, and Change within Departments

A number of sociologists have examined competition, conflict, and strategic change in the university (e.g., Slaughter 2002). A strand of this research tradition extends to the internal work of departments.

For example, Jeffrey Pfeffer and colleagues have extensively examined the ways that departments allocate scarce resources among competing faculty. Pfeffer and Nancy Langton (1988) found that several factors apparently contribute to increased dispersion in faculty salaries inside a department: private institutional control, larger departmental size, and a greater tendency to work alone. Contributing to more equal salary distributions, Pfeffer and Langton suggest, are greater social contact among departmental members, more democratic and participative departmental governance, and greater demographic homogeneity. The authors conclude that social factors, as well as predictable individual factors, are influential in wage dispersion: "There are important connections between social relations in a department, how work is organized and administered, and salary inequality" (p. 603). Thus, they suggest, their results are consistent with social-psychological theories of how norms, social contact, and social relations affect reward systems.

Later, A. M. Konrad and Jeffrey Pfeffer's 1990 analysis of data from more than 5,000 academics across 200 colleges and universities provided further support for that perspective. They found that faculty productivity and faculty pay are most strongly related in departments that have stronger norms emphasizing research; are located in private and higher-prestige institutions; are in institutions governed by collective-bargaining agreements; exhibit more research collaboration and social contact among faculty; are in academic fields with more highly developed scientific paradigms; and have chairpersons with shorter, fixed-length terms.

Having established the factors apparently contributing to wage dispersion in departments, Pfeffer and colleagues next turned to examining its effects. Pfeffer and Langton (1993) found that faculty in departments with high levels of wage dispersion tended to be less satisfied, less productive in research, and less likely to collaborate on research. The negative effects of wage dispersion on satisfaction appeared to be reduced for faculty with longer tenure, faculty in fields with more developed scientific paradigms, and faculty in units with salaries based more on experience and scholarly activity. Even in these cases, however, dissatisfaction was predictably greater among those earning less. Also predictably, wage dispersion has a smaller negative effect on satisfaction at private colleges and universities, because in those settings salaries are less likely to be known. Overall, Pfeffer and Langton's results suggest that one's position in the salary structure, the availability of information about wage inequality, and a socially legitimated basis of reward allocation will affect the extent to which wage dispersion produces adverse effects.

Salary levels and annual increments make plain the results of competition in departments. Another result of internal competition, unfortunately, can be ethical lapses. Melissa Anderson, Karen Seashore Louis, and Jason Earle (1994) provide evidence that competitive and individualistic social climates in departments can contribute to scholarly misconduct by graduate students and faculty. Large research projects, for example, may be especially likely to breed such conditions and thus misconduct. Interestingly, Anderson, Louis, and Earle's results suggest that departments' social climates are more important than their structural characteristics and that both, in turn, are more important than the department's home discipline in creating the conditions for misconduct.

Results from my own research with Anderson (Hearn and Anderson 2002) also emphasize the importance of structural factors in creating conditions for conflict episodes. We note that the familiar three-domain model of organizational conflict—relationship-based, task-based, and process-based—can oversimplify by conflating a conflict's cause, manifestation, and effects. Arguing that "the most productive approach to understanding conflict in academic departments is via underlying structural factors, rather that via manifested disputes around personalities, tasks, and process" (pp. 506–7), we studied disagreements regarding faculty promotion and tenure decisions. We found that departments with larger instructional loads and lower levels of internal curricular specialization were more likely to have split votes over promotion and tenure. Interestingly, beyond these structural effects, our results highlight significant disciplinary roots in conflicts: departments from disciplines with a "soft" knowledge base were more likely to evince conflict in promotion and tenure decisions.

Moving from the causes to the effects of conflict episodes, some analysts have examined how departments deal with problems such as those posed by research misconduct. Again, social and structural characteristics are important. Braxton (1991), for example, found in his study of units responding to violations of scientific norms among their faculty that a department's place in a national prestige hierarchy positively related to the formality of the actions it took in response to scientific violations. Braxton suggests several possible reasons for this result: a stature-related tendency toward greater formalization, a desire for protection against potential federal sanctions in grant awards, and an effort to maintain prestige in the face of negative publicity.

Regardless of units' underlying structural tendencies toward consensus or conflict, they must adapt to changing circumstances. Using budgetary and curricular records at Stanford University, Curtis Manns and James March (1978) explored the relation between changing financial conditions and departments' modifications of their curricula. They hypothesized that (1) departmental efforts to increase the attractiveness of their curriculum will be greater in times of financial adversity than in times of prosperity and (2) curriculum-change efforts pursued during times of adversity will be weaker in departments with strong research reputations than in departments with weaker reputations. To test these hypotheses, they studied eight attributes of departmental curricula: variance in course enrollment; variance in average units; length of course descriptions in the catalog; proportion of undergraduate courses taught by full professors; proportion of courses given at noncompetitive times; proportion of courses not requiring a prerequisite; average number of units earned in courses; and average grades earned in courses. In keeping with the hypotheses, the results suggest that departments' curricula respond notably to declines in financial conditions and that departments with strong research reputations were somewhat less responsive than departments with weak reputations.

In emphasizing the organizational context of units' curricular changes, Manns and March avoided some familiar traps in traditional analyses of such change. Sheila Slaughter (2002) has convincingly argued that work on curricular change has too often ignored or downplayed the social context of academic disciplines and units. Published histories of disciplines and fields, for example, tend to ignore the power of the extant reward system under which scholars work, i.e., faculty's vested interests in theories and methods that bring them prestige, position, and resources. Among higher education scholars, analyses of curriculum change recognize the importance of demographic change and changing skills requirements in the economy but tend to lack attention to organizational mechanisms of change. Market-oriented narratives focus productively on human capital investments and students as consumers of educational products but tend to overlook the social (noneconomic) structures of power and status that shape market influences. Noting these deficiencies, Slaughter presents an alternative, sociologically informed model of curricular formation and change, focusing on disciplinary developments influencing professors' research interests, social movements surrounding such newer fields as women's and ethnic studies programs, and powerful organizations in the political economy. Of these forces, Slaughter is inclined to emphasize the significance of powerful external organizations as suppliers of jobs and research directions. At the level of schools and departments, curricular change may be driven more by such worldly forces than by more abstract ideals.

Resource Dependencies and Power Relations

A number of prominent sociological analysts have examined the factors contributing to departmental success in resource distributions within universities. As noted in the introductory material in this chapter, these studies are in some respects more institutional than departmental in orientation. What is more, these works overlap with others covered elsewhere in the chapter. Still, they are important and prominent enough to merit separate mention here.

Jeffrey Pfeffer and colleagues have used academic departments as a primary empirical setting in their research program on resource dependencies in organizations. In that work, they have paid particular attention to how power relations help drive universities' resource allocations among departments. Pfeffer and Gerald Salancik (1974) found that units' relative political/particularistic power (for example, their representation in campus governance activities) and their strength in terms of bureaucratic/universalistic criteria (for example, workload, national rank, and number of faculty) are both important in determining departmental fates in university budget decisions. Interestingly, Pfeffer and Salancik's results suggest that the more politically powerful an academic department, the less its allocated resources are a direct function of departmental workload and student demand for course offerings. Pfeffer and Salancik conclude that departmental power influences organizational decisions only to the extent that such decisions are not constrained by other factors—for instance, by other organizations, state legislatures, or governmental agencies.

In another analysis in the same year, Salancik and Pfeffer (1974) hypothesized that a department instrumental in obtaining critical resources for the university would be especially successful in obtaining the critical and scarce resources of the organization. The results suggest that a department's ability to obtain outside grants and contracts is critical to its fate in internal budgetary decisions. Also important are national prestige and the relative size of the graduate programs. Each of these factors relates to institutional dependencies on certain critical resources: research dollars, prestige, and tuition dollars. One might expect that departments with lower success in obtaining outside resources would fare better in internal resource distributions. In effect, they would be compensated for their differential access to outside resources. In fact, however, Salancik and Pfeffer suggest that the internal resource-allocation system exacerbates resource inequalities by granting the most internal support to the subunits with the most outside support.[5]

Later work by Pfeffer and others confirmed the "power of power" in university operations. Pfeffer, Salancik, and Huseyin Leblebici (1976) found that departments' total grant allocations from the National Science Foundation (NSF) were significantly related to departmental representation on NSF advisory boards. This result provides an external analog to the 1974 finding of Pfeffer and Salancik that departmental representation in campus governance is associated with more favorable outcomes in internal budgetary systems. Back on the internal side, Moore and Pfeffer (1980) found that departmental political power on campus appeared to speed the frequency with which departmental faculty move through ranks toward tenure and promotion. The proportion of departmental faculty at more senior ranks also facilitated swift movement through ranks. On the other hand, the rate of departmental growth, the level of the department's scientific paradigm, and a department's national prestige had no effect on advancement. Additional work by Pfeffer and colleagues explored the extent to which the effects of political power are contingent on particular circumstances. Pfeffer and Moore (1980b), for example, found that departmental political power

5. The pattern provides another example of Merton's (1968) "Matthew Effect," in that the richer departments become still richer. Cordes and Walker, in a 1996 *Chronicle of Higher Education* article, suggest that the pattern persists.

appears less important when resources are scarce. In those times, universalistic, nonpolitical criteria may ascend in importance.

In a separate line of research, Sheila Slaughter and colleagues (Slaughter 1993; Slaughter and Leslie 1997) have presented findings suggesting that resource-reallocation patterns in higher education parallel the ongoing redistribution of wealth and power in the larger society. Using neo-Marxian, postmodernist, and feminist theories, Slaughter interprets patterns of faculty retrenchment in higher education as strongly shaped by the same class-based political/economic conflicts that are restructuring the broader economy. While these changes are often defended as market driven, Slaughter and colleagues argue that retrenchment is also, in important ways, socially constructed. Evidence presented in these analyses suggests that the fields least likely to be cut in internal reallocation processes were those best able to attract external resources and represent themselves as close to the market. Often, those favored units also had majority male student bodies. Slaughter's work suggests that postsecondary education is being restructured rather than retrenched and that new budgetary resources are being disproportionately provided to departments and schools that are already resource rich. In such an environment, departments seeking to attract funding may be pressured to move toward matching the characteristics of more successful units in their disciplines on other campuses and in other disciplines on their own campuses.

In later work, Slaughter paid particular attention to the social implications of these allocative patterns in public institutions, noting that "supply-side institutional resource allocation policies tend to bestow fewer state resources on departments and/or fields of study that have large numbers of women and minority faculty" (1998, p. 234). She concludes that "universities as communities should address explicitly the growing resource disparities among departments" (p. 239) and should rethink mission, market, internal resource allocation patterns, and beliefs about what kinds of knowledge merit resources. Still later, C. S. Volk, Slaughter, and S. L. Thomas (2001) carried the theme to an analysis of departments in a public research university. Noting that earlier work had not paid sufficient attention to departments as opposed to institutions or individuals, they stress that departments powerfully mediate individual faculty's performance and ability and chances to accrue institutional resources. "Faculty delivering some curricula may not receive the same resources as faculty associated with other curricula, just as faculty in departments preparing students for certain careers may not be given the same support as faculty in other, more favored departments" (p. 338). Volk, Slaughter, and Thomas contrast rational/political theory, which suggests that "funds flow to departments that are central to mission and workload, are productive in terms of student credit hours, grants and contracts and faculty scholarship, and are high in quality" (2001, p. 389), with critical/political theory, which suggests that departmental resource allocations are influenced by gender, race, power, and service to dominant external constituencies. The findings provide support for both models, but the authors also note that a number of findings, such as a loss of resources for upper-division student credit hours, fit neither model and can be interpreted variously. The authors conclude: "Colleges and universities often try to clarify missions by focusing on markets. But markets are, like missions, multiple, complex, and sometimes conflicting. . . . There is not a linear market logic that dictates how state dollars are allocated to departments, so we cannot rely exclusively on market models" (p. 407).

Organizational Implications of Disciplinary Differences

Sociologists have long theorized about the relationships between specific academic fields and the organizational features of academic departments housing them. There can be little question that departments reflect their individual disciplinary roots as the faculty go about their work. Tony Becher (1989) stresses the distinctive training, initiation, and socialization of new members of disciplines and the consequently distinctive nature of interactions within the associated fields and academic units. Similarly, Clark notes that faculty in academic departments

> are not organized to carry out the will of nominal superiors in organized hierarchies; instead they develop their own incentives and their own forms of cooperation around a subject matter and its problems. In fact, it is their intentions and strivings and not those stated as the broad aims of higher education which determine the real goals of the many departments, schools, and sub-colleges that make up the operating levels of universities and colleges. The operating units are as much if not more the arms of the disciplines as they are the arms of the institutions, especially when research is emphasized over teaching and specialized training is more important than liberal education. (1987b, p. 381)

Seeing differences, sociologists often expect to find stratification, and this line of inquiry is no exception. Clark viewed departments as being at the intersection of two stratification systems. Their unit's prestige will vary according to the stature of the discipline they represent as well as their own department's stature within the field: "A high-rated department in a prestigious discipline has doubly powerful grounds for autonomous decision making," while "a low-rated department in a subject lacking prestige is likely to exist on the margin of trust and power, given access only to crumbs left at the far end of the table" (Clark 1987b, pp. 169–70).[6] Of course, these external referents for authority are far more important in the university sector than in others. Clark notes that "at the extreme of the two-year institution, the local district framework, with its genetic imprint of school trusteeship and administration, makes institutional controls much more powerful than disciplinary influences. Whether academics are in English or physics or business administration has little effect. What matters most in determining their authority is that they are in a community college" (1987a, p. 174).

Prestige appears to parallel what has been termed the "level of knowledge development" in a field. A prominent line of sociological inquiry suggests that a field's knowledge development has significant implications for the organizational functioning of the field's associated academic departments. Some of the earliest research in this tradition was by Lodahl and Gordon (1972, 1973a, 1973b), who explored the usefulness of Thomas Kuhn's concept of "paradigm" by studying teaching and research activities within the university.[7] Hypothesizing that a high level of knowledge (paradigm) development in a discipline facilitates research and teaching through improved processes of communication and access to stored information, they found that physicists and chemists (representing faculty in high-paradigm fields) exhibited more agreement over field content and were more willing and satisfied to spend

6. Clark (1987a, p. 170) suggests that the "phenomenon of 'the more, the more,' in which the powerful become more powerful, occurs also within departments as well as among them." For example, faculty with power owing to prestigious, well-rewarded lines of research tend to be disproportionately rewarded over time in salary, grants, and recognition.

7. At about the same time, Anthony Biglan (1973) applied a psychological approach to disciplinary differences, identifying pure-applied, soft-hard, and life-nonlife as critical dimensions of difference among fields. Many analyses of academic departments have utilized Biglan's approach, but his work is decidedly less sociological than that of the investigators whose work is highlighted in this chapter.

time with graduate students than were sociologists and political scientists (representing faculty in low-paradigm fields).

In terms of power and decision making, Lodahl and Gordon found that in teaching decisions (i.e., who teaches what and when?), faculty in the physical sciences rely more heavily on committees and consensus formation, while faculty in the social sciences rely more on negotiations conducted by department chairs. Interestingly, Lodahl and Gordon found that while physical science departments enjoy greater autonomy from central administrations, owing to their higher prestige, social science departments grant more autonomy to their individual members on a variety of workload and administrative matters.

In later work, Judith Adkison (1979) found support for Lodahl and Gordon's conclusion that paradigm development affects interaction patterns within and across departments; she related her findings to the extent of *normative crystallization* (that is, the level of agreement around a field's core norms). As noted earlier, Hearn and Anderson (2002) found that conflict over promotion and tenure cases was especially likely in low-consensus fields. Thus, there is support for Clark's (1987a) observation that greater consensus is achievable in departments with well-developed, accepted bodies of knowledge and thus shared views on the definition of quality. Together, these results indicate that disciplinary differences go to the heart of teaching and research in academic units. Any attempt to change the university must take into account the close relations between structures in different fields and the notably different styles with which university departments operate.[8]

In an impressive line of studies on university decision making, Pfeffer and colleagues repeatedly found evidence that the level of knowledge development in a field significantly affects departmental functioning. Pfeffer, Leong, and Strehl (1976) found publication productivity more clearly connected to departmental prestige in fields with the highest levels of paradigm development. In fields with low paradigm development, publications are less closely tied to productivity, a finding that suggests greater consistency in the quality of publications in the high-paradigm fields. Similarly, Pfeffer, Leong, and Strehl (1977) found that departmental representation on boards of prestigious journals has a

---

8. For additional work on related issues from a sociological perspective, see Neumann and Boris 1978, Neumann 1979, and Bresser 1984.

bigger effect on publication rates in departments with high consensus than in those with lower consensus. Pfeffer and Moore (1980a) found that units claiming a higher, more widely shared disciplinary paradigm benefit from longer tenure among their departmental heads. Interestingly, smaller (and thus presumably more cohesive and integrated) departments also had longer-serving chairs. Both results suggest that consensus enhances administrative stability. Pfeffer and Moore (1980b) found that the level of paradigm development behind a unit adds to explanations of budget allocations, thus improving the explanatory model produced earlier by Pfeffer and Salancik (1974). Specifically, high levels of paradigm development can apparently augment the budgetary benefits that departments draw from campus political power and improvements in enrollment.

In similarly strong work, Salancik, B. M. Staw, and L. R. Pondy (1980) found in their study of 20 departments in a single university that administrative turnover in departments (i.e., chair appointments and resignations) was an interactive function of the paradigm development of the department's field, the resource interdependence among departmental members, and the degree of unrest during the historical period of an administrator's headship. This work was rooted in a classic proposition from James Thompson (1967) regarding the connections between organizational uncertainties and managerial stability. The results also fit Pfeffer and Salancik's (1974) proposition that organizational control is adjusted to align organizations with their emerging environments.

It is important to note that the work of Pfeffer, Salancik, and their colleagues considers paradigm development empirically as a variable in sophisticated multivariate models representing theories for explaining certain departmental outcomes. Thus, its effects in those models are contextualized rather than univariate. In other words, rather than mere bivariate correlations, the results suggest convincingly that disciplinary roots may play a causal role in departmental outcomes.

Reviewing the literature on the operational effects of departmental knowledge development, J. M. Braxton and L. L. Hargens (1996) concluded that, compared to units in low-consensus fields, departments in high-consensus fields tend to be more efficient, change and adapt more easily, are less conflicted, have less turnover, are more collaborative in publications, and are more effective in achieving certain goals and obtaining financial and human resources. These authors caution analysts, however, not to overstate the differences: they suggest that departmental consensus does not appear to matter for success in achieving under-graduate education goals or satisfying students and faculty, and con-sensus is not associated with disagreements on the primacy of research or certain other values.

Having established the effects of, or at least associations with, depart-mental disciplinary roots, it is important to consider how and why such differences arise. As Braxton and Hargens (1996) argue, we need to look at the *causes* of departmental differences as well their consequences. Is consensus driven by features of social structure (Fuchs 1992), research technologies (Collins 1994), the nature of the field itself (Cole 1994), or the personality types associated with the field (Smart, Feldman, and Ethington 2000)? Is it possible that there is substantial reciprocal causa-tion among consensus, disciplinary social structures, and research tech-nologies (Pfeffer 1993)? At present, these questions are unanswered, but some hints may be drawn from observations of what might be consid-ered informal natural experiments, such as the birth of new units on campus.

Z. F. Gamson (1966) analyzed the collective conceptions and norms emerging among faculty in two departments at a newly founded small college. The two dominant departments there, the natural sciences and social sciences, exhibited sharp differences that crystallized into two different belief systems. The natural science department pursued a pre-dominantly "utilitarian" approach, emphasizing cognitive effects on students with little concern for encouraging students' commitment to the college or faculty interaction with students. In contrast, the social science department pursued a "normative" approach, encouraging stu-dent commitment and faculty efforts to "reach" students personally as well as intellectually. These results suggest that certain aspects of depart-mental differences may be, in a sense, genetic—products of the prior socialization of faculty as well as their values and personal styles.

Gumport (1988) provides evidence on unit births that were more difficult. Suggesting that curriculum development efforts reveal the ways that scholarly interests on a campus intersect and conflict, she studied interest groups, interdisciplinary programs, and departments in the field of women's studies. In new fields like this, she suggests, faculty become mediators among new intellectual ideas, local organizational oppor-tunities, and political commitments rooted in external cultural move-ments. Emerging subcultures of scholars potentially conflict with con-ventional academic understandings, making organizational recognition of those subcultures less likely. Although knowledge itself is unquestionably dynamic, she suggests that the task of *organizing and reorganizing academic knowledge* is difficult because disciplinary structures within campuses tend to resist change, or at least tend to be self-sustaining.

Regardless of one's understandings of the roots and implications of disciplinary differences, those differences cannot be ignored. Analysts of department-level data often find these differences among the most, if not the most, striking aspects of their findings (Peterson 1976; Braxton and Hargens 1996; Smart, Feldman, and Ethington 2000; Hearn and Anderson 2002). The challenge is to provide theoretical tools to "pick the lock" to the mysteries of the differences' pervasiveness.

Compositional Patterns

The work of a number of sociologists suggests that compositional factors such as a department's gender, age, seniority, and racial/ethnic distributions may affect departmental functioning. For example, these factors may influence salary distributions or decision styles. The theoretical logic behind such propositions holds that "the context of social relationships, defined by the distribution of status characteristics among organizational members, often determines the impact of the characteristics on individual and organizational outcomes" (Tolbert and Bacharach 1992, p. ix).

The growing body of research from this perspective suggests strongly that a unit's demographic profile is an influential *organizational* variable (see Pfeffer 1983; Stewman 1988; Bacharach and Bamberger 1992; Mittman 1992; Hearn and Anderson 1998). That is, demographic factors have notable organization-level consequences and are not merely the aggregated demographic characteristics of the individuals within the organization.

The "ur-text" for demographically framed organizational analysis is Ken McNeil and J. D. Thompson's (1971) article in the *American Sociological Review*. Although this theoretical work set the stage for later work in a variety of organizational settings, it is noteworthy that McNeil and Thompson focused their initial theorizing and analysis on academic units.[9] The operative mechanism in their propositions is what they call a

9. It should be stressed that McNeil and Thompson (1971) were not the first to consider the effects of faculty demography in academic departments. Two years earlier, Corwin (1969) presented findings suggesting that older, homogeneous, and relatively stable faculties

unit's *metabolism*: its stability and regeneration as members enter and leave the organization. The authors view faculty socialization as a centerpiece of organizations' "social regeneration," or patterns over time in the ratio of newcomers to veteran members. They argue that a healthy rate of regeneration, neither too high nor too low, conveys that a sense of stability prevails in an organization, even though people inevitably enter and leave. Obviously, McNeil and Thompson argue, the socialization process tends to be easier during slow and steady regeneration. If an organization is stable, more attention can be paid to meeting its fundamental goals. As regeneration rates go higher, however, the proportion of members who know the organizational culture declines, and the need for socialization and routinization necessarily increases. A smaller proportion of veterans must socialize newcomers, and although veterans have leverage, new customs and norms are likely to develop among the ascendant pool of newcomers. Thus, when units are forced to recruit heavily among the younger population—that is, to pursue rapid regeneration—departmental turmoil may result.

McNeil and Thompson's arguments have been echoed by later analysts, who have observed that age, rank, and length-of-service distributions can affect departmental functioning in a variety of ways. In a particularly interesting study in this genre, Bruce McCain, Charles O'Reilly, and Pfeffer (1983) found that university academic departments with substantial gaps among cohorts were characterized by increased rates of voluntary retirements, resignations, involuntary removal, and expired appointments. Their explanation for the finding was that people who enter an organization together or at about the same time tend to view the organization similarly. Identifiable discontinuities or bulges in the organization's demographic distributions thus can create ripe conditions for turnover.

Younger and more junior faculty tend to fare differently from their more senior counterparts in the competition for research funding, and departments with a rather junior demographic composition overall may tend to have rather disparate patterns of funding. Over time, therefore, movement from senior to junior composition or vice versa may affect the overall pattern of funding in a department. In a study of

---

may be especially willing to enforce strong socialization regimes and expel nonconforming new members. The theoretical scope and detail of McNeil and Thompson's consideration of the topic, however, propelled it to greater visibility and recognition.

departments at a large research institution, M. S. Anderson (1990) found that the accumulated years of experience within an academic department may affect the group's ability to shield itself from internal budget cuts and its capacity for mustering external research support. As departments become more senior, they become more dependent on a limited range of relatively critical sources of support. For example, in departments that were heavily dependent on federal research dollars at a given time, the proportion of funding from federal sources grew as departmental faculty increased in seniority. In contrast, when faculty in such units became more junior, departments tended to shift away from traditional federal funding sources. Such shifts have differing implications for departments' ongoing financial arrangements and relationships over time.

Beyond seniority and the related constructs of age and length of service, analysts have studied other demographic compositional factors. Of these, gender has been the most frequent focus. As is well known, women faculty tend to be concentrated in disciplines with the least lucrative labor-market conditions and tend to have less education and experience and fewer journal publications than men (Bellas 1994). All of these differences contribute to their having significantly lower salaries than men (Bellas 1994) as well as salary growth lower than men's (Bellas 1997). Although distinctive life choices undoubtedly contribute to these disadvantages, M. L. Bellas (1994, 1997) argues that unmeasured internal factors within institutions also contribute to unequal salary distributions in higher education. One can infer that departments' salary-distribution practices for their faculty may be one of Bellas's implicated internal factors. But the problem may also lie in the treatment of departments with large numbers of women faculty. Slaughter (1993) provides evidence that departments with a majority of male students (and thus, usually, a majority of male faculty and male members of the occupation) tend to fare better in resource allocations within universities.

Some work on gender issues has examined male-female proportions' effects on internal departmental operations and behaviors. Focusing on students, my research (Hearn 1980), my investigation with Susan Olzak (1981, 1982), and that of V. D. Alexander and P. A. Thoits (1985) found that the student gender composition of units can influence student performance and attitudes in college. Focusing on faculty, Pamela Tolbert et al. (1995) examined gender composition in 50 sociology departments over an 11-year period. They found that as the proportion of women faculty in a majority-male department grew, turnover among women also increased, suggesting that increases in the relative size of a minority will result in increased intergroup competition and conflict. Once women hit a threshold of around 35–40 percent, however, turnover began to decrease in departments.

All of these analyses were inspired and informed by the pioneering theorizing of sociologist Rosabeth Moss Kanter. Kanter (1977) theorized that gender ratios within organizations are important factors for understanding and predicting a large number of behavioral phenomena, from the degree of power women and men feel at work to the ways they cope with professional and personal stresses. Most memorably, Kanter suggests that when the gender composition of units within organizational settings reaches certain "tipping points," work relations change dramatically. Kanter's ideas regarding the effects of gender composition have been persuasively extended by others (e.g., Wharton and Baron 1991) and remain influential for work in higher education and other settings.

For theory and research, the composition concept raises important measurement issues. Kanter's analysis and its successors in the gender-composition literature focus on tipping points, i.e., percentages at which the effects of demographic factors begin to change. Efforts to specify tipping points across organizations may founder on the variations in the activation point across settings and across time. For example, changing societal gender attitudes may move the point up or down exogenously to the organization itself. Pfeffer and Moore's (1980a) study of the tenure of academic department chairs used a rather straightforward indicator of seniority composition to capture average faculty rank in a department: the department-level mean of a variable whose value for an individual is 1 for an assistant professor, 2 for an associate professor, and 3 for a full professor. Although the indicator had effects in the work of Pfeffer and his colleagues, Anderson and I (Hearn and Anderson 2002) attributed its failure to show any effects in their study of departmental conflict to the possibility that it oversimplifies compositional influences. For example, a departmental score of 2.0 could be achieved on the indicator through three very different compositional profiles: a department with an even mix of assistant and full professors, a department with an even mix of assistant, associate, and full professors, or a department with all associate professors.

McCain, O'Reilly, and Pfeffer's (1983) study of unit turnover employed a somewhat more sophisticated indicator of academic composition. That study's distinctiveness lies in the particular aspect of faculty demographic distributions it considered: hiring cohorts of faculty and the gaps between them. The authors' primary demographic indicator was the number of five- to eight-year periods in a department's history during which no new faculty were hired. For that indicator, a value of 0 indicates a relatively even distribution of entry dates, and higher values signify increasing numbers of well-defined cohorts by date of hire. McCain, O'Reilly, and Pfeffer also employed a second, simpler demographic indicator: the proportion of faculty in the most senior group, as measured by length of service.

Obviously, the potential indicators of compositional characteristics of units are numerous. Analysts could devise and apply quantitative indicators of diversity, of salary inequalities, of bimodal seniority systems, and beyond. The organizational measurement literature (see Price and Mueller 1986) provides many directions for such work. Before one embarks on such ventures, however, specifying a theoretical rationale for the indicator formulation is essential. Otherwise, the process of indicator creation and testing is far more likely merely to represent wasted effort.

Departments as Contexts for Student Development and Socialization

Because students spend so much time in them and depend so heavily on them for the success of their postsecondary experiences, academic departments unquestionably can influence students' values, attitudes, personal styles, and career outcomes as well as their knowledge. These capabilities have made the effects of departments on students a long-standing focus of sociological attention. Early work in this tradition focused on socialization effects in undergraduate, graduate, and professional education, while later work emphasized faculty-student interactions and connections to occupations and stratification systems.

In a classic series of studies in the 1950s and 1960s, Howard Becker and colleagues examined social-psychological factors in socialization processes in graduate and professional school. In postbaccalaureate education, the department or individual school within a university is demonstrably more central to student development than it is at the undergraduate level. Becker and J. W. Capper's (1956) interviews with graduate students in physiology, philosophy, and mechanical engineering departments indicated that changes in students' social participation around the department in the course of graduate work lead to the acquisition or maintenance of specific kinds of occupational identities. Becker and Capper concluded that social participation affects students' identity through the operation of the several social-psychological mechanisms relating to socialization: development of interest in problems and pride in skills, acquisition of ideologies, investment, the internalization of motives, and sponsorship.

In similar work later, Becker and Blanche Geer (1958) and Becker et al. (1961) traced the paths of medical-school freshmen from unalloyed idealism to a wavering mixture of idealism and cynicism over their four years of medical training. Most notably, these analyses suggested that idealism and cynicism are situational rather than stable traits possessed by individuals to a greater or lesser degree. What is more, Becker and his colleagues suggested that in educational units like medical schools, idealistic and cynical attitudes may be productively viewed as collective rather than individual attributes.

In parallel work on the socialization of graduate students, David Gottlieb (1961) found that the nature of students' integration and communication with faculty in their home departments was central to students' subsequent changes in career plans toward or away from employment in research-oriented departments. Clark (1983) took the next step, relating graduate-school socialization to the capability of college and university faculty to govern themselves. Working with their graduate professors, new entrants to a scholarly field see and internalize the field's norms for research and teaching as well as the supporting values of academic life in general, including commitment to peer review and academic freedom. Disciplinary cultures are perpetuated through faculty's early and enduring socialization to the profession, which is passed along in turn to novitiates.

Rebecca Vreeland and Charles Bidwell (1966) turned research attention toward the socialization of undergraduate students. Citing the limited evidence for the differential impacts of major departments, these University of Chicago sociologists argued that systematic theorizing was essential for the study of departmental impacts on undergraduates. Their essay represented an attempt to provide that theoretical basis for the research. Vreeland and Bidwell argued first that disciplinary differences alone cannot explain different student outcomes across departments. With that as a first assumption, they hypothesized that the two critical factors promoting student attitude and value changes toward the goals of major departments are the departments' normative goal structure ("technical" versus "moral") and its affective climate (faculty interest in and interaction with undergraduates). Their normative hypothesis was that the greater the weight assigned by a department to moral goals, the more consistent values and attitude change should be among its student members. Their affective hypothesis was that the greater the extent of faculty interest, student-faculty interaction, and student peer interaction in the department, the more extensive should be value and attitude change among its student members.

Under Vreeland and Bidwell's theory, similar departments might have quite different effects. For example, a German languages department and a philosophy department are both in the humanities, but faculty in the German department might emphasize technical goals and have limited interactions with students, while the philosophy faculty might have ambitious socialization goals and pursue extensive and intensive interactions with undergraduates. Thus, the philosophy department would be much more likely to influence attitudes because its engaging social climate reinforces its broad normative goals.

John Weidman (1974, 1979) empirically tested Vreeland and Bidwell's claim that "the department . . . is the principal workplace of the college, has relatively well-defined goals and expectations for students, and commands powerful normative and utilitarian sanctions" (1966, p. 238). Results from Weidman's analysis of data from a large national sample of departments in nine disciplines suggest that the intensity and frequency of departmental faculty-student contact had important positive impacts on certain student values ("helping others," "creativity," "career values"). The normative climate had significant but somewhat less powerful impacts on values, and the normative climate was correlated with affective climate. Specifically, departments emphasizing moral goals had more frequent and more intense faculty-student contacts and fostered value changes more often than departments with technical goals, a finding consistent with Vreeland and Bidwell's predictions. Contrary to Vreeland and Bidwell, however, Weidman (1974) found that the affective climate did not appear to have significant effects as a mediator of normative climate.

Vreeland, Bidwell, and Weidman's contributions may be extended through more explicit attention to linkages between departments and larger social systems. As the societal context of departments varies, it seems likely that the degree and kind of impact they have vary as well. John Meyer has maintained that

> the most important effect colleges have on the typical student is on his career choice . . . A distinction of great importance to the society and to the colleges is the extent to which training for the occupation is rooted in the structure of the college. Do students learn about the occupation and form an image of it in college or elsewhere? Are members of the occupation on the faculty of the college, and is there a department composed of members of the occupation which specializes in teaching occupationally relevant material? Or, on the other hand, is college work regarded (by students and practitioners) as of only peripheral or preparatory significance to real training or practice? Do students and practitioners regard the quality of work in college as indicating the quality of later occupational performance, or only as affecting the likelihood of getting admitted to the occupation advantageously? (1965, pp. 14–15)

Meyer (1965, 1970) stresses that many scientific and scholarly occupations almost exclusively require employment in specific academic departments. Unlike law, medicine, and business, these occupations have no firm home outside the academy. What is more, there are few opportunities for young people outside of colleges to identify with and aspire to these occupational roles, which are growing in numbers and practitioners. For Meyer, this implies that the college assumes a greater role in socializing students bound for scientific and scholarly occupations and thus that college characteristics are more salient for students in these areas. "For students who will be scholars or scientists, occupational identity is developed and controlled in and by the colleges" (1965, p. 17). In these scholarly and scientific major and occupational choice areas, (1) playing the role and interacting with role occupants are necessary for student identity formation, since the larger, cultural definitions of the occupations are so vague that the interactional supports of the college must be stronger in these fields, and (2) the rewards and evaluations in the academic structure of the college are more important gratifications and deprivations for students, because the basis of their future occupational role is there, not outside. In other words, "since [these students] put more of their egos into the collegiate arena, maintaining them requires more positive evaluations and support than is the case with most students" (Meyer 1965, p. 18). As elements of this kind of support, Meyer mentions peer interactions in the department and, most important, supportive faculty interaction with students on personal and vocational issues.

The unique feature of these scientific and scholarly major departments is thus that they can have a more direct socializing effect on students than other departments can, because they are recognized as being the locus of their fields by the students, the professors, and the outside society. In other departments, Meyer suggests, sociological certification effects would be more powerful: "college effects on student values or other private qualities are more likely to occur through the application of institutionalized definitions to actors than through some direct effects of interaction in the college itself" (Meyer 1972, p. 116). That is, graduates acquire their distinctive values not through experiences in major departments or schools more generally but rather through expectations and interactions they experience through being defined as college students and graduates in the larger society. In contrast, in the scientific and scholarly disciplines, institutionalized definitions emanate from the college itself, and affect students.

An example of Meyer's perspectives can be drawn from a comparison of two undergraduate major programs. A business administration program does not have the same links to the outside society as a history major program does, since the student in the business major is being trained by business *professors* (not businesspeople) for the "real" test in the "natural order" outside, while the undergraduate aspiring to be a historian is trained by practicing historians. The history major aspiring to stay in the field must either continue in the academic setting toward the Ph.D. or enter a history-oriented occupation outside (e.g., teaching high school history), in which case his or her role is similar to that of history professor. Thus, Meyer would argue, a history professor is capable of greater impacts than a business professor, because he or she works in a more vocationally salient occupation. Clearly, different undergraduate majors have different certifying and gatekeeping functions for the larger society.

The evidence is clear that different majors produce different socioeconomic outcomes. Engineering majors have long earned more than philosophy majors upon graduating, and the reasons may lie as much in the societal prestige of the field as in the technical knowledge imparted in its undergraduate major. Kenneth Wilson (1978) and Wilson and Lynn Smith-Lovin (1983) present evidence that vocation- and status-targeted undergraduate majors positively affect income, occupational, and prestige outcomes.

A series of studies in the 1980s found that both the social-psychological and social-structural aspects of departments may be influential for undergraduate outcomes other than income or occupational prestige levels. Studies I carried out alone and with Olzak (Hearn 1980, 1987; Hearn and Olzak 1981, 1982) found that the level and kinds of associations that departments maintain with the larger social structure of occupations can influence students' affective well-being, satisfaction levels, aspirations, and plans for graduate education. Also influential in those outcomes, however, were individual factors such as students' background characteristics, their academic performance in college, and parental supportiveness, as well as social factors such as the gender composition of the department, faculty-student interaction, and major department climate. The relative role of these various factors differed by gender, suggesting a need for further attention to gender differences in department-effects research.

Conclusions: Directions for Future Theory and Research

Thirty years ago, Marvin Peterson bluntly appraised the state of knowledge about academic departments: "While the literature on academic departments is voluminous, most is nontheoretical and not based on research. Myths about academic departments abound, controversies about their adequacy and inadequacy continue, and an intriguing and easy topic becomes at once frustrating and difficult" (1976, p. 22). This chapter was undertaken as an attempt to update Peterson's appraisal and perhaps even refute his charge, at least in reference to sociological work on departments. Well, as the saying has it, "one out of two isn't bad." The body of theoretically based work on departments is now indeed substantially greater, but the work remains insufficiently developed for us to view these settings as easily understood.

In his essay, Peterson (1976) identified the following as areas needing more research attention: the external environments of departments (organization-environment relations, boundary transactions, etc.), the formation and meaning of departmental goals, determinants of productivity, managing departmental activity, strengthening human resources, departmental boundary transactions, and change and adaptation. He lamented the absence of research on departmental effects, change, and adaptation. Among the issues he identified for future research were the growth of collective bargaining, the development of management information systems, the increasingly rationalized resource allocation systems, the impacts of shifting enrollments and budgetary priorities, and the growing emphasis on innovative academic programming, delivery, and technology.

Unquestionably, notable gains in the sociological understanding of departments have been made since Peterson's article appeared. We now have a host of results from respected sociological scholars like Clark, Pfeffer, Gumport, and Slaughter regarding departmental resources, structures, processes, change, and adaptation. Still, scanning the literature on departments as a whole, one would be hard pressed to argue that Peterson's laments have been adequately addressed.

Perhaps this field of inquiry suffers from a lack of ambition and scope. As noted by Charles Perrow (1986) and many others, organizational analyses tend to be rooted in one or another rather easily identifiable theoretical and disciplinary perspective. Interestingly, analysts using a distinctive perspective tend to focus empirically on certain kinds of organizations associated with that perspective. For example, organizational ecologists have tended to study dynamic arenas like the newspaper industry, breweries, and wineries (Carroll 1988). At the same time, certain settings tend to be viewed from certain perspectives. As G. T. Allison (1971) persuasively illustrated, governments have too often been viewed solely from a rational-actor perspective. As a subject of study, academic departments generally fit the pattern of being examined from a limited array of theoretical and disciplinary perspectives. Investigators have studied departments employing nonsociological lenses, and there is variation in the particular lenses sociologists have employed, but this review suggests that the range of sociological thinking employed in work on departments might be expanded.

As a start, little attention has been paid to symbols, rituals, and other aspects of organizational culture at the departmental level. Clark (1972) wrote convincingly of "distinctive colleges" that evinced strong collective understanding of their historical accomplishments, identity, and purpose. Institutions with this organizational "saga" have engaging rituals, symbols, and traditions and inspire intense loyalty among their students, staff, faculty, and alumni. This theoretical perspective has not been applied systematically to academic departments, yet one can discern parallel themes in reading the memoirs and other popular writings of accomplished academics. At almost every major institution, one can find a department with a particularly stirring history seeming to fit the "saga" concept. Consider, for example, the Department of Economics at

Chicago (see http://economics.uchicago.edu/about__history.shtml), the Department of Electrical Engineering at Stanford (see www-ee.stanford.edu/history.php), or the Institute of Child Development at the University of Minnesota (see http://education.umn.edu/ICD/about/default.html). Research on departments could unquestionably benefit from more exploration of the cultural underpinnings of departments as organizations.

The sociological notions of institutionalization and legitimation also have been little considered at the departmental level. By definition, such analyses would require longitudinal designs. Blau (1973) was among the first to note that too much work on higher-education organization is cross-sectional. To this day, longitudinal research on departments is still rare. Much can be learned by tracking departments over time as they respond to developing threats and opportunities. Much can also be learned by studying the birth and death of programs and departments. Today, new departments are emerging representing either hybrid fields, like genetic engineering, or professionalized multidisciplinary fields like management or public health. At the same time, because of retrenchment and restructuring, new departments are also being created by accretion, the merging of formerly independent units into one.[10] Among contemporary analysts, Gumport and Snydman (2002) and Volk, Slaughter, and Thomas (2001) have contributed perceptive and valuable longitudinal analyses of departmental issues.[11] More such work is needed.

For our understanding of departments to advance, it is critical that useful longitudinal data on departments, especially data comparable across institutions, become available—such is surely not the case now.[12] It is also critical that research designs and methods for investigating departments reflect the increasing depth and breadth of organizational theory and of sociology more generally. As mentioned earlier, attention must be paid to the measurement of departmental structures and processes. Although this has improved in recent years, studies in the field still

10. The merging of formerly independent higher education and school administration departments into new "educational leadership and policy" units is an example familiar to faculty in schools of education.

11. Again, Gumport and Snydman stress the point, sometimes ignored by analysis, that departments and programs are not identical constructs. It is thus important to study program change as well as departmental change.

12. For a review of publicly available datasets for departmental research, and consideration of the problems of data availability, see Hearn and Gorbunov 2005.

frequently lack the measurement detail and range of studies in other realms of organizational studies (e.g., see Price and Mueller 1986). Just as important, researchers on departments show little indication of employing the newer time-series/cross-sectional, event-history, and survival-analysis designs that are becoming increasingly popular in sociology, policy studies, political science, and economics (e.g., see McLendon, Heller, and Young 2005).

Even more fundamentally, the internal workings of departments also merit more detailed theoretical and empirical attention. One angle that has been little explored in recent years is the connection between scholarly fields and various aspects of department organization. It may be that, as Cole (1994) has noted, departmental functioning (e.g., the success of efforts to achieve faculty consensus) is affected by the nature of the phenomena a field studies. Adopting particular research technologies may produce replicable results and build accumulation and elaboration in fields and in this way bring the seeds of consensus. An inability to agree on research approaches, however, may contribute to conflict (Collins 1994). With just a few exceptions (e.g., Smart, Feldman, and Ethington 2000), the disciplinary and epistemological roots of departments' structural and functional differences have not been explored much recently.

Disciplines bring socioeconomic as well as epistemological influences to departments. Few attempts have been made to examine the anticipatory effects of the societal connections of students' major departments. The goal would be to explore further the extent to which different academic departments have different degrees and kinds of effects on their students depending upon the larger societal context of their parent disciplines. Work from Meyer's provocative institutional theory perspectives has focused mainly on the campus and social-system levels of analysis, with little study regarding whether there are differences in departmental effects on students due to variations in the nature and clarity of links between a degree in a given subject and a high-status or otherwise distinctive occupation after graduation (see Meyer 1970, 1972, 1977; Kamens 1971).

In bringing such perspectives to bear, it is important to consider the fit between current organizational arrangements and assumptions, on one hand, and emerging external conditions on the other. Gumport and Snydman (2002, p. 402) have raised a provocative question: "is there a widening gulf between departmental structures and vital educational processes," including teaching and learning? That is, is the form becoming maladaptive? In a similar vein, Volk, Slaughter, and Thomas have argued,

> We need to rethink our models of resource allocation as well as our ideas about mission and market. To do this, we will have to refine the categories we now use: for example, rather than teaching, we need to reconceptualize around lower-division teaching, upper-division teaching, and graduate education. We need to think about how teaching relates to degree completion and how that should be rewarded. . . . When we think about research, we have to factor in how close departments are to federal research markets —in other words, are there substantial federal programs that can support research in the field—and if not, we have to decide whether to compensate such departments rather than penalize them. . . . We need to break open the models of resource allocation we have used in the past because these are no longer adequate to complex, bureaucratic institutions with multiple missions and multiple markets. (2001, pp. 407–8)

Future research on departments should also address the increased momentum toward interdisciplinarity, especially in research universities. In the emerging research and teaching context, where internal structures and traditions are confronting external opportunities and pressures in unprecedented ways, it is not at all clear what is adaptive and what is maladaptive. In the entrepreneurial university, for example, matrix forms of organization may become more prevalent, with teaching organized programmatically rather than by departments, and with faculty assigned to more than one program. In such a scenario, the viability of the departmental form becomes uncertain. Which departmental functions would remain? As Gumport has put it, "What would a department be for?"[13] Identifying such prospective organizational ambiguities, and pursuing research to address them, merits analytic attention.

Beyond defining and refining research agendas, however, it may be wise to consider a return to some familiar research agendas of the past. Sociological research on students in departments may be a case in point. It appears that research in that arena has taken an ironic turn. Two decades ago, Clark (1983) characterized higher education research as focused disproportionately on "people-processing" functions and insufficiently focused on knowledge processing, which, he suggested, forms

---

13. I am indebted to Patricia Gumport (personal communication, November 16, 2004) for this question, and more generally, for pointing me toward this line of reasoning.

the heart of academic organization. In a statement that has influenced numerous subsequent analysts and analyses, Clark observed that "educational structures, in effect, are a theory of knowledge, in that they help define what currently counts as knowledge" (1983, p. 26). Clark was right: as a central structural element in higher education, the department certainly is critical for knowledge processing, and many sociologists (including Rhoades, Slaughter, and Gumport) have heeded his call for more attention to knowledge processing. Unquestionably, knowledge processing remains inadequately studied and inadequately understood. Yet this review suggests that at least at the department level, knowledge processing has occupied more sociological attention in recent years than has people processing. With the exception of recent work by Austin (1996, 2002), Gumport (2000), and Weidman et al. (2001), I found little recent, sociologically framed research on departments' roles in teaching, socializing, and certifying students, at either the undergraduate or graduate level. It has been decades since the pioneering work of Becker, Vreeland, and Bidwell on academic units' effects on students, and this topic has lain largely unexamined by sociologists in recent years. Work on the knowledge-processing functions of higher education should continue to grow, but perhaps it is time to reemphasize the parallel significance of the people-processing aspect of departmental work.[14]

Limits and Possibilities of the Sociological Lens

An effort to review existing sociological theory and research focused on any particular organizational domain, including the academic department, is doubly vulnerable to the charge of incompleteness. Such an effort attends neither to nonsociological perspectives on the subject nor to sociological perspectives not yet applied to the department as a social organization. That is, one may view sociological perspectives as one of a number of legitimate, useful across-setting theoretical perspectives, and one may view academic departments as one of a multitude of legitimate targets of theoretical attention, but considering the task a matter of seeing what exists now at the intersection of the two views may do justice to neither. Academic departments have been considered profita-

14. Gumport's 2000 analysis is the most sociologically provocative of the recent investigations in this arena. That work examines ways institutional prestige and resources distinctively influence graduate training and socialization in different fields, beyond the well-researched influences of disciplinary differences and departmental composition and practices.

bly through a wide variety of lenses, and sociological considerations of organizations have been applied only selectively to departments. So if the point is to understand academic departments more completely, one needs to move away from the narrow focus of this chapter and toward two different horizons: toward the perspectives of other disciplines and toward sociological theories of organizations not yet considered in this setting.

But reaching even those two horizons is probably still not enough. There is a third way: truly interdisciplinary work. The call for such work is perhaps too familiar, and the prospects for success perhaps too slight, but the rationale is strong. Interstitial collaborations and migrations have become familiar in the sciences in recent years. Biologists have begun to study genetic determinants of group behaviors. Psychologists and neuroscientists have sought to understand individual reasoning in business transactions, long a focus of economists. Sometimes to the surprise of other social scientists, economists have applied their models to such new territories as marriage and voting behaviors. Such work can devolve into mere academic territoriality, as seen in the disputes over the claims of sociobiologists to have contributed an explanation of social behavior superior to those proffered by sociology, psychology, and anthropology. But such work can also point to breakthroughs of real power and scope. The work of Daniel Kahnemann and Amos Tversky (1979) provides the most spectacular example: building on sources from organizational theory and psychology, as well as economics, their contributions won the Nobel Prize in economics. Might the emergence of sophisticated interdisciplinary thinking about departments be a real possibility?

Concluding Thoughts

In a provocative essay, sociologist Andrew Abbott (2002) has argued that we may tend to overestimate the power of contemporary pressures on university organization. Abbott suggests that demographic and economic changes in the larger society may, in the end, have limited impact on the conduct of academic research in the disciplines, at least in scholarship's major home, the research universities. In Abbott's view, commercial competition may erode academic autonomy, structures, and traditions in less prestigious colleges and universities, but the established organizational structures and forms of academic life will endure elsewhere for foreseeable decades. This impermeability poses a buffer that may be simultaneously both comforting and troubling. That is, departments in well-established colleges and universities may continue to exist in heavily institutionalized internal and external environments capable, for better or worse, of resisting pressures for change.[15] Thus, one can envision a future of significant change in some academic units but relative constancy in others.

In such a mixed scenario, sociological ideas about academic departments will ideally maintain some "usefulness" for future theory, policy, and practice. Perhaps that usefulness may even extend beyond higher education. This essay is aimed toward improving understanding of departments, but academic departments may have characteristics of increasing relevance to sociological organization theory in general. Departments are largely professional in composition, exhibit fluid participation in governance and leadership activities, and rely often on changing, adaptive team configurations. The contours of the emerging national economy may make such characteristics more typical of organizations *generally* now than in the twentieth century. If academic departments were earlier considered organizational outliers of limited general interest, perhaps they will prove far less so in the future.

References

Abbott, A. 2002. "The Disciplines and the Future." In *The Future of the City of Intellect*, ed. S. Brint. Stanford, CA: Stanford University Press.

Adkison, J. 1979. "The Structure of Knowledge and Departmental Social Organization." *Higher Education* 8 (1): 41–53.

Alexander, V. D., and P. A. Thoits. 1985. "Token Achievement: An Examination of Proportional Representation and Performance Outcomes." *Social Forces* 64 (2): 332–40.

Allison, G. T. 1971. *Essence of Decision: Explaining the Cuban Missile Crisis.* Boston: Little, Brown.

Allison, P. D., and S. J. Long. 1990. "Departmental Effects on Scientific Productivity." *American Sociological Review* 55 (4): 469–78.

Anderson, M. S. 1990. "Resource Dependencies and Organizational Demography: A Study of Academic Departments." Paper presented at the annual meeting of the Association for the Study of Higher Education, Portland, OR.

Anderson, M. S., K. S. Louis, and J. Earle. 1994. "Disciplinary and Departmen-

15. Thus, a pattern described earlier by Meyer and Rowan (1978) endures.

tal Effects on Observations of Faculty and Graduate Student Misconduct." *Journal of Higher Education* 65:331–50.

Austin, A. E. 1996. "Institutional and Departmental Cultures: The Relationship between Teaching and Research." In *Faculty Teaching and Research: Is There a Conflict?* ed. J. M. Braxton. New Directions for Institutional Research 90. San Francisco: Jossey-Bass.

———. 2002. "Preparing the Next Generation of Faculty: Graduate School as Socialization to the Academic Career." *Journal of Higher Education* 73 (1): 94–122.

Bacharach, S., and P. Bamberger. 1992. "Alternative Approaches to the Examination of Demography in Organizations." In *Research in the Sociology of Organizations*, ed. P. Tolbert and S. B. Bacharach, 10:875–111. Greenwich, CT: JAI Press.

Baird, L. 1986. "What Characterizes a Productive Research Department?" *Research in Higher Education* 25:211–25.

Bayer, A. E. 1991. "Career Publication Patterns and Collaborative 'Styles' in American Academic Science." *Journal of Higher Education* 62 (6): 613–36.

Becher, T. 1989. *Academic Tribes and Territories: Intellectual Enquiry and the Cultures of Disciplines*. Buckingham, UK: Society for Research into Higher Education and Open University Press.

Becker, H. S., and J. W. Capper. 1956. "The Development of Identification with an Occupation." *American Journal of Sociology* 41 (4): 289–98.

Becker, H. S., and B. Geer. 1958. "The Fate of Idealism in Medical School." *American Sociological Review* 23 (1): 50–56.

Becker, H. S., B. Geer, E. C. Hughes, and A. Strauss. 1961. *Boys in White: Student Culture in Medical School*. Chicago: University of Chicago Press.

Bellas, M. L. 1994. "Comparable Worth in Academia: The Effects on Faculty Salaries of the Sex Composition and Labor-Market Conditions of Academic Disciplines." *American Sociological Review* 59:807–21.

———. 1997. "Disciplinary Differences in Faculty Salaries: Does the Gender Bias Play a Role?" *Journal of Higher Education* 68 (3): 299–321.

Bellas, M. L., and R. K. Toutkoushian. 1999. "Faculty Time Allocations and Research Productivity: Gender, Race and Family Effects." *Review of Higher Education* 22 (4): 367–90.

Biglan, A. 1973. "The Characteristics of Subject Matter in Different Academic Areas." *Journal of Applied Psychology* 57 (3): 195–203.

Blau, P. M. 1973. *The Organization of Academic Work*. New Brunswick, NJ: Transaction.

Braxton, J. M. 1983. "Department Colleagues and Individual Faculty Publication Productivity." *Review of Higher Education* 6 (2): 115–28.

———. 1991. "The Influence of Graduate Department Quality on the Sanctioning of Scientific Misconduct." *Journal of Higher Education* 62 (1): 87–108.

Braxton, J. M., and L. L. Hargens.1996. "Variations among Academic Disciplines: Analytical Framework and Research." In *Higher Education: Handbook of Theory and Research*, vol. 11, ed. J. C. Smart. New York: Agathon.

Bresser, R. K. 1984. "The Contexts of University Departments: Differences between Fields of Higher and Lower Levels of Paradigm Development." *Research in Higher Education* 20 (1): 3–15.

Carroll, G. R., ed. 1988. *Ecological Models of Organizations*. Cambridge, MA: Ballinger.

Cartter, A. 1966. *An Assessment of Quality in Graduate Education*. Washington, DC: American Council on Education.

Clark. B. R. 1972. "The Organizational Saga in Higher Education." *Administrative Science Quarterly* 17 (2): 178–84.

———. 1983. *The Higher Education System*. Berkeley: University of California Press.

———. 1984. "The Organizational Conception." In *Perspectives on Higher Education*, ed. B. R. Clark. Berkeley: University of California Press.

———. 1987a. *The Academic Life: Small Worlds, Different Worlds*. Princeton, NJ: Carnegie Foundation for the Advancement of Teaching.

———, ed. 1987b. *The Academic Profession: National, Disciplinary, and Institutional Settings*. Berkeley: University of California Press.

Cole, S. 1994. "Why Sociology Doesn't Make Progress." *Sociological Forum* 9 (2): 133–54.

Cole, S., and J. R. Cole. 1967. "Scientific Output and Recognition: A Study in the Operation of the Reward System in Science." *American Sociological Review* 32:377–90.

———. 1968. "Visibility and the Structural Bases of Awareness of Scientific Research." *American Sociological Review* 33:397–413.

Collins, R. 1994. "Why the Social Sciences Won't Become High-Consensus, Rapid-Discovery Science." *Sociological Forum* 9 (2): 155–77.

Cordes, C., and P. V. Walker. 1996. "The Widening Gap: Departments' Clout at Universities Depends on Grantsmanship." *Chronicle of Higher Education* 42 (40): A014, available at http://chronicle.com/prm/che-data/articles.dir/art-42.dir/issue-40.dir/40a01401.htm

Corwin, R. G. 1969. "Patterns of Organizational Conflict." *Administrative Science Quarterly* 14:507–20.

Finkelstein, M. 1984. *The American Academic Profession: A Synthesis of Social Scientific Inquiry since World War II*. Columbus: Ohio State University Press.

Fox, M. F. 1996. "Publication, Performance, and Reward in Science and Scholarship." In *Faculty and Faculty Issues in Colleges and Universities*, 2nd ed., ed. D. E. Finnegan, D. Webster, and Z. F. Gamson, 408–28. Needham Heights, MA: Simon and Schuster Custom Publishing.

Friedkin, N. E. 1978. "University Social Structure and Social Networks among Scientists." *American Journal of Sociology* 83 (6): 1444–65.

Fuchs, S. 1992. *The Professional Quest for Truth: A Social Theory of Science and Knowledge.* Albany: State University of New York Press.

Gamson, Z. F. 1966. "Utilitarian and Normative Orientations toward Education." *Sociology of Education* 39:46–73.

Gottlieb, D. 1961. "Processes of Socialization in American Graduate Schools." *Social Forces* 40 (2): 124–31.

Gumport, P. J. 1988. "Curricula as Signposts of Cultural Change." *Review of Higher Education* 12 (1): 49–61.

———. 2000. "Learning Academic Labor." In *Comparative Social Research*, vol. 19, ed. R. Kalleberg, 1–23. Stamford, CT: JAI Press.

Gumport, P. J., and S. K. Snydman. 2002. "The Formal Organization of Knowledge: An Analysis of Academic Structure." *Journal of Higher Education* 73 (3): 375–408.

Hackman, J. D. 1985. "Power and Centrality in the Allocation of Resources in Colleges and Universities." *Administrative Science Quarterly* 30:61–77.

Hagstrom, W. O. 1971. "Inputs, Outputs, and the Prestige of American University Science Departments." *Sociology of Education* 44:375–97.

Hearn, J. C. 1980. "Major Choice and Well-Being of College Men and Women: An Examination from Developmental, Organizational, and Structural Perspectives." *Sociology of Education* 53:167–78.

Hearn, J. C. 1987. "Impacts of Undergraduate Experiences on Aspirations and Plans for Graduate and Professional Education." *Research in Higher Education* 27 (2): 119–41.

Hearn, J. C., and M. S. Anderson. 1998. "Faculty Demography: Exploring the Effects of Seniority Distribution in Universities." In *Higher Education: Handbook of Theory and Research*, vol. 13, ed. J. C. Smart. New York: Agathon.

———. 2002. "Conflict in Academic Departments: An Analysis of Disputes over Faculty Promotion and Tenure." *Research in Higher Education* 43 (5): 503–29.

Hearn, J. C., and A. V. Gorbunov. 2005. *Funding the Core: Understanding the Financial Contexts of Academic Departments in the Humanities.* Occasional Paper of the American Academy of Arts and Sciences. Cambridge, MA: American Academy of the Arts and Sciences.

Hearn, J. C., and S. Olzak. 1981. "The Role of Major Departments in the Reproduction of Sexual Inequality." *Sociology of Education* 54:195–205.

———. 1982. "Sex Differences in the Implications of the Links between Education and the Occupational Structure." In *The Undergraduate Woman: Issues in Educational Equity*, ed. P. Perun, 275–99. Lexington, MA: Lexington.

James, E., and E. Neuberger. 1981. "The University Department as a Non-profit Labor Cooperative." *Public Choice* 36:585–612.

Kahneman, D., and A. Tversky. 1979. "Prospect Theory: An Analysis of Decision under Risk." *Econometrica* 47:263–91.

Kamens, D. H. 1971. "The College 'Charter' and College Size: Effects on Occupational Choice and College Action." *Sociology of Education* 44 (3): 270–96.

———. 1972. "Commentary on Hagstrom's 'Inputs, Outputs and the Prestige of American University Science Departments.'" *Sociology of Education* 45 (4): 446–50.

Kamens, D. H., and G. Sarup. 1980. "Departmental Organization, Legitimacy, and Faculty Militancy: Structural Sources of Pro-union Sentiment in a Public University." *Research in Higher Education* 13:244–59.

Kanter, R. M. 1977. "Numbers: Minorities and Majorities." In *Men and Women of the Corporation*, 206–42. New York: Basic Books.

Keith, B. 1999. "The Institutional Context of Departmental Prestige in American Higher Education." *American Educational Research Journal* 36 (3): 409–45.

Konrad, A. M., and J. Pfeffer. 1990. "Do You Get What You Deserve? Factors Affecting the Relationship between Productivity and Pay." *Administrative Science Quarterly* 35 (2): 258–85.

Lodahl, J. B., and G. Gordon. 1972. "The Structure of Scientific Fields and the Functioning of University Graduate Departments." *American Sociological Review* 31:355–65.

———. 1973a. "Differences between Physical and Social Sciences in University Graduate Departments." *Research in Higher Education* 1:191–213.

———. 1973b. "Funding the Sciences in University Departments." *Educational Record* 54:74–82.

Manns, C., and J. G. March. 1978. "Financial Adversity, Internal Competition, and Curriculum Change in a University." *Administrative Science Quarterly* 23 (4): 541–52.

Massy, W. F., A. K. Wilger, and C. Colbeck. 1994. "Overcoming 'Hollowed' Collegiality." *Change* 26 (4): 10–20.

Massy, W. F., and R. Zemsky. 1994. "Faculty Discretionary Time: Departments and the 'Academic Ratchet.'" *Journal of Higher Education* 65 (1): 1–22.

McCain, B., C. O'Reilly, and J. Pfeffer. 1983. "The Effects of Departmental Demography on Turnover: The Case of the University." *Academy of Management Journal* 26:626–41.

McLendon, M. K., D. E. Heller, and S. Young. 2005. "State Postsecondary Education Policy Innovation: Politics, Competition, and the Interstate Migration of Policy Ideas." *Journal of Higher Education* 76 (4): 383–400.

McNeil, K., and J. D. Thompson. 1971. "The Regeneration of Social Organizations." *American Sociological Review* 36: 624–37.

Merton, R. K. 1968. "The Matthew Effect in Science." *Science* 159:56–63.

Meyer, J. W. 1965. "Working Paper on Some Non-value Effects of Colleges." Manuscript, Bureau of Applied Social Research, Columbia University.

———. 1970. "The Charter: Conditions of Diffuse Socialization in Schools." In *Social Processes and Social Structures: An Introduction to Sociology*, ed. W. R. Scott, 564–78. New York: Henry Holt.

———. 1972. "The Effects of Institutionalization of College in Society." In *College and Student: A Sourcebook in the Social Psychology of Education*, ed. K. A. Feldman. New York: Pergamon.

———. 1977. "The Effect of Education as an Institution." *American Journal of Sociology* 83:55–77.

Meyer, J. W., and B. Rowan. 1978. "The Structure of Educational Organizations." In *Environments and Organizations*, eds. M. Meyer et al., 78–109. San Francisco: Jossey-Bass.

Mittman, B. 1992. "Theoretical and Methodological Issues in the Study of Organizational Demography and Demographic Change." In *Research in the Sociology of Organizations*, vol. 10, ed. P. Tolbert and S. B. Bacharach. Greenwich, CT: JAI Press.

Moore, W. L., and J. Pfeffer. 1980. "The Relationship between Departmental Power and Faculty Careers on Two Campuses: The Case for Structural Effects on Faculty Salaries." *Research in Higher Education* 13 (4): 291–306.

Neumann, Y. 1979. "Determinants of Faculty Salary in Prestigious versus Less-Prestigious Departments: A Comparative Study of Academic Disciplines." *Research in Higher Education* 10 (3): 221–35.

Neumann, Y., and S. Boris. 1978. "Paradigm Development and Leadership Style of University Department Chairpersons." *Research in Higher Education* 9:291–302.

Parsons, T., and G. M. Platt. 1974. "The Core Sector of the University: Graduate Training and Research." In *The American University*, 103–62. Cambridge, MA: Harvard University Press.

Perrow, C. 1986. *Complex Organizations: A Critical Essay.* 3rd ed. New York: Random House.

Peterson, M. W. 1976. "The Academic Department: Perspectives from Theory and Research." In *Examining Departmental Management*, ed. J. R. Smart and J. R. Montgomery, 21–38. New Directions for Institutional Research 10. San Francisco: Jossey-Bass.

Pfeffer, J. 1983. "Organizational Demography." In *Research in Organizational Behavior*, vol. 5, ed. L. Cummings and B. Staw, 299–357. Greenwich, CT: JAI Press.

———. 1993. "Barriers to the Advance of Organizational Science: Paradigm Development as a Dependent Variable." *Academy of Management Review* 18:437–55.

Pfeffer, J., and N. Langton. 1988. "Wage Inequality and the Organization of

Work: The Case of Academic Departments." *Administrative Science Quarterly* 33:588–606.

——. 1993. "The Effects of Wage Dispersion on Satisfaction, Productivity, and Working Collaboratively: Evidence from College and University Faculty." *Administrative Science Quarterly* 38:382–407.

Pfeffer, J., A. Leong, and K. Strehl. 1976. "Publication and Prestige Mobility of University Departments in Three Scientific Disciplines." *Sociology of Education* 49 (3): 212–18.

——. 1977. "Paradigm Development and Particularism: Journal Publication in Three Scientific Disciplines." *Social Forces* 55:938–51.

Pfeffer, J., and W. L. Moore. 1980a. "Average Tenure of Academic Department Heads: The Effects of Paradigm, Size, and Departmental Demography." *Administrative Science Quarterly* 25:387–406.

——. 1980b. "Power in University Budgeting: A Replication and Extension." *Administrative Science Quarterly* 25 (4): 637–53.

Pfeffer, J., and G. R. Salancik. 1974. "Organization Decision Making as a Political Process: The Case of a University Budget." *Administrative Science Quarterly* 19:135–51.

Pfeffer, J., G. R. Salancik, and H. Leblebici. 1976. "The Effect of Uncertainty on the Use of Social Influences in Organizational Decision Making." *Administrative Science Quarterly* 21:227–45.

Price, J. L., and C. W. Mueller. 1986. *Handbook of Organizational Measurement.* Marshfield, MA: Pitman.

Russell, S. H., R. C. Cox, J. M. Boismier, and J. T. Porter. 1990. *A Descriptive Report of Academic Departments in Higher Education Institutions: 1988 National Survey of Postsecondary Faculty.* Contractor survey report NSOPF-88, January. Washington, DC: National Center for Education Statistics.

Salancik, G. R., and J. Pfeffer. 1974. "The Bases and Uses of Power in Organizational Decision Making: The Case of a University." *Administrative Science Quarterly* 19:453–73.

Salancik, G. R., B. M. Staw, and L. R. Pondy. 1980. "Administrative Turnover as a Response to Unmanaged Organizational Interdependence." *Academy of Management Journal* 23 (3): 422–37.

Slaughter, S. 1993. "Retrenchment in the 1980s: The Politics of Prestige and Gender." *Journal of Higher Education* 64 (3): 250–82.

——. 1998. "Federal Policy and Supply-Side Institutional Resource Allocation at Public Research Universities." ASHE presidential speech. *Review of Higher Education* 21 (3): 209–44.

——. 2002. "The Political Economy of Curriculum-Making in American Universities." In *The Future of the City of Intellect*, ed. S. Brint. Stanford, CA: Stanford University Press.

Slaughter, S., and L. L. Leslie. 1997. *Academic Capitalism: Politics, Policies, and the Entrepreneurial University.* Baltimore: Johns Hopkins University Press.

Smart, J. C., K. A. Feldman, and C. A. Ethington. 2000. *Academic Disciplines: Holland's Theory and the Study of College Students and Faculty.* Vanderbilt Issues in Higher Education. Nashville: Vanderbilt University Press.

Stewman, S. 1988. "Organizational Demography." In *Annual Review of Sociology*, vol. 14, ed. W. Scott and J. Blake, 173–202. Palo Alto, CA: Annual Reviews.

Thompson, J. D. 1967. *Organizations in Action.* New York: McGraw-Hill.

Tolbert, P. S., and S. B. Bacharach. 1992. Introduction to *Research in the Sociology of Organizations*, vol. 10, ed. P. S. Tolbert and S. B. Bacharach. Greenwich, CT: JAI Press.

Tolbert, P. S., T. Simons, A. Andrews, and J. Rhee. 1995. "The Effects of Gender Composition in Academic Departments on Faculty Turnover." *Industrial and Labor Relations Review* 48 (3): 562–79.

Trow, M. 1976. "The American Academic Department as a Context for Learning." *Studies in Higher Education* 1 (1): 89–106.

Volk, C. S., S. Slaughter, and S. L. Thomas. 2001. "Models of Institutional Resource Allocation: Mission, Market, and Gender." *Journal of Higher Education* 72 (4): 387–413.

Vreeland, R., and C. Bidwell. 1966. "Classifying University Departments: An Approach to the Analysis of Their Effects upon Undergraduates' Values and Attitudes." *Sociology of Education* 39:237–54.

Weick, K. 1976. "Educational Organizations as Loosely-Coupled Systems." *Administrative Science Quarterly* 21 (1): 1–19.

Weidman, J. C. 1974. *The Effects of Academic Department on Changes in Undergraduates' Occupational Values.* Final Report. Washington, DC: National Center for Educational Research and Development.

———. 1979. "Nonintellective Undergraduate Socialization in Academic Departments." *Journal of Higher Education* 50 (1): 48–62.

Weidman, J. C., D. J. Twale, and E. L. Stein. 2001. *Socialization of Graduate and Professional Students in Higher Education: A Perilous Passage?* ASHE-ERIC Higher Education Report 28 (3).

Wharton, A. S., and J. N. Baron. 1991. "Satisfaction? The Psychological Impact of Gender Segregation on Women at Work." *Sociological Quarterly* 32 (3): 365–87.

Wilson, K. L. 1978. "Toward an Improved Explanation of Income Attainment." *American Journal of Sociology* 84 (3): 684–97.

Wilson, K. L., and L. Smith-Lovin. 1983. "Scaling the Prestige, Authority, and Income Potential of College Curricula." *Social Science Research* 12:159–86.

9 The Sociology of Diversity

ANTHONY LISING ANTONIO AND
MARCELA M. MUÑIZ

In 1973, racial and ethnic minority students constituted less than 10 percent of all college students in the United States (Snyder and Hoffman 1991). Not surprisingly, Burton Clark, in his assessment of the sociology of higher education, did not identify a line of inquiry that was centrally focused on race[1] in higher education. Race as a specific concern did appear in one of the two primary "streams" of study, the study of inequality beyond high school, as one of a trio of bases for stratification (social class, sex, and race). The seminal and prominent work in the stream identified by Clark, however, predominantly concentrated on examining the effects of social class on social mobility (e.g., Lynd and Lynd 1929; Warner and Lunt 1941; Hollingshead 1959; Clark 1960; Sewell and Shah 1966). The promising developments he identified for the future of the field—cross-national studies and historical analyses—also did not encompass race as a central concern for inquiry.

At the time of his assessment, Clark could not have predicted the rapid growth of racial and ethnic minority populations on campuses in subsequent decades, nor the effect that dramatic change would have on the study of higher education. Fueled by a combination of immigration, enhanced educational access, and economic demand for postsecondary credentials, the racial makeup of the undergraduate population quickly evolved from overwhelmingly white to substantially nonwhite. Already 17 percent of all undergraduates in 1980, minority student representation swelled to over 25 percent by 1993 (Snyder 1995). In some states, demographic change was even more striking. At the University of California, for example, white students were already down to 72 percent of

---

1. We use the terms *race* and *ethnicity* interchangeably in this chapter to reflect current usage in this research area and to avoid the more cumbersome term *race/ethnicity*.

all undergraduates in 1980, and a decade later they had dropped to a slim majority—only 55 percent of all students.[2] Enrollment data for 2004 indicated that white undergraduates were a *minority* at six of the eight undergraduate campuses of the university. Similar trends are evident in other rapidly diversifying states like New York, Texas, Florida, and New Mexico.

This demographic change is significant. As Clark observed, changes in the landscape of higher education and of the country in the 1950s and 1960s (specifically the move toward mass higher education and the demands of a growing, advanced economy) greatly increased the importance of higher education for the general public, business, and the government and thus spurred the growth of research activity in the field. The radical change in the social and cultural geography of college campuses we are experiencing at the beginning of the twenty-first century is no less profound a shift. And this diversification of the student body is occurring coincident with record levels of aspiration and participation in higher education. For example, nine out of ten tenth-graders plan to attend college (Wirt et al. 2004), and 75 percent of high school graduates actually do matriculate within two years of graduation (Berkner and Chavez 1997). At a time when the student body is changing rapidly, the number of concerned stakeholders is increasing with equal speed.

These trends translate into new challenges for higher education, challenges that have elicited lines of sociological inquiry quite different from what Clark expected thirty years ago. These challenges include achieving equitable access to higher education for multiple racial groups; fostering the learning and development of the unprecedented number of "new" students that characterize a diverse student body; managing campus tension and conflict brought about by diversity; diversifying a predominantly white faculty to better serve diverse students; and reconciling conflict surrounding the dominance in the general education curriculum of a white, male, European, and European American canon over works by non-Western and racial minority scholars. The emergent lines of inquiry that have surfaced in response to these challenges are not necessarily novel; they reflect the concerns of established subfields in sociology such as stratification and inequality, socialization, intergroup relations, the professions, and the sociology of knowledge. The press of

2. Enrollment data from the California Postsecondary Education Commission website, *www.cpec.ca.gov/*.

demographic change, however, has evoked considerable study in which racial and ethnic diversity is essential if not central to the problems addressed and the analyses conducted. This emergent area of sociological scholarship on higher education is the focus of this chapter.

While sociological inquiry of the diverse campus remains, in a general way, within the broad categories identified by Clark in 1973, the centrality of diversity in many recent studies characterizes an area of inquiry with a distinct analytical perspective. Four taken-for-granted assumptions commonly undergird this work:

1. Demographic shifts have created new challenges associated with racial diversity and necessitate a reexamination of sociological problems in higher education.
2. Racial *diversity* is integral to the framing of sociological problems; a black-white binaristic approach to race is no longer appropriate.
3. Race and ethnicity are central constructs of analysis; they are not simply background or control variables.
4. The educational challenges that derive from the diversity created by demographic change need to be addressed within a framework of institutional change or transformation.

Fundamentally, therefore, the sociology of diversity seeks first, to understand how students, faculty, and institutions experience, react to, or are affected by a racially diverse student body, and second, to apply scholarly knowledge toward institutional change. We have identified five lines of inquiry: access and diversity, the impact of diversity on students, intergroup relations, diversity in the curriculum, and diversity in the professoriate. In this still-emerging area of scholarship, the bulk of the work has been conducted in just the last 10–12 years and primarily along two lines, the impact of diversity and intergroup relations. The work does not have a traditional disciplinary center; it is being conducted by sociologists, social psychologists, and higher education scholars independently as well as in collaboration.

Readers familiar with the scholarship on racial diversity in higher education will note that a few very good compilations and syntheses of much of this work have been published in recent years. These include "The Educational Benefits of Diversity: Evidence from Multiple Sectors" (Milem 2003), "College Environments, Diversity, and Student Learning" (Hurtado, Dey, Gurin, and Gurin 2003), "The Benefits of Racial and Ethnic Diversity in Higher Education" (Milem and Hakuta 2000), and *Diversity Works: The Emerging Picture of How Students Benefit* (Smith and associates 1997). Each of these reviews competently exhausts the current knowledge in question surrounding the learning outcomes associated with ethnically and racially diverse student bodies, and our goal in this chapter is not to replicate or update their work. Rather, our task is to describe the sociology of diversity as an active, emerging area of scholarly inquiry in higher education. For each of the five aforementioned lines of inquiry, we summarize the questions pursued by researchers, discuss previous and current contributions, and reflect on the prospects for future research activity.

Access and Diversity

Inequality has been a central concern in the sociology of education since its early beginnings in the 1930s and 1940s. In the field of higher education, the study of inequality seeks primarily to describe, understand, and explain differential rates of educational access, achievement, and attainment by race, class, and gender. As Patricia McDonough explains in Chapter Three of this volume, scholars have studied inequality at the individual, organizational, and field levels. Individual-level work has dominated this line of inquiry, however, with the literature predominantly populated by studies of stratification in access (primarily focused on educational aspiration and college choice) and in educational attainment (progression through college and attainment of bachelor's and graduate degrees). Organizational- and field-level approaches are more recent and less prolific in the literature.

The onset of racial diversity in the college-age cohort of the 1970s and 1980s served to highlight the continued underrepresentation of African American, Latino, and Native American students, as enrollments grew rapidly but movement toward proportional representation was much slower (Astin 1982; Trent 1991; Trent et al. 2003). At the same time, however, Asian Americans (primarily those of East and South Asian descent) were gaining entry into selective research universities at a rate that would soon surpass the proportion of their presence in the general population, while white student representation continued to decline. This juxtaposition of radically divergent educational access for different racial groups, along with a series of federal Office of Civil Rights investigations into apparent quotas on Asian American admissions at a number of prominent elite institutions, created the context for new studies of inequality focused on diversity (Takagi 1992). The context featured conservative critics aggressively seeking the legal or legislative dismantling of race-based affirmative action admission policies, which they criticized as nonmeritocratic, with liberal educators defending their policies by appealing to the educational efficacy of a diverse student body and the need to address the continuing problem of minority underrepresentation.

This newer line of work departs from student-focused research and instead focuses on institutional practices and outcomes. The bulk of this activity has emerged since 1996, the year the Fifth Circuit Court of Appeals declared the use of race in admissions unconstitutional in *Hopwood v. University of Texas*, and the year after the regents of the University of California voted to end affirmative action on their campuses. Studies of admission practices and their impact on the racial diversity of admitted classes address specific policy responses to the loss of affirmative action. The small but growing body of work uses descriptive statistics as well as more complex predictive models to examine the impact on diversity in admissions when race is excluded from consideration. Scholars have looked at the impact of substitute criteria such as class-based affirmative action (Kane 1998; Karabel 1998; Kahlenberg 1996), class rank (Geiser 1998; Horn and Flores 2003; Marin and Lee 2003; Tienda et al. 2003), or traditional academic indicators only (Bowen and Bok 1998; Chapa and Lazaro 1998; Karabel 1998; Koretz et al. 2001). Generally, these studies are characterized by the use of predictive, quantitative analyses and a common sociological framework.[3] Most common to the research in this area is a clear intent to inform public debate on admissions policy in higher education with the presentation of rigorous, empirical social science. Though most of the scholars work in academic departments rather than policy research centers or public policy schools, they identify clearly the policy arena in which they are writing and their intent to provide data-based analyses for public discussion and in most cases, a set of unequivocal, actionable conclusions on the policy at issue. This type of specific policy-oriented research, though reminiscent of the sociological

---

3. Though not always explicit, each of the studies assumes a classic status attainment model—student admission to college is dependent on socioeconomic status, individual characteristics (academic achievement and ability), and school characteristics (usually socioeconomic context, urbanicity, and racial composition)—under the constraints of the admissions policy in question.

work on school segregation in the 1960s and 1970s, represents a major departure in style and objective from the sociology of higher education discussed by Clark in 1973.

Studies of college choice and status attainment continue to be a staple of the literature on inequality, although with the recognition of diversity, an increasing number of studies focus specifically on African Americans, Asian Americans (in aggregate and as separate ethnic groups), and Mexican Americans (Ceja 2001; Freeman 1999; Freeman and Thomas 2002; McDonough and Antonio 1996; McDonough, Antonio, and Trent 1997; Perna 2000; Teranishi 2002, 2004; Teranishi et al. 2004; Teranishi, Gomez, and Allen, 2002; Lee 1997). A few studies are emerging, however, that again approach the access literature with diversity as a point of departure. Rather than framing college choice as a problem centrally concerned with the effects of student characteristics (socioeconomic background, gender, race, academic achievement, and aspirations) or school characteristics (resources, control, and urbanicity) on postsecondary destinations, these scholars focus on the effects of colleges and universities. As we noted above, the politics of diversity in the late 1990s has created a volatile environment with respect to admissions policy. Researchers are concerned with how this environment is affecting application behavior—and ultimately, the racial diversity among those gaining access to specific higher education institutions. This area of activity predictably coincides with the implementation of major policy changes such as Georgia's HOPE scholarship program (Cornwell and Mustard 2002; Dynarski 2002), Texas' Top 10% Plan (Tienda, Cortes, and Niu 2003), California's Eligibility in Local Context policy (Student Academic Services 2002), and the outlawing of affirmative action in California (Card and Krueger 2004) and Texas (Chapa 1997; Chapa and Lazaro 1998; Finnell 1998). Signs indicate that the future will bring continued changes in admissions, and with it, continued research along this line.

Two developments are noteworthy. First, in 2003 the Supreme Court ruled constitutional the use of race in admissions in *Gratz v. Bollinger* and *Grutter v. Bollinger*, declaring affirmative action legal but also setting an implied 25-year timetable on its legality. And in 2002, Richard Atkinson, president of the University of California, began pushing the UC in the direction of dropping the SAT as an admission requirement, a move that has generated much discussion about the future of the SAT in selective admissions (Bollinger 2002). Each of these policy developments promises continued volatility in admissions policies and practices in the near future, and consequently, further scholarly focus on how institutions are changing to address issues of access and diversity.

The Impact of Diversity on Students

As Clark noted in 1973, scholarship on college impact constituted a formidable strain of work within the sociology of higher education. Research activity continued to be vigorous in subsequent decades, as study in this area expanded from a focus on the effects of institutional characteristics such as size, control, and selectivity to the impact of within-institution environments defined by students' involvement in both academic and social activities in college (see chapter 4 in this volume). E. T. Pascarella and P. T. Terenzini (1991) identified and reviewed some 2,600 studies of college impact conducted in the 1970s and 1980s, a number surpassing the output of the previous four decades. Upon examining their voluminous review at the end of the 1990s, however, the two scholars concluded that dramatic demographic change was an important factor in the U.S. college scene that researchers in this area had previously neglected (Pascarella and Terenzini 1998). Researchers increasingly focused on student diversity in the 1990s, responding both to the fact that current research did not apply well to the new generation of college students and to the legal challenges to affirmative action surfacing middecade. While there was an increase in the number of studies examining college effects on nontraditional (minority, first-generation, reentry) students in the 1990s, studies that focused on how diversity affects student outcomes emerged as a new line of inquiry in the large and expansive field of college impact.

Studies on the impact of diversity are primarily quantitative—of both large and small scale—because they fall within the strongly quantitative tradition of research on college impact. Many studies within this line of inquiry aim to inform the debates over affirmative action in admissions, the educational benefits of diversity, and the value of diversity-related program offerings such as campus cultural centers and ethnic theme dorms. In addition, they look carefully at the role of cognitive or social environments in student development and rely on frameworks rooted in social psychology and sociology. The vast majority of work on the impact of diversity has been conducted within the last 10 years; on the whole, it is the most active line of inquiry within the sociology of diversity. We categorize the work into three areas: the impact of structural diversity, interpersonal interactions with diversity, and diversity in the curriculum and cocurriculum.[4]

The first of the three research areas examines the impact of structural diversity on student outcomes. The structural diversity of an institution has to do primarily with the racial and ethnic composition of a student body (Hurtado et al. 1998, 1999). This work examines the impact of a diverse educational setting and draws comparisons across universities to determine the impact of a diverse context on student outcomes. Multi-institutional databases are required of this work; since such databases are limited, studies in this area are less common. Alexander Astin's 1993 work, a general study of college impact, was among the first large-scale, multi-institutional studies to examine the effects of undergraduate racial composition on outcomes such as educational attainment, political identification, and career choices. Astin was followed by work that places racial diversity at the center of analysis and is more extensive. Two prominent examples are Mitchell Chang's (1996, 1999) dissertation research and Patricia Gurin's (1999) work conducted as expert testimony for the *Grutter v. Bollinger* and *Gratz v. Bollinger* affirmative action court cases. Chang's work comprehensively examines the relationship between various structural measures of diversity and student outcomes, including satisfaction, retention, grade point average, intellectual and social self-concept, and the frequency of discussing racial issues and socializing with someone from a different race. Gurin expanded this area further by looking at a larger array of outcomes (both learning and civic outcomes), near- and long-term impact (four and nine years after college entry), and separate effects on white, African American, and Latino students. Although both Chang and Gurin measured a wide variety of effects, they recommended further examination along this line to clarify the positive and negative effects on different subpopulations and the impact of differently composed racially diverse environments.

Astin (1993), like other researchers, concluded from his study of structural diversity that the racial composition of a college creates the context for interaction with diversity and that in those interactions the most direct effects of diversity are realized. Many studies of interracial interaction and interpersonal engagement with racial issues have been

---

4. Scholars working from an interdisciplinary perspective have developed similar categorizations. See Gurin et al. 2002, Milem 2003, Milem and Hakuta 2000, and Smith and associates 1997.

conducted in the last decade, and they have given rise to the most comprehensive empirical knowledge base in the sociology of diversity. Literature reviews of this work testify to the volume of activity in this area (Milem 2003; Hurtado et al. 2003; Milem and Hakuta 2000; Smith and associates 1997), and the list of educational outcomes that are examined is impressive: intellectual and social self-concept; critical thinking and problem solving; grades; retention and graduation; aspirations for graduate study; positive racial attitudes; participation in civic life; diversity of postcollege relationships and friendships; satisfaction with college; leadership skills; and sense of community on campus. And even though the results in this area are fairly consistent in illustrating the positive effects of socialization across race, research activity continues to be vigorous. Recently published work addresses the impact of interactional diversity on gender roles (Bryant 2003); complex thinking (Antonio et al. 2004); personal, vocational, and intellectual development (Hu and Kuh 2003); and in medical education (Whitla et al. 2003).

A third area within this line of inquiry examines the impact of diversity in the curriculum and cocurriculum. Increasing racial diversity in student bodies contributed to the development of new courses in ethnic studies and American cultures, as well as to the growth and development of diversity-related cocurricula such as ethnic student organizations, cultural awareness workshops, and race dialogues (Milem and Hakuta 2000). Many scholars view these curricular and cocurricular initiatives as interconnected, or part of the "diversity agenda" in higher education (Chang 2002; Smith and associates 1997; Baez 2000). Consequently, research soon followed, including multi-institutional studies that evaluated the impact of general student participation in these activities (Astin 1993; Chang 1996; Gurin 1999; Springer et al. 1996; Villalpando 2002; Whitt et al. 2001) and single-site studies that evaluated the efficacy of specific programs (Gurin 1999; Neville and Furlong 1994; Zuñiga et al. 1995). The outcomes examined in this area are quite varied, ranging from positive racial attitudes (Hyun 1996; Milem 1994) and civic involvement (Astin 1993) to critical thinking skills (Hurtado 2000) and persistence (Chang 1996).

The emergence of research on the impact of diversity on students is significant for several reasons. First, it is the most active among the lines of inquiry we identify within the sociology of diversity. The sheer volume of work along this line has lent it substantial visibility. Second, much of the work along this line is conducted in response to policy debates concerning the educational efficacy of diversity in higher education, and as a result, it receives considerable attention outside the usual academic circles. Its emergence as a vital line of inquiry, however, highlights the lack of serious theoretical work on the phenomenon of diversity. The need for theoretical work is significant, because it reflects the social conditions in which much of the inquiry was conducted. The legal battle for affirmative action, though a lengthy process, elevated to high visibility the demand for empirical evidence of the relationship between racial diversity and student outcomes. Consequently, researchers responded appropriately and earnestly—but at the expense of prior theorizing on how diversity "works." Nevertheless, entering the new millennium, we have a substantial foundation of work upon which to base our pursuit of greater understanding as to why and how interaction with diversity contributes to student development, and some researchers recently have begun this work (e.g., Gurin et al. 2002).

Finally, whereas research on the impact of diversity has focused extensively on how students affect one another and how institutions affect students, this line of inquiry has spoken relatively little about institutional transformation in light of student diversity. Because this work falls within the literature on college impact, it builds from the well-accepted conclusion regarding the importance of student effort and involvement in garnering the outcomes of college. Not surprisingly, this work too places the onus of learning and development on students rather than on institutions. More recent work has begun to look at how diversity in the student body affects the cultural life of the institution, including the development of subcultures (Gonzalez 2002), the transformation of social spaces (Gonzalez 2000–2001), and the alteration of friendship networks (Antonio 2004). These studies, all of them qualitative, are early examples of what is likely to be a productive direction within this line of inquiry, as interest in institutional transformation grows and an increasingly diverse and complex student population demands a greater variety of methodological tools and approaches with which to understand student development in college (Pascarella and Terenzini 1998).

Intergroup Relations

Like the study of inequality, the study of intergroup or racial/ethnic relations has a long history in sociology as one of the foundational areas of the field. The subfield is generally concerned with the nature of relations in multiethnic societies (e.g., conflict, cooperation, and competition), the social hierarchy of groups (origins and consequences), intergroup power dynamics (how group dominance is sustained and challenged), and the long-range outcomes of multiethnic relations (e.g., assimilation, segregation, pluralism—Marger 1991). Each of these concerns came into play quite prominently in U.S. higher education in the 1980s, a decade that saw campus diversity swell even as progress faded in terms of proportional access and retention for students of color (Altbach 1991; Astone and Nuñez-Womack 1990; Richardson and Skinner 1991; Trent 1991). Perhaps as a consequence, the 1980s also saw increasingly frequent campus racial conflict (Ferrell and Jones 1988; Green 1989).

Socially, campuses were no longer contending with the black-white, minority-majority issues of the late 1960s. Multiple cultural groups were seeking social space, legitimacy, and status on campus, and as with student unrest in the 1960s, the tense racial climate spurred researchers to revisit the college campus, this time intentionally focused on the multicultural context. Many institutions conducted self-studies; one in particular captured with striking clarity the character and complexity of problems experienced on a diverse campus. At the UC Berkeley Center for the Study of Social Change in 1991, Troy Duster and his colleagues published the final report of their two-year investigation of diversity at Berkeley. Prompted by a campus commission on "responses to a changing student body," these researchers consciously placed rapid demographic change at the forefront of their research problem to ask, how are undergraduate students experiencing the new ethnic and racial diversity of the campus? This qualitative study of students' reactions and feelings in response to—and experiences and perceptions of—ethnic and racial diversity at the Berkeley campus marked the advent of serious scholarly engagement with campus diversity (Institute for the Study of Social Change 1991). Though the report discussed a number of findings regarding intergroup perceptions, tensions, and behavior, the finding that students retreat into ethnic enclaves upon encountering a multicultural campus—that the diverse campus is a racially "balkanized" one—found its way to the *New York Times*, CNN, and other media outlets, triggering both national dialogue and further sociological inquiry into campus diversity.

Inquiry along this line has addressed a variety of new questions in higher education. Like Duster and his colleagues, many have asked broad questions about the nature of ethnic relations on their own campus. Literally hundreds of institutions have conducted self-studies of their campus climate for diversity in the last fifteen years. These studies query students, faculty, and staff about their perceptions of racial tension and friendliness; observations of racist behavior, material, and graffiti; and experiences with racial isolation and interaction. As locally focused investigations, such studies generally have not had much impact on the field. They are an indicator, however, of sustained engagement with the area, as institutional studies of campus racial climates appeared as early as the late 1980s (e.g., UCMI 1989) and are continuing across the country.[5] Larger studies, and those focused on a scholarly audience, ask more theoretical questions in efforts to understand intergroup relations. These studies have addressed the nature of racial stratification and affiliation on campus, the origins of tense racial climates and the ways in which they affect students, and new conceptualizations of community and intergroup relations for a multicultural context.

Earlier studies of intergroup relations on campus primarily focused on black-white racial dynamics; they investigated African Americans' experience of isolation and alienation on predominantly white campuses and the effect of that experience on academic success (e.g., Fleming 1984; Allen 1985, 1992; Allen, Epps, and Haniff 1991). Diversity in the late 1980s introduced a new image of race relations on campus—multiple, self-segregated ethnic enclaves. In response, scholars attempted to understand the extent to which diverse campuses were segregated and why students of various racial backgrounds did or did not socialize across race. Studies of interracial contact and social segregation appeared throughout the 1990s, approached with a range of research methods: qualitative (Institute for the Study of Social Change 1991), quantitative (Hurtado, Carter, and Sharp 1995; Hurtado, Dey, and Treviño 1994), and mixed (Antonio 1998; UCMI 1989). More recent work in this area focuses specifically on interracial friendships among students, addressing the role of race in friendship formation and development (Antonio 2004; Martínez Alemán 2000).

The concept of campus racial climate was derived from organizational sociology as an analytical tool for studying the diversifying campus. Pioneered by Sylvia Hurtado and her colleagues, the campus

5. See, for example, the University of Michigan Student Study (*www.umich.edu/oami/ mss/about/index.htm*), a 2004 study designed to compare to a similar study of diversity conducted ten years earlier.

racial climate is characterized by contemporary perceptions, attitudes, and expectations regarding race relations and racial attitudes held by the institution and its students, faculty, and staff; interpersonal interactions with diversity; and institutional history and structure with regard to race relations. (Hurtado 1992, 1994; Hurtado et al. 1998, 1999). Initially, studies of campus racial climate were aimed at reducing racial tension and as such were focused on the institutional factors that predict racial tension (Hurtado 1992, 1994). More recent work has treated climate as an independent variable, to study its effect on academic (retention and grades) and psychological (stress, alienation, isolation, well-being) outcomes (e.g., Allen and Solórzano 2001; Hurtado and Carter, 1997; Lewis, Chesler, and Forman 2000; Loo and Rolison 1986; Nora and Cabrera 1996; Smedley, Myers, and Harrell 1993; Solórzano, Ceja, and Yosso 2000). Researchers also considered the role of racial climates in promoting interracial friendliness and contact (e.g., Antonio 1998; Hurtado, Dey, and Treviño 1994; Institute for the Study of Social Change 1991; Tanaka 2003).

Diversity and racial tension also brought the need to envision alternative models of campus community and the roles of students and faculty in its development. Two of the more prominent works offering alternative conceptions were developed by Troy Duster (1993) and William Tierney (1993). Duster outlines the shift from a white-majority-dominated campus to one without a racial or ethnic majority as a process in which subcommunities of students move beyond relationships based upon competition for economic, social, and cultural resources and learn to value cultural difference as contributing to a common collective experience. Tierney uses a more anthropological approach but is cited here because, like sociologists of culture, he is centrally interested in the nature and role of meaning systems in interpersonal interaction and formal organizations. In *Building Communities of Difference*, Tierney develops a notion of community similar to that of Duster, using postmodernism and critical theory to describe multicultural campus communities built upon cultural difference, agape, and hope and characterized by cultural border crossing and dialogue. A later contribution offering a vision of multicultural campus relations posits intersubjective understanding reached through intercultural dialogue as the central organizing feature of the campus community (Tanaka 2003). Other recent work, while not offering complete models of campus community and intergroup relations, analyzes minority student resistance and adaptation to campus racial climates to critique current social arrangements and propose strategies for institutional change (e.g., Gonzalez 2002; Solórzano, Ceja, and Yosso 2000; Solórzano and Villalpando 1998). The future of this line of inquiry clearly lies in the theoretical and conceptual work necessary to envision and enact institutional changes that foster alternative models of multicultural community.

Diversity in the Curriculum and the Professoriate

Although the impact of diversity is wide ranging, reaching across the entire higher education enterprise, scholars have responded most often to the challenges that relate most directly to students. Consequently, the previous three lines of inquiry are relatively well developed compared to the final two lines discussed here: diversity in the curriculum and in the professoriate. We introduce them here as lines of inquiry that emerged with the onset of diversity but that are clearly still in their infancy.

Clark says that higher education institutions are perceived as places "where society recreates (and develops) itself in the young" (1973, p. 13 in this volume). According to Clark, society has a vested interest in transmitting values and in developing personal character in its citizens, and higher education is a critical institution where such development takes place. The curriculum plays a particularly important role, as the level of contention evident in the "culture wars" of the 1980s easily demonstrates (Berman 1992). As seen through a sociological lens, the advent of racial diversity among college students (and in American culture more broadly) has raised questions regarding the functions of the curriculum, particularly as related to notions of identity and citizenship development (Giroux 1995) and to the legitimation of academic knowledge (Aronowitz 1990).

Scholarly interest in diversity in the curriculum appears to have been initiated again by a new "problem" in higher education, one that garnered national attention. In 1987, Allan Bloom published *The Closing of the American Mind*, a book that severely criticized the increasing inclusion of noncanonical (non-Western) texts in the nation's colleges and universities. Bloom argued that the growing incorporation of non-Western thought threatened the stability of the culture and values that form the basis of U.S. democratic society. At Stanford University, a faculty debate on the content of the Western Civilization requirement triggered campus demonstrations among its increasingly diverse stu-

dent population, giving the issue a human face and drawing the attention of the national press (Bernstein 1988; Vobejda 1988). In response, a
number of scholars published essays, both philosophical and polemical,
weighing in on the ills and virtues of a more diverse curriculum (e.g.,
Gates 1992; Hirsch 1987; Nussbaum 1997; Ravitch 1990; Schlesinger 1991).
The vast majority of these writers are humanists, however, and their
normative arguments do not venture deeply into the sociological questions arising from the debate. Unlike scholarship in K–12 education, the
sociological literature here is still nascent. The few notable publications
include R. A. Rhoads's (1995) work on general education and cultural
legitimation, Stanley Aronowitz's (1990) examination of cultural studies
and knowledge legitimation in the academy, and M. R. Olneck's more
recent (2001) essay applying Pierre Bourdieu's ideas of social distinction
to the struggle to diversify the curriculum.

Clark noted that "research on institutional and system capacities to
embody certain values in the thought and life styles of an evolving
group" was lagging (1973, p. 13 in this volume). More than thirty years
later, such work—particularly with respect to diversity—is still limited
and in need of further development. Although the curricular debates
that garnered national attention in the late 1980s are not currently in the
public eye, the issues underlying that debate are still very much present
in the early years of this century and will continue to persist in light of
ongoing student diversification. Future scholarship on diversity in the
curriculum, however, rests on the degree to which faculty and institutions feel the press of demographic change for curricular reform; the
emergence and the origin of direct pressure for change are difficult to
predict. Sheila Slaughter (1997) notes that demographics alone may not
trigger reform and that curricular formation may require accompanying political and social forces. Nonetheless, it is apparent that whether
pressure for reform emanates directly from student demand, from reform movements originating in progressive departments, or via social
movements occurring outside the university, scholarly attention to the
meaning and impact of the challenges such reforms present to higher
education is likely to follow.

In 1973, the relatively nascent study of the "academic man" held great
potential for further growth as the sociology of professions was just
beginning to grow in earnest. The explosion of diversity in the undergraduate population was just under way, however, when Clark himself
contributed to the growth of that emergent area with the publication of

The Academic Life: Small Worlds, Different Worlds in 1987. Student diversity, juxtaposed to the relatively small (10%) and stable representation of full-time undergraduate faculty of color in the 1990s (Sax et al. 1999), initiated new questions for the study of faculty. Questions concerning faculty of color—a term not in existence in 1973—explore not only issues of representation in academe but also issues relating to academic culture, diversity in the workplace, and conceptions of knowledge.

A fair amount of work has been conducted on the factors behind low minority representation among faculty; these include low Ph.D. production and tenure rates among faculty of color, subtle forms of personal and institutional racism in recruitment and promotion processes, and inhospitable departmental climates (see Turner and Myers 2000 for a comprehensive review). This line of work continues, as the lack of even incremental progress defines representational equity as a persistent problem. The specter of student diversity, however, has prompted a smaller number of researchers to investigate how faculty of color are changing our institutions. Some scholars have studied the roles played by diverse faculty, whether as role models, effective mentors to minority students, or contributors to a more student-centered value system in academe (Mickelson and Oliver 1991; Washington and Harvey 1989; Antonio 2002). Others have looked at the impact of diverse faculty on student learning and exposure to diverse ideas (Milem 1999; Smith 1989); their distinct contributions to institutional missions (Milem 1999; Allen et al. 2002); and their role in broadening conceptions of scholarship beyond research and publishing (Antonio 2002). Still others examine bidirectional socialization, showing how faculty of color influence change in academic culture by raising issues pertaining to their marginalization, introducing conflict, and providing leadership for change (Tierney and Bensimon 1996; Reyes and Halcon 1988; Turner and Myers 2000). The continuing theme within this emergent line of inquiry is the presence of diverse faculty as an impetus for institutional transformation, for such presence not only alters the conception of scholarship, teaching, and service performed within the academy but also raises the question of who is entitled to define those conceptions (Baez 2002).

A second, related topic examines the intersection between faculty diversity and conceptions of knowledge. The relatively recent presence of faculty of color in academe has prompted scholars to consider not only how minority faculty are faring as productive thinkers in the academy but also how their work raises basic questions of epistemology, of knowledge production itself. Patricia Hill Collins, in her discussion of black female sociologists, initiated this discussion with her argument that racial and gendered oppression provides a distinctive perspective among women scholars of color, one with the potential to affect disciplinary knowledge profoundly and "reveal aspects of reality obscured by more orthodox approaches" (1986, p. S15). Dolores Delgado Bernal (1998) has continued this line in her work focused on Chicana scholars. Like Collins, Delgado Bernal challenges the notion of a universal foundation of knowledge; she proposes a feminist epistemological framework that places Chicana cultural intuition and experience at the core of knowledge production by Chicana scholars (Delgado Bernal 1998). More recently, Delgado Bernal and Octavio Villalpando (2002) explore "ways of knowing" related to race and ethnicity, arguing that faculty of color bring a foundational, unique epistemological perspective to the academy, a question also pursued by others (Scheurich and Young 1997). Thus far, the impact of these studies on the field has been limited, an outcome undoubtedly related to the oppositional stance of their theses and their call for transformation of the structures supporting the epistemological dominance of scientific positivism. Renewed interest among young scholars of color in higher education, however, is a sign that the line of inquiry is gaining momentum and will continue in the coming era.

Prospects for Future Inquiry

We have described the sociology of diversity as a discrete area of inquiry arising from and responding to challenges in an era of rapid demographic change in the student bodies of U.S. colleges and universities. Emerging acute educational problems related to diversity, we argue, catalyzed the inception of this research as well as its subsequent growth. Racial and ethnic diversity continues to challenge higher education with respect to providing equitable access, safe and effective learning environments, a faculty representative of its students, and a curriculum relevant for the education of a diverse society. Demographic projections indicate that these challenges will persist, if not intensify, over the next decade. By 2015, not only will undergraduate enrollment grow by approximately one and a half million students, but 80 percent of those students will be African American, Asian American, and Latino. Indeed, in ten states, minority students will constitute at least 40 percent of the undergraduate population (Carnevale and Fry 2000). These projections suggest that the sociology of diversity will indeed grow as an active area in the sociology of higher education.

Additional factors will shape the nature of the inquiry as well. The sociology of diversity is strongly linked to the social, cultural, and policy environments that affect higher education. Public concern and political struggle over issues such as campus unrest, minority underrepresentation, educational quality, and—most recently—affirmative action in admissions have driven the research agenda examined in this chapter. In many cases, scholarly inquiry was aimed at specific policy initiatives such as ending affirmative action, top X-percent admissions plans, diversification of general education course requirements, and the implementation of diversity-focused cocurricula (e.g., cultural awareness workshops, race dialogues, ethnic theme dorms). Certainly, policy debates will continue to drive the focus of inquiry into the second decade of this century. In the first decade of the century, much of the work being conducted addresses student outcomes, because of the continuing dispute over the legality of affirmative action and a rising tide of debate over standards and high-stakes assessment in higher education. Work in faculty diversity has seen less activity, and activity on the curriculum is waning. Demographic projections almost assure abundant activity on the impact of diversity on students, but as ethnic studies programs continue to grow, debate and study related to diversity and the curriculum should grow as well (Chang 1999).

The attention to policy that characterizes the sociology of diversity has contributed to vitality in the area by attracting scholars beyond departments of sociology into the domain. The scholars cited in this chapter work in charitable foundations, research centers, and departments of economics, education, ethnic studies, public policy, psychology, and sociology. Although the legacy of sociology is clear from the nature of the problems studied and the prominent focus placed on race, intergroup relations, and stratification, the many vantage points from which the collective work is being pursued should help to keep the area intellectually fresh and sustainable. Clark admonished us to be watchful lest our work become a "managerial sociology" where we become preoccupied with refining the educational system and addressing specific policy concerns of the day. The sociology of diversity, since its inception, has aimed to address specific educational problems and policies but has not shied away from broader sociological questions about, for example, the nature of social order and intergroup relations in nonhierarchical multicultural communities. Intellectual diversity, in part, has kept the field from becoming singularly focused and solely preoccupied with contemporary educational challenges. With microscopic and macroscopic lenses, qualitative, quantitative, and mixed methodologies, and functionalist as well as interpretive frameworks, the research as a whole takes a broad approach to specific educational problems.

The Legacy of Institutional Change

We describe the sociology of diversity as an "emerging" area of inquiry because the majority of the activity within the area has occurred within the last 10 to 12 years. We are only now achieving the temporal distance necessary to identify a cohesive and stable body of work. However, we also describe the work as emerging because a close look at the objectives of the inquiry leads to a related conclusion—the social transformation of higher education initiated by diversity remains a work in progress.

The lines of inquiry described in this chapter not only focus on bringing data to bear on the challenges of diversity but also, at a deeper level, assert the necessity of institutional transformation if those challenges are to be met successfully. Work in the area of access and diversity, for example, emphasizes the limiting role of institutions rather than of student characteristics, thereby designating institutions as the site of intervention and improvement. Research on intergroup relations also consistently places institutions at the center of race relations phenomena, implicating administrators as orchestrators of campus climate through policies affecting intergroup cooperation, racial attitudes, diversity in the curriculum and cocurriculum, and opportunities for formal and informal interracial interaction. The lines on faculty and the curriculum are perhaps the most transparent. Focusing on recruitment, tenure, and promotion practices and the processes of knowledge legitimation, these research lines also maintain the necessity for institutional change as a premise for any genuine response to the challenges of diversifying the faculty and curriculum. Research on the impact of diversity, because of its student development legacy, has the least discernible emphasis on institutional transformation and is exceptional in that regard. The majority of the research in this area presumes a student agent navigating a given, an essentially stable campus environment; most often the task then is to estimate the impact of existing conditions (diversity) and practices. The literature is changing, however, as more researchers examine the impact of students *on* institutions (see Chapter 4 in this volume).

The stance toward institutional transformation inherent in this body of work is not surprising. Philip Altbach compared the challenges of diversity in the 1990s to those posed by the civil rights movement 30 years earlier, writing, "In the 1960s it was possible to support the Civil Rights movement without that support having any significant implications for the universities. In the 1980s, issues related to race had a direct impact on campus—for intergroup relations, for the curriculum, for the professoriate and perhaps more important, for the allocation of resources" (1991, p. 4). As previous scholars have noted, diversity in higher education is not limited to concerns of underrepresentation and race in admissions but in fact pervades the entire educational enterprise of a university with goals for democratization (Chang 2002; Smith and associates 1997; Baez 2000). Rapid demographic change, in other words, has made it impossible to ignore the structural failings of higher education with regard to equitable access, disparities in academic success, and intercultural socialization and learning, or the role of diverse faculty and curriculum in achieving those and other educational outcomes.

In our examination of the sociology of diversity, we have found that scholars have recognized the transformative potential of the challenges of diversity and have oriented their research accordingly. The work described in this chapter is an emerging area of research because institutional change is still forthcoming. Although sociological inquiry has helped to highlight the vital role of institutional transformation in the successful future of higher education, change has been slow, and the calls for transformation continue. This bodes well from a scholarly standpoint, as work in this area will continue to emerge as the student body further diversifies, and institutional change remains a critical strategy for meeting the challenges forthcoming.

References

Allen, W. R. 1985. "Black Student, White Campus: Structural, Interpersonal, and Psychological Correlates of Success." *Journal of Negro Education* 54 (2): 134–47.

——. 1992. "The Color of Success: African-American College Student Outcomes at Predominantly White and Historically Black Public Colleges and Universities." *Harvard Educational Review* 62 (1): 26–44.

Allen, W. R., E. G. Epps, E. A. Guillory, S. A. Suh, M. Bonous-Hammarth, and M. L. A. Stassen. 2002. "Outsiders Within: Race, Gender, and Faculty Status in U.S. Higher Education." In *The Racial Crisis in American Higher Education: Continuing Challenges for the Twenty-first Century*, ed. W. A. Smith, P. G. Altbach, and K. Lomotey. Albany: State University of New York Press.

Allen, W. R., E. G. Epps, and N. Z. Haniff, eds. 1991. *College in Black and White: African American Students in Predominantly White and in Historically Black Public Universities*. Albany: State University of New York Press.

Allen, W. R., and D. Solórzano. 2001. "Affirmative Action, Educational Equity, and Campus Racial Climate: A Case Study of the University of Michigan Law School." *La Raza Law Journal* 12:237–363.

Altbach, P. G. 1991. "The Racial Dilemma in American Higher Education." In *The Racial Crisis in American Higher Education*, ed. P. G. Altbach and K. Lomotey. Albany: State University of New York Press.

Antonio, A. L. 1998. "The Impact of Friendship Groups in a Multicultural University." Ph.D. dissertation, University of California–Los Angeles.

———. 2002. "Faculty of Color Reconsidered: Retaining Scholars for the Future." *Journal of Higher Education* 73 (5): 582–602.

———. 2004. "When Does Race Matter in College Friendships? Exploring the Role of Race within Men's Diverse and Homogeneous Friendship Groups." *Review of Higher Education* 27 (4): 553–75.

Antonio, A. L., M. J. Chang, K. Hakuta, D. A. Kenny, S. Levin, and J. F. Milem. 2004. "Effects of Racial Diversity on Complex Thinking in College Students." *Psychological Science* 15 (8): 507–10.

Aronowitz, S. 1990. "Disciplines or Punish: Cultural Studies and the Transformation of Legitimate Knowledge." *Journal of Urban and Cultural Studies* 1 (1): 39–54.

Astin, A. W. 1982. *Minorities in American Higher Education*. San Francisco: Jossey-Bass.

———. 1993. *What Matters in College: Four Critical Years Revisited*. San Francisco: Jossey-Bass.

Astone, B., and E. Nuñez-Wormack. 1990. *Pursuing Diversity: Recruiting College Minority Students*. Washington, DC: School of Education and Human Development, George Washington University.

Baez, B. 2000. "Diversity and Its Contradictions." *Academe* 86 (5): 43–47.

———. 2002. " 'Race' Work and Faculty of Color: Changing the Academy from Within." Plenary paper presented at Keeping Our Faculties: Addressing the Recruitment and Retention of Faculty of Color, University of Minnesota, April 21–23.

Berkner, L. K., and L. Chavez. 1997. *Access to Postsecondary Education for the 1992 High School Graduates*. Washington, DC: U.S. Department of Education, Office of Educational Research and Improvement.

Berman, P. 1992. *Debating P.C.: The Controversy over Political Correctness on College Campuses.* New York: Dell.

Bernstein, R. 1988. "In Dispute on Bias, Stanford Is Likely to Alter Western Culture Program." *New York Times,* January 19, A12.

Bloom, A. 1987. *The Closing of the American Mind: How Higher Education Has Failed Democracy and Impoverished the Souls of Today's Students.* New York: Simon and Schuster.

Bollinger, L. 2002. "Debate over the SAT Masks Perilous Trends in College Admissions." *Chronicle of Higher Education,* July 12, B11.

Bowen, W. G., and D. Bok. 1998. *The Shape of the River: Long-Term Consequences of Considering Race in College and University Admissions.* Princeton, NJ: Princeton University Press.

Bryant, A. N. 2003. "Changes in Attitudes toward Women's Roles: Predicting Gender-Role Traditionalism among College Students." *Sex Roles: A Journal of Research* 48 (3–4): 131–42.

Card, D., and A. B. Krueger. 2004. *Would the Elimination of Affirmative Action Affect Highly Qualified Minority Applicants? Evidence from California and Texas.* Working Paper 10366. Cambridge, MA: National Bureau of Economic Research.

Carnevale, A. P., and R. A. Fry. 2000. *Crossing the Great Divide: Can We Achieve Equity When Generation Y Goes to College?* Princeton, NJ: Educational Testing Service.

Ceja, M. 2001. "Applying, Choosing, and Enrolling in Higher Education: Understanding the College Choice Process of First-Generation Chicana Students." Ph.D. dissertation, University of California–Los Angeles.

Chang, M. J. 1996. "Racial Diversity in Higher Education; Does a Racially Mixed Student Population Affect Educational Outcomes?" Ph.D. dissertation, University of California–Los Angeles.

———. 1999. "Expansion and Its Discontents: The Formation of Asian American Studies Programs in the 1990s." *Journal of Asian American Studies* 2 (2): 181–206.

———. 2002. "Preservation or Transformation: Where's the Real Educational Discourse on Diversity?" *Review of Higher Education* 25 (2): 125–40.

Chapa, J. 1997. "The Hopwood Decision in Texas as an Attack on Latino Access to Selective Higher Education Programs." Manuscript.

Chapa, J., and V. A. Lazaro. 1998. "*Hopwood* in Texas: The Untimely End of Affirmative Action." In *Chilling Admissions: The Affirmative Action Crisis and the Search for Alternatives,* ed. G. Orfield and E. Miller. Cambridge, MA: Harvard Education Publishing Group.

Clark, B. R. 1960. *The Open Door College.* New York: McGraw-Hill.

———. 1987. *The Academic Life: Small Worlds, Different Worlds.* Princeton, NJ: Carnegie Foundation for the Advancement of Teaching and Princeton University Press.

Collins, P. H. 1986. "Learning from the Outsider Within: The Sociological Significance of Black Feminist Thought." *Social Problems* 33:S14–S32.

Cornwell, C., and D. B. Mustard. 2002. "Race and the Effects of Georgia's HOPE Scholarship." In *Who Should We Help? The Negative Social Consequences of Merit Scholarships*, ed. D. Heller and P. Marin. Cambridge, MA: Civil Rights Project at Harvard University.

Delgado Bernal, D. 1998. "Using a Chicana Feminist Epistemology in Educational Research." *Harvard Educational Review* 68 (4): 555–82.

Delgado Bernal, D., and O. Villalpando. 2002. "An Apartheid of Knowledge in Academia: The Struggle over the 'Legitimate' Knowledge of Faculty of Color." *Equity and Excellence in Education* 35 (2): 169–80.

Duster, T. 1993. "The Diversity of California at Berkeley: An Emerging Reformulation of 'Competence' in an Increasingly Multicultural World." In *Beyond a Dream Deferred: Multicultural Education and the Politics of Excellence*, ed. B. W. Thompson and S. Tyagi. Minneapolis: University of Minnesota Press.

Dynarski, S. 2002. "Race, Income, and the Impact of Merit Aid." In *Who Should We Help? The Negative Social Consequences of Merit Scholarships*, ed. D. Heller and P. Marin. Cambridge, MA: Civil Rights Project at Harvard University.

Ferrell, W. C., and C. K. Jones. 1988. "Recent Racial Incidents in Higher Education: A Preliminary Perspective." *Urban Review* 20:211–33.

Finnell, S. 1998. "The Hopwood Chill: How the Court Derailed Diversity Efforts at Texas A&M." In *Chilling Admissions. The Affirmative Action Crisis and the Search for Alternatives*, ed. G. Orfield and E. Miller. Cambridge, MA: Harvard Education Publishing Group.

Fleming, J. 1984. *Blacks in College*. San Francisco: Jossey-Bass.

Freeman, K. 1999. "The Race Factor in African Americans' College Choice." *Urban Education* 34 (1): 4–25.

Freeman, K., and G. E. Thomas. 2002. "Black Colleges and College Choice: Characteristics of Students Who Choose HBCUs." *Review of Higher Education* 25 (3): 349–58.

Gates, H. L. 1992. *Loose Canons: Notes on the Culture Wars*. New York: Oxford University Press.

Geiser, S. 1998. *Redefining UC's Eligibility Pool to Include a Percentage of Students from Each High School: Summary of Simulation Results*. Oakland: University of California Office of the President.

Giroux, H. A. 1995. "National Identity and the Politics of Multiculturalism." *College Literature* 22 (2): 42–57.

Gonzalez, K. P. 2000–2001. "Towards a Theory of Minority Student Participation in Predominantly White Colleges and Universities." *Journal of College Student Retention: Research, Theory, and Practice* 2 (1): 69–91.

———. 2002. "Campus Culture and the Experiences of Chicano Students in Predominantly White Colleges and Universities." *Urban Education* 37 (2): 193–218.

Green, M. F. 1989. *Minorities on Campus: A Handbook for Enhancing Diversity.* Washington, DC: American Council on Education.

Gurin, P. 1999. "The Compelling Need for Diversity in Higher Education. Expert Testimony in *Gratz et al. v. Bollinger et al.*" *Michigan Journal of Race and Law* 5:363–425.

Gurin, P., E. L. Dey, S. Hurtado, and G. Gurin. 2002. "Diversity and Higher Education: Theory and Impact on Educational Outcomes." *Harvard Educational Review* 72 (5): 330–66.

Hirsch, E. D. 1987. *Cultural Literacy: What Every American Needs to Know.* Boston: Houghton Mifflin.

Hollingshead, A. B. 1959. *Elmtown's Youth.* New York: John Wiley.

Horn, C. L., and S. M. Flores. 2003. *Percent Plans in College Admissions: A Comparative Analysis of Three States' Experiences.* Cambridge, MA: Civil Rights Project at Harvard University.

Hu, S., and G. D. Kuh. 2003. "Diversity Experiences and College Student Learning and Personal Development." *Journal of College Student Development* 44 (3): 320–34.

Hurtado, S. 1992. "The Campus Racial Climate: Contexts of Conflict." *Journal of Higher Education* 63:539–69.

———. 1994. "The Institutional Climate for Talented Latino Students." *Research in Higher Education* 35:21–41.

———. 2000. "Linking Diversity and Educational Purpose: How the Diversity of the Faculty and the Student Body Impacts the Classroom Environment and Student Development." In *Diversity Challenged: Legal Crisis and New Evidence*, ed. G. Orfield. Cambridge, MA: Harvard Publishing Group.

Hurtado, S., and D. F. Carter. 1997. "Effects of College Transition and Perceptions of the Campus Racial Climate on Latino Students' Sense of Belonging." *Sociology of Education* 70 (4): 324–45.

Hurtado, S., D. F. Carter, and S. Sharp. 1995. "Social Interaction on Campus: Differences among Self-Perceived Ability Groups." Paper presented at the annual meeting of the Association for Institutional Research, Boston, May.

Hurtado, S., E. L. Dey, P. Y. Gurin, and G. Gurin. 2003. "College Environments, Diversity, and Student Learning." In *Higher Education: Handbook of Theory and Research*, vol. 18, ed. J. C. Smart. New York: Agathon.

Hurtado, S., E. L. Dey, and J. G. Treviño. 1994. "Exclusion or Self-Segregation? Interaction across Racial/Ethnic Groups on College Campuses." Paper presented at the annual meeting of the American Educational Research Association, New Orleans, April.

Hurtado, S., J. F. Milem, A. R. Clayton-Pedersen, and W. R. Allen. 1998. "En-

hancing Campus Climates for Racial/Ethnic Diversity: Educational Policy
and Practice." *Review of Higher Education* 21 (3): 279–302.

———. 1999. *Enacting Diverse Learning Environments: Improving the Climate for Racial/Ethnic Diversity in Higher Education.* Washington, DC: George Washington University, Graduate School of Education and Human Development.

Hyun, M. 1996. "Commitment to Change: How College Impacts Changes in Students' Commitment to Racial Understanding." Ph.D. dissertation, University of California–Los Angeles.

Institute for the Study of Social Change. 1991. *The Diversity Project: Final Report.* University of California–Berkeley.

Kahlenberg, R. D. 1996. *The Remedy: Class, Race, and Affirmative Action.* New York: Basic Books.

Kane, T. J. 1998. "Misconceptions in the Debate over Affirmative Action in College Admissions." In *Chilling Admissions. The Affirmative Action Crisis and the Search for Alternatives*, ed. G. Orfield and E. Miller. Cambridge, MA: Harvard Education Publishing Group.

Karabel, J. 1998. "No Alternative: The Effects of Color-Blind Admissions in California." In *Chilling Admissions. The Affirmative Action Crisis and the Search for Alternatives*, ed. G. Orfield and E. Miller. Cambridge, MA: Harvard Education Publishing Group.

Koretz, D., M. Russell, D. Shin, C. Horn, and K. Shasby. 2001. *Testing and Diversity in Postsecondary Education: The Case of California.* Chestnut Hill, MA: National Board on Educational Testing and Public Policy.

Lee, S. J. 1997. "The Road to College: Hmong American Women's Pursuit of Higher Education." *Harvard Educational Review* 67 (4): 803–27.

Lewis, A., M. Chesler, and T. A. Forman. 2000. "The Impact of 'Colorblind' Ideologies on Students of Color: Intergroup Relations at a Predominantly White University." *Journal of Negro Education* 69:74–91.

Loo, C. M., and G. Rolison. 1986. "Alienation of Ethnic Minority Students at a Predominately White University." *Journal of Higher Education* 57:58–77.

Lynd, R. S., and H. M. Lynd. 1929. *Middletown.* New York: Harcourt, Brace.

Marger, M. N. 1991. *Race and Ethnic Relations: American and Global Perspectives.* 2nd ed. Belmont, CA: Wadsworth.

Marin, P., and E. K. Lee. 2003. *Appearance and Reality in the Sunshine State: The Talented 20 Program in Florida.* Cambridge, MA: Civil Rights Project at Harvard University.

Martínez Alemán, A. M. 2000. "Race Talks: Undergraduate Women of Color and Female Friendships." *Review of Higher Education* 23 (2): 133–52.

McDonough, P. M., and A. L. Antonio. 1996. "Ethnic and Racial Differences in Selectivity of College Choice." Paper presented at the annual meeting of the American Educational Research Association, New York, April.

McDonough, P. M., A. L. Antonio, and J. W. Trent. 1997. "Black Students, Black

Colleges: An African-American College Choice Model." *Journal for a Just and Caring Education* 3 (1): 9–36.

Mickelson, R. A., and M. L. Oliver. 1991. "Making the Short List: Black Candidates and the Faculty Recruitment Process." In *The Racial Crisis in American Higher Education*, ed. P. G. Altbach and K. Lomotey. Albany: State University of New York Press.

Milem, J. F. 1994. "College, Students, and Racial Understanding." *Thought and Action* 9 (2): 51–92.

———. 1999. "The Importance of Faculty Diversity to Student Learning and to the Mission of Higher Education." Paper presented at the American Council on Education Symposium and Working Research Meeting on Diversity and Affirmative Action.

———. 2003. "The Educational Benefits of Diversity: Evidence from Multiple Sectors." In *Compelling Interest: Examining the Evidence on Racial Dynamics in Higher Education*, ed. M. Chang, D. Witt, J. Jones, and K. Hakuta. Palo Alto, CA: Stanford University Press.

Milem, J. F., and K. Hakuta. 2000. "The Benefits of Racial and Ethnic Diversity in Higher Education." In *Minorities in Higher Education: Seventeenth Annual Status Report*, ed. D. Wilds. Featured Report. Washington, DC: American Council on Education.

Neville, H., and M. Furlong. 1994. "The Impact of Participation in a Cultural Awareness Program on the Racial Attitudes and Social Behaviors of First-Year College Students." *Journal of College Student Development* 35 (5): 371–77.

Nora, A., and A. F. Cabrera. 1996. "The Role of Perceptions of Prejudice and Discrimination on the Adjustment of Minority Students to College." *Journal of Higher Education* 67 (2): 119–48.

Nussbaum, M. C. 1997. *Cultivating Humanity: A Classical Defense of Liberal Education.* Cambridge, MA: Harvard University Press.

Olneck, M. R. 2001. "Re-naming, Re-imagining America: Multicultural Curriculum as Classification Struggle." *Pedagogy, Culture, and Society* 9:333–55.

Pascarella, E. T., and P. T. Terenzini. 1991. *How College Affects Students: Findings and Insights from Twenty Years of Research.* San Francisco: Jossey-Bass.

———. 1998. "Studying College Students in the Twenty-first Century: Meeting New Challenges." *Review of Higher Education* 21:151–65.

Perna, L. W. 2000. "Differences in the Decision to Attend College among African Americans, Hispanics, and Whites." *Journal of Higher Education* 71:117–41.

Ravitch, D. 1990. "Multiculturalism: E Pluribus Plures." *American Scholar* 59 (3): 337–54.

Reyes, M. L., and J. J. Halcon. 1988. "Racism in America: The Old Wolf Revisited." *Harvard Educational Review* 58 (3): 299–314.

Rhoads, R. A. 1995. "Critical Multiculturalism, Border Knowledge, and the

Canon: Implications for General Education and the Academy." *Journal of General Education* 44 (4): 256–73.

Richardson, R. C., and E. F. Skinner. 1991. *Achieving Quality and Diversity: Universities in a Multicultural Society.* New York: Macmillan.

Sax, L. J., A. W. Astin, W. S. Korn, and S. K. Gilmartin. 1999. *The American College Teacher: National Norms for the 1998–1999 HERI Faculty Survey.* Los Angeles: Higher Education Research Institute, University of California–Los Angeles.

Scheurich, J. J., and M. D. Young. 1997. "Coloring Epistemologies: Are Our Research Epistemologies Racially Biased?" *Educational Researcher* 26 (4): 4–16.

Schlesinger, A. M. 1991. *The Disuniting of America: Reflections on a Multicultural Society.* Knoxville, TN: Whittle Direct.

Sewell, W. H., and V. P. Shah. 1966. "Socioeconomic Status, Intelligence, and the Attainment of Higher Education." *Sociology of Education* 40:1–23.

Slaughter, S. 1997. "Class, Race, Gender, and the Construction of Postsecondary Curricula in the United States: Social Movement, Professionalization, and Political Economic Theories of Curricular Change." *Journal of Curriculum Studies* 29 (1): 1–30.

Smedley, B. D., H. F. Myers, and S. P. Harrell. 1993. "Minority-Status Stresses and the College Adjustment of Ethnic Minority Freshmen." *Journal of Higher Education* 64 (4): 434–52.

Smith, D. G. 1989. *The Challenge of Diversity: Involvement or Alienation in the Academy?* ASHE-ERIC Higher Education Reports 5. Washington, DC: School of Education and Human Development, George Washington University.

Smith, D. G., and associates. 1997. *Diversity Works: The Emerging Picture of How Students Benefit.* Washington, DC: Association of American Colleges and Universities.

Snyder, T. D. 1995. *Digest of Education Statistics 1995.* NCES 1995–029. U.S. Department of Education, National Center for Education Statistics. Washington, DC: U.S. Government Printing Office.

Snyder, T. D., and C. M. Hoffman. 1991. *Digest of Education Statistics 1990.* NCES 1991–660. U.S. Department of Education, National Center for Education Statistics. Washington, DC: U.S. Government Printing Office.

Solórzano, D., M. Ceja, and T. Yosso. 2000. "Critical Race Theory, Racial Microaggressions, and Campus Racial Climate: The Experiences of African American College Students." *Journal of Negro Education* 69:60–73.

Solórzano, D., and O. Villalpando. 1998. "Critical Race Theory, Marginality, and the Experience of Minority Students in Higher Education." In *Emerging Issues in the Sociology of Education: Comparative Perspectives*, ed. C. Torres and T. Mitchell. New York: State University of New York Press.

Springer, L., B. Palmer, P. T. Terenzini, E. T. Pascarella, and A. Nora. 1996. "Attitudes toward Campus Diversity: Participation in a Racial or Cultural Workshop." *Review of Higher Education* 20 (1): 53–68.

Student Academic Services, Office of the President, University of California. 2002. *Eligibility in the Local Context Program Evaluation Report.* www.ucop.edu/news/cr/report02.pdf (accessed October 10, 2004).

Takagi, D. Y. 1992. *The Retreat from Race. Asian-American Admissions and Racial Politics.* New Brunswick, NJ: Rutgers University Press.

Tanaka, G. K. 2003. *The Intercultural Campus. Transcending Culture and Power in American Higher Education.* New York: Peter Lang.

Teranishi, R. T. 2002. "Asian Pacific Americans and Critical Race Theory: An Examination of School Racial Climate." *Equity and Excellence in Education* 35 (2): 144–54.

———. 2004. "Yellow and Brown: Residential Segregation and Emerging Asian American Immigrant Populations." *Equity and Excellence in Education* 37 (3): 255–63.

Teranishi, R. T., M. Ceja, A. L. Antonio, W. R. Allen, and P. M. McDonough. 2004. "The College-Choice Process for Asian Pacific Americans: Ethnicity and Social Class in Context." *Review of Higher Education* 27 (4): 527–51.

Teranishi, R. T., G. Gomez, and W. R. Allen. 2002. "Social Capital and the Stratification of College Opportunities for Southeast Asian Students." Paper presented at the annual meeting of the Association for the Study of Higher Education, Sacramento, CA, November.

Tierney, W. G. 1993. *Building Communities of Difference: Higher Education in the Twenty-first Century.* Westport, CT: Bergin and Garvey.

Tierney, W. G., and E. M. Bensimon. 1996. *Promotion and Tenure: Community and Socialization in Academe.* Albany: State University of New York Press.

Tienda, M., K. Cortes, and S. Niu. 2003. "College Attendance and the Texas Top 10 Percent Law: Permanent Contagion or Transitory Promise?" Princeton, NJ: Princeton University. www.texastop10.princeton.edu/publications/tienda101803.pdf (accessed July 23, 2004).

Tienda, M., K. Leicht, T. Sullivan, M. Maltese, and K. Lloyd. 2003. "Closing the Gap? Admissions and Enrollments at the Texas Public Flagships before and after Affirmative Action." Princeton, NJ: Princeton University. www.texastop10.princeton.edu/publications/tienda041501.pdf (accessed July 23, 2004).

Trent, W. T. 1991. "Student Affirmative Action in Higher Education: Addressing Underrepresentation." In *The Racial Crisis in American Higher Education*, ed. P. G. Altbach and K. Lomotey. Albany: State University of New York Press.

Trent, W. T., D. Owens-Nicholson, T. K. Eatman, M. Burke, J. Daugherty, and K. Norman. 2003. "Justice, Equality of Educational Opportunity, and Affirmative Action in Higher Education." In *Compelling Interest: Weighing the*

Evidence on Racial Dynamics in Higher Education, ed. M. J. Chang, D. Witt-Sandis, J. Jones, and K. Hakuta. Palo Alto, CA: Stanford University Press.

Turner, C. S. V., and S. L. Myers Jr. 2000. *Faculty of Color in Academe: Bittersweet Success.* Needham Heights, MA: Allyn and Bacon.

UCMI (University Committee on Minority Issues). 1989. *Building a Multiracial, Multicultural University Community: Final Report of the University Committee on Minority Issues.* Stanford, CA: Stanford University.

Villalpando, O. 2002. "The Impact of Diversity and Multiculturalism on All Students: Findings from a National Study." *NASPA Journal* 40 (1): 124–44.

Vobejda, B. 1988. "Bennett Assails New Stanford Program: Change in Cultural Readings Called Capitulation to Pressure Politics." *Washington Post*, April 19, A05.

Warner, W. L., and P. S. Lunt. 1941. *The Social Life of a Modern Community.* New Haven, CT: Yale University Press.

Washington, V., and W. B. Harvey. 1989. *Affirmative Rhetoric, Negative Action: African-American and Hispanic Faculty at Predominantly White Institutions.* ASHE-ERIC Higher Education Report 2. Washington, DC: School of Education and Human Development, George Washington University.

Whitla, D. K, G. Orfield, W. Silen, C. Teperow, C. Howard, and J. Reede. 2003. "Educational Benefits of Diversity in Medical School: A Survey of Students." *Academic Medicine* 78 (5): 460–66.

Whitt, E. J., M. I. Edison, E. T. Pascarella, P. T. Terenzini, and A. Nora. 2001. "Influences on Students' Openness to Diversity and Challenge in the Second and Third Years of College." *Review of Higher Education* 72 (2): 172–204.

Wirt, J., S. P. Choy, P. Rooney, S. Provasnik, A. Sen, and R. Tobin. 2004. *The Condition of Education 2004.* NCES 2004–077. U.S. Department of Education, National Center for Education Statistics. Washington, DC: U.S. Government Printing Office.

Zuñiga, X., B. A. Nagda, T. D. Sevig, and E. L. Dey. 1995. "Speaking the Unspeakable: Student Learning Outcomes in Intergroup Dialogues on a College Campus." Paper presented at the annual meeting of the Association for the Study of Higher Education, Orlando, FL, November.

10 Sociological Frameworks for Higher Education Policy Research

MICHAEL N. BASTEDO

The study of policy and politics is quickly becoming a central subfield in higher education research. As public policy becomes more salient in the evolution and development of higher education systems, research on policy, politics, and governance has increased concomitantly. Researchers and students are seeking new and compelling concepts and frameworks to help explain policy dynamics in higher education. However, of the available analyses, few have proved useful. Although policy process models from political science have recently been promoted to fill this gap, theories drawn from sociology and organization studies have enormous potential to advance our understanding of higher education policy. Just as theories of firms and nonprofit organizations have been invaluable to our understanding of the behavior of universities, comparable sociological theories can be used to analyze the policy process. Policymakers do not function in a vacuum; they are embedded in organizations—legislatures, boards, and agencies—all of which develop influences, practices, and habits that help determine policymakers' behavior. As a result, concepts derived from the sociological study of organizations can be used profitably to analyze political behavior and enhance our knowledge of the policy process.

This chapter looks at several concepts in organization theory and sociology that can be used to study higher education policy and politics. These include concepts of organizational strategy, the role of interests and agency in the organizational process, the use of symbols and symbolic behavior by organizational leaders, and the analysis of institutional logics applied to organizational fields. This is certainly not an exhaustive review of the possibilities, but each of these organizational processes is worth careful examination given its salient effects on the policymaking process in higher education. In order to establish a foundation for considering sociological frameworks, I will first review some of the extant theories of policy process drawn from political science, beginning with those that have been strongly influenced by sociological theories of organization.

Policy Process Theories

Policy process theories are rooted in the institutional school in political science, which is related to but somewhat distinct from sociological institutionalism (March and Olsen 1984; Scott 2001). Both schools look closely at the impact of organizational structures, environments, and behavior on organizational decision making, as opposed to simply examining the interaction of individual actors or interest groups. For obvious reasons, political institutionalism is focused primarily on political behavior, while sociologists have a broader focus on a wide variety of institutional types, of which political institutions are only one special type.

In the study of higher education politics and policymaking, theories of policy process have gained ascendancy as researchers have attempted to fill this vacuum (McLendon 2003a; 2003c; Pusser 2003, 2004). Descriptive analyses of the policy process have been available for some time, but these emphasized a sequential, incremental approach (Bendor 1995; Easton 1965; Lasswell 1948; Lindblom 1959). A range of new possibilities have now also become available, from garbage can models to punctuated equilibrium theory and advocacy coalitions, to help guide education researchers in their studies of the policy process (Sabatier 1999). However, as these models have emerged so recently, the usefulness of their application to higher education policy has yet to be fully explored. These new theories will undoubtedly inspire more and significant new work to enhance our understanding of the politics of higher education.

Policy process theories are often rooted in theoretical frameworks or methodologies familiar to sociologists and organization theorists. One prominent case, a broad theory of political agenda setting, is quite familiar to those who study higher education. Michael Cohen, James March, and Johan Olsen (1972) developed garbage can theory to understand the process by which university presidents manage the complex dynamics of contemporary universities. It was then appropriated by John Kingdon for application to a compelling and enduring mystery of political science: how issues reach salience in political agendas (Kingdon

1984/2003). It has since been expanded, critiqued, and reformulated and is now commonly referred to as the "multiple-streams framework" (Mucciaroni 1992; Zahariadis 2003).

Garbage can theory, at the simplest level, saw various streams of problems, solutions, technologies, and people interacting with reference to organizational issues and recognized that certain combinations of these streams could yield choice opportunities—the chance to make an acceptable decision. In the case of college presidents, the more the president could control the interactions among those elements and create "garbage cans" to attend to specific issues, the higher the probability of a successful solution (Cohen and March 1974). (Or, taken from the cynic's point of view, garbage cans could be used to keep constituents busy while the real work was taking place elsewhere.) In the case of agenda setting, Kingdon saw problems, ideas (or policies), and politics as three streams coming together to yield similar choice opportunities for political actors.

Other policy process theories are less rooted in established organization theory. Punctuated equilibrium theory, for example, takes its inspiration from ecology models of biological development (Baumgartner and Jones 1991; Jones, Baumgartner, and True 1998; True, Jones, and Baumgartner 2003). Evolutionary biologists—most famously, Stephen Jay Gould—noted that species transformations tended to occur in brief, intense periods of change rather than gradually over time. This process was called "punctuated equilibrium" to denote long, fallow periods of incremental change followed by dramatic, rapid change over short periods of time. Social scientists, seeking an alternative to the standard incrementalist theories of political change offered by Charles Lindblom, David Easton, and others, borrowed this theory to understand radical changes in policy development that failed to adhere to the incremental model.

Frank Baumgartner and Bryan Jones (1991) consider that equilibria in political systems occur because "policy monopolies" have been created among the various overlapping subsystems in politics. These policy monopolies create established structures, political roles, and interest group mobilization efforts that lead to incremental change. Radical policy changes—called policy punctuations—occur when these policy monopolies are systematically destroyed. Baumgartner and Jones see these as occurring due to variations in public or policymaker interest in various issues, although the factors behind changes in public interest and the attention of political actors are still largely unclear.

The group behavior of political actors is addressed by Advocacy Coalition Theory, or ACT (Sabatier 1988; Sabatier and Jenkins-Smith 2003; Schlager 1995). According to ACT, politics is generated by rival coalitions of political actors who share a set of normative and causal beliefs and engage in nontrivial, coordinated activity over a period of time. ACT is thus a kind of interest group mobilization that occurs *within* political institutions. Major policy change can occur only when the dominant coalition of actors is unseated through shifts in public opinion or other environmental conditions, but minor, incremental change occurs through routine shifts in opinion or attention among members of the dominant coalition.

A number of other political theories are available for policy researchers in higher education. Policy innovation and diffusion models use econometric models to analyze the translation of policy ideas across institutional, state, or international contexts (Berry and Berry 1990, 1999; McLendon, Heller, and Young 2005). Institutional choice theory examines the degree to which policy changes are influenced by the implicit selection of decision makers to implement them (Clune 1987; Gormley 1987). Political utilities analysis looks at how particular organizational structures or implementation strategies have usefulness for political actors beyond their substantive importance (Malen 1994; Weiler 1990). Finally, similar to garbage can models, arena models examine how participants, interests, and ideals contend for a place on the political agenda, but these models go further to examine how the arena itself legitimizes participants and policy ideas (Mazzoni 1991; Fowler 1994).

The application of these theories to higher education is a relatively new phenomenon and limited to a small but burgeoning set of researchers (McLendon 2003c). Nonetheless, the theories have wide applicability to problems in governance and higher education policy and could be profitably used alone or combined with other ideas (see below). The emergence of these frameworks will undoubtedly lead to demystification of the process of higher education policy and agenda setting, but as yet it is unclear which of the frameworks will prove most useful and provide the most understanding for higher education researchers and practitioners. Simultaneously, we need to consider other frameworks from alternative traditions that may enhance our knowledge.

The Policymaking Environment for Higher Education Organizations

To understand more fully higher education as an organization, we must first consider the university as an open system. An open-systems approach acknowledges that organizations are embedded in multiple environments, both technical and institutional, to which the organization must respond (Scott 2001). Organizations are not monolithic in their responses to the environment; part of the variance in their responses can be explained by differences in the degree of complexity and uncertainty of environmental demands (Lawrence and Lorsch 1967; Thompson 1967) and by the nature, quantity, and source of organizational resources (DiMaggio 1983; Pfeffer and Salancik 1978). Another part of this variance, however, can be explained by differences in individual and organizational capacity—enabled through leadership ability, interest mobilization, and value commitments—to engage in strategic action (Child 1972; Oliver 1991).

The technical and institutional environments for public higher education are exceedingly complex due to the multiple constituencies that higher education must serve, including parents, alumni trustees, state boards, legislators, and governors. Internal actors, including faculty, staff, and students, present their own demands for organizational adaptation to their needs. In addition, higher education must accommodate multiple, occasionally competing demands from the environment to increase access, lower costs, improve quality, and increase effectiveness (Gumport and Pusser 1999). A great deal of research was conducted throughout the 1980s and 1990s on the relationship between the field of higher education and its environment (Peterson 1998).

Societal demands regarding the role of higher education have shifted dramatically in recent years, pressuring campuses to think of themselves largely as an industry rather than as a social institution (Gumport 2000). As a result, academic restructuring and retrenchment efforts were prominent throughout the 1990s, as public universities responded to the demands of state governments to eliminate unproductive and duplicative academic programs (Gumport 1993; Slaughter 1993). While state-level attention to academic programs was hardly new, the degree of heat and attention increased dramatically since its inception, and the impact on faculty has been substantial.

In addition, we have seen increasing pressure to "systematize" public systems of higher education, as state boards use their coordinating authority to eliminate duplicative programs and move underprepared students to lower levels of the system (Bastedo and Gumport 2003; Gumport and Bastedo 2001). The source of these demands is not only political and economic, as it surely is, but also institutional, the result of cognitive theories and preconceptions about the proper role of government in public higher education. Institutional actors, however, may engage in strategic action to manipulate these environments and their organizational impact. As the next section shows, power and authority play an important mediating role in the capacity to act strategically.

Policy as Strategy

In recent years, strategy has been considered an important component of institutional action. The traditional function of institutional theory has been to explain the powerful capacity of the environment to promote the similarity of structures and practices across organizations (Meyer and Rowan 1977; DiMaggio 1983; DiMaggio and Powell 1983). The theory provides a compelling explanation for pervasive similarities among organizations and implies that the isomorphic process increases the stability of organizations over the long term and thus improves their odds for survival. Over the past fifteen years, however, institutional theory has been criticized for paying more attention to the roots of stability in organizations than to the sources of organizational change or the indubitable role of power in organizational development (Covaleski and Dirsmith 1988; DiMaggio 1988; Fligstein 1997; Perrow 1986; Powell 1991).

Recent work in neoinstitutional theory has provided a much-needed space for conceptualizing the role of strategic action within an institutional framework. Traditional strategic decision-making models have tended to emphasize the unfettered ability of leaders to influence organizations and their environments within a specific set of constraints. Another line of scholarship, however, has tried to recognize the role of environmental pressures on the process of strategic action (Child 1972; Hitt and Tyler 1991; Hrebiniak and Joyce 1985). Similarly, resource dependence theories have accounted for strategic action by the successful manipulation of task constraints and organizational environments (Pfeffer and Salancik 1978). Christine Oliver (1991) integrated the institutional and resource dependence perspectives to identify a continuum of strategic action ranging from acquiescence to manipulation. She argued that variation in the degree of institutionalization provides room for varying degrees of "resistance, awareness, proactiveness, influence, and self-interest" in organizational decision making (Oliver 1991, p. 151). Nevertheless, from this perspective, strategic action is still completely dependent on external factors—namely, the degree of institutionalization in the organizational field—that are outside the control of individual actors.

A role for leadership and power within institutional theory can be buttressed by insights from theorists of strategic choice. Strategic choice theory developed in direct response to the highly deterministic organization theories that predominated during the 1960s (Child 1972, 1997). Organizational design, structure, and performance were seen as determined by the operational demands presented in the environment. An organization's size, governance, technologies, and resource constraints severely limited the choices that could be made by its managers. Strategic choice theory, on the other hand, has emphasized the role of organizations and individuals within organizations in engaging actively to construct organizational structures and processes. Strategic choice is defined as the process whereby those with authority and power within the organization decide upon courses of action. The focus is therefore on the political process developed among organizational actors that leads to strategic decision making by the organization. Thus, according to John Child, "strategic choice articulates a political process, which brings agency and structure into tension and locates them within a significant context" (1997, p. 44). Effective strategic choice requires the exercise of power and directs attention toward those who possess power and toward the limits upon that power imposed by the environment.

Criticisms of this new perspective have inevitably emerged, and they have been substantial. Although the theory was perhaps ahead of its time in focusing upon agents and their relationship to the organizational environment, decision making was seen as determined by how agents could preserve their own autonomy by meeting performance expectations. This conception of agents' ability to actively manipulate the organizational environment was therefore severely limited, an artifact of the deterministic theories that strategic choice theory was designed to confront. In addition, strategic choice was seen only within the limits of constraints imposed by the environment, not in relation to the limits imposed by the actors themselves. This has led some theorists to posit that organizations fully "select and interpret their environment, respond to those elements that are fixed, and attempt to shape the remaining elements to their advantage" (Hitt and Tyler 1991, p. 331; see also Keats and Hitt 1988). As a result, Child, the founder of strategic choice theory, has acknowledged that "organizational actors often create choice possibilities through their relationships with people who are formally outside of the organization" (Child 1997, p. 57).

Oliver, in 1991, laid the groundwork for future work by developing an influential taxonomy of possible strategic actions—acquiescence, compromise, avoidance, defiance, and manipulation—that organizations could utilize in response to isomorphic pressures in the institutional environment. Subsequently, there have been attempts to flesh out this perspective theoretically, often with a continued focus on the role of isomorphism in creating opportunities for change (Goodrick and Salancik 1996; Suchman 1995). Only a few have begun to look at the intra-organizational dynamics related to strategic action and organizational change.

Recent empirical work in institutional theory has been promising to develop our understanding of how actors within organizations engage in strategic action. Mark Covaleski and Mark Dirsmith (1988), in their groundbreaking study of the deteriorating relationship between the University of Wisconsin and its state benefactors during a budget crisis, articulated the ability of powerful state actors to mandate institutional compliance from the university when their interests were at stake. Lauren Edelman (1992) highlighted the ability of business leaders to maintain their managerial autonomy by mediating the impact of institutional pressures to implement civil rights law. Jerry Goodstein (1994) demonstrated that organizational response to institutional demands in the environment varies depending on the nature of the pressure and the organization. Finally, Margarete Arndt and Barbara Bigelow (2000) used content analysis of hospital annual reports to argue that senior administrators were using references and evidence of pressures in the institutional environment to justify their decision making to shareholders. This work has moved far beyond strategic choice theory to develop nuanced models of interactions between actors and institutions that produce strategic change.

Strategic planning models have been quite popular in the higher education literature since the early 1980s, perhaps reaching their zenith with the publication of *Academic Strategy*, still widely considered a classic in the field (Keller 1983). Organization theorists also played with the concept, developing models for strategic planning and conducting empirical research on the effectiveness of strategic orientations for colleges and universities, particularly in response to scarce resources (Cameron 1983; Cameron and Tschirhart 1992; Chaffee 1985; Leslie and Fretwell 1996). None of these works, however, has seriously considered the institutional environment or the role of campus leaders in managing it. Almost uniformly, these authors see strategic planning as a highly rational, top-down process by which leaders consider alternatives, make hypotheses, conduct feasibility analyses, make decisions, and see that organizations carry out their decisions per their instructions. A neoinstitutional perspective, however, encourages us to consider the myriad cultural, cognitive, regulative, and normative pressures in the environment and to investigate why behavior that is ostensibly nonoptimal persists.

Policy as Entrepreneurship

Leaders can play an important role in institutional processes. Radical organizational change requires leadership in the early stages of the institutionalization process, through the building of organizational sagas, the development of resources and legitimacy, and the migration of new organizational models (Clark 1970; DiMaggio 1991; Kraatz and Moore 2002; Maguire, Hardy, and Lawrence 2004; Rao 1998). Leaders must also successfully negotiate the institutionalization process, by recognizing that institutions constrain the choices that are possible or legitimate (Greenwood and Hinings 1996; Selznick 1957). During such times of radical change, staff often play an important and disproportionate role in the institutionalization process, as discontinuous change upsets existing hierarchies and forces leaders to rely upon staff for expertise (Barley 1986; Bastedo 2005a).

Early formulations of institutional theory—now usually regarded as the "old institutionalism"—acknowledged that organizations could have leadership and engage in strategic action within the limits of the institutional structure. According to Phillip Selznick (1957), institutional actors may act as leaders by providing a "guiding hand" that steers the organization among the multitude of institutional constraints. While the organization would undoubtedly be buffeted by these existing constraints, and may well drift among them in the appropriate direction, a leader can guide the organization more smoothly by developing its mission and distinctive competence, and by personally acting as the embodiment of institutional purpose (Selznick 1957). This tradition is strong in higher education research, from Burton Clark's case studies of a junior college and three unusual liberal arts colleges (Clark 1960, 1970) through to Steven Brint and Jerome Karabel's (1991) more recent account of the transformation of the U.S. community college.

The "new" institutionalism that developed during the 1970s, however, tended to treat institutional constraints as so deterministic that the concept of strategic action was hardly credible (Meyer and Rowan 1977). According to R. A. Colignon (1997, p. 8), the behavioral assumptions underlying the new institutionalism were that "people are irrational, affectively driven, cognitively and morally diminished, and lacking in interpretive competence and practical consciousness." While this critique is undoubtedly exaggerated, institutional analysts began to conceptualize a role for individual agency that allowed organizational change to occur beyond routine adaptation (Covaleski and Dirsmith 1988; DiMaggio 1988; Perrow 1986; Powell 1991). In a particularly influential essay, P. J. DiMaggio (1988) argued that the concept of institutional entrepreneurs—derived from Stuart Eisenstadt (1980)—could provide leverage for understanding the role of strategic action in creating new institutions. Although the concept was barely mentioned by DiMaggio, it has been used as a conceptual framework in a number of subsequent articles (Colomy 1998; Fligstein 1997; Rao 1998). Also, the concept of "policy entrepreneurs" has gained ascendancy in political science literature (Kingdon 2003; Mintrom 1997).

Indeed, the concept of institutional entrepreneurship can also provide leverage for understanding the role of leaders in creating new institutions (DiMaggio 1988; Fligstein 1997; Selznick 1957). In the case of higher education governance, multiple institutions hold sway, each with its own set of embedded values, interests, and shared norms. Legislators, campus and system administrators, and faculty all have institutionalized sets of values and norms that must be negotiated by policymakers in the higher education field. Statewide governing and coordinating boards themselves have a set of institutionalized values and practices that have become legitimate over time in the field (Berdahl 1971; Richardson et al. 1999). Successful institutional entrepreneurs are able to use their social capital, political power, and leadership skills to negotiate these multiple and often conflicting institutional demands. As Hayagreeva Rao, Calvin Morrill, and Mayer Zald have said, institutional entrepreneurs "spearhead collective attempts to infuse new beliefs, norms, and values into social structures" (2000, p. 240). They are disproportionately influential in setting policy agendas, framing events, and managing political conflict, thus reinforcing the legitimacy and credibility of their actions. Nevertheless, the role of leaders and policy entrepreneurs is underdeveloped in institutional theory to date.

Policy as Symbolic Action

Like all organizational actions, policy must be understood as having both substantive and symbolic components. This is not to say that the only role of institutions is to engage in "impression management" of organizational behavior through the use of symbols or other nonsubstantive actions (Arndt and Bigelow 1996; Powell 1991). Rather, it is to emphasize that organizational action often has an important symbolic component, and those components may have real importance, even primary importance.

On a substantive level, policy decisions are often the result of political exigencies, resource allocation dilemmas, and other practical issues that play a part in the political process. All organizations face similar dilemmas of external constraints, resource and power dependence, and other aspects of the organizational environment that contrive to restrict decision making. Indeed, it is often the case that competing environmental demands and associated resource constraints result in situations where it is impossible for the organization to produce outcomes that are desirable to constituents. In the case of policy, disappointed constituents are usually the public or powerful political actors.

In such cases, symbolic behavior is often the result (M. Edelman 1962; Pfeffer 1982). These can be attempts at managing the impressions of external actors or may simply signal an attempt at meeting needs. The success of all symbolic behavior is measured by the degree to which it serves to maintain organizational legitimacy. This can be viewed cynically, as public relations—or even worse, as fakery or lies. But from the point of view of the organization, symbolic behavior reflects an attempt at survival or a need to maintain resources or values in the face of untenable environmental demands.

A fascinating series of studies by Lauren Edelman at the University of California at Berkeley has explicated these processes in various legal contexts (Edelman 1992; Edelman, Uggen, and Erlanger 1999; Edelman and Petterson 1999). In studies of federal civil rights law, Edelman found that managers used symbolic compliance to create the impression that they were in accord with affirmative action mandates while maintaining maximum managerial autonomy in personnel decisions (Edelman 1992). The establishment of EEO (equal employment opportunity) offices and written affirmative action plans bears no statistical relationship to changes in workforce composition at those corporations (Edelman and Petterson 1999). The hiring of affirmative action officers at colleges and universities yields similar results (Edelman, Petterson, Chambliss, and Erlanger 1991). Edelman concludes that organizations use various structures and established positions to maintain symbolic compliance with legal demands while maintaining the organization's resources, legitimacy, and autonomy.

Symbolic compliance often occurs through a process of decoupling, the process by which certain organizational behaviors are disassociated from core organizational activities. (This is not to be confused with loose coupling among subunits of an organization.) Early work in organization theory attempted to explicate the dynamics underlying the decoupling of organizational units and processes. John Meyer and Brian Rowan (1977) theorized that organizations decouple their formal structures and processes from inspection to prevent any resulting losses in legitimacy. Meyer and Rowan saw many of these decoupling procedures acting as "rational myths"—symbols of efficiency and effectiveness that actually lack those qualities under closer scrutiny. Organization charts, academic grades, and degree structures all may have these qualities.

Although decoupling was one of the earliest articulated processes in the institutionalization of formal organizations, empirical research on decoupling has been extremely rare. Recently, a series of intriguing papers has investigated decoupling in corporate finance structures, finding that business firms often adopt innovations viewed favorably by shareholders and boards of directors, like CEOs' long-term incentive plans, stock repurchase plans, and poison pills, but then fail to implement them (Westphal and Zajac 1995, 1998, 2001). C. E. Coburn (2004) found that although the classroom is widely viewed as a structure that decouples instruction from environmental pressures through teacher autonomy, a more nuanced process occurs in which teachers use their preexisting beliefs about quality instruction to translate environmental pressures into instructional behavior. In the field of higher education, Robert Birnbaum (2001) argues that whereas management fads, like

Total Quality Management (TQM) and Zero-Based Budgeting (ZBB), were considered and used by various colleges, most cases resulted in only "virtual adoption" of these practices until the fad subsided. Despite these excellent studies, however, our understanding of the underlying dynamics of the decoupling process, and how it is often employed strategically, has yet to be fully developed.

Policy as Logic

Policy change can also be seen as a form of institutional change, which emphasizes the powerful and adaptive role of norms, values, and beliefs in the process of institutionalization (e.g., Meyer and Rowan 1977; DiMaggio and Powell 1991). Recently, the concept of *institutional logics* has become a popular means for scholars to articulate the dominant theories of action underlying institutional processes. Institutional logics are the "belief systems and associated practices that predominate in an organizational field" (Scott et al. 2000, p. 170). These are the "organizing principles" that organizations use when making decisions within a specified arena (Friedland and Alford 1991, p. 248).

Analysis of institutional logics is increasingly common in the organizational literature, and education has often been the context for analysis. Scholars have recently examined the role of institutional logics in changing conceptions of the higher education publishing industry (Thornton and Ocasio 1999; Thornton 2002), on an urban school's response to state accountability standards (Booher-Jennings 2005), on academic health center mergers (Kitchener 2002), on performance assessment in Canadian colleges and universities (Townley 1997), and on the responsiveness of community colleges to environmental demands (Gumport 2003). Further studies have looked at institutional logics in market reactions to stock repurchase plans (Zajac and Westphal 2004), in the deinstitutionalization of the nineteenth-century thrift industry (Haveman and Rao 1997), and in a novel study, in the nouvelle cuisine movement in French restaurants (Rao, Monin, and Durand 2003).

Institutional logics convey the idea that a single idea or approach dominates a policy system. But logics can also be a template for action, a set of characteristics that identify the theory of action to be used in policy development. In this way, the work of Royston Greenwood and C. R. Hinings (1993) is very helpful. They develop the concept of an archetype, "a set of structures and systems that consistently embodies a single interpretive scheme" (Greenwood and Hinings 1993, p. 1053). An archetype is an array of multiple, interrelated features that need to cohere in order to provide direction for strategic action by the organization. The development of an archetype is the result of intraorganizational processes, as advantaged groups or individuals consolidate their political position and gain control over organizational resources. Policies can thus be analyzed in a dual manner. At once they are a logic that is compelling to policy actors in the organization, and they are a set of organizational characteristics that are adapted to support the emerging logic (Bastedo 2005b).

Institutional logics can draw upon concepts not only from contemporary institutional theories but also from power and strategic choice perspectives. This would view policy systems as arenas in which institutions and actors are engaged in dynamic processes that create and recreate social structures. There is room to understand the agency of individuals and organizations as well as the powerful influences of institutional structure on policy development and implementation processes. Interactions between institutions and actors refine the structure of the policy system and influence policy outcomes. Inside the organization, actors with interests and value commitments use their leadership skills and power. Logics thus provide space both for institutional constraints and for human agency.

Conclusion: Doing Research in Higher Education Policy and Politics

This chapter has sought to provide at least a taste of the various sociological theoretical and conceptual possibilities open to researchers in higher education policy and politics. For the graduate student seeking a conceptual framework for a dissertation or a practitioner seeking greater understanding of seemingly mystifying political behavior, these frameworks can guide us to more nuanced understandings of the political process and models for predicting future behavior. Nonetheless, a great deal of work remains to be done, methodologically and conceptually.

The complexity of political behavior requires study that uses a wide variety of research methodologies. In higher education, case study methods have been used predominantly, with the state as the usual unit of analysis (e.g., Bastedo 2005a, 2005b; McLendon 2003b; Pusser 2003; Richardson et al. 1999). Further qualitative work is needed, particularly work that uses different levels of analysis. Research at the federal level is still needed (e.g., Cook 1998; Parsons 1997), as is work looking specifically at legislators, governors, and other important policymakers (e.g., Berdahl 2004; Conklin and Wellner 2004; Ruppert 1996, 2001). Unfortunately, international and comparative work on policy formation in higher education is still very rare (Enders 2004). Across all levels of analysis, studies that are methodologically ambitious, with large numbers of cases and subjects, would be most welcome.

Quantitative work on policy formation, politics, and governance remains highly descriptive in nature (e.g., Ruppert 2001; Schwartz and Akins 2005). As a result, this work lacks the methodological sophistication of quantitative studies of policy outcomes, although some exceptions are notable (Hearn and Griswold 1994; McLendon, Heller, and Young 2005). This is not simply a question of interest; existing data is often poor, establishing new datasets is both time consuming and expensive, and policy formation is not a topic that generally attracts substantial grant funding. Nonetheless, numerous research questions can be addressed only with better data and sophisticated quantitative methods.

Regardless of the method used, the politics of higher education is a growing field, attracting new researchers and conceptual frameworks from across the social sciences. The sociological concepts and frameworks reviewed here provide opportunities to leverage new and important insights into the policy formation process. An enhanced understanding of the political environment facing colleges and universities will provide both researchers and practitioners with better tools to address the complex tasks facing contemporary higher education.

References

Arndt, M., and B. Bigelow. 1996. "The Implementation of Total Quality Management in Hospitals: How Good Is the Fit?" *Health Care Management Review* 21 (1) 93–94.

——. 2000. "Presenting Structural Innovation in an Institutional Environment: Hospitals' Use of Impression Management." *Administrative Science Quarterly* 45:494–522.

Baldridge, J. V. 1971. *Power and Conflict in the University: Research in the Sociology of Complex Organizations.* New York: John Wiley and Sons.

Barley, S. R. 1986. "Technology as an Occasion for Structuring: Evidence from Observations of CT Scanners and the Social Order of Radiology Departments." *Administrative Science Quarterly* 31:78–108.

Bastedo, M. N. 2005a. "The Making of an Activist Governing Board." *Review of Higher Education* 28:551–70.

———. 2005b. "Metapolicy: Institutional Change and the Rationalization of Public Higher Education." Paper presented at the annual meeting of the American Educational Research Association, Montreal, Canada, April 11–15.

Bastedo, M. N., and P. J. Gumport. 2003. "Access to What? Mission Differentiation and Academic Stratification in U.S. Public Higher Education." *Higher Education* 46:341–59.

Baumgartner, F. R., and B. D. Jones. 1991. "Agenda Dynamics and Policy Subsystems." *Journal of Politics* 53:1044–74.

Bendor, J. 1995. "A Model of Muddling Through." *American Political Science Review* 89:819–30.

Berdahl, R. O. 1971. *Statewide Coordination of Higher Education*. Washington, DC: American Council on Education.

———. 2004. "Strong Governors and Higher Education." Manuscript, University of Maryland.

Berry, F. S., and W. D. Berry. 1990. "State Lottery Adoptions as Policy Innovations: An Event History Analysis." *American Political Science Review* 84:395–416.

———. 1999. "Innovation and Diffusion Models in Policy Research." In *Theories of the Policy Process*, ed. P. Sabatier. Boulder: Westview.

Birnbaum, R. 2001. *Management Fads in Higher Education*. San Francisco: Jossey-Bass.

Booher-Jennings, J. 2005. "Below the Bubble: 'Educational Triage' and the Texas Accountability System." *American Educational Research Journal* 42:231–68.

Brint, S., and J. Karabel. 1991. "Institutional Origins and Transformations: The Case of American Community Colleges." In *The New Institutionalism in Organizational Analysis*, ed. W. W. Powell and P. J. DiMaggio, 337–60. Chicago: University of Chicago Press.

Cameron, K. S. 1983. "Strategic Responses to Conditions of Decline: Higher Education and the Private Sector." *Journal of Higher Education* 54:359–80.

Cameron, K. S., and M. Tschirhart. 1992. "Postindustrial Environments and Organizational Effectiveness in Colleges and Universities." *Journal of Higher Education* 63:87–108.

Chaffee, E. E. 1985. "The Concept of Strategy: From Business to Higher Education." In *Higher Education: Handbook of Theory and Research*, vol. 1, ed. J. C. Smart, 47–99. New York: Agathon.

Child, J. 1972. "Organizational Structure, Environment, and Performance: The Role of Strategic Choice." *Sociology* 6:1–22.

———. 1997. "Strategic Choice in the Analysis of Action, Structure, Organizations, and Environment: Retrospect and Prospect." *Organization Studies* 18:43–76.

Clark, B. R. 1970. *The Distinctive College.* Chicago: Aldine.

Clune, W. H. 1987. "Institutional Choice as a Theoretical Framework for Research on Educational Policy." *Educational Evaluation and Policy Analysis* 9:117–32.

Coburn, C. E. 2004. "Beyond Decoupling: Rethinking the Relationship between Institutional Environment and the Classroom." *Sociology of Education* 77:211–44.

Cohen, M. D., and J. G. March. 1974. *Leadership and Ambiguity: The American College President.* New York: McGraw-Hill.

Cohen, M. D., J. G. March, and J. Olsen. 1972. "A Garbage Can Model of Organizational Choice." *Administrative Science Quarterly* 17:1–25.

Colignon, R. A. 1997. *Power Plays: Critical Events in the Institutionalization of the Tennessee Valley Authority.* Albany: State University of New York Press.

Colomy, P. 1998. "Neofunctionalism and Neoinstitutionalism: Human Agency and Interest in Institutional Change." *Sociological Forum* 13:265–300.

Conklin, K., and J. Wellner. 2004. *Linking Tuition and Financial Aid Policy: The Gubernatorial Perspective.* Boulder: Western Interstate Commission for Higher Education.

Cook, C. E. 1998. *Lobbying for Higher Education: How Colleges and Universities Influence Policy.* Nashville: Vanderbilt University Press.

Covaleski, M., and M. Dirsmith. 1988. "An Institutional Perspective on the Rise, Social Transformation, and Fall of a University Budget Category." *Administrative Science Quarterly* 33:562–87.

DiMaggio, P. J. 1983. "State Expansion and Organizational Fields." In *Organizational Theory and Public Policy*, ed. R. H. Hall and R. E. Quinn, 147–61. Beverly Hills, CA: Sage.

——. 1988. "Interest and Agency in Institutional Theory." In *Institutional Patterns and Organizations*, ed. L. Zucker, 3–22. Cambridge, MA: Ballinger.

——. 1991. "Constructing an Organizational Field as a Professional Project: U.S. Art Museums, 1920–1940." In *The New Institutionalism in Organizational Analysis*, ed. W. W. Powell and P. J. DiMaggio, 267–92. Chicago: University of Chicago Press.

DiMaggio, P. J., and W. W. Powell. "The Iron Cage Revisited: Institutional Isomorphism and Collective Rationality in Organizational Fields." *American Sociological Review* 48 (2): 147–60.

——. 1991. Introduction to *The New Institutionalism in Organizational Analysis*, ed. W. W. Powell and P. J. DiMaggio, 1–40. Chicago: University of Chicago Press.

Easton, D. 1965. *A Systems Analysis of Political Life.* New York: Wiley.

Edelman, L. B. 1992. "Legal Ambiguity and Symbolic Structures: Organizational Mediation of Civil Rights Law." *American Journal of Sociology* 97:1531–76.

Edelman, L. B., and S. M. Petterson. 1999. "Symbols and Substance in Organizational Response to Civil Rights Law." *Research in Social Stratification and Mobility* 17:107–35.

Edelman, L. B., S. M. Petterson, E. Chambliss, and H. S. Erlanger. 1991. "Legal Ambiguity and the Politics of Compliance: The Affirmative Action Officers' Dilemma." *Law and Policy* 13:73–97.

Edelman, L. B., C. Uggen, and H. S. Erlanger. 1999. "The Endogeneity of Legal Regulation: Grievance Procedures as Rational Myth." *American Journal of Sociology* 105:406–54.

Edelman, M. 1964. *The Symbolic Uses of Politics*. Urbana: University of Illinois Press.

Eisenstadt, Stuart N. 1980. "Cultural Orientations, Institutional Entrepreneurs, and Social Change: Comparative Analysis of Traditional Civilizations." *American Journal of Sociology* 85:840–69.

Enders, J. 2004. "Higher Education, Internationalisation, and the Nation-State: Recent Developments and Challenges for Governance Theory." *Higher Education* 47:361–82.

Fligstein, N. 1997. "Social Skill and Institutional Theory." *American Behavioral Scientist* 40:397–405.

Fowler, F. C. 1994. "Education Reform Comes to Ohio: An Application of Mazzoni's Arena Models." *Educational Evaluation and Policy Analysis* 16:335–50.

Friedland, R., and R. R. Alford. 1991. "Bringing Society Back In: Symbols, Practices, and Institutional Contradictions." In *The New Institutionalism in Organizational Analysis*, ed. W. W. Powell and P. J. DiMaggio, 232–66. Chicago: University of Chicago Press.

Goodrick, E., and G. R. Salancik. 1996. "Organizational Discretion in Responding to Institutional Practices: Hospitals and Cesarean Births." *Administrative Science Quarterly* 41:1–28.

Goodstein, J. D. 1994. "Institutional Pressures and Strategic Responsiveness: Employer Involvement in Work-Family Issues." *Academy of Management Journal* 37:350–82.

Gormley, W. T., Jr. 1987. "Institutional Policy Analysis: A Critical Review." *Journal of Policy Analysis and Management* 6:153–69.

Greenwood, R., and C. R. Hinings. 1993. "Understanding Strategic Change: The Contribution of Archetypes." *Academy of Management Journal* 36:1052–81.

———. 1996. "Understanding Radical Organizational Change: Bringing Together the Old and the New Institutionalism." *Academy of Management Review* 21:1022–54.

Gumport, P. J. 1993. "The Contested Terrain of Academic Program Reduction." *Journal of Higher Education* 64 (3): 283–311.

——. 2000. "Academic Restructuring: Organizational Change and Institutional Imperatives." *Higher Education* 39:67–91.

——. 2003. "The Demand-Response Scenario: Perspectives of Community College Presidents." *Annals of the American Academy of Political and Social Science* 586:38–61.

Gumport, P. J., and M. N. Bastedo. 2001. "Academic Stratification and Endemic Conflict: Remedial Education Policy at the City University of New York." *Review of Higher Education* 24:333–49.

Gumport, P. J., and B. Pusser. 1999. "University Restructuring: The Role of Economic and Political Contexts." *Higher Education: Handbook of Theory and Research*, vol. 14, ed. J. C. Smart, 146–200. New York: Agathon.

Haveman, H. A., and H. Rao. 1997. "Structuring a Theory of Moral Sentiments: Institutional and Organizational Coevolution in the Early Thrift Industry." *American Journal of Sociology* 102:1606–51.

Hitt, M. A., and B. B. Tyler. 1991. "Strategic Decision Models: Integrating Different Perspectives." *Strategic Management Journal* 12:327–51.

Hearn, J. C., and C. P. Griswold. 1994. "State-Level Centralization and Policy Innovation in U.S. Postsecondary Education." *Educational Evaluation and Policy Analysis* 16:161–90.

Hrebiniak, L., and W. F. Joyce. 1985. "Organizational Adaptation: Strategic Choice and Environmental Determinism." *Administrative Science Quarterly* 30:336–49.

Jones, B. D., F. R. Baumgartner, and J. L. True. 1998. "Policy Punctuations: U.S. Budget Authority, 1947–1995." *Journal of Politics* 60:1–33.

Keats, B. W., and M. A. Hitt. 1988. "A Causal Model of Linkages among Environmental Dimensions, Macro Organizational Characteristics, and Performance." *Academy of Management Journal* 31:570–98.

Keller, G. 1983. *Academic Strategy.* Baltimore: Johns Hopkins University Press.

Kingdon, J. W. 2003. *Agendas, Alternatives, and Public Policies.* 2nd ed. New York: Longman.

Kitchener, M. 2002. "Mobilizing the Logic of Managerialism in Professional Fields: The Case of Academic Health Center Mergers." *Organization Studies* 23:391–420.

Kraatz, M. S., and J. H. Moore. 2002. "Executive Migration and Institutional Change." *Academy of Management Journal* 45:120–43.

Lasswell, H. B. 1948. *The Analysis of Political Behavior.* New York: Oxford University Press.

Lawrence, P. R., and J. W. Lorsch. 1967. *Organization and Environment: Managing Differentiation and Integration.* Boston: Harvard Business School Press.

Leslie, D. W., and E. K. Fretwell Jr. 1996. *Wise Moves in Hard Times: Creating and Managing Resilient Colleges and Universities.* San Francisco: Jossey-Bass.

Lindblom, C. 1959. "The Science of Muddling Through." *Public Administration Review* 19:79–88.

Maguire, S., C. Hardy, and T. B. Lawrence. 2004. "Institutional Entrepreneurship in Emerging Fields: HIV/Aids Treatment Advocacy in Canada." *Academy of Management Journal* 47:657–79.

Malen, B. 1994. "Enacting Site-Based Management: A Political Utilities Analysis." *Educational Evaluation and Policy Analysis* 16:249–67.

March, J., and J. Olsen. 1984. "The New Institutionalism: Organizational Factors in Political Life." *American Political Science Review* 78:734–49.

Mazzoni, T. L. 1991. "Analyzing State School Policymaking: An Arena Model." *Educational Evaluation and Policy Analysis* 13:115–38.

McLendon, M. K. 2003a. "The Politics of Higher Education: Toward an Expanded Research Agenda." *Educational Policy* 17:165–91.

———. 2003b. "Setting the Governmental Agenda for State Decentralization of Higher Education." *Journal of Higher Education* 74:479–515.

———. 2003c. "State Governance Reform of Higher Education: Patterns, Trends, and Theories of the Public Policy Process." *Higher Education: Handbook of Theory and Research*, vol. 18, ed. J. C. Smart, 57–144. New York: Agathon.

McLendon, M. K., D. Heller, and S. Young. 2005. "State Postsecondary Policy Innovation: Politics, Competition, and Interstate Migration of Policy Ideas." *Journal of Higher Education* 76 (4): 363–400.

Meyer, J., and B. Rowan. 1977. "Institutionalized Organizations: Formal Structure as Myth and Ceremony." *American Journal of Sociology* 83:340–63.

Mintrom, M. 1997. "Policy Entrepreneurs and the Diffusion of Innovation." *American Journal of Political Science* 41:738–70.

Mucciaroni, G. 1992. "The Garbage Can Model and the Study of Policy Making: A Critique." *Polity* 24:459–82.

Oliver, C. 1991. "Strategic Responses to Institutional Processes." *Academy of Management Review* 16:145–79.

Parsons, M. D. 1997. *Power and Politics: Federal Higher Education Policy Making in the 1990s.* Albany: State University of New York Press.

Perrow, C. 1986. *Complex Organizations: A Critical Essay.* New York: McGraw-Hill.

Peterson, M. W. 1998. *Improvement to Emergence: An Organization-Environment Research Agenda for a Postsecondary Knowledge Industry.* Stanford, CA: National Center for Postsecondary Improvement.

Pfeffer, J. 1981. "Management as Symbolic Action: The Creation and Maintenance of Organizational Paradigms." *Research in Organizational Behavior* 3:1–52.

———. 1982. *Organizations and Organization Theory.* Boston: Pitman.

Pfeffer, J., and G. R. Salancik. 1978. *The External Control of Organizations: A Resource Dependence Perspective.* New York: Harper and Row.

Powell, W. W. 1991. "Expanding the Scope of Institutional Analysis." In *The New Institutionalism in Organizational Analysis,* ed. W. W. Powell and P. J. DiMaggio, 183–203. Chicago: University of Chicago Press.

Pusser, B. 2003. "Beyond Baldridge: Extending the Political Model of Higher Education Organization and Governance." *Educational Policy* 17:121–45.

———. 2004. *Burning Down the House: Politics, Governance, and Affirmative Action at the University of California.* Albany: State University of New York Press.

Rao, H. 1998. "Caveat Emptor: The Construction of Nonprofit Consumer Watchdog Organizations." *American Journal of Sociology* 103:912–61.

Rao, H., P. Monin, and R. Durand. 2003. "Institutional Change in Toque Ville: Nouvelle Cuisine as an Identity Movement in French Gastronomy." *American Journal of Sociology* 108:795–843.

Rao, H., C. Morrill, and M. N. Zald. 2000. "Power Plays: How Social Movements and Collective Action Create New Organizational Forms." *Research in Organizational Behaviour* 22:239–82.

Richardson, R. C., Jr., et al. 1999. *Designing State Higher Education Systems for a New Century.* Phoenix: Oryx.

Rowan, B. 1982. "Organizational Structure and the Institutional Environment: The Case of Public Schools." *Administrative Science Quarterly* 27:259–79.

Ruppert, S. S. 1996. *The Politics of Remedy: State Legislative Views on Higher Education.* Washington, DC: National Education Association.

———. 2001. *Where We Go from Here: State Legislative Views on Higher Education in the New Millennium.* Washington, DC: National Education Association.

Sabatier, P. A. 1988. "An Advocacy Coalition Framework of Policy Change and the Role of Policy-Oriented Learning Therein." *Policy Sciences* 21:129–68.

———, ed. 1999. *Theories of the Policy Process.* Boulder: Westview.

Sabatier, P. A., and H. C. Jenkins-Smith. 2003. "The Advocacy Coalition Framework: An Assessment." In *Theories of the Policy Process,* ed. P.A. Sabatier, 117–68. Boulder: Westview.

Schlager, E. 1995. "Policy Making and Collective Action: Defining Coalitions within the Advocacy Coalition Framework." *Policy Sciences* 28:242–70.

Schwartz, M., and L. Akins. 2005. *Policies, Practices, and Composition of Governing Boards of Public Colleges and Universities.* Washington, DC: Association of Governing Boards of Universities and Colleges.

Scott, W. R. 2001. *Institutions and Organizations.* 2nd ed. Thousand Oaks, CA: Sage.

Scott, W. R., M. Ruef, P. J. Mendel, and C. A. Caronna. 2000. *Institutional Change and Healthcare Organizations: From Professional Dominance to Managed Care.* Chicago: University of Chicago Press.

Selznick, P. 1949. *TVA and the Grass Roots*. Berkeley: University of California Press.

——. 1957. *Leadership in Administration*. New York: Harper and Row.

Slaughter, S. 1993. "Retrenchment in the 1980s: The Politics of Prestige and Gender." *Journal of Higher Education* 64:250–82.

Suchman, M. C. 1995. "Managing Legitimacy: Strategic and Institutional Approaches." *Academy of Management Review* 20:571–610.

Thompson, J. D. 1967. *Organizations in Action*. New York: McGraw-Hill.

Thornton, P. H. 2002. "The Rise of the Corporation in a Craft Industry: Conflict and Conformity in Institutional Logics." *Academy of Management Journal* 45:81–101.

Thornton, P. H., and W. Ocasio. 1999. "Institutional Logics and the Historical Contingency of Power in Organizations: Executive Succession in the Higher Education Publishing Industry, 1958–1990." *American Journal of Sociology* 105:801–43.

Townley, B. 1997. "The Institutional Logic of Performance Appraisal." *Organization Studies* 18:261–85.

True, J. L., B. D. Jones, and F. R. Baumgartner. 2003. "Punctuated-Equilibrium Theory: Explaining Stability and Change in American Policymaking." In *Theories of the Policy Process*, ed. P. A. Sabatier, 97–116. Boulder: Westview.

Weiler, H. N. 1990. "Comparative Perspectives on Educational Decentralization: An Exercise in Contradiction?" *Educational Evaluation and Policy Analysis* 12:443–48.

Westphal, J. D., and E. J. Zajac. 1995. "Substance and Symbolism in CEOs' Long-Term Incentive Plans." *Administrative Science Quarterly* 39:367–90.

——. 1998. "The Symbolic Management of Stockholders: Corporate Governance Reforms and Shareholder Reactions." *Administrative Science Quarterly* 43:127–53.

——. 2001. "Decoupling Policy from Practice: The Case of Stock Repurchase Programs." *Administrative Science Quarterly* 46:202–28.

Whittington, R. 1988. "Environmental Structure and Theories of Strategic Choice." *Journal of Management Studies* 25:521–36.

Zahariadis, N. 2003. "Ambiguity, Time, and Multiple Streams." In *Theories of the Policy Process*, ed. P. A. Sabatier, 73–96. Boulder: Westview.

Zajac, E. J., and J. D. Westphal. 2004. "The Social Construction of Market Value: Institutionalization and Learning Perspectives on Stock Market Reactions." *American Sociological Review* 69:433–57.

IV LOOKING AHEAD

11 A Note on Pursuing Things That Work

BURTON R. CLARK

There is no longer any doubt about it. The disconnect between researchers and practitioners in understanding universities remains acute. Researchers write mainly for one another, armed with disciplinary and interdisciplinary perspectives. Early in their careers, they test hypotheses generated from a review of the literature. As they grow older, they aim to generate "theory," ensuring turgid prose. Ruminating among broadly stated schemes, as presently practiced in the sociology of higher education, they publish articles in journals that practitioners do not read. For their part, practitioners turn to one another to gain insight into how to handle ongoing specific concerns. For them, academic theorizing is imprecise and remote—a case of talking the talk far removed from local operating complexities. Researchers aim too high and attempt to explain too much. Practitioners—the staffs of U.S. foundations included—aim too low and fall into ad hoc discussions. When questions of how change comes about in universities take the stage, the gap widens.

This disconnect in how the university is analyzed is similar to how business firms were studied up to the 1960s. But in the ensuing four decades, faculty in business schools closed the gap between research and practice by means of case-study analysis, concentrating on exemplary institutions and best practices. The resulting literature on General Electric alone is a subspecies, filling bookshelves and classroom assignments. Case studies of firms, good and bad, today constitute the basic tools of instruction.

Recently, researchers studying American education levels K–12 have seriously tackled the research-practice disconnect. Ellen Condliffe Lagemann observed in a 2001 Spencer Foundation annual report that by operating close to practice, "use-driven" or "practice-based" research on elementary and secondary education has sought to link fundamental understanding with immediate application (Lagemann 2001). Beyond education studies, in the wider scientific scene, Donald E. Stokes challenged the old dichotomy between basic and applied research. In the late 1990s, he stressed combining research for understanding with research for use, using as "a model case the fundamental yet use-inspired studies by which Louis Pasteur laid the foundations of microbiology a century ago" (Stokes 1997). Stokes asserted a modern "dynamic paradigm" that would help renew the compact between science and government and, even more broadly, the connection between basic science and American democracy.

A new approach, then, has spread throughout many societal sectors and realms of analysis. It centers on use-inspired, practice-driven research that can serve also as research for basic understanding.

We who study university change can reduce the research-practice disconnect by two means immediately at hand. First, we can reason inductively from the experience of on-the-ground practitioners. We can convene seminars on what works. We can give primacy to the hard reality of observed practices in defined settings: from departments and research centers to broader schools and faculties, to all-encompassing central administrators, academic senates, and coalitions of faculty and managers. Only secondarily do we glance at broad frameworks developed in the study of business and public administration—resource dependency, path dependence, isomorphism, management by objectives, total quality management. These borrowed approaches never get to the point of how decisions are collectively fashioned in complex universities, each loaded with unique features in an extended portfolio of missions and programs, general and specific, that need rebalancing from year to year.

In the complex realities of practice, we can pursue what works. We find out what significant organizational changes Stanford made in the last half of the twentieth century to become an outstanding university (undergraduate education included) noted for talent-attracting magnetism. We find out how Michigan and Wisconsin continue to prosper in research *and* in teaching *and* in service as public U.S. universities, even as they extend themselves to include new populations and outside business and professional groups. We watch North Carolina State University experimentally fashion a separate niche alongside Duke University and the University of North Carolina, to give the state of North Carolina increasing strength in its research triangle. We take seriously the question of how U.S. universities raised themselves up to a collective posture whereby they dominate in international assessments—recently carried out in Switzerland (Herbst, Hagentobler, and Snover 2002), Britain (*Times Higher Education Supplement* 2004), and China (Institute of Higher Education, Shanghai Jiao Tong University 2004)—of the top 50, top 100, top 200, top 500 universities in the world. Other nations have long come—and continue to come—to the United States to find out what works, before carrying home lessons that can be integrated with home country constraints and opportunities. The world of actual university reform is a very busy place.

Researchers of changing university practice can also greatly extend the insights of inductive reasoning by pursuing case studies internationally. The time is long overdue for researchers and practitioners alike to escape nationalistic tunnel vision as fully as possible: the French, from the tunnel of unique traditional structures and practices in a national higher education system defined originally by Napoleon a century and a half ago (Christine Musselin, in her recent book, has brilliantly shown the way out—Musselin 2004); the Russians, from their particularly rocky road of modernizing old authoritarian structures while government support collapses; the Germans, from the frozen ice of interlocked local and national interests glorified by Humboldtian ideals; and the Americans, most arrogant of all, from thinking the whole world must also be captivated by the grinding problem of remedial education, the never-ending debate over the fate of general/liberal education in megauniversities, and the corruption of big-time sports, all uniquely embedded in a particular U.S. combination of weak elementary-secondary education and highly differentiated, sharply competitive higher education.

Reducing our own deep disconnect between research and practice is not easy. But young scholars who put their minds and enthusiasms to it could make a difference in a decade. They need to see practitioners as their primary teachers. The mantra becomes: sit not with statisticians but with university management groups. They need to patiently pursue case studies of specific universities, forging ethnographic compromises as their narratives bracket newly identified common features amidst institutional specificities. Some among them will need to pursue case studies outside their own country, by field research if possible, by document analysis alone if necessary, to reduce tunnel vision and to determine how common elements vary internationally. Researchers need to catch up with varied practice and then move on as practice moves on. Fast-moving times require adaptive research.

A good example of adaptive research operating at the cutting edge of university change comes from Canada. In a collection of papers given at a 2002 conference on "the changing role of higher education," John R. Evans reported on "the academic-commercial interface in a knowledge-driven economy," as seen specifically in "a view from MaRS"—an example of "clusters" at various stages of development across Canada, six of which have major emphasis on biotechnology (Evans 2005). Details are reported particularly for the promising MaRS cluster (Medical and Related Sciences Discovery District) in Toronto, seen as "a great site to promote the cluster convergence of critical elements" *and* exemplifying the agglomeration effects or critical mass of having a large number of scientists, investors, and firms all in a single location. Among the practitioners at this Canadian cutting edge, *commercialization* is a highly positive term, with its financing and nurturing at the center of attention. This attitude toward university-commerce ventures contrasts sharply with the very negative connotations often assigned to the idea of commercialization by academics in the United States.

Practitioners sit at the crossroads of action. They have to make things work, to experiment and learn in compartmentalized universities, each operating in a particular societal context. What practitioners have variously been able to accomplish in recent decades provides ample ground for optimism. If you want to know how to build a great university in three or four decades, go find out how from MIT and the University of California–San Diego, and on through at least 30 universities in the American system. And go find out from the University of Toronto and the University of British Columbia in Canada; from Cambridge, Warwick, and Strathclyde universities in Great Britain; from fast-developing universities in Singapore, South Korea, Hong Kong, Taiwan, and China, in Asia; from flagship universities in Uganda, Tanzania, and Mozambique that now serve as models for university reform in African nations.

It is not university personnel who lack the grounded capacity to understand how their institutions operate and how they change (they learn as they practice) so much as it is the lagging researchers and observers whose soggy images of asserted glories of universities in simpler times lead them to exaggerate present-day deficiencies.

By invoking the status quo ante of universities during the last 100 years or so, as is commonly done, proponents of the good old days forget that those times may have been the worst. For example, discrimination in access ran successively against Irish and Italian Catholics; Jews (in the 1920s and 1930s, Princeton had a 5 percent and Yale a 10 percent quota)[1]; women (who just a few decades ago were limited to 5 percent or less of enrollment in medical and law schools); and on to the access constraints encountered in recent years by present-day minorities. And Joe College remained firmly in control of student life until the arrival of mass higher education after World War II.

What old-time colleges were like is worth perhaps half a cheer. Today we can give two cheers for modern universities and the many types of colleges that pursue productive paths of adaptive development in an age of universal access. From community colleges to research universities, from one country and one continent to another, a host of informed practitioners know how things work. What they have figured out on the spot—and go on figuring out anew in changing webs of interacting programs and practices—constitutes a largely untapped pool of resources for researchers who seriously want to explain the workings of higher education in the twenty-first century.[2]

Amid the current extensive diffusion of analytical interests and self-sustaining subfields in the sociology of higher education, a focus on the realities of successful practice, at the least, will help narrow the stubborn gap that has long persisted between the understandings of researchers and the concerns of practitioners. A more integrated pursuit of things that work should also bolster optimism and hope for the future of universities and colleges in the twenty-first century.

References

Clark, B. R. 1988. *Creating Entrepreneurial Universities: Organizational Pathways of Transformation.* Oxford: Pergamon-Elsevier Science.
——. 1998. *Creating Entrepreneurial Universities: Organizational Pathways of Transformation.* Oxford: Pergamon/IAU.

1. For the classic, pathbreaking work on discrimination against Jews, see Wechsler 1977; see also McCaughey 2003. Historians have a particularly fine eye for the details of documented practice.

2. My comments on pursuing practices that work flow from research that began in the mid-1990s to examine case studies of university change. I worked first in Britain and continental Europe, then from the findings of other scholars in countries elsewhere in the world, and finally back to the United States. The results were reported in two books; the first took up five case studies (Clark 1998), the second ranged over fourteen (Clark 2004).

———. 2004. *Sustaining Change in Universities: Continuities in Case Studies and Concepts.* Maidenhead, UK: Open University Press and Society for Research into Higher Education.

Evans, J. R. 2005. "The Academic-Commercial Interface in a Knowledge-Driven Economy: A View from MaRS." In *Creating Knowledge: Strengthening Nations: The Changing Role of Higher Education*, ed. G. A. Jones, P. L. McCarney, and M. L. Skolnick, 273–82. Toronto: University of Toronto Press.

Herbst, M., U. Hagentobler, and L. Snover. 2002. *MIT and ETH Zurich: Structures and Cultures Juxtaposed.* CEST 2002/9. Berne, Switzerland: Center for Science and Technology Studies.

Institute of Higher Education, Shanghai Jiao Tong University. 2004. "Top 500 World Universities." Available at http://ed.sjtu.edu.cn/rank/2004/2004Main.htm.

Lagemann, E. C. 2001. "Report of the President." In *Spencer Foundation Annual Report. April 1, 2000–March 31, 2001,* 5–6. Chicago: Spencer Foundation.

McCaughey, R. A. 2003. "Jews at Columbia." In *Stand, Columbia: A History of Columbia University in the City of New York, 1754–2004,* 256–76. New York: Columbia University Press.

Musselin, C. 2004. *The Long March of the French Universities.* English ed. (French orig. 2001). New York: Routledge/Falmer.

Stokes, D. E. 1997. *Pasteur's Quadrant: Basic Science and Technological Innovation.* Washington, DC: Brookings Institution.

Times Higher Education Supplement. 2004. "World University Rankings." November 5 issue.

Wechsler, H. S. 1977. *The Qualified Student: A History of Selective College Admission in American, 1870–1970.* New York: Wiley.

12 Reflections on a Hybrid Field

Growth and Prospects for the Sociology of Higher Education

PATRICIA J. GUMPORT

The sociology of higher education has been steadily expanding along distinct lines of inquiry in the thirty-plus years since Clark's 1973 map of the field. The preceding chapters show developments in streams of research that were evident back then, as well as in emerging topics that we can surmise reflect ideas both intellectually engaging and professionally meaningful to researchers in these past few decades. Across the board, developments in the field show deepening interest in perennial questions about higher education, including its social organization, purposes, structures, practices, and divergent impacts on participants in the enterprise and on society at large. These developments also attest to the rich legacy of sociological theories, concepts, and methods. The field has indeed come a long way since Clark's general characterization of the research as reflective of a convergence between a sociological concern and a practical problem.

At the same time, we note considerable variation in the extent and depth of the convergence between sociology and higher education, with some research anchored explicitly in both and other research leaning more toward one than the other. Whether studies have both sociological and educational import or are at either end of the continuum, the possibilities for advancing these lines of inquiry continue to be exciting: sociological concepts and methods deepen our understanding of higher education's realities just as higher education, in its diverse forms and with its vexing challenges, continues to be a rich site for sociological analysis.

In this last chapter of the volume, I step back from the particulars addressed by my colleagues in their chapters, with two objectives: to reflect on the field's cumulative changes and to consider the prospects for the field's future. To do the former, I highlight some substantive developments. To do the latter, I pick up where I left off in Chapter Two's discussion of the societal and organizational contexts that have shaped the field's development.

Here I consider a number of salient factors within the professional contexts of researchers who contribute to the sociology of higher education—that is, within their local campus settings and professional associations, which mediate a range of intellectual, organizational, and political pressures, and which—on a daily basis—signal to researchers the categories of ideas that are worth pursuing. I argue that there is much interest and support for particular lines of inquiry, as seen in the earlier chapters in this volume. But I am also concerned about the sociology of higher education *as a field,* as it faces major factors working against its visibility and vitality, against its institutionalization. The bases for this writing are my own experiences working on these topics over the past 20 years and my observations of dynamics in research universities—especially within professional schools of education where, like me, many faculty who have been conducting research in this field teach and work.

Finally, I conclude by proposing some ideas worthy of future research, important themes within the sociology of higher education that have been understudied—indeed, whose time is well nigh—and I will suggest that, however unpredictable the formal constructs of sociology of higher education may be, many promising and rewarding arenas for study beckon, and through those the future of the field will be determined.

Reflections on Substantive Developments

The major lines of inquiry in sociology of higher education as reflected in the chapters in this volume represent sustained interests in core questions across the four domains visible to Clark as of 1970. Since then, the organizing categories have been reshaped, as important new avenues of inquiry and dimensions for analysis have captured researchers' interest. As in other fields, lines of inquiry are propelled by what researchers find interesting and problematic. Although it could be presumed from its name that the sociology of higher education is primarily driven by sociological ideas, the preceding chapters cover many examples of research propelled by concern over contemporary realities. These range from studies where the questions are problem driven to those that are practice oriented in their conclusions and implications. Features of higher education with longevity and institutionalization provide rich subject matter for inquiry, while much of the newer work is stimulated by the perception that change is under way. Particularly in this field, in the past two decades, proclamations of rapid and unprecedented change have prompted researchers to inquire about it with curiosity if not urgency. Major changes in the practical realities of higher education—both on campuses and in the wider environment—have supported this interest. While some research is inspired by visible structural changes, such as expansion and differentiation, other studies address more normative changes, such as changes in values and priorities of groups on campuses.

As researchers have pursued the study of inequality, they have examined the role of higher education in perpetuating inequalities in the wider society and the inequalities inherent in higher education itself—that is, in stratified social orders that associate status markers with students, faculty, and the institutions themselves. The study of inequality has extended into research on students' academic preparation in K–12 education; patterns of access and financial aid; and the policy levers with the most direct impact on inequality before, during, and after higher education.

Indeed, inquiry into these topics has been taken up with urgency. The range of interest is reflective of the political continuum, from those interested in improving higher education's effectiveness in meeting society's workforce training needs to those with a progressive agenda, who are propelled by concerns that higher education continues to fall far short of its ideals of access to and success for students from all backgrounds. Some emerging lines of research have curiously been dubbed "K–16 issues," though the main focus there is to understand how to facilitate the transition from high school to college—a crucial juncture, especially in that large proportions of students begin college in need of basic skills in math and literacy. At the national level, estimates show that approximately 63 percent of students in two-year colleges and 40 percent of those entering four-year universities take some "remedial" or developmental courses (U.S. Department of Education 2001).

Rhetorically, in policy circles, critics have also proposed that higher education take greater responsibility in rectifying these inadequacies, including more directly supporting improvements in K–12 education. Yet the research on what works organizationally and educationally to promote equity and equality has not kept up with this policy agenda. Several reasons account for this, including the fact that many researchers do not want to orient their research to an advocacy agenda, whether to identify solutions or to evaluate alternative strategies for improvement. Some researchers do not want to contribute to the study of what are often termed "best practices." Another reason is rooted in the ideological stance underlying the dominant policy discourse. Currently, research by educational policy analysts, often trained in economics or political science, has acquired a firm hold on inquiry about many of these topics. Some observers regard these dominant approaches as unduly narrow when they are grounded in rationalist presumptions from economics and political science, employ methods that strive for parsimony, and uncritically align with neoliberal educational reform agenda and policy models such as are exemplified by the No Child Left Behind Act. This is a powerful reminder of how political economic realities shape what is viewed as problematic, the types of research that can appropriately shed light on it, and what are conceived as potential solutions. Simultaneously, it should also be noted that researchers with a critical sensibility do work that resists the prevailing discourse, such as those who are studying inequality by examining the negative effects of the prevailing policy approaches as well as the incompatibilities and contradictions between capitalism and democracy.

With a similar air of urgency, the study of college impact has also proliferated since 1970, into many new topics for inquiry: beyond determinants of college student experience to conceptual lenses for analyzing campus climates, especially as student enrollments reflect more diverse backgrounds in terms of race, class, and gender. Research on college students also reflects a wide range of interests and approaches. In terms of data, a valuable resource has been the National Longitudinal Surveys (NLS), which have tracked the eighth-grade class since 1988. A common lament is nonetheless the absence of large-scale datasets that track student characteristics and pathways through higher education. Advances in methodological approaches, from qualitative inquiry into students' perceptions and experiences to quantitative tools for measurement, such as hierarchical linear modeling (HLM), have provided new leverage for researchers to distinguish among sets and levels of explanatory factors. In spite of growing interest in HLM and "mixed methods" research designs, these are not (yet) prominent among articles in peer-reviewed journals. Given the influx of new topics for inquiry and new methodological approaches, many would likely acknowledge Clark's earlier admonition that research on college effects can be time consuming and costly but would most likely refute his concerns about its be-coming "tunnel vision riveted on the trivial" and "an inbred tradition of work"—or at least not find it any more inbred than research in other subfields.

In the early twenty-first century, questions related to diversity have become more central for practitioners and researchers at campuses of all types, as they wrestle with changing interpretations of the parameters of affirmative action guidelines and reorient their practices to the Supreme Court dictate to demonstrate the educational benefits of diversity broadly defined. This has occurred alongside a movement advocating "intellectual diversity," or the diversity of ideas, which implicitly or explicitly casts the academy as left-leaning and dominated by faculty pushing narrow political beliefs. Regarding these issues, the impetus for research is more from "the practical problem" than from sociological concerns, even though there remain important social-psychological questions about the contexts that support student development, identity formation, and social networks, among other topics.

Interest in measuring college student learning outcomes—not simply changes in their attitudes and beliefs—has been spurred by the develop-ment of assessment instruments that have gained currency in the wider context of accountability demands, means that open up new avenues for research into student learning. The possibilities for integrating tech-nological advancements with instructional materials—whether on cam-pus or at a distance—have generated even more interest in studying student learning and the effectiveness of different instructional ap-proaches. The assessment of student learning outcomes is still in its infancy, in part because methodological standards for validity are not well established or uniformly heeded by otherwise well-intentioned practitioners—many of whom are interested in examining the potential learning gains in innovative forms of instruction (including technology-mediated forms) over traditional instruction. Some of this work has the flavor of "program evaluation" rather than working toward the cumula-tive advancement of knowledge; the latter typically references prior con-ceptual frameworks and findings established by pioneer researchers in college effects. Again here we can note the development of a line of inquiry ostensibly driven more by practical problems than by sociologi-cal interests.

The study of the academic profession has also kept pace with chang-ing realities, from the general external scrutiny of higher education's alleged organizational inefficiencies to changes in the nature of faculty work across institutional types. Especially in public higher education, it has become commonplace for critics imposing an institutional performance paradigm to express concern about "deadwood"—unproductive and uneven quality among faculty—or, alternatively, to scrutinize the hiring of "star faculty" who have decreased teaching responsibilities yet command unprecedented high salaries. Structurally, no one presumes any longer that departments will automatically be granted permission to fill vacancies in tenure-line positions; instead "off-track" hiring is widespread—both part-time and full-time fixed-term appointments, with different mixes of rights and responsibilities (Schuster and Finkelstein 2006). Indeed, the many different conditions and forms of academic work in the contemporary era challenge even recent functionalist accounts of "small worlds, different worlds" from the 1980s (Clark 1987; Ruscio 1987). More tensions in academic workplaces have emanated from (and further aggravated ambiguity in) the jurisdictions of authority between faculty and administrators, with discretionary power and legitimacy increasing for campus officials to pursue strategic initiatives, including those that reach deeply into academic departments and faculty appointments. At a practical level, these changes are tied to complex collective bargaining agreements where unions exist.

Indeed, the expectations for faculty work have been changing at a fundamental professional level. Views are divergent—even among faculty—as to what is expected, whether the traditional roles of sage and scholar have been displaced by expectations that faculty embrace an entrepreneurial spirit and pursue revenue-generating opportunities (including commercialization) that will in turn support research, graduate education, and broader institutional functions. Divergent views of what work is most valued call into question the presumption of a community of scholars with shared norms, the basis of their professional authority secured in self-regulating quality via peer review, in criteria for decision making that anchored faculty governance mechanisms (such as senates), and in long-held entitlements to academic freedom, disinterested inquiry, and organized skepticism. Such deep changes in what is believed to be faculty work suggest the need for frameworks that can shed light on these practical problems, by drawing on sociological concepts to understand changes in the nature of professional authority in large-scale organizations as well as the endemic conflict in academic organizations. Other profound questions also beckon, including the dynamics of professional socialization during graduate education within different institutional and disciplinary settings—"learning academic labor," as I have called it (Gumport 2000b)—using sociological insights about how identity and career aspirations are formed in a stratified system of higher education. These processes are also integrally related to the dynamics of knowledge legitimation within and across the disciplines, as I discuss below.

In contrast to robust advances in the studies of inequality, college impact, and the academic profession, studies of governance have been far less visible, especially compared to research on academic organizations, with which Clark initially linked governance. With the exception of some descriptive work on state-level coordination, the research has focused on local governance arrangements and patterns of shared authority, including formal structures such as governing boards, and less formal divisions of responsibilities between administrators and faculty —who have historically had purview over the curriculum and academic programs. While those interests have continued over the past few decades, the study of governance came to reflect more interest in politics and policymaking, with some consistent concern about the effects of external factors on institutional autonomy, such as economic and political changes in state contexts and public scrutiny of higher education. These and related lines of inquiry remind us to be careful not to simplify unduly the organizing categories and labels for lines of inquiry within a field, for substantive developments are ongoing and cumulative, their formation as new trajectories most easily recognized in hindsight.

Finally, among the four initial domains, the study of colleges and universities as organizations has arguably shown the greatest expansion —as a corpus of work and also into diverse lines of inquiry that parallel advances in organizational theory. In the past few decades, organizational theorists have come into their own, and their work has become institutionalized in several types of academic departments (sociology, political science) and professional schools (education, business, engineering) and in a number of highly regarded publications that attract researchers across those fields (Scott 1998). Thematically, the research is distributed between long-standing and newer topics. It is no surprise that more research addresses themes of transformation and dedifferentiation, having moved beyond the growth themes of expansion and massification to examine other types of institutional change as it is manifest in varying ways across academic settings. Decision making conceived in terms of rational and nonrational elements remains of interest, yet organizational learning and establishing "a culture of evidence" to inform decisions have captured the attention of organizational analysts (Cohen, March, and Olsen 1972; March and Olsen 1976; March 1988). During the 1990s, some research emerged that reflected an action agenda—to rationalize (i.e., make rational) the basis for decisions in higher education, such as demonstrating the necessity and value of strategic planning and management reforms to improve quality and efficiency.

As interest in these ideas has been elaborated and the terms themselves have acquired legitimacy, some observations must be made. One is that it is worth studying how words like *rational* and *efficient* have come to be taken for granted as strengths of the organization and how organizational life has been restructured to support them (Gumport forthcoming). Another is that researchers in universities are inescapably at once participants in and observers of the organizational realities, and their experiences no doubt shape what they see as problematic, analytically interesting, or worth drawing out as conclusions and implications.

In higher education over this time, the term *administration* has fallen out of favor as *leadership* has become more central, both in research and in teaching about higher education. Perhaps even more prominently, the term *management* has become widely used to refer to the work done by department chairs, deans, and those occupying other positions in campuses' upper ranks. Researchers have begun to examine managerialism as an ideology that gained legitimacy in this historical period (Enteman 1993), although it should also be noted that characterizing "a managerial revolution" as attempts to rationalize the practices and structures of academic organizations extends back to the mid-1960s (Rourke and Brooks 1966). The earlier writing differed in that it observed "managerial innovation" as an emerging experiment that entailed coordinated data gathering to inform decision making, whereas the contemporary term often refers to a more widespread phenomenon: a strengthening of centralized power in the upper levels of campus positions, which have greater discretion and control over resources—both to pursue strategic market-oriented imperatives and to impose performance metrics on activities at lower levels of the organization. At issue, then, is the shift in interest from coordination to control, and the need to examine concomitant changes and consequences for professional authority. These questions become more important as deans in particular have been expected to put more time and effort into fundraising activities, yet in the process they accrue more resources and the discretionary authority to use them.

These changes are significant as subjects of study in their own right, as well as for creating possible consumers of research in the sociology of higher education. In fact, the trajectory of research *on* higher education leaders can be seen as a developing line of inquiry, one that looks more like a "sociology of managers" than a "managerial sociology." Research related to the former can be seen as advancing inquiry that bridges studies in the academic profession and in governance, focusing on changes in the nature of professional authority in academic organizations. (It remains for the researcher to determine whether to conceptualize faculty as within the scope of managers and practitioners to whom Clark refers.) However, the latter term brings to the fore a broader question: what are the aims of research in the sociology of higher education? Given the wide range of topics evident by the end of the twentieth century, the answer could presumably be a plurality of aims, from the more sociological to the practical, and can be conceptualized superficially as a matter of the relative weight given to each.

A more serious answer, however, requires revisiting Clark's 1973 caution against framing research instrumentally to meet the needs of practitioners (in this case, managers). The danger he noted was to pose questions too narrowly, in order to meet the needs of managers. There is also the risk of framing research within the taken-for-granted parameters in use by campus leaders. Yet in Chapter Eleven of this volume, Clark criticizes researchers in the field for being out of touch with practitioners and producing work that is impenetrable to them. He urges researchers to reorient their work to the needs of practitioners. In his own words, he underscores the turnabout and calls for the study of university change via case study methods: "I realize that my final note on pursuing things that work jars against what I said 30 years ago. But I have learned much since then and have been born again around the great utility of case study narratives if we are going to get a better understanding of interacting elements in university change. I would be pleased if just one or two young people entering the field were to be convinced. The point is simple: how do we study the interaction of elements in university change if we tear the elements apart and study them one by one? Practitioners have to take them up on the run in on-the-spot interaction" (personal correspondence, January 10, 2006).

Given this clear framing, the reader concerned with the future of the field faces a choice to accept or reject this call. Advancing the line of inquiry Clark advocates would entail shaping research questions to speak directly to the concerns of higher education managers, studying problems they encounter in their real-life settings, and developing concepts to help illuminate the nature of the problems and appropriate solutions. An alternative priority is to work from a critical sensibility that problematizes the interests and needs of higher education practitioners and offers interpretations that challenge the status quo, whether conceptually or in practice. This approach allows for scrutiny of espoused purposes and consideration of alternative means available for achieving those or other purposes. Yet another priority is to let the research questions be driven by ideas from the discipline of sociology; for it is very different to think about education from sociology in contrast to thinking sociologically about education from education. In fact, one could view this tack as absolutely essential for the field to be regarded as a distinct, legitimate field within sociology. Either way, the field must take seriously the fact that the work of people who self-identify as sociologists of higher education may reflect not merely a plurality of research interests but also genuinely divergent views over the purposes of inquiry and the methods and discourse styles that are appropriate for pursuing them. This remains an open question for faculty and students in the field, as well as for funding agencies that have the resources to support research in the field.

This recognition is all the more important in light of methodological developments in the social sciences and in educational research. As specialization has become more valued, especially for faculty in research universities, the goal of advancing research methods per se has become a priority for some researchers in their studies and in their professional identities. It is worth noting some evidence in the sociology of higher education of another trajectory Clark (1973) cautioned against—a preoccupation with measurement in quantitative research, and in qualitative work, the production of vignettes that are primarily descriptive or that lapse into play without making the most of their inherent analytical purchase. Researchers working in both traditions, quantitative and qualitative, have shown interest in critiquing research methodology as an object of study. Particularly among those with a qualitative bent, some scholars have sustained the scrutiny of paradigmatic dominance, delving deeply with a critical eye into problematizing objectivity and prevailing conceptions of how we know what we know about higher education (Denzin and Lincoln 2005). These themes were commonly taken up—not only by educational researchers but also within selected communities in the social sciences and humanities—throughout the 1990s.

Indeed, self-ascribed qualitative research approaches gained legitimacy through the 1980s and 1990s among those with a bent toward studying culture, human agency, life histories, and self-reflexivity. Similarly, researchers studying higher education ventured beyond more generic case-study approaches to undertake projects examining patterns of beliefs, values, decisions, affinities, and aspirations among undergraduates, graduate students, faculty, and administrators and across a wide range of campuses. Contributions have ranged from illuminating divergent perspectives in the face of conflict to identifying cultural dynamics within colleges and universities or shedding light on the nature of marginalization and anomie. Intellectual undertakings from these perspectives often generated new lines of inquiry with distinctive aims, particularistic rather than universalistic, explicitly subjective rather than objective, via inductive rather than deductive analysis. As to the nature of their contribution to the field, these studies have appealed to the rationales of describing and understanding a phenomenon (often a process) in context, providing necessary correctives to prevailing theory (by showing what is missing, neglected or ill-conceived), and proposing concepts and measures for others to study more systematically or in other settings. Among educational researchers, a subgroup has self-identified as doing "grounded theory," reflecting a resurgence of interest in work popularized by Barney Glaser and Anselm Strauss (1967), who, among other things, articulated the merits of an inductive process of "constant comparison" through iterations between data and concepts. Even though schools of education ostensibly expanded their tolerance for methodological pluralism from the mid-1980s through the late 1990s, most research that reflected qualitative approaches, especially if cast as purposefully subjective, still faced scrutiny, unless the research was ethnographic and situated within a more traditional anthropological frame. Questions ranged from whether the research questions were worthwhile to whether the design and methods were valid, reliable, and "rigorous" and whether the result constituted "real research" that would advance the knowledge base of the field.

As was the case for the rest of the social sciences, which showed some blurring of genres (Geertz 1983), the qualitative research activities in higher education across these topics did not always lend themselves to neat classifications within prevailing categories of analysis. This complicates the struggle for legitimacy for researchers who are expected to position their work in the field. For an individual, this entails establishing the significance of a research focus and making the case for the phenomenon as a worthwhile subject of inquiry, especially if it is a problem in practice. That is, the researcher has to demonstrate that the focus is not simply idiosyncratic, that it derives from or can shed light on an enduring social process or problem. Some substantive foci that have been cast as worthwhile research topics have been institutionalized as recognizable categories (e.g., college student development) in courses and academic specializations in higher education graduate programs, and in professional associations where higher education researchers present their work. In fact, some researchers reach an extreme of linking the subject matter of their research to their identity; that is, even though they produce studies in the field and may be regarded as having a specialization in higher education, they have developed a narrower identity, as someone who studies community colleges, for example. Conversely, what is considered trivial tends to be research that has not been cast as within a category with preestablished significance—that is, not recognized as something we need to know about. It is incumbent on the researchers to establish the category as worthy of study. In the past decade, rethinking racial identity in education has uncovered topics in need of study, such as "whiteness" and multiracial identities.

In sociology departments, topics in higher education are considered important if they are cast as a case, an instance of a broader phenomenon; or higher education can be an appropriate site of study when the researcher is examining other social processes. Research on college students, for example, does not easily find a category standardized as such in the sociological discipline, but it can be framed within related topics of disciplinary interest, such as peer influence, anticipatory socialization, educational aspiration, occupational achievement, and status attainment—to name a few. The same can be said for research on faculty (as a case in the study of the professions) and research on changing academic norms and structures on campuses (as a case of institutional change, whether about education as a social institution or as a case of the changing nature of nonprofits). Earlier in my own research, I examined changes in curricula and academic disciplines by drawing from the sociology of knowledge and the sociology of science. As will be discussed further below, how research in the sociology of higher education is framed is of the utmost importance; finding the appropriate niche, whether in education or in sociology, depends upon locating the research in a category with relevant literature that can be reviewed for what is already known about the topic and that has enough proximity to a line of inquiry deemed worthy of study, perhaps even institutionalized as such.

Prospects for the Future: Professional Contexts

The challenge of finding suitable ground in which to plant the seeds of fertile professional endeavors in sociology of higher education must be considered in its own right, by examining the contextual forces that facilitate or constrain the elaboration of ideas in the field. Establishing the space for particular ideas can be viewed as an intellectual, organizational, and political achievement (Gumport 2002), one that requires recognition, with some visibility—which in turn creates the opportunity to make the case for the work's intellectual vitality, resulting in greater visibility. These interdependencies constitute a self-fulfilling cycle (usually seen as virtuous, if one is a winner). As a research interest is perceived as viable for a research agenda, it gains more momentum. Faculty become invested in cultivating these interests in the next generation, and this increases the perceptions of prospective vitality for the field. The converse is also the case, whereby any given work may be conceived of as off the edge instead of cutting-edge and may be devalued or dismissed. In this way a field can develop with persistent omissions and silences, areas of nonknowledge so to speak, where some ideas fail to get traction and visibility, reinforcing the notion that they are not vital or viable to pursue academically. (A tremendous amount can be at stake in such determinations!)

These dynamics are more complicated than they may initially appear, given powerful yet potentially divergent forces in the academic workplace. The pattern here is not simply that incentive-driven faculty members pay attention to the signals that certain types of research will bring academic rewards in the short run or successful career trajectories in the long run. One complexity is that the value attributed to the subject matter (to the phenomena that are the subject of inquiry) is *itself* always changing, framed as it is by higher education's own institutional and political interests. This means that a researcher's agenda and accomplishments are valued differently depending on how his or her work is situated among vying interests—and depending on which peer reviewers are asked to comment on the merits and deficiencies of the work.

Against this backdrop, and given the societal and organizational contexts reviewed in Chapter Two, this section of the chapter looks more closely at the professional contexts for researchers in the sociology of higher education. One contribution of this book is to bridge the divide between researchers in sociology and in education. In addition to the field's relative lack of visibility *as a field* in either location, not much cross-talk has taken place between faculty across these locations on most campuses. (One exception to this is Stanford University, where interchange among faculty has been facilitated by courtesy appointments—and more generally, by highly permeable boundaries among the Sociology Department in the School of Humanities and Sciences, the School of Education, and the Graduate School of Business.) But precisely because many ideas in this field straddle these professional arenas, there is potential for ongoing intellectual exchanges and infusions of distinctive energies from faculty in different locations with different training: from sociological researchers with interests in higher education as a social institution or as a site to study sociological phenomena, to higher education researchers working in schools of education with some training in sociology, to higher education researchers trained in education yet interested in applying ideas from sociology.

This is to say, in other words, that in spite of the dramatic expansion within distinct lines of inquiry in this field over the past 30 years—and perhaps because the research is pursued by individuals from different professional contexts—the visibility of sociology of higher education *as a field* remains questionable. The fact remains that the researchers still reside primarily in one world or the other, and the incremental currents in each do not advance sociology of higher education as a field of study. In each academic silo, faculty and graduate students work in contexts that convey what are to be their primary obligations, including norms vis-à-vis the ideas that should occupy them in research and in classes. The forms that their respective work takes differ—especially how their research is framed differs, because they are socialized to different norms in graduate school. One unfortunate side effect of this separation is that the intellectual resources each draws upon may be unduly narrow and partial by neglecting prior work on a topic, such that the research fails to make a cumulative contribution that is seen by researchers working from these different locations. Powerful countervailing forces drive the strategically minded individual to frame his or her research for a primary audience that corresponds to their academic department, if they want to be reviewed favorably by peers.

With a caveat regarding the danger of generalizing, given the variation in departments across universities, I sketch here some further distinctions between higher education and sociology as two academic contexts in which researchers work (or academic locations in which faculty reside), and thereby I reflect upon the obstacles to and possibilities for sociology of higher education as a field.

Differences in Professional Socialization

Higher education doctoral students are commonly encouraged to frame research as practice-driven questions—albeit with a conceptual framework, often at least nominally drawn from sociological constructs—leading to conclusions that help inform or shed light on educational problems. The conceptual risks therein include unduly narrowing the research question and framing it with too many taken-for-granteds about the current terms of practice. What is sacrificed in such work is not only the originality possible through using sociological concepts to frame the research problem in new and illuminating ways but also the analytical leverage that sociological theorizing and sensibilities can provide. (Exceptions include the chapter authors in this volume, whose doctoral training immersed them in sociological ideas, journals, and conferences.)

In sociology, the message is for research to be framed to advance established lines of inquiry in the discipline, such that higher education, if an interest at all, is considered as an instance or site of study for sociological phenomena or as a major social institution on a par with K–12 education, religion, the family, and the economy. The risk is a lack of historical awareness of higher education's legacies and complexities as a site of study. Moreover, sociologists tend not to locate their research within the corpus of work covered in higher education journals. Thus their research may not recognize propositions already substantiated by higher education researchers and may not take into account or contribute to a line of inquiry already established in the study of higher education.

The risk of missed opportunities thus goes both ways. For example, higher education researchers have for the past few decades done substantial work on college effects and published it in higher education and student affairs journals. For sociologists interested in launching a study on college effects to overlook these journals would mean they would not benefit from nor build on the state of the art of the inquiry in higher education. Conversely, in another example, sociologists have made major advances in the study of nonprofits that would be missed by higher education researchers studying emerging partnerships if they fail to familiarize themselves with prior research on interorganizational collaboration, social networks, and changing organizational forms.

Aside from the potential for missed opportunities to build on established knowledge in the field, we need to consider the dynamics of professional positioning within each academic home. Sociology and education each have contexts and perspectives that tend to marginalize expertise in the sociology of higher education. In education, especially in higher education programs, drawing primarily on sociology to frame research questions or propositions may be seen as too theoretical. To sociologists, studies of higher education may be seen as insufficiently grounded in theory and too oriented to practice. Granted, a researcher is more likely to make a successful academic career being too theoretical in a school of education than by being too practical in a sociology department, because professional schools tolerate—and some even value—disciplinary expertise more than sociology departments have regard for practice. Clearly, for a researcher in an academic career, the pursuit of the sociology of higher education needs to be understood at levels beyond the obvious engagement in this rich conceptual enterprise. It entails many professional challenges, especially for faculty who seek the currency required for academic success in ascending the faculty ranks in research universities, where original contributions to knowledge are expected.

Differences in Academic Contexts

To consider prospects for the future of the sociology of higher education, we need to address more systematically how these professional contexts define the work of faculty who are major contributors of research in the field. Clark's 1973 discussion of prospects for the young field did not address the impact of changing professional pressures on faculty: the bulk of research he reviewed as of 1970 was produced by researchers who identified primarily as sociologists. He did not foresee the increase, by the 1980s and through the 1990s, in disciplinary-oriented research produced by faculty in schools of education, including faculty in higher education programs, many of whom are chapter authors in this volume. One must presume that research contributed by faculty from each academic location reflects distinctive pressures to foreground what is expected from either sociology or higher education and to address those audiences accordingly. In the past few decades, three sets of forces have been in play: disciplinary specialization, different sets of incentives for faculty in sociology from those for faculty in education, and challenges to the academic legitimacy of higher education as a scholarly pursuit. These three forces together have both accounted for and resulted in professional contexts that have supported research in one or more lines of inquiry in the subfields but that do not support the advancement of the sociology of higher education as a field.

In terms of specialization, within the academy, broader trends have encouraged faculty to frame their research within a narrower niche. As disciplinary specialization has resulted in highly specialized areas of expertise, some observers quip that faculty have come to know more and more about less and less; and by extension it would be reasonable to surmise that they know less and less about each other. In any given department, when the time comes for promotion reviews, local colleagues may have little to no substantive knowledge of each other's field, especially in smaller academic units with only one or two people in an academic specialty. The result of these conditions is that more weight is put on external letters from referees (who are most valued if they come from high-prestige universities) and on the publication record (especially in peer-reviewed journals), which signals to strategically minded faculty that they should develop cosmopolitan profiles within a recognized specialty. This is a high-stakes venture, as is well known among assistant professors in research universities with a notoriously high bar for tenure.

For faculty in sociology, over the past 30 years, the study of education has sustained some visibility—although not as a mainstream area—while the study of higher education has achieved very little visibility, and only then typically as a site for the sociological study of organizations or occupations—or more recently for the surging interest in studies of science, knowledge, and technology fueled by enthusiasm abroad.

As one indicator, among the 40 specialty areas listed as sections in the American Sociological Association (ASA), sociology of higher education is not listed—although there are some related categories within which researchers study higher education either as a site of study or as a context for the sociological phenomenon they are exploring: "sociology of education," "organizations, occupations, and work," and "science, knowledge, and technology," to name a few. (At the time of this writing, the ASA requires 200 members to establish a section, a fact worthy of note in case the reader is motivated to participate in establishing a section on the sociology of higher education.) At the risk of stating the obvious, the contributions most valued by sociology *qua discipline* are those that advance the theoretical, empirical, or methodological foundations of the discipline—rather than applied research, such as the application of a theory to shed light on a practical problem in a particular organizational domain.

Sociologists studying higher education face an additional challenge of publication venues. Sociology proffers only a handful of very highly regarded journals, and the competition for publication within them is fierce. (See Table 12.1.) Some faculty have indicated that they feel fortunate to be given the opportunity to "revise and resubmit" for several rounds rather than be turned down at the outset—even if the process takes two or more years. To be a contender for a top sociology journal, an article on higher education would have to be grounded in established lines of inquiry within the discipline of sociology and would have to demonstrate its original contribution therein.

What is specifically sociological about a study is a perennial question for some observers of the discipline. C. Wright Mills proposes that it lies in the scholar's sociological imagination, which is instilled through training (Mills 1959). Mills also correctly notes the blurring of distinctions and boundaries among the social sciences, which he casts as beneficial to a researcher's "capacity to shift" (p. 7) from one analytical perspective to another and from the individual level of analysis to society without losing sight of the complexities in between. Yet what is considered important analytical work, irrespective of a topical area worthy of study in its own right, must be framed as a key dimension of social structure or an instance of vital or enduring social processes or practices.

Arguably the consensus reflected in these messages creates a clearer terrain in sociology for researchers to navigate than in education. For faculty in education, the expectations have been far more ambiguous over the past few decades. It is readily acknowledged that schools of education have "a muddled mission" and lack consensus about what they should be and do (Judge 1982; Clifford and Guthrie 1988; Tierney

Table 12.1. Sociology of Higher Education: Selected Journals by Founding Date

Subject	Pre-1970		1970–1979		1980–1989	
	Title	Year	Title	Year	Title	Year
Sociology	American Journal of Sociology	1895				
	Social Forces	1922				
	Sociology of Education	1927				
	American Sociological Review	1936				
Organizations	Administrative Science Quarterly	1956	Academy of Management Review	1976	Organizational Studies	1980
	Academy of Management Journal	1957				
Higher Education	Journal of Higher Education	1970	Higher Education	1972	Higher Education: Handbook of Theory and Research	1985
			Research in Higher Education	1973		
			Review of Higher Education	1978		
Applied Higher Education	Journal of College Student Development	1959	Planning in Higher Education	1972		
	NASPA Journal	1963				
Other Higher Education	Daedalus	1955	Change	1972		
			Academe	1979		
Education	Comparative Education Review	1957	American Journal of Education	1979	Educational Policy	1987
	American Educational Research Journal	1964	Educational Evaluation and Policy Analysis	1979		
	Curriculum Studies	1968				

2001). In the last two decades of the twentieth century, several schools of education in top research universities attempted to improve their status vis-à-vis graduate departments in the social sciences, either by attracting scholars from social science disciplines into education or by encouraging more explicitly discipline-based scholarship from their own faculty. In spite of strong conviction among the proponents of this strategy, the emphasis on disciplinary-based research has not been widely shared among schools of education nationally and at times not even upheld uniformly among faculty within their own schools of education.

Since what counts as appropriate scholarship in education has been contested, faculty in education have had to interpret mixed signals. This challenge is seen poignantly in the expectations for assistant professors, who often need unanimous approval from their faculty for promotion. Given the heavy emphasis on practice in professional schools—by definition—faculty there are expected to develop a research agenda addressing problems of educational practice or policy, with the additional aim of improving the preparation of leaders for educational settings. In research-oriented schools of education that aspire for disciplinary legitimacy, other young faculty are told that they must meet the same research productivity and standards as those in the disciplines. The result is an ambiguous set of expectations regarding how to frame their research and where to publish, with little certainty that their contributions will be valued and rewarded locally by their colleagues. Of course, one way to handle this is to cultivate a larger and more diverse portfolio, but the additive model is not always feasible under the time constraints of the tenure clock. In this scenario, straddling two worlds means twice the work to satisfy both sets of expectations and networks of potential peer reviewers, with the payoff unclear for a research track record of such Janus-like character.

Within schools of education, faculty who study higher education are located for the most part in graduate programs of higher education that produce college and university administrators, institutional researchers, and higher education faculty. Among the several hundred faculty in the United States who do research and guide advanced study in higher education, very few self-identify as sociologists of higher education and seek to publish in sociology journals. Yet many of them use articles and books that we consider within the sociology of higher education for their own research or teaching. In fact, many significant disciplinary legacies from sociology are the implicit analytical building blocks of the research that fills higher education journals and courses today. Authors often invoke distinctions that are Weberian, Durkehimian, Parsonian, or even Marxist without realizing it, or they use concepts (e.g., differentiation and integration, bureaucratic and professional authority, resource dependence and organized anarchy, legitimacy and institutionalization) without explicit attribution to their sociological roots.

The careers of those higher education faculty who do aspire to develop research in the field, like several chapter authors in this volume, can grow from a strong foundation of sociological perspectives with which to anchor and elaborate their research interests. Methodological framing can certainly be significant in a research project's standing. The more scientific pursuits with empirical data and a sophisticated methodology tend to carry more weight among educational researchers. Those who pursue qualitative approaches are still often seen as engaging in softer scholarship that risks being perceived as journalism or merely "playful" vignettes—what Clark admonished against. Bias there persists, in spite of the increased visibility of qualitative studies in education generally. Qualitative research is more likely to be taken seriously when it is located within an appropriate tradition, such as when focused upon a more general sociological problem. Many frames are possible—for example, within functionalist parameters of shared values or conflict, within explanations of more macro structural determinants, or as reflecting the normative tensions in systemic adaptations (Parsons 1951; Smelser 1962; Durkheim 1893); with theoretical underpinnings and interpretive methodologies initially developed within Weberian sociology (Weber 1922; Gerth and Mills 1946; Shils and Finch 1949) or in the Chicago school of sociology (Abbott 1999); or even aligned with disciplinary efforts to link macro and micro theory (Huber 1991), advance cultural analysis (Alexander and Seidman 1990), or refine case study methodologies (Ragin and Becker 1992). Indeed, those who conduct contemporary field research in higher education can perhaps strengthen their work and how it is perceived by drawing a more explicit link between their own premises (or rationales) and one or more of these foundational resources. Incorporating such lines can contribute to their legitimacy among the more disciplinary-based faculty in schools of education. (Again, many of the chapter authors in this volume are examples.)

Whether faculty within higher education programs are drawing on sociological resources to study problems in practice or policy or developing research on some aspect of higher education as a phenomenon to study in its own right, very few of them aim to reach an audience of sociologists. For them higher education, or perhaps education more generally, is the main stage. Since Clark's 1973 article, two new U.S. professional associations (in 1976 the Association for the Study of Higher Education and in 1981 Division J of the American Educational Research Association) have provided ready audiences for this type of research, including studies that selectively apply sociological theory or concepts to practical problems in colleges and universities or to policy problems for state and national systems. These associations have provided significant venues for advancing the academic careers of higher education researchers through opportunities for networking and presenting papers at their annual conferences.

Like faculty in sociology departments, higher education faculty in schools of education know that publishing articles in the top peer-reviewed journals carries the greatest currency for promotion. There is no journal on the sociology of higher education per se. A brief look at the landscape of journals suggests several possibilities, yet the general terms in the titles belie the very precise standards of discourse form and content required to get past the gatekeepers. (See Table 12.1). Six new journals devoted to publishing higher education research were founded in the 1970s and quickly achieved visibility in the field. However, it is worth noting that having an article accepted by one of the higher education journals has at times required sacrificing sociological content, as anonymous peer reviewers on occasion have expressed impatience with discussions of sociological theory or methods and requested that they be cut back or cut out entirely to allow more space for the practical problem, findings, and implications. Moreover, when the time comes for tenure review, it is not clear whether publishing articles in that form in these venues will be sufficient for promotion. Young faculty who have sought guidance on these matters have often received contradictory advice.

The above discussion of sources of ambiguity and strain in the professional contexts for researchers in a position to contribute to sociology of higher education has touched on some additional legitimacy challenges that may emerge for faculty who study topics that correspond with their daily lives: research on faculty roles and rewards, faculty culture, community, identity politics, marginality, and alienation. Each of these areas corresponds to powerful scholarly legacies in sociology, so it is also no stretch to extend these interests into scholarship that advances the sociology of higher education as a field of study. Yet this is not often done—nor viewed as necessary to do—by colleagues from education, researchers who are deeply devoted to the improvement of practice.

Whether in schools of education or departments of sociology, the study of higher education is often regarded as marginal compared to the study of elementary and secondary schools, classroom practices, school administration, and public policy issues. This lack of visible interest in higher education as an area of study can seem surprising, given that academic social scientists live amidst the problems of colleges and universities as well as the issues of higher education systems writ large, and as such their workplace provides an endless supply of research questions and data possibilities. Yet this very immediacy may also be a deterrent, as faculty across the university are less likely to see higher education as a scholarly pursuit because they think they already know about it, having spent years studying and working in academic settings. Alternatively, the study of higher education is considered "navel gazing" or myopic (too focused on everyday life) rather than important analytical work.

When faculty do take advantage of the opportunity to study higher education problems on their own campuses, complex issues may and do arise. Faculty may be especially inclined to undertake such work if they are training college and university administrators or institutional researchers in their graduate programs in higher education. If the research is done to serve the immediate needs of the campus, faculty may not see fit to take a critical stance. There may be other political consequences to studying one's own campus—for example, for researchers who are explicit about a social change agenda, where the primary commitments are to reform colleges and universities or to advance specific dimensions of social justice. When work with these purposes is packaged within a critical theory framework, the analytical approach and dense narrative have—ironically—been criticized by practitioners looking for something more transparent and immediately relevant. In a similar vein, if the research puts the campus in a negative light or generates concern within the campus community or its constituents, the researcher is vulnerable to criticism—or worse yet, retaliation. Even if one avoids these pitfalls, the work might be seen at best as a service activity rather than as research, and if it lacks conceptual development and systematic inquiry, it would be far from what we would consider sociology of higher education.

This discussion of the constraining factors experienced in professional contexts would be incomplete without mention of the fact that faculty are not the only actors in universities who advance a field. Faculty make choices about which work to pursue; and they communicate these determinations in their mentoring of junior faculty and graduate students. However, their research can find vital support from administrators (department chairs, deans, and provosts) who are in a position to make choices about where to allocate resources and in what form (e.g., faculty billets; postdoctoral or doctoral fellowship funding; designating a set of ideas as suitable for a course, major, or degree program). So local institutional support must be forthcoming. Grants from funding agencies have significance too, both material and symbolic. Beyond the campus, a field of study grows through exchanges among scholars and in venues for presenting works in progress and for publication. There is no question that important disciplinary legacies are implicit in much of the research that has filled higher education journals over the past 30 years. For these reasons, ongoing examination of the vitality of this field will be instructive and will most certainly take into account the bodies of work by those who do not self-identify or who have not been identified as direct contributors to the sociology of higher education.

Happily, a number of exemplary scholars in the field—Burton Clark, John Meyer, Neil Smelser, and James March, for example, who have been cited time and again in this volume—have had long careers of studying higher education and successfully straddling both academic worlds in their faculty positions. Their work provides a benchmark of the substance and sweep possible within the nexus of our field. Nonetheless, the various divergent expectations for faculty in their respective academic locations would suggest that we continue to think purposefully—and, I am suggesting, openly—about whether and how we cultivate contributions to the field, along with a sense of community and membership in the field as a whole. In the context of these ongoing determinations, the sociology of higher education may be seen as an area of academic knowledge whose continued vitality will result from difficult individual and institutional choices.

Promising Avenues for Inquiry

As many challenges as the professional contexts within sociology and education pose to the potential future growth of sociology of higher education as a field, efforts to surmount the obstacles and persevere in this richly rewarding area would seem well worth it. Not only has sociology of higher education produced profound scholarship, both within and without the rubric, but given current developments in the larger society—reflected in and fed by higher education—sociology of higher education may be perfectly situated to produce research that addresses and advances some of the most cutting-edge questions facing us today, questions that to this point have been underdeveloped.

At the very least, the above reflections on the unique (and somewhat daunting) professional contexts of potential contributors to the sociology of higher education can be seen as highlighting this field of study as a possible site to explore how higher education settings (whether purposefully or inadvertently) constrain and support knowledge growth in academic specializations that transcend one discipline. The evolution of sociology of higher education could teach us much about the continued vitality of academic fields that straddle two or more academic units, professional orbits with distinct expectations for preferred forms and areas of research.

Inspired by the Sociology of Knowledge

Among lines of inquiry that for some time have been underdeveloped in the field, none seems more worthy of pursuit than research inspired by the sociology of knowledge, a tradition that queries how social contexts shape ideas—and more concretely, how material conditions support prevailing beliefs and do so at different levels, from the very local setting of groups in organizations to more macro settings beyond higher education, such as wider political and economic forces. As mentioned at the outset, premises in the sociology of knowledge view the advancement of knowledge in a field as shaped not only by the ideas themselves but also by the settings in which researchers work. The above discussion surveying the professional contexts of researchers contributing to the sociology of higher education illustrates this vantage point. It is itself an undeveloped line of inquiry in the sociology of higher education.

By calling out "knowledge" as a generative topic of inquiry for this field, I mean that researchers seriously examine the various forms of knowledge legitimated in higher education and the knowledge functions of higher education in society. This means looking at ideas that come to be recognized as worth knowing, teaching, credentialing, advancing through research, and the like. Higher education is seen as a major social institution that, among other things, defines areas of expertise that are worthwhile to society, behaviors that are appropriate among precollege youth for competitive admission, parameters for creating new knowledge through research—all key societal currents essential to explorations in the sociology of higher education.

By the 1990s in sociology and in education, some explicit interest in these questions had emerged among researchers. Although the bulk of research about higher education cast the enterprise as principally engaged in people-processing activities, the newer research with much untapped potential sees higher education as a knowledge-processing system, a system that legitimates categories of ideas worthy of teaching in curriculum, worthy of credentials in degree programs, and worthy of expertise to be valued in society. Placing knowledge at the center of higher education is a significant conceptual departure from most social science frameworks used in the study of higher education.

For the most part, higher education is still seen as a people-processing system, as literally processing people, with its goals and structures reflecting a conception of the college or university as a place where students undergo personality development, learn skills, develop human capital, or use the degree for status attainment and upward mobility. Yet Clark, following Meyer (1977), observes that higher education is composed of knowledge-bearing groups organized into categories that have legitimacy based on knowledge's weighty legacies: "the notion that certain ideas are the best and survive because they deserve to last forever is a powerful sustaining myth, especially in the humanities" (Clark 1983, p. 16). Some of these categories are so embedded in our cognitive constructs that they go unnoticed, and yet their continuity and the processes whereby they change are eminently worthy of study.

Such social theorists have paved the way for this notion of knowledge as socially organized, located, produced, and legitimated. The idea of reality as socially constructed and selectively achieving "facticity" has been well established by Peter Berger and Thomas Luckmann, who elaborated the premise of interdependence between self and society (Berger and Luckmann 1967). In sociology Meyer, among others advancing institutional theory, has cultivated an awareness that the legitimation of knowledge is central to wider environmental forces promoting rationalization (Meyer 1977). This set of ideas has been used as a framework to study knowledge change in higher education—for example, in a case study of institutional and individual commitments to create what became known as feminist scholarship (Gumport 2002). Within neoinstitutional theory, researchers have explored the potential for strategic organizational behavior likely to garner legitimacy (Oliver 1991; Suchman 1995). While it is interesting to consider how legitimacy may be sought at all levels, from the organization and its subunits to the interpersonal and the cognitive taken-for-granted notions carried and elaborated on by individuals, the application of these concepts to higher education has additional significance for practitioners who seek possible courses of action as organizational responses to environmental change.

As mentioned in Chapter Two of this volume, additional lines of inquiry in sociology offer a more refined understanding of the idea that knowledge is socially constructed. Sociologists of science have made great strides in characterizing science as a social institution, as socially organized, with social structures, communication patterns, and networks critical to sustaining lines of research. They have characterized faculty's knowledge-production activities as taking shape within specific contexts, with resources and standard operating procedures that set the parameters for discovery. In other words, by focusing on science as a type of knowledge, they furthered the idea that knowledge is made, not found, and legitimated rather than timelessly established as truth. From a different angle, sociologists of culture conceptualize that institutions produce culture—including higher education, which legitimates the ideas and designates what is thinkable for society. It would be worth studying the impact of the forthcoming college generation, currently students in middle school and high school, dubbed Generation M for the multiple forms of media they use to multitask and digest information; the expectation that higher education meet student demand becomes more daunting in this light.

Each of these traditions offers intellectual resources to problematize the knowledge functions of higher education and how they play out for individuals, organizations, and society at large, helping to formulate questions about how things change, or not, how new things are sustained, or not, and what consequences emanate from those processes.

In higher education, several practical realities have converged with these sociological sensibilities to substantiate these lines of inquiry as worth pursuing in the sociology of higher education. As teaching the disciplinary canons and the general education curriculum became a site of conflict, whole orders of knowledge and categories of expertise showed signs of destabilizing, constructs that were previously presumed to be authoritative knowledge. Traditional views of knowledge as universalistic, objective, and value free were challenged by multicultural critiques tied to ideologies competing in social movements, identity politics among students and faculty, and shifts in faculty members' affinity groups. This contested terrain became all the more apparent given the cycles of financial constraints, when budget cuts were cast as unavoidable. What knowledge was most worth knowing, teaching, and investing in came to be explicitly discussed on campuses, in departments, in dissertation committees, and even in classrooms. In some academic settings, financial considerations have achieved a taken-for-granted status, taking shape as an industry logic that pervades the discourse on what should be taught and which faculty positions are worthy of short-term or long-term investment. The constellation of prevailing beliefs can be understood as an institutional logic. Through this framework, changing interpretations of higher education's mission can be examined, with the rationale for societal investment. This seems especially pertinent given that in the early twenty-first century, the view seems increasingly taken for granted that higher education should solve societal problems in several arenas (such as medical, environmental, and economic). Core concepts of neoinstitutional theory can illuminate practical realities by providing a frame for studying the nature of structural and normative changes in higher education (Gumport forthcoming).

Similar generative possibilities apply in considering changes in knowledge production. Higher education organizations, especially research universities, are becoming more widely recognized as dedicated to knowledge production, an activity all the more valued in contemporary society, which is cast as having shifted to a knowledge economy. (In Chapter 7, Meyer et al. refer to this shift as becoming a knowledge society.) In a knowledge economy, the production of ideas is central, more than the production of things. This recognition has been clearly symbolized by such gestures as the creation of a Distinguished Professor of Knowledge position in 1997 in the business school at the University of California–Berkeley, an endowed chair made possible by a $1 million grant from the Xerox Corporation and its Japanese affiliate (Sterngold 1997). The core expertise required of the professor was that he or she know how corporations can create and then use innovative ideas— criteria perfectly fitting the times in putting a premium on the creation of intellectual property, the centrality of intellectual capital, employees as knowledge workers, and knowledge itself as revenue generating. The fact that this faculty position served to further the interests of companies was all the more telling for higher education, making evident that higher education holds no monopoly on either knowledge production or knowledge transmission—yet more evidence of the changing political economic environment for higher education. Put more starkly, knowledge has become a competitive arena, and higher education's authoritative position is in jeopardy as never before. The nice irony in this illustration (and further testimony to higher education's centrality in the knowledge society) is that Xerox chose to advance this agenda by investing in a faculty position at one of the country's best public research universities.

In spite of these fascinating dynamics in higher education and the rich legacy of sociological concepts probing the content of teaching and research—and the nature of these, higher education's core knowledge functions—the sociology of knowledge has not yet been recognized and supported as a major line of inquiry in the field, nor has it been nurtured from an assured base in either sociology or higher education programs. Some researchers have worked to extend particular lines of inquiry in this domain; for example the knowledge production angle, especially changes in the nature of research activities and intellectual property in university-industry collaboration and changing organizational forms (e.g., Owen-Smith and Powell 2001; Rhoades and Slaughter 2004; Slaughter and Leslie 1997; Gumport and Snydman 2006). Others have begun to examine how the academic structure generates its own momentum for perpetuating the existing social organization of knowledge as it defines curricula, faculty work, and career paths (e.g., Gumport and Snydman 2002) and how consumer tastes are a powerful force for reorganizing the curriculum (Brint 2002). Some researchers have inquired into challenges to the disciplinary system of classification and self-ascribed interdisciplinary agendas of faculty (e.g., Lattuca 2001; Abbott 2002). Each line of inquiry is taking early steps that attest to the enormous value in exploring questions about knowledge, in framing them at the convergence of sociological concepts with practical problems in higher education. Questions to consider include what conditions facilitate knowledge creation; what organizational forms are appropriate to sustain and advance interest in ideas deemed worthy of longevity; and whether the traditional "discipline"-based system of classifying knowledge is effective for organizing teaching and learning while faculty career paths, research agendas, and emerging areas of intellectual expertise diverge into new, sometimes different pursuits. These and other related questions could yield studies of great interest for years to come.

And finally (to be methodologically clear), the above discussion of the sociology of knowledge as an example of an understudied line of inquiry in the sociology of higher education indicates several conditions that can support a line of inquiry: problems or challenges recognized as important enough to be studied; conceptual tools or substantive expertise institutionalized in either higher education programs or sociology departments; faculty colleagues in those units who would be collaborators or at least an interested audience, either at conferences or as peer reviewers of publications; and researchers with the resources (even if only time) to support such study. Indeed, it would seem that these conditions apply to a number of key and timely venues of study that the sociology of higher education is uniquely configured and situated to bring to light.

Inspired by Higher Education Phenomena

In addition to the sociology of knowledge, other promising future lines of inquiry, some not (yet) established as categories of research, bode well for rich and satisfying studies to come in our field. Mentioned earlier in passing are emerging higher-education phenomena such as the accountability-driven assessment of student learning and the impact of advances in information and communications technology on different facets of higher education (teaching, learning, administration, research, student life, scholarly communication, organizational collaboration). These should be studied in different campus settings, and then examining the variation among them, for research universities have most often been the subject of research, followed by community colleges, leaving "the missing middle"—a term currently in use to refer to the large set of colleges and universities with moderate to low selectivity. The ideological underpinnings of higher education warrant deeper analytical attention, not only because they signal interests at work across the contemporary political and religious spectrum but also because they are playing a role in campus life as faculty and student activities are monitored by critics and proponents alike.

Key topics in the policy arena also have an unlimited set of questions, not simply the purview of policy analysts, including research to examine privatization and challenges to the publicness of public higher education, governance dynamics that reflect shifting political interests and spans of control, and legislative and legal mandates that set new limits for the behavior of higher education organizations and participants. Researchers should take care not to accept uncritically the master narratives that dominate in any one period—for example, the belief that global competition and adaptation to market forces is the most pressing contemporary challenge—for to do so carries the danger of reinforcing the dominant discourses that legitimate contemporary forms in higher education. Researchers in this field are well situated to examine a wider set of forces at work, their causes and consequences, their manifest and latent dynamics.

If we are to examine some of these key societal currents, more conceptual work is needed. Primary among the societal trends in need of analysis is the changing relationship between higher education and society, not simply as a social charter that changes or needs reinterpretation but as it reflects fundamental shifts in the institutional division of labor, recognizing that higher education is positioned in an inescapable interdependence with other social institutions whereby changes in one affect the purview of the other. For example, how are we to understand the nature of change and attendant consequences in higher education as colleges and universities have become expected to take on family functions (e.g., childcare, socialization) or to assume primary responsibility for workforce training, instead of industries' training in house? Conversely, what societal functions move out of higher education and where do they go, and with what consequences? For example, for-profit organizations cherry-pick profitable academic programs and instructional software, and industry expands its investment in research and development, even defining knowledge creation as within its domain. Clearly, the relationship between higher education and society has changed dramatically since Jencks and Riesman 1968 and Parsons and Platt 1973.

At the most macro level, the comparative study of national higher education systems must be further elaborated, not simply for Clark's several-decades urging of it but for the widespread acknowledgment of global interdependence, which puts the need for research on national and transnational patterns in a new light. Aside from being interesting and valuable in its own right, cross-national and comparative study, as Clark points out, can be an essential corrective to American myopia and engender conceptual and practical insight into patterns of state control, institutional autonomy, professional authority, faculty careers, and student pathways in other countries. Beyond that, within sociology, moving up to the transnational level of analysis yields evidence of field-level dynamics that provide scholars with opportunities to rethink and refine established theories (e.g., Meyer, Drori, and Hwang 2006.) An important line of inquiry is how the global diffusion is facilitated by Weberian rationalization, to examine diffusion of student culture, faculty research norms, entrepreneurial revenue strategies, and performance metrics organizations, for example. But it is also important to examine the sources of tension among such worldwide forces for change and the forces for continuity (such as historical legacies within higher education in any given country), as these produce distinctive variation worthy of study.

Increased globalization creates even more fertile ground for study of changes in higher education practices. Through the lens of the sociological concepts of structural forms (such as collaboration or networks) and political-economic forces (government mandates, shifting markets), researchers have opportunities to study changing patterns in scientific communication and institutional partnerships and the attendant consequences for teaching and research. Also ripe for study are changes in scholarly networks spanning a larger geographic range than ever before. We can examine emerging patterns in the international flow of students, not simply study-abroad opportunities but cross-national educational experiences that aim to be genuinely collaborative degree programs.

Moreover, unprecedented cooperation among nations, as promoted in the European Union for instance, can be explored through comparative research on academic collaboration among universities in different countries. Under what conditions are universities likely to collaborate rather than compete, and what is known about how to maximize the anticipated benefits while reducing the likelihood of potential liabilities? This is a question to be asked at both national and transnational levels. Aside from the growing awareness of such interesting developments worthy of study, practically speaking, research on these issues as they manifest in different countries should be easier now that more collaborative relationships have flourished among colleagues located in different countries and advances in technology enable direct communication as well as more widespread dissemination of information about higher education activities from campuses to transnational levels.

Next Steps

Having considered some of the deterrents to and several promises possible within the development of our hybrid field, I return to Clark's 1973 foundational conception of sociology of higher education as a convergence of a sociological concern and a practical problem in higher education. By this point, we are more aware that a variety of aims may propel research in the field and researchers' particular academic training and departmental home may lead them to be interested in different substantive foci. For those who would be stewards of the field, I offer some questions to work toward a more nuanced definition of what constitutes research in the field: Must it be an original contribution that advances sociological theory (or method) and also advances our understanding of a problem (contemporary or otherwise) in higher education —or can it do only one or the other? Must it have the earmarks of research from both sociology and higher education, as reflected in citations or discourse patterns expected in each arena? Must it be published in a venue acceptable to both, or may it be for only one or the other? How important are any of these features if the ideas are generative and promise to illuminate what was previously unknown?

In conceptualizing the promising possibilities for future lines of inquiry, we should make a concerted effort to look at the topics around which there are persistent silences and omissions. Who and what are understudied and why? Where is fertile ground from neighboring fields? What concepts from related disciplines inspire our imagination to see higher education and its unique facets in a different light? One might be concerned that this would cause us to stray too far from the sociological foundations and sensibilities of the field, but scholarly imagination and creative research ideas can be nurtured from many—even unexpected— sources.

If we proceed with a more inclusive definition that acknowledges the value of incremental contributions, faculty in either sociology or education may be apt to contribute to further developments in the field. Faculty in sociology departments are poised to do so, although that research may benefit from more grounding in the historical development of particular higher education systems or the contemporary problems that plague them. Faculty in education may receive training in sociological theory and methods, which may make them good consumers of sociological research, but they would benefit from better training in how to be good producers of it. So researchers from each arena may have predictable limitations. And this brings us back to the question of professional socialization in graduate school: are graduate programs in either sociology or higher education adequately preparing the next generation to advance this field, even to locate their research within the rich legacies of developments in the field's major lines of inquiry? I think that support at this intellectual intersection has been missing, and the professional conditions for faculty in each academic location do not provide sufficient incentives for generating or consolidating efforts in this regard.

Straddling the different academic locations and professional audiences, the sociology of higher education as a field of study poses an opportunity for universities to be proactive in fostering dialogue among faculty in separate academic units and with disparate theoretical predispositions or, conversely, to wait and see what incremental advancements emerge from scholars mining in their specialty tunnels. Interested stakeholders, like philanthropic foundations, can also play a role in galvanizing a field of study, just as they have on occasion promoted dialogue between academic researchers and policymakers or practitioners. One question on the minds of faculty in research universities concerns uncertainty in the future of funding for research in the field—which by the turn of the twenty-first century had sent researchers scrambling to seek funding from new sources, not simply philanthropic foundations but the National Science Foundation, the U.S. Department of Education, and other government agencies. In the wider communities into which higher education organizations are increasingly becoming integrated, activities supported by financial resources and local organizational settings can yield intellectual breakthroughs while simultaneously cultivating a sense of community. Indeed, purposeful efforts to foster cooperation, even collaboration, among researchers in different academic units and with external audiences are increasingly discussed as an antidote to today's unprecedented competition, fragmentation, individualism, and insularity among university faculty. Faculty, students, administrators, campus leaders, and audiences beyond the academy—how all these regard this field and its future is thus an immediately practical matter with significant intellectual consequences.

References

Abbott, A. 1999. *Department and Discipline: Chicago Sociology at One Hundred.* Chicago: University of Chicago Press.

——. 2001. *Chaos of Disciplines.* Chicago: Unviersity of Chicago Press.

——. 2002. "The Disciplines and the Future." In *The Future of the City of Intellect: The Changing American University,* ed. S. Brint. Stanford, CA: Stanford University Press.

Alexander, J., and S. Seidman. 1990. *Culture and Society: Contemporary Debates.* Cambridge: Cambridge University Press.

Berger, P., and T. Luckmann. 1967. *The Social Construction of Reality.* Garden City, NY: Doubleday.

Brint, S. 2002. "The Rise of the Practical Arts." In *The Future of the City of Intellect: The Changing American University,* ed. S. Brint. Stanford, CA: Stanford University Press.

——. 2005. "Creating the Future: 'New Directions' in American Research Universities." *Minerva* 43:23–25.

Clark, B. R. 1973. "Development of the Sociology of Higher Education." *Sociology of Education* 46:2–14.

——. 1983. *The Higher Education System.* Berkeley: University of California Press.

——. 1987. *The Academic Life: Small Worlds, Different Worlds.* Princeton, NJ: Carnegie Foundation for the Advancement of Teaching.

——. 1998. *Creating Entrepreneurial Universities: Organizational Pathways of Transformation.* Oxford: IAU and Pergamon.

Clifford, G. J., and J. W. Guthrie. 1988. *Ed School: A Brief for Professional Education.* Chicago: University of Chicago Press.

Cohen, M. D., J. G. March, and J. P. Olsen. 1972. "A Garbage Can Model of Organizational Choice." *Administrative Science Quarterly* 17:1–25.

Denzin, N., and Y. Lincoln. 2005. *The Sage Handbook of Qualitative Research.* 3rd ed. Thousand Oaks, CA: Sage.

Durkheim, E. 1893/1960. *The Division of Labor in Society.* Glencoe, IL: Free Press.

Enteman, W. F. 1993. *Managerialism: The Emergence of a New Ideology.* Madison: University of Wisconsin Press.

Geertz, C. 1983. "Blurred Genres: The Refiguration of Social Thought," In *Local Knowledge: Further Essays in Interpretive Anthropology,* ed. C. Geertz, 19–35. New York: Basic Books.

Gerth, H. H., and C. W. Mills, eds. 1946. *From Max Weber: Essays in Sociology.* London: Routledge & Kegan Paul.

Glaser, B., and A. Strauss. 1967. *The Discovery of Grounded Theory: Strategies for Qualitative Research.* New York: Aldine.

Gumport, P. J. 2000a. "Academic Restructuring: Organizational Change and Institutional Imperatives." *Higher Education: The International Journal of Higher Education and Educational Planning* 39:67–91.

———. 2000b. "Learning Academic Labor." *Comparative Social Research* 19:1–23.

———. 2002. *Academic Pathfinders: Knowledge Creation and Feminist Scholarship.* Westport, CT: Greenwood.

———. Forthcoming. *Academic Legitimacy: Institutional Tensions in Restructuring Public Higher Education.* Baltimore: Johns Hopkins University Press.

Gumport, P. J., and S. K. Snydman. 2002. "The Formal Organization of Knowledge: An Analysis of Academic Structure." *Journal of Higher Education* 73 (3): 375–408.

———. 2006. "Higher Education: Evolving Forms, Emerging Markets." In *The Non-Profit Sector: A Research Handbook,* Second Edition, eds. W.W. Powell and R. Steinberg. Hartford, CT: Yale University Press.

Huber, J., ed. 1991. *Macro-Micro Linkages in Sociology.* Newbury Park, CA: Sage.

Jencks, C., and D. Riesman. 1968. *The Academic Revolution.* New York: Doubleday.

Judge, H. G. 1982. *The American Graduate Schools of Education: A View from Abroad.* New York: Ford Foundation.

Lattuca, L. 2001. *Creating Interdisciplinarity.* Nashville: Vanderbilt University Press.

March, J. G. 1988. "Organizational Learning." *Annual Review of Sociology* 14:319–40.

March, J. G., and J. Olsen. 1976. *Ambiguity and Choice in Organizations.* Bergen, Denmark: Universitetstsforlaget.

Meyer, J. W. 1977. "The Effects of Education as an Institution." *American Journal of Sociology* 83:55–77.

Meyer, J. W., G. Drori, and H. Hwang. 2006. "World Society and Organizational Actor." In *Globalization and Organization*, ed. J. W. Meyer, G. Drori, and H. Hwang. Oxford: Oxford University Press.

Mills, C. Wright. 1959. *The Sociological Imagination.* New York: Oxford University Press.

Oliver, C. 1991. "Strategic Responses to Institutional Processes." *Academy of Management Review* 16:145–79.

Owen-Smith, J., and W. W. Powell. 2001. "Careers and Contradictions: Faculty Responses to the Transformation of Knowledge and Its Uses in the Life Sciences." *Research in the Sociology of Work* 10:109–40.

Parsons, T. 1951. *The Social System.* Glencoe, IL: Free Press.

Parsons, T., and G. M. Platt. 1973. *The American University.* Cambridge, MA: Harvard University Press.

Ragin, C., and H. Becker, eds. 1992. *What Is a Case? Exploring the Foundations of Social Inquiry.* Cambridge: Cambridge University Press.

Rhoades, G., and S. Slaughter. 2004. *Academic Capitalism and the New Economy: Markets, State, and Higher Education.* Baltimore: Johns Hopkins University Press.

Rourke, F. E., and G. E. Brooks. 1966. *The Managerial Revolution in Higher Education.* Baltimore: Johns Hopkins University Press.

Ruscio, K. P. 1987. "Many Sectors, Many Professions." In *The Academic Profession: National, Disciplinary, and Institutional Settings,* ed. B. Clark, 331–68. Berkeley: University of California Press.

Schuster, J., and M. Finkelstein. 2006. *The American Faculty: Restructuring Academic Work and Careers.* Baltimore: Johns Hopkins University Press.

Scott, W. R. 1998. *Organizations: Rational, Natural, and Open Systems.* 4th ed. Upper Saddle River, NJ: Prentice-Hall.

Shils, E., and H. Finch, eds. 1949. *The Methodology of the Social Sciences.* Glencoe, IL: Free Press.

Slaughter, S., and L. L. Leslie. 1997. *Academic Capitalism.* Baltimore: Johns Hopkins University Press.

Smelser, N. J. 1962. *Theory of Collective Behavior.* New York: Free Press.

Sterngold, J. 1997. "Professor Knowledge Is Not an Oxymoron." *New York Times,* June 1, Week in Review, 5.

Suchman, M. 1995. "Managing Legitimacy." *Academy of Management Review* 20 (3): 571–610.

Tierney, W. G. 2001. *Faculty Work in Schools of Education.* Albany: State University of New York Press.

U.S. Department of Education. 2001. *The Condition of Education.* Washington, DC: National Center for Education Statistics.

Weber, M. 1922/1968. *Economy and Society.* New York: Bedminster.

Contributors

anthony lising antonio is Associate Professor at the Stanford University School of Education. From his studies in the college choice process, antonio has published research on the choice of historically black versus predominantly white colleges, racial and class-based organizational influences of high schools on college aspirations, and the role of news-magazine college rankings in the dissemination of college knowledge. His latest work in this area appears in *From High School to College: Improving Opportunities for Success in Post-secondary Education* (Jossey-Bass, 2004). antonio has also studied the impact of racial and cultural diversity on college students and the status of faculty of color in academe. He received the Early Career Award from the Association for the Study of Higher Education in 2004. antonio earned his Ph.D. in Education at the University of California–Los Angeles.

Michael N. Bastedo is Assistant Professor at the Center for the Study of Higher and Postsecondary Education at the University of Michigan. His research examines public policy, governance, and organization of public higher education. His articles have been published in the *Review of Higher Education*, *Higher Education*, and *American Higher Education in the Twenty-first Century* (2nd ed., Johns Hopkins University Press). He holds the A.B. with honors from Oberlin College, a master's degree in education from Boston College, a master's degree in sociology, and a Ph.D. in administration and policy analysis from Stanford University.

Burton R. Clark is the Allan M. Cartter Professor Emeritus of Higher Education and Sociology, Graduate School of Education and Information Studies, University of California–Los Angeles. He has held successive faculty posts at Stanford University, Harvard University, University of California–Berkeley, Yale University, and University of California–

Los Angeles, in departments of sociology and graduate schools of education. His major publications include *The Open Door College* (1960), *The Distinctive College* (1970), *Academic Power in Italy* (1977), *The Higher Education System* (1983), *The Encyclopedia of Higher Education*, 4 volumes (coeditor, 1992); *Places of Inquiry* (1995); *Creating Entrepreneurial Universities* (1998), and *Sustaining Change in Universities* (2004). Clark received his Ph.D. in sociology from the University of California–Los Angeles.

Amy J. Fann has research interests that focus on the barriers to college access for the most underrepresented and underinvestigated group in higher education, Native American high school students. Fann has conducted research projects on outreach needs from the perspective of California's American Indian high school students from diverse tribes and has carried out case studies on tribal attitudes toward education, educational organizations, and tribal needs relating to education. She is currently engaged in postdoctoral research in how tribal sovereignty and economic development needs shape college aspirations and behaviors of tribal citizens from both nongaming and gaming tribes. She received her Ph.D. from the Graduate School of Education and Information Studies at the University of California–Los Angeles.

David John Frank is Associate Professor of Sociology and, by courtesy, Education at the University of California–Irvine. Along with Jay Gabler, he recently completed a detailed study of transformations in the university's teaching and research priorities worldwide, examining how changing academic emphases correspond to globally institutionalized models of reality. *Reconstructing the University: Global Changes in the Academic Core over the Twentieth Century* will be published by Stanford University Press in 2006. Frank earned his Ph.D. in sociology at Stanford University.

Patricia J. Gumport is Professor of Education and Director of the Stanford Institute for Higher Education Research (SIHER). As a sociologist of higher education, she has examined how institutional practices and organizational contexts reshape the content, structure, practice, and relative legitimacy of academic fields. She has studied the conditions in which new knowledge emerges and becomes institutionalized, the professional socialization that occurs during graduate education, and the tensions arising in academic workplaces during organizational restructuring. Her forthcoming book on academic legitimacy portrays the ascendance of industry logic and its consequences within public higher education during the last quarter of the twentieth century. Gumport earned two master's degrees (sociology and education) as well as a Ph.D. in education from Stanford University.

James C. Hearn is Professor of Public Policy and Higher Education at Peabody College, Vanderbilt University. Hearn's work focuses on post-secondary education organization and policy. He has investigated faculty workforce issues in colleges and universities; organizational and financial developments affecting the humanities in higher education; trends toward marketization and performance accountability in post-secondary-education policy, finance, and management; federal and state policies affecting governance and decision making in postsecondary institutions; and federal and state policies directed toward financing student access, choice, and persistence in postsecondary education. In addition to an M.B.A. in finance from the University of Pennsylvania (Wharton), he holds a master's in sociology and a Ph.D. in the sociology of education from Stanford University.

Sylvia Hurtado is Professor and Director of the Higher Education Research Institute at the University of California–Los Angeles, in the Graduate School of Education and Information Sciences. Before that, she served as Director of the Center for the Study of Higher and Postsecondary Education at the University of Michigan. Hurtado's primary interest is in student educational outcomes, campus climates, college impact on student development, and diversity in higher education. She is coauthor of the books *Enacting Diverse Learning Environments* and *Intergroup Dialogue*, which focus on diversity in the teaching and learning process. Hurtado obtained her master's in education from the Harvard Graduate School of Education and her Ph.D. in education from the University of California–Los Angeles.

Patricia M. McDonough is Professor of Education in the Higher Education and Organizational Change Division of the Graduate School of Education and Information Sciences at the University of California–Los Angeles. McDonough has conducted research on students' college-choice decision making, high school counseling, the impact of college rankings on students' college choices, access for African American and Latino students, rural college access, the impact of financial aid knowledge on college choice, access to historically black colleges, private college counselors, affirmative action, and college admissions officers. Her book *Choosing Colleges: How Social Class and Schools Structure Opportunity* examines how students choose colleges and the influence of parents, schools, and colleges on that decision-making process. McDonough earned a Ph.D. from Stanford University.

John W. Meyer is Professor of Sociology and (by courtesy) Education, emeritus, at Stanford University. He has contributed to organizational theory (e.g., *Organizational Environments*, with W. R. Scott, Sage, 1983) and to the sociology of education, developing lines of thought now called sociological institutional theory. Since the late 1970s, he has studied the impact of global society on national states and societies (e.g., Thomas et al., *Institutional Structure*, Sage, 1987). He recently completed a collaborative study of worldwide science and its impact on national societies (Drori et al., *Science in the Modern World Polity*, Stanford University Press, 2003). Another collaborative project, on the impact of globalization on organizational structures, is in publication (Drori et al., eds., *Globalization and Organization*, Oxford University Press, 2006). He is now engaged, with colleagues, in studies of the rise and impact of the world human rights regime and in comparative research on the curriculum and global expansion of higher education. Meyer received his Ph.D. in sociology from Columbia University.

Marcela Muñiz is a doctoral candidate in higher education at Stanford University. Prior to beginning her doctoral studies, Muñiz worked in Stanford's Office of Undergraduate Admission, where she was Assistant Dean of Admission and oversaw diversity outreach. While in graduate school, Muñiz has served as a research assistant with the Stanford Institute for Higher Education Research, the Provost's Advisory Committee on the Status of Women Faculty at Stanford, and the Aspen Institute's Program on Education in a Changing Society. Her research interests extend from the role of multicultural campus environments in college student development to affirmative action, access, and equity in higher education, and institutional change. She holds bachelor's degrees in sociology and Spanish from Stanford University.

Marvin W. Peterson is Professor of Higher Education and former Director of the Center for the Study of Higher and Postsecondary Education at the University of Michigan. His scholarly interests and publications have focused on organizational behavior; management and leadership; institutional research and planning; institutional and system change and transformation; and organizational research methods and issues. Peterson made major contributions to the work of the Kellogg Forum on Higher Education Transformation and the National Center for Postsecondary Improvement. He has been President of the Association for the Study of Higher Education, the Association for Institutional Research, and the Society for College and University Planning, and he has received outstanding career awards from all three associations. Peterson holds an M.B.A. from Harvard and a Ph.D. in higher education from the University of Michigan.

Francisco O. Ramirez is a Professor of Education and (by courtesy) Sociology at Stanford University. Ramirez has conducted cross-national studies on the role of education in the formation of world society and on the influence of world society on educational developments. These studies include topics such as women's access to higher education; the role of education and science in economic development; universities in comparative perspective; and the interrelationships among education, citizenship, and human rights. Major grants from the National Science Foundation, the Spencer Foundation, and the Bechtel Initiative on Global Growth and Change have supported these studies and led to publications in the *American Sociological Review*, *American Journal of Education*, *Sociology of Education*, and *Comparative Education Review*. He has headed the sociology of education sections for both the American Sociological Association and the American Education Research Association. Ramirez earned his Ph.D. in sociology from Stanford University.

Gary Rhoades is Professor and Director of the University of Arizona's Center for the Study of Higher Education. His research focuses on the sociology of higher education, the restructuring of professions and higher education institutions, academic unions, and comparative higher education. His work has been published, among other places, in *Academe*, *Journal of Higher Education*, *Review of Higher Education*, *Higher Education*, *Sociology of Education*, *Tertiary Education and Management*, and *Thought & Action*. Recent books include *Managed Professionals: Unionized Faculty and Restructuring Academic Labor* (SUNY, 1998) and (with Sheila Slaughter) *Academic Capitalism and the New Economy: Markets, State, and Higher Education* (Johns Hopkins University Press, 2004). Rhoades earned his Ph.D. in sociology at the University of California–Los Angeles.

Evan Schofer is Assistant Professor of Sociology at the University of Minnesota. His work traces the historical expansion of education and science, examining how these institutions serve to rationalize society and reshape political and economic activity. His cross-national research on science and educational systems has appeared in *ASR*, *Social Forces*, and a coauthored book titled *Science in the Modern World Polity: Globalization and Institutionalization* (Stanford University Press, 2003). He also conducts research in comparative political sociology and globalization, on topics ranging from political participation and civil society to the origins and expansion of the global environmental movement. He is currently engaged in examining the long-term impact of educational expansion on the degree of economic inequality within societies. Schofer received his Ph.D. in sociology from Stanford University.

Index